The Man in the Woods

The Recapitulation Diaries

Year One

by

J. E. Ketchel

Riverwalker Press

Cover art and design by J. E. Ketchel

Riverwalker Press
PO Box 101
Red Hook, NY 12571
www.riverwalkerpress.com

ISBN: 978-0-9800506-3-9

MEDICAL DISCLAIMER: The information in this book is intended for educational and informational purposes only. It is not meant to diagnose or treat any mental health disorder whatsoever, nor is it intended to replace treatment with a competent mental healthcare provider. Please seek appropriate support and put the book aside if it proves to be too disruptive. Any application of the material presented in this book is at the reader's discretion and is his or her sole responsibility. The author and publisher are in no way responsible or liable for misuse of this information.

Table of Contents

Intent

My intent in publishing *The Recapitulation Diaries* is to demonstrate the validity of the ancient shamanic practice of *recapitulation* as a means to completely heal from the long term impact of severe trauma. I undertook a recapitulation under the guidance of Chuck Ketchel, LCSW, a psychotherapist and *Tensegrity* practitioner who was taught the *Magical Pass* of recapitulation while immersed in the shamanic world of Carlos Castaneda. This book is based on the copious notes I kept during the first year of my three-year-long recapitulation process.

Recapitulation has been a formal shamanic practice for eons. Imbued with the intent of ancient seers it is used to remember and relive all the events of a lifetime in order to gain clarity and insight into experiences, as well as to reclaim personal energy lost during those experiences. As shamans recapitulate, they practice a side to side sweeping breath to both reclaim lost personal energy and to release the outside energy that gets attached during life experiences and interactions with others.

When I first met Chuck I'd never heard of the shamanic practice of recapitulation. Three years later, I emerged from my personal recapitulation process a totally different person, fully released from the lifelong impact of sixteen years of brutal sexual abuse which began at the age of two. During those three years of deep inner work, I successfully recovered and relived hundreds of traumatic events, physically, emotionally, and cognitively. It was a life changing three-year period, transformational on many levels.

Though I'd spent my entire life dealing with the traumatic repercussions of the events of my childhood, I had no memory of them. Today I have full access to all those memories, but they no longer carry any emotional or physical charge. They no longer inhibit nor control me as they once did, they are simply facts of my life, fully understood and released, on all levels. I have shed my personal history, retrieved my personal energy, and emerged from the experience healed. I am free to experience and live my life in a new way.

In successfully resolving and understanding my childhood experiences on the deepest level, my most innocent self was freed from the past and allowed the freedom to truly live without fear, to joyfully embrace all that life offers. On a spiritual level, recapitulation opens the door to experiences of the magical dimension of being human, to the innate skills inherent in all of us. My recapitulation honed my ability to enter different energetic states at will, to shape shift, and to develop the ability to channel an energy being no longer in human form.

Recapitulation is a serious practice, not to be undertaken lightly, though it is available to anyone who sets the intent to recapitulate. That being said, the guidance of a knowledgeable shamanic practitioner and teacher was of the utmost importance as I did my recapitulation. I strongly recommend seeking professional support, as the reliving of trauma can be both riveting and terrifying.

I stress, *emphatically*, that this is an adult book. Although the exposition of sex abuse is not the sole purpose of this book, it is the parallel journey I encountered as my personal recapitulation naturally unfolded. In order to fully grasp the complexities of recapitulation, sexually explicit and physically torturous events are included, as they emerged, in the way they emerged. In my case, the repressed memories of terrifying abuse intertwined with the deeper intent of the process: *to solve the riddle of the unknown self.* Furthermore, it is not my intention to expose, blame, or reveal anything that is not pertinent to the reader's ability to fully understand what it means to recapitulate.

This book and the two volumes to follow document the full truth of the experiences of my life. These experiences are not meant to be read by children, and they may even trigger extreme discomfort in the mature adult reader. I wish to point out however, that I refuse to hide the true facts of sexual abuse perpetrated upon children, ugly as they are and difficult though they may be to believe. Disbelief has already had its time. In perpetually covering up the real truth of what happens when children are sexually abused, far too many children continue to suffer. Whether a seemingly insignificant case of touching or a far more obvious case of total personal invasion, as was my case, the truth is that intrusion of any sort can be traumatic. I know, from my own experience, that childhood sexual abuse results in a severely restricted life. Far too many adults continue to carry the burden of childhood trauma as a result of the secrecy they must uphold, placed on them by both their abusers and society. It's time to face the truth.

I am able to write this book because I no longer carry any personal attachment to the past or to this story, even though the pages of this book reveal deeply personal experiences. At this point in my life, I have indeed fully healed. I write now to help others. Indeed, I consider this to be a universal story that *must* be shared. I cannot, in good conscience, withhold it from anyone who may have the possibility of healing as a result of my daring to disclose it.

For those who suffer: *I dedicate this book to you*—for the journeys you have already taken and the journeys you have yet to take. I know you are strong and that, above all, you desire freedom. It is my greatest hope that you may muster the courage to face your own traumas. Know that you are supported in that effort by your own spirit and the intent of the shamans of ancient Mexico.

I know there are many people, men and women alike, who are tortured by many of the same issues that I struggled with for most of my life. I say to you: *there is a way to achieve total healing and new life*. It is my hope that *The Recapitulation Diaries* may inspire you to begin a journey of not only recovery and healing, but transformation as well. I also hope that my book may broaden the knowledge of healing options available to the many who suffer from lifelong trauma, whether stemming from physical invasion, as in my case, or for other reasons. Those reasons are as varied as life itself, but, as I hope my story illustrates, people can truly heal from even the most devastating of traumatic experiences. The healing potential of recapitulation is truly magical—to that I can personally attest.

So, what is recapitulation? Read on, but also be aware that every journey is unique and must be encountered on its own terms. I can only attest to the value and truth of my own experiences and so, I humbly offer *The Man in the Woods—The Recapitulation Diaries: Year One*—as encouragement to those who seek transformation in this lifetime.

From here on, the actual diaries that I kept, during the first year of my three-year-long shamanic recapitulation, are presented. Rewriting has been done to cohesively pull together quickly jotted notes, thoughts, insights, and experiences into a more readable format, without change to actual content; to clarify certain terms and processes; as well as to protect the innocent.

Chapter One

An Invitation

December 30, 2000

I'm out for an early morning jog. It's snowing quite heavily and because of the weather I decide to circle around the neighborhood rather than run the longer route out into the countryside. Up ahead, through a veil of blowing snow, something reddish darts across the road, a cat perhaps.

As I jog around a curve in the road I see the flash of red once again, more clearly this time: a fox! I watch as it darts back and forth across the road. Brilliant reddish-orange energy in motion, it runs up the snow bank on one side of the road then back down across the road to the bank on the other side. With its long tail pointing straight back, its nose pointing forward, it looks very much like a fox on a mission. I slow down as it runs back into the middle of the road and stands skittishly, as if confused, facing in my direction. I wonder if it's rabid.

I watch as it prances lightly on its little black feet; its large ears pointy and alert; its red color vivid against the winter whiteness. Its delicate black legs are like thin charred sticks dancing in the road. It's slightly comical in appearance, and I can almost imagine a red bandana wrapped around its neck, a feathered Robin Hood cap on its head. It seems to be waiting for me, expecting me. I take a step towards it and it runs off again, climbs the snow bank, and runs down the other side and out of sight.

I begin jogging again. I don't want to frighten the fox if it's still nearby, nor do I want to appear frightened myself, though I am concerned. Suddenly, it runs out into the road again and stops a few yards in front of me. It plants its feet and faces me with a defiant and confrontational aire. I stop at a safe distance to study this nervy little creature blocking my path.

"Is it threatening me or challenging me?" I wonder.

"All I want to do is go for a little run, Mister Fox," I whisper, "to start my day with a little exercise, which is my habit, to get my energy up for the day ahead."

It's early enough that no one else is out, no cars passing; snowing heavily enough that people are staying inside, cold and blustery enough that only the heartiest or most routine of people are out at this hour on this wintry Saturday morning. The fox doesn't appear to be rabid. But what's up with it?

"Come on, don't you recognize me?" it seems to ask.

I stand my ground and wait to see what it's going to do. It appears to beckon me to follow as it turns and trots up the road, glancing back over its shoulder to see if I'm following. Slowly, a little reluctantly, I jog after it, keeping a safe distance. It turns around again to make sure I'm following as it begins crisscrossing back and forth again from snow bank to snow bank, zigzagging with intent. Now I'm concerned again that it might be rabid.

It stops once again in the middle of the road and turns and stares at me through the veils of falling snow. I stop in my tracks, sure that this time it will attack. I wonder if I should turn and run or simply stand my ground. As I raise my arms to protect myself, it flips its bushy white-tipped tail and, holding its head high, leaps the snow bank on the left side of the road, landing in deep snow up to its belly. It turns one last time, gives a final nod and bounds off across the snowy yard between two houses, heading towards the woods. On the edge of the woods, it seems as if a small door opens and in the blink of an eye I watch the comical little fox scamper through it before a gust of swirling, blinding snow slams it shut.

I can't explain how I know this, but in that split second everything about my life suddenly becomes crystal clear. I know that everything is about to change; that I'm going to take a new path. I have no idea what this really means, I just know it's time. Somehow I understand that the fox is showing me the way, telling me that it's time to stop running in circles.

It's time to shift the wheel of time, and step out of the mind and body numbing survival mode that I've operated from my entire life. It's time to take a different approach. The fox is guiding me, showing me how to retrace my steps. It's showing me that I must go back and forth, slowly and thoughtfully, that I must stop and thoroughly examine where I've been. I must study myself intently and find out why I feel so disconnected, so foreign in this world, why I don't fit in. The fox is instructing me to find out why I'm so depressed all the time, and to finally seek the answer to the question that has puzzled me my whole life: *What is wrong with me?*

I understand, on this snowy day, two days before the turn of the New Year, that I must change my life. I know I must pursue that red fox through that door into the woods, even though I have no idea where it's going to lead me or why—I just know it's absolutely imperative that I follow it. Somehow I know that something is waiting for me behind that door at the edge of the woods. And I know it's time to finally pay attention to the voices behind the door of my own awareness.

"You may not like it, but it's time for you to hear the truth," they seem to be saying. They've been saying this for years, I just haven't been ready to listen.

These are the truths I acknowledge as I finish my jog, half wondering if I'll encounter the fox again on the other side of the woods, but I know there's no reason to. I already know what I have to do.

Chapter Two

Heeding the Call

May 1, 2001

My husband set up an appointment for couples therapy today, hoping to save our rapidly deteriorating marriage. I recognize the name of the therapist he's chosen, a man who lives in a nearby town. Though we've never met, his name has haunted and puzzled me from the moment I first set eyes on it. I have no idea why I have such a reaction, but whenever I see the name of this man, Chuck Ketchel, a wave of intense fear rolls right through me.

May 8, 2001

We went to a couples therapy session today. My reaction to meeting Chuck Ketchel in person was not one of fear at all. He seems like a nice man, intelligent, calm, and professional, and it's very clear that he's extremely good at what he does.

May 22, 2001

I meet for a session alone with Chuck. I tell him that the marriage is over, that I already knew that the first day we met him, that I've known it for a long time. I know I must face my husband, my children, my family, but even more than that I know I must face something inside myself. Something has been eating away at me for decades, calling me, asking me to pay heed. I just haven't wanted to listen, instead I've been on the run from it; constantly moving as if I'm being chased by something.

"Something's been nagging at me," I say. "I'm not sure what it is, but it's been bothering me for years. Your name was the name that I always saw whenever I thought about calling a therapist, so when my husband set up that appointment with you, I knew it was significant. Now that I've started talking, I know I need to keep talking. I don't even know what it is that I have to talk about, but I do know that something's wrong with me and, if I don't do something about it, I'll die. Something is warning me that I'm dying, not in a physical way, I'm not ill or anything, but in a spiritual way. I'm dying inside. I've been dying for decades."

"In December of 1999," I tell Chuck, "one year prior to encountering the fox, I had made the decision to set up a painting studio with another artist in an old factory building, taking my art studio out of the house for the first time in years, a declaration of independence on my part, threatening a major challenge to a sixteen year relationship. That was probably the real beginning of the ending of our marriage."

I'm both nervous and excited as I realize that I'm taking the first actual steps toward real change, since the sighting of the fox. I'm curious to see what happens as I embark on this journey. I now understand that what began on my husband's part as a deeply sincere attempt to save our marriage has ended with him delivering me to my destiny. He has led me to the office of Chuck Ketchel, but more importantly to that mythical door in the woods, the place I most certainly need to be.

"Your own spirit has been calling you," Chuck says as we set up an appointment for next week.

When I leave Chuck's office I feel both relieved and burdened. I'm choosing to heed the call of my spirit for the first time in my life, and that feels incredibly right, while at the same time I'm intensely aware that in so doing I will be hurting the people I love the most. I'm asking them all to take a journey they haven't asked for and never anticipated.

May 29, 2001

When I meet with Chuck I feel fragile and yet utterly determined. I realize that in choosing divorce my own desire for deep personal change is finally being given life. I'm already feeling the weight of my decision as pragmatic issues arise almost daily, but still, there's something inside me hungry for life. I still can't clearly articulate what it is, but I can't pause for even a second to reconsider my decision.

"*This is something I have to do!*" I tell Chuck. "Something is pushing me so hard that I must heed its call. Now that the ball is rolling nothing can stop the momentum."

"Well," says Chuck, "let's see what happens."

"I'm grateful to my husband for leading me to your office, but now it's time for me to go to work on myself.

Chapter Three

The Usher

June 13, 2001

In a dream I'm on a city bus sitting next to an old man who appears to be about seventy or eighty years old. I'm acutely aware that he's going to touch me. I'm trying to keep from brushing up against him in any way, holding my arms tightly against my chest. He reaches out and touches my cheek with one hand and puts his other hand on my breast. Angrily, I push his hands away. Shaking and afraid, I sink into an old state of paralysis. The man seems familiar in a disturbing way. As his hand comes toward me yet again I'm triggered into a déjà vu experience of this same dream some thirty years ago, when I was a young woman living in Philadelphia. I'm on the same bus, sitting next to him as his hand comes toward me. Too paralyzed to protect myself I just let him touch me. This déjà vu experience jolts me. As he now reaches to touch me again I'm determined to react differently. I immediately push his hand away and tell him to stop; quietly hissing at him under my breath because I don't want to draw attention to myself or to what's happening. I'm embarrassed and ashamed, but also indignant. He leans over and tries to kiss me, his mouth brushing against my lips and cheek as I turn away. Again, I react. I get up and walk away in a huff. As I move away, I suddenly realize I don't have any personal belongings with me, no money, no purse, no identification whatsoever. Eventually, the bus stops and I get off. Overwhelmed with feelings of loss, I wander around the city until I'm finally walking along a familiar path, one that I've walked along many times before in dreams. I wander this path until I wake up and, still drowsy, scribble this dream in my journal.

June 19, 2001

It's evening, the supper dishes are cleaned up and I'm in the kitchen making chocolate chip cookies for the end of the year school parties. I measure the ingredients into a large bowl and begin stirring with a wooden spoon. As I stir, the thoughts in my head stir too. I can't stop thinking about that disturbing dream I had the other night. I had discussed it in a session with Chuck today, but I just couldn't get clarity on it, though something about it remains so viscerally familiar.

I haven't been able to get the image of the old man in that dream out of my head; he's been puzzling me all day. I ponder his actions as I stir the cookie dough, the thoughts in my head tumbling, stirring too, until of their own accord they settle on this phrase: *He who abuses has been abused; he who abuses has been abused; he who abuses has been abused.*

These words take over; I can't stop them. They incessantly march through my head, stomping across my brain, smashing aside all other thoughts until I'm bent over the bowl of cookie dough gasping for air, dizzy and nauseous. I can't breathe!

In the next second, I'm jolted to the floor. In front of me, at the end of a long narrow tunnel, I see something that looks no bigger than a tiny television screen, the size of a deck of cards, and I watch as poorly lit images project onto this tiny screen. It's as if someone is thumbing through a small flipbook or a stack of cards, showing me things I should know. Something about each scene on each card is dimly recognizable and then it's gone, flipping to the next one. My knees and elbows dig into the floor; the wooden spoon, still clenched in my hand, stands like a sentinel, witness to this strange and frightening phenomenon.

I squint into the screen at the end of the tunnel and glimpse scene after scene of something so far away and so fleeting that I can barely grasp the meaning. The screen seems to pause on one vision, the genitals of a little friend from childhood. I don't know how I know this part of her so well. She's so small, tiny almost, the labia are pulled apart and I'm clipping bobby pins onto them. We're playing the game of Operation, a game she taught me. It was just a game, one that I hated, but a game only, though now I gather that it must have been more than that. Not simply a game, it meant that something was wrong—terribly, shockingly wrong.

Stricken, caught in the terrifying strangeness of the moment, I watch as more visions of childhood quickly flip before me, some vaguely recalled, others totally unfamiliar. And then, just as quickly, it's gone and I can't recall the details so finely presented an instant ago, but I know that something has shattered inside me.

Something has crashed through an ancient door and shown me what I have long forgotten.

With the screen gone, the tunnel dissolves and I find myself still hunched on the floor, shaking, drooling, and gasping for air, my heart pounding, head throbbing, and in the next instant a new wave of scenes spew out of me and I remember that strange game of Operation more clearly. It started at a very early age, maybe when I was three or four. In a quick sequence of visions I see it being played out hundreds of times over many years, a bedraggled string of memories, shocking in their detail. They are presented to me so briefly that I can't hold onto them—I know, however, that they are true.

As the memory of this game returns, I understand that there was something else behind it and, for the first time in my life, I wonder where that game originated and why we played it so often. I remember that my strange little friend did things to me and I did things to her, but now I wonder if someone was abusing her. And did someone abuse me as well? Shame, very old shame, always present though kept at bay, now totally smothers me under its old familiar mantle. I know where it comes from. I know now what I always sensed was true: *I wasn't a normal little girl.*

With a sense of dread, knowing I will have to come back to investigate these memories later, that I won't be able to push them away as easily as I once did, I force myself to stand up straight, to finish making the cookies, to be the perfect mother, appearing as if everything is fine. But the disturbing scenes lurk in the background of my awareness now, along with the stark and bitter realization that sexual abuse of some sort was part of my childhood. I grasp what I was never able to clearly see before: that I was most likely participating in a young child's acting out of her sexual abuse, the abused child acting out on another child what was happening to her. Someone was doing something horrific to her, and perhaps to me. Or did it originate with me? Did I instigate the acting out? Was I sexually abused as a child?

This is all too much for me to comprehend at the moment, none of it makes sense, but everything is different now. The past has cracked through the still surface of calm that I have worked so hard to maintain my whole life. At age forty-eight, the long-held illusion of an almost perfect childhood has finally and permanently shattered.

Crushed by the heavy blow of this striking realization, I automatically spoon the dough onto the baking sheets as I've done hundreds of times before. As I put the cookies to bake and wash the bowls and utensils that old mantle of shame turns into a more familiar state of depression. As I struggle to re-establish a sense of inner calm and equilibrium, as I try to keep my body from shaking, I can't help but dwell on the fact that something had always been terribly wrong.

I had been such a quiet child, too quiet, always afraid, always sad. As I ponder where that deep sadness might have come from, the memory of this game, pulled up from the depths of my unconscious, announces itself as the key to everything. And suddenly I'm no longer a mature adult, no longer a mother baking cookies in her own kitchen, but a tiny child completely alienated and totally alone.

I feel a deep sense of sadness for that little girl I once was, who never knew she had lost something, a little girl whose whole life was defined by what happened to her, without her permission, without her realizing it. I understand that every action and reaction, every decision, every moment of paralysis and every moment of reckless abandon, from earliest childhood until this very moment, was influenced by what happened. I always wondered why I was so afraid, why fear was my constant companion. At this moment of clarity I finally know, but what do I really know? It's all still too dim, too frightening to investigate any further. I can't stay with the painful feelings and thoughts that come spilling out of me and by the time the cookies are baked I'm safely sealed in again, feeling somewhat back on familiar ground.

"I'll close the door for the time being," I decide.

I go to bed and soothe myself to sleep, chanting my oldest and dearest mantra: *Let no one in.*

June 20, 2001

Over the years, vague memories of that strange game had popped up quite often, though rather than stop and wonder about them, I'd quickly push them back into the darkness from which they had come, too disturbing to linger over. As a child they were more readily accessible, surprising me often enough with their shamefully strange and curious play, but as I got older and further from that time in my life the memories receded. Later, as a young adult, the instant they appeared I turned away as fast as I could, running like a scared child from the looming monster of horrible secrets that courted me throughout my childhood. The images, laced with confusion and fear, sat quietly behind the closed door of my unconscious until something stirred them again. As time went on and I successfully pushed the memories further into the past, it was as if they had never happened, as if I had never played that strange game with my strange little friend. Finally, I was able to suppress them totally—until now.

June 22, 2001

I feed tacos and birthday cake to five happy little girls at my daughter's tenth birthday party, normal girls. While I watch them eat, talk, and simply enjoy each other's company I remember myself at that age, uncomfortable around other children. Memories emerge of a shy and painfully quiet little girl, standing off on the side, watching life from the sidelines, rarely partaking. I was never quite present. I hated crowds, felt distant and lost out in the world, my feet never quite touching the ground.

I slept in a tight little ball, the covers pulled over my head, away from the monsters under the bed. I preferred my solitude where I could safely allow myself to get lost in the bubble of my own creativity. Being alone was my protection; with no one else around I could often relax.

I had always been shy, it was just accepted that I was painfully withdrawn and quiet, naturally a loner. My mother once commented that I never needed disciplining or quiet times when I was little because I was always quiet. In fact, I was painfully quiet, too frightened to move, fearful that I would do something wrong and be punished, far better to be still and silent. And, luckily, I could volitionally disappear into deep recesses of quiet within myself, and I was quite happy to do so.

At other times, a familiar yet inexplicable feeling would come over me and I would find myself involuntarily disappearing, shrinking deeper and deeper into a dark, narrow tunnel. I would crawl in as far as I could possibly go and then turn around and look out from its depths. It was like looking through the tiny aperture of a telescope from deep within the cave that was me. At times like those I didn't particularly like the experience, but it was very familiar, and so I wasn't frightened when it happened, odd as it felt.

I remember that I couldn't stand being touched or being too near anyone, especially adults. I mostly stayed away from boys too, until I was in my twenties, rarely dating in high school and college. If I did, the dates were brief, highly tense and nervous occasions. I dreaded the time spent in those uncomfortable circumstances with an unfamiliar person who I knew wasn't really interested in me but only in trying to touch my body, to kiss me or get inside my pants. I was afraid of physical touch. I suspected that I was pretty odd, that something was wrong with me because I wasn't sexually interested, as other girls seemed to be. I tried not to let it bother me too much, though it disturbed me that I always felt so dead inside.

I had a boyfriend when I was in my twenties, an older man, almost twenty years older. After my first marriage ended I spent four years with him in his world of travel, wine, and sex. He roused me from the dead, awakening feelings I never knew I could experience, and I loved him for it. He taught me that everything was permissible, that it was actually fun to be beautiful and to enjoy pleasures.

I gained weight and looked like a woman for the first time in my adult life. My breasts filled out and my body began to move differently. He took me dancing, dining, and filled me with sensual delights, but he also controlled me. At one time I was not even allowed to leave the apartment we shared. He brought freelance illustration jobs home for me to work on and basically kept me imprisoned. He knew where I was and what I was doing every minute of every day. In the end, I discovered he kept me under such tight control to keep hidden the truths of his own exploits. He told me strange stories of why he was coming home so late, or why he needed to work all weekend, or travel so frequently to other cities on business. I believed him, naively so, but I wanted to. For a long time it was an agreeable arrangement.

I was always a runner and a walker and once, while walking around the city in the evening, I saw his car parked in front of an apartment building—where I knew his old girlfriend lived—when he was supposed to be in another city. I finally reacted, the message too clear to ignore or excuse. I kicked his car door and smeared dog feces on the windshield in a fit of anger, and stomped away to await his return. In the end, when I told him I could no longer believe a word he told me, he announced that he was done with me. At the time, I felt I was being tossed back to the dead, that I had been used, but I also knew that, in spite of my disappointment in him, he had shown me that I did have the capacity to feel, to receive and give love. But I also understood that he couldn't fight the truth; that truth was stronger than words and by finally accepting it myself, that time, I was free to move on.

June 23, 2001

I wake up each morning expecting everything to return to normal, back to the way it used to be, but it's as if I'm in a strange new world where everything is slightly askew. The present is fading and that dim past I had glimpsed is sharpening, coming into focus as more memories of my child self begin to emerge. Today I wake up with a whole new perspective on that child. For the first time I feel connected to her trials and I deeply mourn that four-year-old girl who was buried alive, that ten-year-old who was so confused, that thirteen-year-old who was so silent, that fifteen-year-old who was so angry, that eighteen-year-old who was so afraid. Even so, I still don't know why I was always so sad and frightened.

More memories are emerging, but I don't dare write them down. However, I'm beginning to understand that there was a good reason for some of the mysteries of why I was the way I was as a child.

Someone once told me that when he first met me he thought I looked so young, at thirty-two more like twenty-two, but when he had looked into my eyes he was shocked.

"I saw great depths of sadness, as if you have lived one hundred hard years," he later told me.

I never forgot that. I took it as a riddle, that I was supposed to figure out something about myself; that I was supposed to uncover those one hundred hard years. After he said that, I went home and peered into my eyes, gazing into a mirror for a long time, trying to solve the riddle of me, but only darkness looked back.

June 24, 2001

We broke the news of the divorce to our two children and our families today. We've decided to spend the next year living together in our rather large house, working through childcare and financial issues as we take steps to the final break. I'm determined that our children remain the most important considerations as we go through this process. My husband is agreeable and the fact that he works out of a home office will help greatly in realizing this. It's not an easy decision and may prove to be exceedingly challenging for all of us, but I'm hopeful that in the long run it will work well for everyone. I know we have many months of conflict, change, anxiety, fear, and sadness to slog through as we take this journey together.

June 27, 2001

I wake up in shock, not feeling anything and yet feeling the weight of everything. Not sleeping much, I get up early, run for a few miles, make some coffee and go to the studio. I work there all day, numbing my feelings by painting, preparing for the art classes I teach, talking to clients and gallery owners, and working on prepping furniture for painting. I've mastered several faux finish techniques now and, along with my children's furniture painting business and illustration work, I'm branching out into painting murals and faux finishes in people's homes. This is how I make a living and so far business is pretty good. Some days people walk in and out of the studio throughout the day, a large and airy space with sun streaming through the windows, crammed full of art supplies, furniture, paintings and a variety of works in progress.

I've never been very extraverted, but I can usually rustle up some bright words of invitation and greeting to visitors. However, lately, I'm pretty depressed and outwardly I'm sure it shows. I feel glum and distant and I'm not sure how to handle the intrusion of this old stuff while at work, these memories that are suddenly staring me in the face. How do I get rid of them long enough to appear normal, to do what I have to do? All of a sudden the most important thing seems to be to rid myself of these horrors that I've successfully kept out of sight for so long; to get them out of mind, out of body, and out of memory, as quickly as possible.

I thought I was doing okay with my life—until now. I thought I was sailing along pretty nicely, but now I realize I've just existed all these years, just made it through life, barely living really. I wonder if simply seeing the past from a new perspective is enough to let it go. If I change my view of my life, will that make me feel better?

I admit that right now I feel terrible, wound so tight I can hardly feel my body at all. My emotions, tightly crammed inside, are ready to erupt. I'm finally ready to spew them out, but I don't really know how. It might sound like the easiest thing in the world to just let out a scream or shout of anguish, but I've never been able to do that. I just hope it doesn't happen at work, on a job, or when I'm teaching a painting class. And even though I may want to let loose, I'm afraid, because underneath I know I'm not allowed to; somebody told me that a long time ago, to never make a sound. My voice is caught, strangled by those old commands.

June 28, 2001

I meet with Chuck and try to talk about what happened to me when I was making the cookies. I stare at my clenched hands in my lap, agonizing for a long time about how to begin, stalling, clearing my throat.

"I have to talk," I say, "but I can't. It feels impossible."

"It's okay, take your time, whenever you're ready," Chuck says gently.

Finally, after what feels like hours, unable to lift my eyes and look at him, I bow my head, put my hands over my face, and haltingly speak of the disturbing visions, the old stuff that I remember. I speak words that I can't believe I'm saying while invisible hands clench my throat, trying to strangle me, not wanting me to speak the ancient secrets, but I get the words out, somehow, in staccato-like phrases that fall on the floor between us, dried tidbits of shameful memories.

"Her game."

"Operation."

"We went wherever we could."

"Locked the bathroom door."

"Went into the woods."

"Took off our clothes."

"Lie down and spread your legs, she said."

"We spread labia apart with bobby pins."

"Put things in vagina."

"Sticks."

"I hated the game."

"Knew it was wrong."

"Hated going to her house."

When I finish talking, it dawns on me that I've always had access to these memories, but repeatedly suppressed them, too ashamed and embarrassed by what they might mean about me. Perhaps I was a deviant, a sadistic personality. It's equally disgusting to imagine that I was so weak and pliable that I couldn't say no and just walk away from my strange little friend.

"Why didn't you call me when you were in the throes of it?" Chuck asks.

"I couldn't," I say, feeling deeply ashamed. "I just figured I'd handle it. I didn't know what to say, how to describe what was happening to me, it was too bizarre. I felt like I was going crazy."

"You entered a state of *non-ordinary reality*, had an experience, and returned to tell about it," he says. "This is the time of *the usher*. The shamans would call it the moment when everything changes. This is a very important moment."

Who are these shamans that he speaks so knowingly about? I wonder, and even though I don't completely understand what he's talking about, I nod, because what he says makes perfect sense. I know I've just been ushered into a part of my hidden self; something inside me has been revealed after long silence and I sense that this is indeed the moment when everything changes.

"It's frightening to put it down on paper, to make it so real," I say. "I feel numb, sad, so alone and yet I'm so practiced at those feelings, they're like good old friends come to keep me company."

Chuck asks if there's anything else I remember about that time.

"I get a stab in my heart every time someone uses the phrase *spread your legs*," I say. "I remember swimming in the community pool and another girl innocently wanting to dive down and swim between my legs and when she said *spread your legs,* I almost panicked. But, in true form, I recovered quickly and spread my legs, but only a little bit, only enough. As an adult on the gynecologist's table I had the same experience. When the doctor would say the same thing, *spread your legs*, disturbing chills would course through me. I knew there was something associated with that phrase, but I couldn't figure it out at ten years old or even thirty years old."

I feel unburdened, lighter and somewhat enlightened as we talk. I find that after all these years of being secretive and hidden, because I was told to be that way, I'm eager to release myself from those old bonds and truly get to know myself.

"I once tried to confess all of this to a priest, in fourth grade," I say. "I was nine years old. I told him I touched myself 'down there' and sometimes I did it to another girl and she did it to me too, but he didn't quite get it. He said something about how we have to touch ourselves sometimes and then he got up out of the confessional and came around to look at me, a scared little girl in my school uniform, hiding my face in my hands, daring to speak about what I considered the biggest sin in the world. But he disappointed me. I wanted him to tell me that God loved me anyway, that it was all right, that I was a good girl. Instead I felt rejected because all he did was look at me, grunt and return to his seat on the other side of the screen. I closed up even tighter after that, deciding I'd never speak of it again. After I left the confessional and walked out of the little room where confessions were being heard, I had to pass all my little classmates lined up waiting their turns. It was like walking a gauntlet; everyone was staring at me. I was sure they must have heard my confession and I was positive they had heard the priest get up and walk around to look at me, the poor sinner cowering in the confessional. I was mortified and vowed to never confess a real sin ever again."

While I tell these things to Chuck in the privacy of a different kind of confessional, I feel almost safe, as if it's okay to finally come out from under the covers I still hide under at night, to come out of the confessional feeling absolved of my sins. I lift my eyes and peek out from between my fingers and see this nice man sitting there, looking at me with such kindness and compassion that I let my hands drop from my face, where I've held them during the entire session. And as I do so, I feel my child self begin to emerge, daring to peek out from under the safety of my old childhood blankets, and talk to this nice man too. I sense it's okay to tell him these things, and he does not disappoint me.

I tell Chuck that the same older boyfriend who taught me that I could feel also triggered the first flashbacks I ever had, screaming attacks that erupted out of nowhere, simply a touch or a pressure in a certain place and I would flip out, shrieking, creeping us both out. Often they happened when I had been drinking alcohol and my normal state of rigid control was compromised. The thing was, I never felt real until I was in that particular relationship, but even then there were those kinds of episodes that kept me from being fully present and engaged in my body.

"Talking about these memories explains why I've always felt so unreal, so not present." I say, finally understanding something key about myself.

"Don't search for memories, don't agonize," Chuck says, as our time comes to an end. "They'll come on their own, when they're ready."

When I get up to leave I feel like a zombie; no feelings, I'm just numb. I can barely walk but somehow stumble to the door and down the short flight of steps to the ground.

"Lift one leg. Lift the other. Do that again and again until you get to the car," I tell myself, as I lift my concrete feet and walk haltingly, stiff-legged, toward the street where I've parked my car.

Later in the day, I notice that the old feelings are still stuck; those hands still choke me. I still can't cry or release anything, though I desperately want to. I want to scream or laugh, anything would help, but I can't. I don't know how. I remain so quiet on the outside, yet screaming on the inside. Everything is buried so deeply; there's no release lever, no button to push for escape though I'm tightly wound up, desperately yearning for release.

"May it come soon," I beg.

I can't eat much and I feel ill for most of the day. I try not to think too much, but I can't stop the images from slipping out of their own accord. Objects and words emerge repeatedly, haunting every hour: *sticks, operation, legs, genitals, bobby pins, hair curlers—not a game.* I write down as much as I can, jotting these notes but keeping the fullness of the images inside, safe from prying eyes, from the old judges: scolding priests, nuns, and parents. Even though I've opened my mouth and started talking about all of this stuff with Chuck, I'm still afraid to write out the truth. I must still uphold the silence of my child self to a certain extent. I must respect her lifelong control of the situation; after all, it kept me alive and sane.

I'm constantly struck by the ability of that child self to keep everything in for so long, because I remember that I was really hurting back then, but I also know that keeping it to myself was really my only protection. I remember feeling safe inside my silence, away from others, keeping myself isolated because other people and other children were so threatening. I was anti-social to a fault, withdrawn and alone, but there was a desperate underlying purpose: *to remain in one piece.*

Observing other kids having fun was a frightening scenario. I couldn't imagine acting as freely as they did, it seemed so unsafe. Always on the alert, I wondered how they could allow themselves be so unguarded, so unprotected, so inattentive to who was around them. Being by myself was safer. I could easily withdraw from the world. I felt happiest alone, reading, drawing, daydreaming, which I did a lot. And in spite of the woods being the setting of some of those disturbing memories with my strange little friend, I still loved the woods. It wasn't the setting that was frightening.

It was not my fault. These words come to me out of nowhere, suddenly falling into my thoughts, a new idea suddenly entering this strange process I'm undergoing. I was not even aware that I had done anything wrong and now here I am with a new mantra. *It was not my fault.*

June 29, 2001

Fantasies fill me; daydreams come to rescue me. I push away the bitter truths that are emerging and focus on memories of a happier childhood, hopeful that there were indeed good times too. I use these softer versions of childhood to help me through the long moments when I'm dragged into sudden turmoil, caught between two worlds, where old memories fight for acknowledgment, too many at once, doing battle with the scared self who wants the status quo to remain in power. I go to war against them with other thoughts, planning meals and things to do with the kids, trying to stay present and busy while at the studio. In an effort to not slip into the deep recesses of the past, I engage in talk with my studio partner, though at times I have no voice, no capacity for sound. I have to force myself to speak out loud, to swim up to the surface of the present day and appear to be normal, alive, but I'm mostly quiet, as usual.

As I battle the old memories that are attempting to emerge after long suppression, and confront the fearful self who is so afraid that the release of them means annihilation, I'm reminded of other times when that silent and fearful self was in control. So afraid to utter a sound, I kept silent when I gave birth to both of my children. I remember the painful silence I upheld as I go into that fragile shell of self once again. I recall that I didn't let loose, cry, scream, or even utter one mighty yell during the entire birthing process of either child. I *quietly* gave birth.

"You're incredible, not a peep," said the head nurse.

"I did groan, a little," I said.

"Honey," she said, "that was nothing. You should hear what goes on in here!"

I lay there quietly throughout the labor and birth of my daughter, half present and half someplace else, lost between two worlds, neither of which was familiar. Two young nursing students, whom I had given permission to be present, stood off to the side, near my feet, their hands clasped in front of them. They were about to witness their first live birth. I noticed them crying at one point, clearly affected, and I wondered what was wrong with me.

"Why can't I be affected too? Why don't I cry too? Something is wrong with me," I thought. "I'm just a wooden woman. I can't feel."

When the nurse handed me my beautiful daughter to hold for the first time I was so stiff and numb, I feared I would drop her. Picturing her rolling out of my wooden arms and onto the floor, I asked my husband to take her from me, sending her all my love after holding her only briefly, telling her I was sorry.

I was in shock, but from what I knew not. I was always that quiet though, always afraid to admit to pain. Why? Even as I undergo this truth-seeking process, delving into myself, I can't admit that I feel anything, that I'm bothered by anything, even the divorce. I'm always fine. People ask how I'm doing and I'm always fine. Well, inside I'm dying. Inside I'm wooden. Inside I'm covered up and buried.

I'm staying by myself a lot at home. I lie on my bed fogged in by thought and memory. Though in separate bedrooms, my husband and I still share the house as we work through the separation agreement. The kids come in and out of my room, visiting me, cuddling in bed. I can't talk to my husband and I don't want to either, I just need to be alone.

I get up every day and go to work and come back to my bed again at the end of the day. I get through the days at work, painting, setting up appointments, scheduling and organizing, always smiling, but underneath numb, trying to concentrate on just remaining present, just doing what needs to be done.

I go to bed early each evening and lie under the covers trying to make sense of this mysterious self that is beginning to haunt me.

June 30, 2001
I'm at a party when, all of a sudden, I'm talking and laughing so hard that I feel like I won't be able to stop. Funny comments come pouring out of quiet me in rapid fire. I make people laugh, and then I make them laugh some more. I can't stop myself.

I feel like I'm losing it.

Chapter Four

I am Powerful

July 1, 2001

There's a lump in my throat. It's stuck there, trying to force me to let go and cry, but I still can't. Feeling only slightly detached from last week's memories, I'm not experiencing any relief, none whatsoever.

The knot of pain lodges ever more firmly as the day goes on, hurting as it grows bigger and bigger. I wonder when relief will finally come so I can start again, so I can start over from a new place, feeling better, feeling like me again. I'm used to being in control, used to being a doer, a helper, but now I'm the one needing help and it's so hard to ask for, so hard to say, "I need," and hard to accept what is so kindly and genuinely offered.

July 3, 2001

It's Tuesday and I meet with Chuck first thing in the morning. I feel better today, not so heavy and laden. We do EMDR—Eye Movement Desensitization Reprocessing, a psychotherapeutic treatment tool—around the lump in my throat. I put the headphones on and the soft bi-lateral thudding in my ears helps decrease the intensity of it. It actually feels less present, less painful, though I'm too afraid to release it completely because I'm afraid I'll have a total breakdown if I do. It acts like a plug; holding everything down that wants to come out. I need to keep it in place until I'm ready to let go of whatever might be behind it. It's frightening to imagine myself going off the deep end, so to speak, or even acting slightly out of character. I must be in control at all times.

Chuck doesn't try to dissuade me from holding onto it, but, sensitive to my dilemma, suggests that I choose a relaxed and safe place, a place that I could easily visualize and use as a respite from haunting memories or pain, or whatever else arises over the next week, including the lump in the throat. I select a spot I used to hike to as a girl, often alone or with friends. It's a beautiful place high on a mountain overlooking a valley, far from everything familiar and known. I always felt so at home there, so singularly safe. While Chuck works the EMDR machine, I escape to my golden pasture on top of the mountain, far from my strange little friend and her curious games, a place she never went with me. I sit once again under the open blue skies and then lie down spread-eagle in the warm grass, certain that I won't be interfered with or disturbed in any way. I sit on the white bench under the old apple tree basking in my aloneness on top of the world, munching on a tart apple, looking far into the distance, happy. This is my safe place.

July 4, 2001

I force myself to take my usual daily run today, even though I'm not feeling particularly peppy. I know I need the energy boost it gives me, but something disturbing happens as I jog along. Violent spasms begin to erupt from deep within my abdomen. Cramping and nauseous, I urge myself to keep going.

"Just run it off," I say, forcing myself to run upright, concentrating on a point far in the distance, taking my attention off what my body is doing. The painful lump in my throat grows bigger and rises a little higher as I run, until it feels like an angry, unspoken roar stuck in my throat. I almost crawl the last leg of my three-mile run back home and just make it to the bathroom before I'm sick with vomiting and diarrhea. I know I must stop pushing myself, stop torturing myself, but I also acknowledge that I do it so I can feel something, so I can feel *anything*, even pain.

I long for a day of distraction from the memories and, as luck would have it, I have to drive a group of family members to a party at a distant relative's home. The first leg of the drive is an hour long. I pick up my elderly parents and aunt and then continue for another hour before arriving at our destination. Other family members arrive shortly after us. There are cousins for my kids to play with and an in-ground pool for them to swim in.

Feeling distant, I stand leaning against a fence that surrounds the pool, not really interested in talking. I keep my sunhat pulled low over my face, both hiding under it and shading my skin and eyes as much as possible from the bright sunlight. After a while I notice that I'm in an almost catatonic state. I can't really feel my body and everyone else seems really far away, their voices barely reaching me even though they're sitting right in front of me. As I experience this sensation, I understand how an uncle, who is schizophrenic, must feel most of the time. He too tends to stand still in one spot, unmoving, at family gatherings. When you look into his eyes there's no one looking back at you, his dark gaze turned inward, looking at something that no one else can see. For a brief moment I panic, wondering if that's what's wrong with me too, but I quickly shake the thought away when my daughter calls me over to watch her swim across the pool underwater. I shift out of my altered state to cheer her on as she skims along the blue bottom, a small, quick little girl, soaring through the water, emerging breathless but triumphant on the other side.

I had asked my parents if they would mind having my two children stay with them for a few days, after the party.

"I need a break," was all I said when I had spoken to my mother on the phone earlier in the week, but I wanted to rescind my request as soon as I felt the familiar rebuff of her response. I felt judged as she scolded me; sending me soaring into old self-criticism and doubt, as if I were a child again. Did I really need a break? How dare I say I need something? I wanted to harden up in the old manner, stiff upper lip and just carry on, as I had been taught. But, instead, I repeated my request.

"I need a break," I said, "even a day or two."

In the end, my mother agreed. I know she enjoys the company of her grandchildren and when I proposed the idea to my kids they were amenable, provided we could talk on the phone any time. So, after the party, I deliver my children into the hands of my reserved and distant parents and, in spite of feeling almost like I'm deserting them, I drive away with a sense of relief, knowing I'll have a few days to work on myself, to study the memories and what's happening to me. I feel the incredible freedom, however fleeting, of not having to take care of anyone else.

As I drive away from my parent's property, I glance up toward the mountaintop, to my safe place where I used to hike so many years ago. I can't see it from the road and something tells me not to look, to keep facing straight ahead. There are new homes creeping up the mountainside now and what I remember most likely no longer exists. I decide it's best to just have the memory, to only go there in my imagination. After a few miles I leave the winding back roads and get on the parkway, an hour's driving ahead of me.

For long stretches I'm the only one on the road, the parkway nearly empty of traffic. After a while it seems as if I'm being drawn forward, the gray asphalt roadway like a giant magnetic strip, pulling me onward much faster than the actual speed I'm driving. I notice the trees along the edges of the narrow roadway beginning to lose their shape as my peripheral vision blurs considerably. A muffled silence fills the car as I drive hunched over the steering wheel, peering into the twilight. Suddenly, I'm hurtling down that dark tunnel again, where the memories live in flickering old movies, long forgotten.

I remember that I played the game of Operation once or twice with another young girl. We had discussions about whether or not it was a sin—that's why I finally revealed it to the priest. When I told her I'd finally gotten the nerve up to confess, she was amazed that I'd had the guts to do it. She just couldn't bring herself to, though she agonized over the sin of it as much as I did. But when I told her it wasn't worth it, that I hadn't gotten resolution, she was relieved to be absolved of having to go down that same embarrassing road into the confessional.

"Remember that game we used to play?" she'd asked me once, as an adult, when I met her at a party.

"No, no, I don't remember," I said, as disturbing images tried to emerge from darkest memory, but I just stood there, embarrassed, staring at her, shaking my head. Before she could explain any further I got called away. Greatly relieved, I left her standing there with her memories as I went to help set out food.

I remember being together in the bathroom at this girl's house once and her younger brother coming in to use the toilet. He saw what we were doing, but didn't even question it. I remember he told us there was blood on the toilet paper when he wiped his bottom. It seemed significant to me at the time, that he too had something wrong 'down there,' and it scared me. I wondered if all kids had things wrong with them, with their private parts. I remember lying on my back on a bathmat; my legs spread wide exposing my genitals, trying to explain to this girl what to do. I was seven or eight years old. I remember trying to explain to her how the game worked and what we were supposed to feel. I remember she didn't get it; she just couldn't grasp the point of it.

As soon as this memory emerges I feel terrible. I remember that it was a most unsatisfying experience. My sense was that playing the game with her never occurred more than a handful of times and I know that I felt terribly guilty about it. On the tails of that memory another emerges, and I remember I once convinced a young boy to play this game with me as well. I took him into my closet, but he was not set up with the right equipment. I didn't know what to do with the little penis hanging between his legs, so I released him, telling him it was a secret game and not to tell anyone. I heard him walk out of my bedroom and tell his father that I had made him take off his pants. I shouted out that it was a lie, that he did it himself, which was true. I was four at the time. As I begin to feel the enormous weight of shame and guilt at what I had once done to these two young children, the smell of my strange little friend's genitals permeates the entire car and more memories emerge.

As I continue driving down that tunnel, keenly aware and yet simultaneously unaware that I'm actually driving my car, I remember how my strange little friend had everything planned ahead of time when we played Operation. It was her game and she was in control of every detail. Everything had to be arranged and methodically laid out before we started. First we would go into the woods, if that was the place we were to play the game that day. Clearing away rocks and sticks on the ground and smoothing over the dirt, we made a place to lie down. Then we snapped thin twigs into short pieces the lengths of bobby pins. When it was her turn to be the patient she would undress and lie on the ground. As the doctor, the first thing I did was open her up, spreading her legs wide and pulling apart her labia. Then I stuck the short pieces of twigs we had so carefully prepared—each one exactly the same length—crossways, so that her labia were held open by the sticks. I placed as many twigs as possible between her labia, stretching her open as far as possible. The point was that it must hurt. If it didn't hurt, she'd let me know and I had to do more, put more things in her, even poke sticks into her vagina until she got the relief she desired. Then it was my turn to be the patient.

I hated playing this game. I didn't like doing it to her or having it done to me. As the memories of this play emerge, I recall knowing that there was something wrong with this game that we always played so intently. No one else ever played this game or any game like it. I was often furious with myself for being there, for falling into her trap again, for agreeing to play with her at all, yet I was also paralyzed, frozen, mesmerized by the methodical preparations, each detail taking us deeper and deeper into a state I could not easily get out of. I couldn't have gotten myself out of those woods if I had tried. I didn't know how. This was the game I had tried to teach my other little friend.

After the emergence of these memories I'm surprised to find myself still driving along the parkway. I've lost track of time and place, feeling as if years have passed, but by the clock in the car I see that only about ten minutes have gone by.

I'm suddenly struck by how well thought out the game always was, as if my strange little friend spent all of her waking life figuring out how to enact it, plotting what we would do. Because, as soon as I arrived at her house, she took my hand and off we went to either a favorite outdoor spot in the woods, to an old shed, or into the bathroom or some other place inside her house. The energy that went into preparing for the game always carried the same intensity and methodical attention to detail. As we went about setting out the instruments needed for the game our attention was totally focused on what we were doing, the preparations sending us both into an altered state of mind so that by the time the 'operation' began we were both on automatic pilot, not fully present or perhaps only fully present in that strange and disturbing world.

I recall again my anger and frustration at having to play the game each time we met, but I also recall how helpless I was. Once started, I did not have the power to end it. We had to go through with it. We were driven to complete it before we could become normal little girls playing normal games.

I couldn't explain to that other little girl the dire need of playing this game. It didn't translate into the everyday world of play, though in that other world I knew exactly what the point of the game of Operation was. It was what my strange little friend and I did. Without question it was necessary. Eventually the game stopped, when I was about nine, I think. Another girl moved into the neighborhood and shortly thereafter she became my best friend and I didn't play Operation anymore with my strange little friend.

When I arrive home I discover that my husband is out.

"Don't expect me back any time soon," says a note on the kitchen counter.

I'm happy to have the house to myself for the first time in a long time, free to sit and write, to contemplate the events of the drive home without interruption. I'm tense after spending the day in the company of my parents and the relatives and now I notice that the lump in my throat has grown bigger again. With that old stuff pressing against me, hurting to my very core, I try to focus on what happened as I drove through that tunnel of memories. Thankful for the freedom of solitude, with no kids or husband to hear me, I even allow myself to express a little pain. I can't cry, but I squeeze out a few small yelps, as I accept the truth of what I learned about myself today.

Sitting in bed, finally allowing myself a few moments of tenderness toward my child self, I'm jolted out of my reverie by the phone ringing. It's my daughter calling.

"Mommy, I want to come home. I can't sleep."

I tell her she has to do the best she can because it's now ten-thirty and I can't make the long drive again tonight. She starts crying.

"They're so mean," she says. "They won't let us sleep together. Grandpa made us sleep in separate rooms. I don't like it here."

I tell her to be very brave and that she has to stay there tonight, but I'll come back and get them tomorrow. I don't blame her. She says her brother is feeling the same way.

"I know you are very strong and that you can stand it for one night," I say. "I love you. I'll see you in the morning."

They're already feeling the big changes that have been rolling into action over the past few months.

July 5, 2001

As I head out to pick up the kids, I wonder if more memories might emerge, if the drive itself will once again trigger events of the past, as it did last night, but nothing new happens on the way, though I feel my energy draining out of me the closer I get to my parent's house and the old neighborhood.

Although I feel somewhat angry that my parents can't accept and appreciate the tender fears of my children, who just wanted to be together, sharing their experience and needing the closeness of each other last night, I know I have more important things to spend my energy on, so I merely thank them for having them. The kids, much relieved, climb into the car and we head back home. I spend the rest of the day with them, knowing that over the next week they'll be starting summer camps and I'll be working most days.

July 6, 2001

I've spent thirteen hours at the studio today. I've been able to take this time for myself because it's my husband's day with the kids and his night to make dinner. Over the past year and a half the studio has proven to be a godsend, a refuge as well as a place of business. It's also been helpful in establishing a more clearly defined structure at home. Little by little we've reached an agreeable arrangement that seems to be working for all of us. The kids are getting used to separate times with each parent, as we, in turn, share the childcare issues, taking turns driving them to and from activities. My husband also agreed to take over cooking and other duties one night a week so I can work late. I force the issue by not going home, because if I go home the agreement tends to fall apart. Now it's late. I'm still at the studio. The building is quiet as I take some moments to reflect on the day.

As I worked today, I noticed how sore my arms were after gripping the steering wheel so tightly while driving home the other night, as I peered into the tunnel, into the past. Throughout the day, more dark memories appeared, taking every opportunity to sneak into my awareness. Even though I kept busy in a conscious effort to hold them back, it was impossible to halt them once they started. I felt like I was under a dark tent most of the day, memories sneaking in, joining me there until it was filled to bursting, the roof a heavy weight above me as more memories sat on it, waiting for their turn. Sometimes I listened to what they had to tell me; sometimes I closed them out. Sometimes I was curious about them. At other times they were extremely difficult to handle and I immediately pushed them away.

No matter how far I go into the past, I still can't fathom where the ideas for the game of Operation came from, how the game itself first started. I wondered all day how my strange little friend could have invented such deliberate and well-planned actions at the tender age of four, or perhaps even younger. As I recalled her focused attention on every detail of the game, I began to hear her sighing. It was as if she was with me, inside that tent, and it sounded like she was actually enjoying the game, sighing pleasurable sighs, not sounding like she was in anguish or distress at all.

Then I remembered another game, the Tree Branch game.

There was a maple tree we used to climb in a field near her house. Following her instructions I'd take off my clothing and, sitting naked, straddle one specific, fairly thick branch that had all of the small branches broken or cut off it, so that it was peppered with small stubs. The game was to drag our bottoms along this branch, rubbing our genitals over the stubs, as we made our way along to the end of the branch before jumping off to the ground. As the memory came through today, I also saw an old chair in the field that we often used to climb up or down from the branch. This game was meant to be fun, but it was also important that we pressed down on each cut off branch nub, that we felt it poking into us.

In the memory, I was age four or five and, again, it was not my favorite game, yet it was better than playing Operation. Often I wore a dress when I played, especially in the summertime, and I recalled holding my dress up and out of the way so I could perform this game to exact instructions, to her instructions, often with her standing beneath me on the ground pointing out that I was not doing it right, telling me to sit on the stubby branches much harder, making me go back and start all over again if I missed one, if I tried to skip one in an effort to hurry the game, or if I fell off the branch. The game was to be played to her specific instructions or I was made to do it again and again. As usual, she was in complete charge.

As the memory emerged I smelled the branch, the field, and my own smell, but mostly I smelled her. All day, after that, I was unable to escape her smell. It clung to me, following me through those memories and right into the present. Now I'm quite nauseated by it.

As I sit and continue reflecting on the process I went through today, I'm struck by the realization that my strange little friend still haunts me as she once did when we were young. I realize she has always haunted me. I wish I knew more. I wish I could remember more details. I wish I could remember why.

It seems to me that her kinky ideas, varied and strange though they were, did seem to be her own ideas. However, I've been puzzled by the same question all day: *Where did those games come from?* When I see her doing some of the things she did, I don't see a scared, abused child. I see someone in complete control, methodically devising bizarre steps in weird games.

The memories don't stop in spite of Chuck telling me to not search for any. They come of their own accord, tumbling out daily, hourly, excruciating minute by excruciating minute. I can't control them; I've given up on that idea. I've gone to that safe place in my mind so many times, seeking brief moments of relief from the endless barrage of memories.

As soon as I step into the cool woods and begin walking along the path that leads to my safe place I feel calm. As I begin the hike to the mountaintop a quiet peaceful happiness begins and it grows more intensely real as I climb higher toward the golden meadow and the blue sky. In my imagination, I throw myself to the ground when I get there and lose myself in the clouds. It's almost as if I'm really there, and this is enough to give me momentary respite from the onslaught of the memories, from the smells, the sensations, and painful pictures of the past.

July 7, 2001
The lump is now a permanent fixture in my throat; a hard rock that won't budge. I almost squeezed a few tears out the other night, but barely. Even though no one was home I still didn't want anyone to hear me, the lump quite effectively blocking any release, of either sound or tears it seems. And I didn't want to lose control either, which is all the power I really have, and have ever had, that and my fierce determination.

Today I remembered learning to ride a bicycle, a two-wheeler. I learned in one day, when I was four years old. I wouldn't give up until I had mastered it. I was that way with everything practical. Toilet training—I was shown the process once and I mastered it. I was the wonder child, outdistancing my older brother, fully ready to tackle the challenges of this world.

As I allow myself to go deeper into the memory of that determined little girl that I was on that long ago day, I remember my mother taking a few minutes to instruct me in how to ride that little bike, a small hand-me-down two-wheeler that a neighbor had given me. It was a rarity to see my mother outside even, a wonder to have her actually running behind me holding onto the back of the seat for a brief few minutes before going back up to the house to take care of my younger siblings. I remember her telling me to sit just like that, in the middle of the seat, to get my balance and just ride away.

I remember how frustrating it was every time I veered into the bank on the side of the dirt road, falling off into the little runoff stream that ran out of the pump house there, and the heaviness of the bike as I picked it up and started again. I spent all day on the rarely traveled road in front of the house, and even though my mother pleaded with me several times to stop, to give it a rest, I would not stop my endeavors. I remember it getting gradually darker, closer to the time when my father would be coming home, my arms aching, my legs bruised and scraped, but I was determined to have that tipsy little bike conquered by then, and, by golly, I did. I think that determination and spirit are what have gotten me through every lonely minute of my life.

July 10, 2001
It's Tuesday, the day I meet with Chuck. I can no longer keep the secret memories to myself. This past, come to greet me after so many years, weighs too heavily. The memories haunt, the images sicken and, although I hear my mother's voice reprimanding that you never, *ever* talk about your personal life, I want to know how it all began. I'm going to finally talk about what I've carried inside me my entire life. I'm going to let it spill out of me. I'm determined.

By the time I get to my appointment with Chuck I'm totally drained, feeling ill, even though it's still early morning. I put the EMDR headphones on as usual and, as I struggle to articulate, to explain what happened all those years ago, I feel like a small child again, ashamed, knowing I've done something really bad. I sit with my head hanging down; unable to look Chuck in the eyes, embarrassed, sure that he'll judge me or consider me a horrible, strangely perverted person. But he doesn't do that at all. Instead, he listens very carefully to each word I speak, as they slowly and wrenchingly emerge from between my tightly clenched teeth.

He gently asks questions in an effort to help me figure out what could have possibly been going on. I tell him everything I've remembered so far. I tell him in gross detail about the strange games we played, more details of Operation, as well as the Tree Branch game. I speak about my frustration at always having to play those horrible games, how I attempted to play them with that other girl and boy too, and how boring they eventually became.

"No one ever looked for us," I say. "No one ever seemed to check on us or care what we did, even at that young age. We just roamed off into the woods, into the world, and did what we wanted. After a certain age, like right out of infancy, there seemed to be no supervision whatsoever. By the age of two we were often out of sight of adults, though we suffered the consequences of our actions, because if we did something wrong we were expected to take full responsibility. But there didn't seem to be anyone actually explaining anything to us about how the world works."

I tell him how proud I am of my child self, for her fierce determination, how I learned to ride that little bike in one day and then how a bigger girl, a foster sister of my strange little friend, broke it one day when she borrowed it. This memory flows out of the other memories as we talk, as the EMDR process does its work.

The foster girl was big for her age, I tell Chuck, perhaps a few years older, awkward, and clumsy. She asked to ride my bike one evening when I was outside in the driveway with some other children. I knew, as soon as I said yes, that it was a mistake. I knew something would happen. Within a few seconds of her taking my bike and hoisting her big body onto it, I heard a snap and the tiny bike literally split in two.

"Oh well," she said, as she stood there with the front wheel and handlebars in one hand and the rest of the bike in the other. "You can probably fix it."

She flippantly tossed the pieces onto the ground and walked away, while I stood there totally devastated. As I tell Chuck the story, I once again feel the wrenching sadness of that little girl self. And yet, I was determined that somehow I would repair it, though try as I might I could not possibly mend the break in the metal frame. Even my older brother—the knower-of-all-things, as I saw him—declared it worthless. I had worked so hard to learn to ride that little bike and it had afforded me a new kind of freedom that now was over because I had been too shy to say no to that bigger girl. This was the first time I understood that a different response on my part would have led to a different outcome, that in one second I could have changed everything, but I had hesitated and thus I could not protect what I knew was at risk. It would be a while before I received another bike.

As I tell Chuck this story the following memory spontaneously emerges.

"I got you a present," my father said when he got home from work one day, as he led me out to the garage.

"What is it?" I asked. I could hardly contain my excitement, a gift for me when it wasn't even my birthday.

"A bike," he said, as I followed him into the garage.

I was thrilled, hoping it was a new blue one, preferably a three-speed, a type that was popular back then. He lifted an enormous old dusty bike out of the trunk of his car, a bike that had belonged to his sister perhaps thirty years before, a nineteen-thirties style bicycle with big balloon tires, made of heavy metal, painted white.

I was so disappointed when I saw this ugly contraption that my desire for a new, fast blue bike instantly collapsed, but it was the only bike I would have for many years to come. I couldn't reach the pedals if I sat on the seat so I rode standing up, always far behind everyone else on their newer, lighter bicycles. Nonetheless, I rode all over the countryside on that bike, my only form of transportation.

As I speak of this memory, yet another emerges, quickly rumbling up from I don't know where, begging to be acknowledged too. It's another incident with that big foster girl, where my inability to speak up to protect something that was important to me would lead to yet another early awareness of how instantaneously things could change.

I had a doll, I tell Chuck, a soft baby doll whose rubber head used to pop off quite suddenly and although I could never get it back on, my mother, after much pushing and twisting, could. One day, while playing dolls with my strange little friend, the head of this doll popped off. When the foster girl saw what happened, she insisted that we have a funeral for it. I pleaded that my mother could fix it, but the bigger girl countered that it couldn't be fixed, showing me how impossible it was, telling me that I was silly to think that my mother could fix the doll when she couldn't. In the end she convinced me that the only thing to do was to have a funeral and burn the doll in the incinerator.

"That's what happens at a funeral," I remember her saying; "you burn in fire."

My strange little friend eagerly agreed to the ritual. We put the doll with her severed head in an old shoebox surrounded by flowers and I, silently screaming inside, knowing full well that my mother could fix the doll, numbly took part in the funeral procession. Caught by the dark power of this older girl, the bike-breaker, all I could do was follow behind as she led the way to the burn barrel. I was not even allowed to carry my doll to her death. Last in line, I walked solemnly behind my strange little friend, head bowed, desperately trying to hold back the tears that wanted to pour out.

The older girl, carrying my dolly in her coffin, instructed us to sing as we marched past the chicken coop and right up to the rusty incinerator barrel, out of which poured black smoke, a fire always smoldering. I don't know what we sang, something somber perhaps. Though I struggled to reach my voice, it was just simply too hard for me to sing. The only thing that would have come out was the sound of crying and I was not going to do that.

The only true mourner, I wanted to grab my doll and run home, to cry out my anger and annoyance at being coerced into this hideous funeral, but I was paralyzed. I could not utter a peep over the horrible fate of the one doll I owned. Voices in my head urged me to grab her and run, but I could not move.

At the burn barrel, I watched in horror as the older girl quickly and unceremoniously tossed the cardboard box into the smoky fire and poked at it with a stick for a few seconds before walking away, telling us that we'd better get out of there quick, that we'd get into trouble if we stayed. I felt the deep loss of my doll, and then, fearful of being reprimanded, I reluctantly turned and walked away with sorrow weighing heavily in my heart.

In that moment, I understood fully the folly of non-action, just as I had when I let this same girl take my bike. Had I acted differently just a few moments before, I could have changed the fortune of my beloved doll and she would still be with me. This was a lesson I would never forget, but it seems that I also had to relearn it many times before I realized it was not just understanding the lesson that was important, but that it was more important to learn how to *take action*, to actually act at the crucial moment. Even at that young age, I saw very clearly that a second could have meant the difference between life and death.

If only I could have acted.

As I tell Chuck the story of this funeral, I recall how frightened I was of the burn barrel. I knew we were not supposed to go near it and, in fact, it was hard to get too close because of the intense heat pouring from it. Full of guilt and remorse, I also worried that my mother would be angry at what had happened, that I would be scolded for allowing my doll to be incinerated. I recall only that my mother had little reaction when I told her—"Oh well, what's done is done!" Secretly I mourned the loss of that little doll for a very long time. Her death haunted me. I felt responsible.

Chuck and I continue processing with EMDR all the memories that came up so quickly, as well as the beliefs that emerged with them: *that I just let things happen, that I still don't fight back or speak up, and the strong feeling that I am totally responsible for everything that happens. Everything is my fault. I alone am to blame.*

The lingering smell of my strange little friend brings up old self-anger and I let it go through me as well. I work through the feelings and old beliefs, visiting them over and over again, with Chuck's promptings to keep going back, until I no longer feel angry with my child self, until I see that it wasn't my fault, that sometimes things just happen, even against my wishes and in spite of my best efforts.

"It was not my fault," I say, tentatively at first, but then I'm able to embrace this declaration of freedom.

"It was not my fault!"

I also realize that back then, when I was just a four-year-old girl, I hadn't really wanted to watch the burning of my doll; it was too painful. I feel such tender sadness for the little girl that I was when I acknowledge this, the little girl who had to stand there while those two other girls took her doll away from her and destroyed it. As I go back into the memory in EMDR, I feel okay as I walk away from the burning barrel this time with my four-year-old self. I take her hand and acknowledge her pain, the two of us united, finally letting our feelings be known, finally speaking the truth to each other.

"The first memory you had in the kitchen baking cookies paved the way for all of these memories to come through," Chuck explains.

"Well, they didn't quite knock me onto the floor like that first one did, like the *usher*, which made it all so real. But they certainly leave me with such old familiar feelings, heavy feelings of inadequacy and numbing fear," I say.

And then I admit that there was something enticing about going to play with my strange little friend, that in spite of the games we played there was something else, something that drew me there. There was a certain allure, a sense of the forbidden, a strangely tainted excitement, because you never knew what could happen there.

The session seems to end abruptly and before I know it I have to stand up and leave the darkness of that old world behind and stumble back out into sunshine, into this reality. I admit to Chuck that I've ignored my feelings for a long time and that I know it's finally time to pay attention to them now.

"Keep going to your safe place; take care of yourself," Chuck says.

"Yes, I'll do what I need to do."

After the session I drive to a nearby park and go for a hike and then sit on a bench overlooking the river for a little while. Taking in the calm expanse of water and the stretch of mountains on the other side helps ground me in this world again, the familiar shapes of the peaks on the far shore comforting, bringing me back to the present. I feel raw and bruised, exposed, as if I've split myself open and poked around inside my chest. I've discovered some strange things about myself, but it feels like I've only scratched the surface. I'm deeply curious about what was really going on back then.

July 11, 2001

I'm with her again, my strange little friend, in the woods. No longer a small girl, I'm eleven or twelve. We're in a strip of woods that separates two fields. She's operating on me. Small broken sticks are used to separate the labia. A large branch is stuck in my vagina and I'm instructed to hold it in place. Its leaves swoop down towards my belly button. She piles things on top of me, ritually laying leaves and sticks in a crisscross pattern, layering dirt on top of that, building up a mound over my pelvic region, out of which pokes the stick. She's humming to herself, in an altered state, an invisible world that I cannot enter. I look up through the leaves of the trees at the blue sky above as she works, not feeling anything, waiting for it to be over. Finally, she's done. I sit up and brush the dirt and debris from my lap, pull the stick out of my vagina and the small sticks one by one from between my labia, and then it's my turn to do this to her, exactly the way she's just done it to me.

I turn toward her lying on the ground, smelling earth and leaves, feeling the dirt beneath my buttocks, smelling her. I put my hand out to pick up a handful of dirt expecting to feel earth, but my hands touch something soft and I'm thrown into confusion. Momentarily lost, I don't know where I am. Surprised and shaking, I sit up to find myself in darkness. Familiar shapes slowly begin to materialize and I discover that I'm in my dark bedroom, touching the sheets on my bed. I realize that the *usher* has come visiting again, sneaking into bed with me; taking me back while I slumbered. It takes me a few minutes to get my bearings, to realize that although I had just been somewhere else, now I'm here in my bedroom.

The memory solidifies, becomes real, and in the same instant thoroughly shatters my original assessment that all of those games stopped at around the age of nine. I can no longer hold onto that hope, because in this memory we're older. I know it's the truth and not a dream. It actually happened over thirty-seven years ago, because I recognize the place, the stretch of woods, and the acting out, too. It's as familiar as the smells that remain with me as I lie back down, curl up on my side and try to fall back to sleep.

When I wake up in the morning, still shaken by the memory in the night, I call Chuck. We talk on the phone for a few minutes. His pragmatism calms me and I'm able to turn my attention to practical methods of dealing with the traumatic impact this process is having on me.

He calls my nighttime experience a *recapitulation*, another shamanic term, meaning to recapture and relive every moment of some aspect of the past, capturing the truth of it. The goal is to eventually be fully freed of it, so that there are no longer any strings of energy attached to it. In reliving my memory last night, he tells me, I was beginning the process of letting it go, letting the energy of it out of my body and my psyche so that it would no longer torment or hold me captive as it has done in the past. It's a process of desensitization that over time will free me of the memory as well as any old feelings or beliefs associated with it. I understand that it will not only take work to go through this process, but it's also going to take some pretty steady nerves if that's the kind of thing that I'm going to be encountering.

"Write it all down," Chuck says. "Acknowledge it, but don't dwell on it, don't try to figure it out. Go to the safe place when you need to."

THE MAN IN THE WOODS

"But those memories keep intruding. It's kind of hard to ignore something like that."

"Make note of them, then move away."

"Okay," I say. "I'm writing it all down, everything that comes to me."

After I hang up the phone, I go directly into another memory. I'm in the narrow passage of our laundry room, where my mother has called me. She's standing with her back to me, sorting dirty laundry into the washing machine. I stand behind her, scrunched against the wall, cowering and fearful of what she's going to say. My heart is beating in my throat. I'm eleven or twelve. She turns around, a pair of my underpants stretched between her two hands. Turning them inside out, showing me the streaks of dirt in the crotch, shaking out woody debris, her voice is sharp, demanding, and accusatory.

"Why is your underwear always so dirty? What are you doing that it looks like this?"

Mortified, unable to look into those glaring eyes only a few inches from mine, wanting to shrink into the wall behind me and disappear, I answer as quickly as possible.

"I go to the bathroom in the woods," I say, and it's only half a lie.

"Don't do that, go to somebody's house and use a bathroom," she commands, and, quickly turning away, she throws my dirty underpants into the washer and goes back to sorting the laundry.

As I stand there once again in memory, behind her turned back, feeling her bristling anger, her hard words echoing again, I clearly remember deciding two things that day. My first reaction was that from that moment on I would do my own laundry. I did not want my privacy so intrusively invaded, my deep inner conflict around the games in the woods so callously dismissed. I would rather shoot myself than get caught in such a humiliating position ever again. I also decided that I would never again communicate anything of personal importance to this bitter and angry woman. There was no real connection to speak of between us, but this totally severed what little there was. From that day on, I decided, I would be a stranger to her.

I slunk out of the laundry room that day feeling as if I had just survived the guillotine, accepting the blatant truth of the fact that I did not like her, as a mother or a person. I clearly remember how seethingly angry I felt; under my breath calling her an idiot for not knowing, not suspecting something, for not even trying to find out what was really going on. I felt justified in punishing her for her lack of attention that had already spanned the greater part of my childhood. I was going to punish her now, by never letting her know anything about me. But the truth was that I couldn't even begin to tell her what really went on. I don't think I knew myself. Maybe if I were still three years old, maybe then I could have said that someone was hurting me, or something like that, but by the time I was a preteen it had gone on far too long. It was too complicated and odd, too deeply embedded in my psyche, both the mortal sin of it and the mystery of it.

As far as what my strange little friend and I did, I would endure it because I knew it would be over, at least until next time. But I remember the pain of it too, the boredom, the humiliation, the frustration, and the anger at myself for being a part of it. And now, after last night's memory, I realize that our games went on for much longer than I had originally thought.

As the day goes on, other incidences emerge, other memories of being with her when we were older, preteens, but also teenagers. I remember seeing her pubic hair, her older face, her larger hands, her older voice instructing.

By evening, I realize I've been back in memory land with my strange little friend for most of the day. The day ends with memories of her other favorite game—aside from Operation—playing house, but even this game is tinged with a strange, unnerving quality. She determined the roles and most often made sure that she was the baby. I had to be the father, though I never knew what fathers did, except go to work and stay away all day, like mine did. Maybe they did operations? If she was in the mood to let him play with us, her little brother would be the mother, but more often than not it was just the two of us playing father and baby. She would be a demanding baby that no one could ever console, with a gratingly annoying cry that I soon hated. The only thing that would soothe her cranky little baby self was to have her diaper changed.

July 12, 2001

"Don't go there. Go to your safe place," I hear Chuck's voice telling me, but I can't keep the memories from coming now. I've opened the door and they're gushing out. I have no control over them. I know I must find a way to attend to them on my own when I'm not in the office with Chuck. I must find a way to handle the onslaught of them, for each memory seems to have numerous others piggybacking along on its ancient energy. I foresee a potentially endless string of memories.

I write down what comes, unleashing it onto paper, letting it sit here in my diary, the truth, in words I never thought I would ever write, of memories I never intended to return to. But here they are. I can't hold them back any longer. They're coming of their own volition. That fox running through the snow may have tricked me into following it into the woods, but I accept it as a necessary move on the part of the universe because, as painful as this recapitulation process is turning out to be, I know it's what I need to be doing.

The time is right for me to resolve the mysteries of my childhood, for although I had assumed they were gone from memory and of no importance, in actuality they've pursued me my entire life, repeatedly chasing me down, tackling me, asking me to go back, to look at what really happened.

I cannot turn from the call of my child self. It's too late for that. I've awoken her and we're taking this journey together now, wherever it may lead.

July 13, 2001

Could I really have had a conversation about what was going on? I didn't even have a name for that part of my body. Not normally a topic of conversation it was simply referred to as: *down there*. I remember being reprimanded by my mother, scolded for touching or scratching myself down there, discovering that it was a most shameful place on my tiny body. You wiped down there after going to the bathroom and that was about it. You were never to let anyone else see it and I learned from that bigger girl—the bike-breaking, doll-burning foster sister of my strange little friend—that blood would come out down there when I was older.

"No, not me!" I said. "Never!"

But she assured me that the terrifying notion would happen to me too, that I was not special, that I would not be spared, though it was all too much to fathom when I heard this at five years of age. There was no name for this most private, shameful, and frightening part of my body that blood would one day pour out of.

None of my friends ever seemed to have a name for it either. How could I possibly have known how to talk about something that never had a name, something that was so shunned that it must not be given any attention, whatsoever, that was not afforded an iota of significance? In the end it became a secret central focus of my childhood, as I played games 'down there' with my strange little friend.

I remember my brothers marching out of the shower stall in my parent's bathroom once as I waited for my turn to go in.

"Don't look at our penises; don't look at our penises!" they chanted, holding their hands over their genitals.

"Don't look at my penis either!" said I, standing naked too, covering myself in the same manner.

"You don't have a penis!" they cried in unison, howling with laughter.

"Well, what do I have?" I asked, embarrassed that I didn't even know it was not called by the same name. It didn't make any sense to me at age nine.

"Nothing, you have nothing!"

And that was all there was to it. I had nothing, so there was really nothing to talk about. But, for the longest time after I received this strange message from my brothers, I called it a penis too. I secretly dubbed it 'my penis' and I became quite fond of it. I even remember the words almost slipping out once or twice, as I caught myself at the last second. It was, by far, the best word I'd ever heard to describe it and since the boys used it I was determined to use it too, much like we all used the same words for features on the face, for instance. I figured what could work for other parts of the body could work down there too. Problem solved, I had a penis! But, as far as I could tell, boys seemed to have a totally different relationship with that part of their anatomy. They knew exactly what it was called. They shouted the word so easily and no one scolded them. They whipped it out of their pants and peed whenever they wanted, and no one scolded them for that either. The adults simply laughed, saying that boys will be boys, but girls were left in the dark, carrying a secret without a name.

For a long time I didn't want to have children because I thought childhood was too scary and I was determined that I would never put anyone through what I had gone through. I worried about my younger brothers and sister as we muddled through our growing up years. The big sister to five younger siblings, I cared for them, loved them, empathized with them, cried when they got hurt and tried to protect them, even if only with well-intentioned worry.

I recall often being angry with my mother for not being available, for not paying attention to what was going on in the world outside of her tightly controlled home environment, and for not being sensitive to a small child's needs and desires for a gentle, protective mother. I was expected to uphold her strict rules, to take total responsibility for every action, to never slip up or do anything childish. I was expected to behave like an adult at all times, and I had adult chores from a very young age.

By the time I was four, I was an expert at changing the diapers of my infant brother, the fourth child in our family that would grow to seven children by the time I was ten. I was fully capable of feeding him and quieting him when no one else could. I remember standing at the stove and heating up his bottle in a little pan of water to just the right temperature, testing it for doneness by shaking a few drops of warm milk onto my wrist. At night I could hear him at the opposite end of the house, fussing and whining, his sharp little fingernails scratching against the tightly tucked-in sheet of his crib. I'd lie awake waiting for my mother to go to him. Eventually, unable to get back to sleep, I'd get out of bed and walk through the dark house to stand beside him in 'the boy's room' where my brothers slept. I'd pat his back and whisper or sing to him until he fell back to sleep. I'd tuck a cloth diaper into his hand so he'd have something to cling to and so he wouldn't scratch his fingernails on the sheet and wake me again. In the morning, if I brought it up with my mother she'd laugh it off, saying she'd heard him, not addressing the fact that I, a five-year-old child, had lain awake waiting for her to do what I eventually did, pay a little attention.

"Okay, don't go there. Leave it for now, that's enough. Go to your safe place," I hear Chuck's voice saying. "Go to your safe place."

I got out of myself a little tonight, out of the darkness of heavy memories. Friends took me out for a drink, a bite to eat, and a chance to relax and forget everything for a few hours. It was good to have those moments of distraction and peace. They made me realize just how intense this recapitulation stuff can be. I've noticed that if I'm not preoccupied with some other mental activity the heaviness and shock of the memories tend to permeate every quiet moment, so that in the end there are no quiet moments.

July 14, 2001

I got up early and spent all day participating in an exhibition, demonstrating my art, as customers piled into the gallery where I sell my work in a nearby city. The effort was worth it. I came away with several new commissions and sold some expensive items through the gallery to some regular customers who I'd never met, though they've been buying my work for years. Afterwards, I went out to dinner with a friend and enjoyed another relaxing evening out. I drove home exhausted, but relieved that I was able to keep the thoughts and memories that popped up throughout the day at bay. There was absolutely no time to dwell on them. They pestered me often enough though, tried teasing me into their territory, but I repeatedly turned away, listening instead to Chuck's voice whispering in my ear, over and over again, reminding me: *Go to your safe place. Go to your safe place. Go to your safe place. Go to your safe place.*

July 15, 2001

I wake up tired, my legs heavy so that I can hardly move. My gaze, when I look at myself in the mirror, is dead. My eyelids hang down, sadly drooping over my empty eye sockets. No one is looking back at me. Although I safely maneuvered away from the memories yesterday, today I wake up back in the midst of them and, try as I might, I can't get beyond them. Memories seep in through the tired cracks in my psyche, permeating every inch of my being. They sweep away my flimsy barricades and fill my very bones with shame and sadness, with long ago fears and angers, with lost feelings. I am the lost me again, confused and struggling in a painful world.

I have no energy today. I can barely get up to make a cup of coffee. I can't muster enough incentive to do my morning run and so I'm consciously deciding to take it easy, but that doesn't mean I'll get any relief. It just means I'll stay in bed and rest and let the feelings sweep over me. I feel I have no choice; that I have to make myself available to this recapitulation process sometimes. It's almost as if I made a deal that I was unaware of; yesterday I got to be free of the memories, but today they demand my full attention. I let myself go to them, I don't force anything, I just let the feelings envelop me.

As I let myself go, I'm able to acknowledge that childhood was hard, painful, though I was somehow strong enough to brave through it. As I recall my youth, I visualize a timeline of events that shaped my life, a timeline that forced me, in my confused and yet imaginative way, to make decisions that kept me going, guided only by my emerging self striving to grow up. With no one to talk to, nowhere to turn, I had to find ways of figuring things out for myself. There was really no one to tell me that life wasn't supposed to be like that. I had no close personal relationships with any adults. I saw them as foreign beings, frightening disciplinarians for the most part. With no one to ask questions of, I invented what and how I should do things, to protect myself but also to keep growing into adulthood with my wits still about me. I was not at all naïve but keenly aware of the world around me, while at the same time I stumbled through almost every day, as if I didn't really belong.

As the day progresses, I'm struck numb by the emergence of more memories. I'm beginning to see that childhood was a most powerful time in my life. No wonder I wanted to grow up as quickly as possible, leaving childhood far behind in the dust of the past.

At an early age, I vowed I would never have sex, never get married, and never have children. I must have been fairly attractive, pretty, but there must have been something else about me, because I seemed to always be pushing away the pawing hands and slobbery kisses of boys, as they groped and grabbed—those shocking attempts to touch my body that left me gasping and afraid. They wanted things from me, but they didn't really want to get to know who I really was. I could push them away and pretend that I didn't care, but, underneath, my sensitive self was crying bitter tears of despair over the truth of the world I lived in; a world that did not allow for realness and for the sensitive girl inside to truly live.

As I connect with the young girl I once was, I see myself as closed off, not connected to the me outside, and not at all connected to my body. I was inside, hiding, closing doors, while the girl that was on the outside presented an equally detached persona; pretending not to care, strangely solitary and aloof.

"You can touch me, but you will never get me," became my mantra when accosted by those boys, and it wasn't only boys; men were interested in me too.

I see men's faces up close, their sagging mouths, quivering lips, almost drooling; their intense stares asking me for things I don't understand. I know they want something. My only reply came from that scared little girl inside me, scampering away into the depths of the tunnel, saying, "You can't get me. I'm in here, so far down you can't ever reach." But I also knew I was so far down I couldn't reach myself either.

I was determined to go through life as if nothing bothered me, but deep inside, I was crying, I was dying. At the same time, at sixteen, a sensitive artist and poet, I was like any young girl with fantasies of having the perfect boyfriend who I could talk to about everything. I envisioned him as a dark-haired boy, a poet, a sensitive soul who would embrace me in all my shyness; who I could whisper my sweet dreams to without being ridiculed; someone who would respect me, the deep soul of me and not just my body. Underneath, I had the same romantic dreams that all young girls have.

July 17, 2001

Layers of heaviness seem to lift as I talk to Chuck, as I tell him everything that's been coming up from the depths of forgotten time, surprising me with such old stuff, coated in dusty cobwebs, barely discernable. Yet, as soon as it appears, I recognize it, knowing I must clean it off, look at it closely and reclaim it as my own. I must acknowledge the memories as my truths, or they'll continue to haunt me in other ways and in other realms.

I tell him that the weekend helped bring me out of myself and out of the darkness of this memory mire for a while, but then I fell headlong right back into it, but not before I'd experienced some personally significant moments of myself in the real world.

"I forgot that I'm likeable," I say. "It's been such a long time since anyone said anything nice to me, but all weekend people said they were enjoying my company and I'm feeling better about myself too. I realize I have a lot to offer."

I speak about the sore lack of self-esteem, how steeped in feelings of ugliness and powerlessness I've always been and how lately I'm waking up to new feelings about myself, long denied. I'm intrigued by the idea that you can only know yourself through other people, as they mirror you.

"If you have no one to reflect back to you," I say, "you slowly die."

I know this because for a long time I had no mirror and I watched as my self-esteem and feelings of self-worth deteriorated greatly, as if the mirror had cracked and I could no longer see myself clearly. It was then that I felt like I was dying and I knew that if I stayed that disconnected from the world and other resonant beings that I would indeed die sooner rather than later. But once I started getting out into my own world, into the world I wanted and needed to be in, I met people who could reflect back the qualities that are inherent in me. I met people who were sensitive, spiritually struggling seekers, not afraid to look closely within, to question who they might be, eager to investigate themselves and question why they do the things they do, looking for truths, not excuses. In recent reflections coming from the world outside of me, I've begun to accept that I might actually be a likeable person, though even now I'm somewhat surprised.

Still, I question why my self-esteem has always been so poor, why I've felt so powerless and stuck most of my life. I've only tended to feel good about myself in tiny blips, momentary occasions throughout my life that I could probably clearly recall and count on one hand, while for the greater part of life I've been deeply depressed. I can say that now, that I've been deeply depressed for most of my life, though at one time I would not have had the nerve to do so. I would have felt guilty for giving myself such a label, even if it were true, and judged it as an attempt on my part to attract attention or pity. And I have no doubt that in my parent's world it would have been perceived that way, as selfish, attention-getting behavior. I would never have dared to excuse my inertia, my lack of energy and enthusiasm for life as anything other than my own fault.

I grew up in a world where you didn't draw attention to yourself in any way, either good or bad. You just existed, plodding on, bearing your woes silently, stoically, never weakening on the outside. You were expected to pick yourself up and just keep going, no matter what was troubling you. And I never felt I was worth worrying about anyway, so why would I allow myself to be declared depressed, even to myself. I didn't feel I was deserving of even that consideration.

I wonder if all the bad childhood experiences are the reason I feel so powerless. Was I brought up to be that way, to treat myself so callously, to have no expectations, to see myself as unworthy of even self-exploration? Did I really have no self-esteem as a small child? I've never really questioned such things before. It was never permissible before, not until I met this man I sit before, this Chuck Ketchel. I leave these questions hanging in the air between us as the session ends.

As I prepare to leave, Chuck gives me a new mantra: *I am powerful!*

"I am powerful," I say, tentatively, timidly at first, just whispering it, but then stronger and stronger. By the time I'm in my car and driving down the street I'm shouting it out. It feels good; it feels right. I can say it easily, truthfully; and I can honestly feel it. I can own it.

I am powerful!

I feel elevated, happier than I've been in a long time for a few hours after the session is over, but as the day goes on other feelings begin erupting, overflowing into the good place I've achieved. Panic teases me with that lump in the throat and that near-breakdown feeling. I hold on tightly as the feelings pass through me without attaching to them, physically girding myself against them, staying in control, as usual.

I follow Chuck's advice and simply note them and let them go. When they're gone, I'm shaky with emptiness. Then I wait for other feelings to collect, to come fill me up again.

July 20, 2001

Why were boys and men so attracted to me when I was young? Was I an exceedingly beautiful child, as was so often remarked, or was I just such a loner that I was a target? I didn't see myself as beautiful or even pretty. The lively blonds with curly hair and happy dispositions were beautiful to me. I was just plain, I thought. At least that's how I felt inside, plain and empty, with no energy or zest for life that I so admired in classically cute little girls with their pretty hair, clothes and shoes, in their princess dresses I so longed to wear, termed tacky by my mother. Instead she dressed me in brown tie-shoes like my brothers wore, plaid dresses, and hand-me-down play clothes. I wore a school uniform every day and so had few other clothes, a dress or two for church or parties, but everything was utterly practical, nothing fancy or frilly. I had a pair of black patent Mary Jane shoes for dressing up and for a long time I begged my mother to let me wear them to school, but to no avail. One day I tossed my ugly brown tie shoes far under my bed, complaining that I couldn't find them, but in the end even that didn't work. My mother found a pair of red rubber boots for me to wear instead.

Though I may have appeared to others to be very self-assured and confident, it was really just a mask. Perhaps though, in the end, I achieved what I set out to do, my fears and weaknesses so well hidden that it was not apparent that inside I was quaking with fear most of the time. The only strong characteristic that I ever felt I had going for me was my fierce inner power, capable of pushing everything else out to the edge of my being, far from feeling, creating a crusty external shell so I could survive. I feel that power still alive inside me, and in spite of feeling sad for the little girl I was, I feel so grateful to her for being who she was back then. I feel that tense, tightly wound up shell of a girl, still holding on for dear life, and at the same time I fear I might splinter at any minute, sending her hurtling into the dark pit of annihilation that she always feared.

I'm fragile now, more on the verge of breaking every day, feeling that I may shatter into a million tiny pieces; the old cracked mirror crashing to the floor. I just can't let that happen. With tremendous concentration and control I keep myself together. I know how to do that.

July 21, 2001
As I look back on my life, I clearly see how all the events, decisions, and choices I've made have led me to this moment, to this time, where once a week now I sit in a chair across from Chuck Ketchel and talk about myself, my fears, my memories, about Carl Jung, Carlos Castaneda and the Seers of Ancient Mexico, the

shamans that Chuck refers to so often in our work together. From this new perspective, I see a long string of choices clearly leading to moments when opportunities were made available. I see that by choosing one path over another, one decision over another—by being in alignment, ready, or just simply brave enough to take the leap—I have, over and over again, been catapulted out of ordinary reality and set upon a path that got me where I am today. Often enough, I clearly saw that a drastic decision was necessary and I made that drastic decision rather than stay on the known and familiar path, though often it was not clear why.

When I was married to my first husband and living in Sweden, I suddenly, one day, saw my life stretching out before me in crisp detail, eminently predictable, right to my death. I knew I couldn't stay there. I had to move on; I needed something different. For reasons I couldn't really understand or clearly articulate at the time, I knew I had to take the other path that was only dimly in sight. I knew that although it was unclear, and even though I didn't know what the heck I was going to do with myself at that point, I had to go in that other direction. I had to step off the well-worn, highly visible and defined path and verge off into the darkness of the unknown.

Now, having taken that dimly lit path so many times, here I am, on it again. This time, however, something is different. This time I feel something walking beside me, something I've long been seeking: *my innocence*. I'm rediscovering my most tender self, the inner spirit self whom I've been disconnected from, whom I've longed for but kept at a distance, having let that part of myself explore only within the confines of my inner world. I've been so afraid to let it out into the world, fearing it would be met with painful rejection and ridicule. I've been so protective of it, keeping it safely encased in my artwork, in my creative writing, in my poetry, neatly hidden, only covertly allowing it expression. But I've also kept others from getting anywhere near that real me, the innocent and truthful self. *Let no one in* was my most powerful and reliable inner prayer, the mantra to remind myself to be cautious: *Let no one in, it's not safe.*

It's too difficult to risk the inevitable rejections, the kicks in the gut, the pain of feeling that I made a mistake again; far better to never open the door at all. I've kept this secret self hidden, for only me, visiting her in her deep cave, but always on my terms. Now, however, I'm revisiting and reuniting with this inner self, gently inviting her to emerge and talk, to join the conversation.

Chuck and I talk about her, especially her innocence and yet, in the same breath, we talk about sex! I guess Freud was probably right, that all personality problems are interruptions in the natural flow of evolving sexuality, if that is what he did indeed say. It does seem as if all my personal frustrations and fears, and a lot of the mentally dysfunctional aspects of my personality are based in my early sexual exploits with my strange little friend. Whatever we did, and why, has caused disturbances inside me. This is the basis of all my fears and, although the deeper meaning is not yet clear to me, I know this to be the case.

July 22, 2001

I wonder how I ever got through those childhood years without cracking up or turning to some vice. I didn't turn to drugs or alcohol, though I did have other, perhaps less obvious obsessions and addictions. I'm thoroughly addicted to details, to tiny patterns, to being in control. I'm addicted to order. Once I make a plan I find it extremely challenging to be confronted with a change. I must be in control or it feels like the world, as I know it, will come to an end.

When I run, I count every step I take. From the moment I step out the door until I return I'm counting, counting, counting. Even while another part of me is thinking other thoughts, the obsessive, controlling part of me is keeping everything in line, putting one foot in front of the other, repetitively counting from one to four as I breathe in and then starting over again, counting from one to four as I breathe out.

In my artwork, I focus intently on tiny details, on decorative patterns, silently counting each stroke, spending hours covering the surface of the paper, canvas, or other medium, controlling even the output of my creative self. The process sends me into trance, offering cooling relief from the stresses and inner tensions that normally plague me.

When I enter the world of my artwork, I'm in total control. From the moment I first learned to draw with pen and ink and learned the techniques of cross-hatching and pointillism, using tiny strokes or pinpoints of ink to build up a picture, I was in heaven. I found an outlet for everything that was inside me, but I only let it out very slowly and methodically, on my terms. The minute I pick up my pen I leave my normal everyday world. I can happily scratch away for hours, perseverating over the placement of every tiny line, spacing them perfectly equidistant apart, producing detailed picture after detailed picture. I realize that this is very obsessive-compulsive behavior, but it's served a most necessary purpose.

At other times, I would find myself doing things absentmindedly, but now, as I go through this recapitulation process, I see them as glaringly compulsive behaviors as well. I'm a compulsive reader, sometimes reading five books a week, gobbling them up, all kinds of subjects, not necessarily retaining everything I read, but losing myself in the reading nonetheless. Sometimes I put one book down and begin a new one already in my lap, immediately forgetting the last story, compelled to keep reading, to keep the world out, controlling what I don't want to know about myself.

As I look back, I see myself doing this year after year from the time I was a small child. One day, when I was in my thirties, I began to notice that I also scratched my head while reading, obsessively picking away at what I perceived as dry skin, picking until my scalp bled. I realized I'd been doing this for years. Somehow it felt good. I gained relief in picking, though I didn't know, at the time, just what it was I needed relief from. As I ponder myself at different times in my life, I see all the obsessive-compulsive behaviors in a bright new light—*as glaring addictions!*

I was safe inside the world I created and upheld, and it worked for a long time. I expected others to live in it too, not out of selfishness on my part, but out of extreme necessity. The strong protective shell I built around myself helped me function, creating an aloof attitude on the outside, providing a false sense of security and strength inside. But really all I was doing was keeping the truths of my life at bay. All I was doing was trying to feel safe in a world that I knew was very unsafe, even though I didn't know how I knew this.

I understand this now, as I recapitulate my early childhood. In my attempt to remain sane, I created a new world to live in so that I could deal with the repercussions of what happened back there in the woods with my strange little friend. Into that self-created, controlled world I could retreat when things got a little too close for comfort, when fears arose and threatened to overwhelm. It was a world of deception, but it was a safe world. I had my art to disappear into. I had access to means of withdrawal and detachment. I had access to that strong inner determination that I've so recently recalled. And I had all my obsessive-compulsive addictions to rely on.

As I recapitulate, I feel myself losing control of that world I created and maintained so well. It actually feels as if the outer crust that surrounds it is about to fall apart, that bit by bit, chunks of hard skin will fall off until raw flesh is exposed. When I get to this point of crumbling, I'm forced to retreat, in dire need of the great relief that withdrawal and isolation afford me. As I return to that old world I'd once created, it doesn't quite hold up the way it used to. The only thing I know for sure is that if I can just remain physically in control I'll be okay.

July 24, 2001

I go to see the dermatologist. He says I look great.

"That beautiful, beautiful nose," he says, referring to the plastic surgery I had done on the bridge of my nose after cancerous skin lesions were removed years ago. Since that time I have obediently followed the original surgeon's orders to have my skin checked yearly. After the dermatologist checks my face, neck, head and back for any signs of cancerous moles or lesions he fixes my hair, which he has ruffled.

"Oh God, why is this old guy doing that," I think, "touching me almost tenderly, stroking my cheek too? Do I just attract these kinds of guys? Do I look so sweetly innocent that he feels he can take such liberties? Do I invite this in some way?"

I realize he's touching me almost absentmindedly, not with any underlying intent and I take it as just part of his caring attention.

"You have such long, thick hair," he says, as I stare into his own highly teased mop of thin frizz.

We talk for a little while and he only charges me twenty-five dollars, as he's done in the past. I only see him once a year and each time I come the receptionist remarks over how little he charges me.

"He must really like you," she says, as I check out.

I'm not sure what that means. I wonder if there's some underlying insinuation in her statement. The doctor knows I have no insurance. I decide that he truly cares about helping people in my situation. But, as I drive home, I investigate the feelings that arose as I stood there in front of the doctor and felt his hands on me. I think about how I felt while he was fussing with my hair and patting my cheek.

I didn't react, nor was I taken aback. I almost liked the attention, but I was also sort of frozen, caught unaware. The room seemed to grow very quiet and I couldn't really hear or take in what was happening. It was almost as if I was in another world. I just stood there rather numbly, woodenly. I wonder if I'm so starved for affection that even the mild attentions of a gnomish old doctor are pleasantly acceptable. Maybe that's why I was so vulnerable as a child, I liked the attention—perhaps I needed it and when it was offered I went for it.

I'm reminded of what it was like growing up. My parents were not demonstrative in the least. My siblings and I took care of our own needs or they weren't attended to at all. Although I was certainly needy as a child, I was never blatantly affection-seeking, nor a show-off, in fact, quite the opposite.

I would see other children, including my strange little friend, practically throwing themselves at people and cringe at the thought of actually doing something like that myself. She, however, liked being the center of attention. By comparison, I shied away from being noticed. I was extremely withdrawn, fearful of even the slightest bit of attention. If someone did show an interest in me, I'd respond with fear and skepticism, even though I knew most people I came into contact with when I was young: relatives, people from the neighborhood or the Catholic school I attended.

I don't ever recall being held by my mother, though I do remember sitting on my father's lap sometimes, until I got "too big," as he called it, until it was no longer comfortable for him. I have no recollection of being hugged, cuddled or touched by my mother. I recall sitting next to her while she read bedtime stories, but I don't recall any exchange of affection. I don't remember ever being kissed by either parent or ever hearing them say they loved me. The words "I love you" were never spoken in our house, *by anyone*. Maybe a deep underlying need for affection made me fair game for the episodes I've recalled while in the company of my strange little friend.

July 25, 2001

In a quiet moment, I think about all the memories that have emerged, the strange and potentially harmful things that happened to me. I realize how destructive they could have been to a small child trying to figure out what life was all about, how confusing, and yet I don't feel too screwed up. I still feel like I can get on with my life, that somehow I'll get through all this; calmly, I hope. I've noticed that this week I've felt much better, even happy sometimes, though still slightly depressed. But at least I don't have any more of those heavy memories coming out of the depths to torture me.

I have a brief conversation with my husband. Then, as he walks away, I have a clear vision of us, as two totally separate beings on two totally different planes that have spent some time together, but now that time is done.

Personally, I feel as if I've gotten over a major hump and that I'll be fine, that I can handle anything on my own. My work is going well—the painting classes, commissions and faux finish work are bringing in sufficient income to pay the bills. At this point, it's enough. More jobs are coming in as word spreads. I feel secure in my abilities, newly confident, while underneath I'm still feeling uncomfortably raw, though I expect that will dissipate over time.

In the evening, I attend a meeting at a local artist's group, a cooperative gallery, and make the decision to join. I need to make some new friends.

July 26, 2001

I wake at 4:40 a.m. out of a dream. I'm with my family in a strange city. My husband goes off leaving me sitting in the car with the kids, which is illegally parked in a parade zone. He didn't leave the keys, so I can't even move it. I'm angry at him for leaving us stranded and worried about getting a ticket. The kids and I get out of the car and stand next to it on the sidewalk. My son says that he wants to go to a museum that we'd passed on the way. I know he can handle being on his own, so I tell him it's fine, to go ahead and that my daughter and I will meet up with him there later.

I watch him walk off down the street, a small thin boy of about five, while my daughter and I wait for my husband to return. Suddenly, several policemen come by dragging a bleeding, naked man who has hundreds of knives stuck in his body. He's yelling loudly, screaming and fighting to get away. Then another group of policemen come past hauling another naked man, fat and pink, also screaming and fighting. I cover my daughter's eyes, trying to shield her from the scenes of these two naked men.

After this event, we stand around a bit longer before we finally decide to give up on my husband. We abandon the car to its fate and head off to find the museum and meet up with my son. We wander around the city, disoriented for a while, but finally reach the museum. It's very crowded. As I look around the lobby I see my mother sitting on a nearby bench, prim and proper, her lips tightly pursed, staring straight ahead, dressed in a matching skirt and jacket with a white blouse. She sits with her knees clamped tightly together, her purse in her lap, her two hands clutching it, a small pillbox hat on her head. She doesn't look in our direction or even acknowledge us. Then I see my son and I know, immediately, that something terrible has happened to him. He's crying and his clothes are disheveled and torn.

"What happened?!" I shout loudly, but with great tenderness and concern.

Rushing over to him, I kneel down and gently hold him in my arms. I see that my mother is watching us now, but she still doesn't acknowledge us or say anything. At that moment, my son turns into a little girl.

"It's okay, tell me anything, no matter what, even if it's bad, or scary, or confusing, or anything," I say.

I'm aware that the little girl is myself, as a child. I'm looking right into her tiny little face, framed by straight dark hair, as her pearly white skin goes ashen gray. I see her shutting down right in my arms, closing her eyes, not able or willing to communicate. I begin to panic, thinking that I'm losing touch with her—she's disappearing and my son along with her.

I wake in a panic, afraid that my son has been sexually abused and that I haven't noticed the signs. But then I shift my thoughts away from him. He's a part of myself in the dream and I'm being shown that there's something deeply wrong with my child self, that there's something I'm still missing.

When I meet with Chuck, I tell him about my dream and the feeling that I'm still missing something, and how sad it felt that the little girl in the dream was pulling away from me, as if rejecting my sincere attempts to help her. I was reacting to her with pure intentions and deep love, but it was as if she saw me like my mother, a coldly distant presence, sitting off on the side, not revealing an ounce of feeling, not reacting at all. The little girl seemed afraid of my mother, and me in turn.

I wondered, in the dream, if my mother would scold me for shouting out in the middle of the lobby, for really paying attention to and reacting to a child in such obvious distress, but I let the old familial expectations go as I turned to the child. The child was more important to me than upholding an old world, as represented by my mother.

In the dream, the child's withdrawal had such a familiar feel to it, as if I were in her body, withdrawing tightly inside, and I knew it was serious, that something had indeed happened to her to cause her to revert to such drastic behavior. I cannot get away from that reality within myself either. I've trained myself so well to withdraw when something bothers me, to in fact disappear, as I feared the girl in the dream was doing. I recognize that I still do it. I think the dream is trying to show me this, that I am still that little girl.

While talking with Chuck, I unravel the truth of how I've used my ability to withdraw as a shield for self-protection, keeping myself in, but also as a barrier to keep others out. I recognize that I've been fairly passive during most of my life. I easily give in to withdrawal, creating a predictable scenario where I feel a certain amount of control, but which really only results in stagnation.

I must challenge myself now to be more assertive, to not back down, to be thoughtful and productive in a more positive way. I must remember: *I am powerful!*

Chapter Five

End of an Era

August 1, 2001
Chuck is away until midmonth. He didn't go into details, but explained, during our last meeting, that he was taking his wife, Jeanne, on a journey to a place down South for some kind of alternative cancer treatment. He sounded apologetic about the need to be away, but I put him off immediately, telling him I'd be fine, that I'm still as practiced as ever at handling things on my own. He said he'd check in to see how I was doing when he had a chance.

"I have my diaries," I tell him, "I'll keep writing everything down."

August 4, 2001
A small, raw chunk of pain sits deep inside where I keep so much hidden. I turn inward and work on building myself up from a pile of nothing, from old remnants of worthlessness to something stronger, staying focused on what's right for the moment.

"Maybe I'll be all right over time," I hope.

As time goes on, however, I find that I'm confronted with the same old negative feelings arising again and again. I grow increasingly unhappy with the way things seem to unravel. It's as if having made this decision to change, the universe is taking up my cause, presenting me with everything that needs to be confronted—*all at once!*

I'm constantly dealing with a myriad of issues: day-to-day life at home and work, the old stuff, the deeply personal mysteries and feelings that arise, along with everything that comes to greet me from outside, but I stick to my convictions that I need to do what I need to do. I acknowledge just how right this process is, both the divorce and the work I'm doing to find my lost self. I eagerly await the emergence of the real me as I go through this painful process, seeking the long-buried self, as of yet still mostly unknown.

Until recently, I ignored the stirrings to change. I let things pass. Now, already open and raw, I'm ready to keep shedding the hard crust of indifference and defeat. As I peel away the old scar tissue of defense, I find that underneath I'm most tender and that I actually hurt, physically.

August 5, 2001
Chuck calls to find out how things are going. We decide to have a phone session on the thirteenth. Until then, I hold onto the chunk of rawness that is now a constant companion, protecting it on the one hand and fearful of releasing it on the other.

August 10, 2001
I have a hard time sleeping most nights and I wake up early each morning, even before the birds are stirring. In the darkness everything is too much. Overwhelmed with all that still lies ahead, with the decisions I have to make, the steps I must take, I lie in the dark and shake.

I dare myself to keep going.

August 13, 2001
When I talk to Chuck, I'm exhausted from not sleeping, battling the old desire to withdraw as the details of the divorce are hammered out, as resentments are bantered about, and decisions are being made. I find myself collapsing, just wanting it to be over, making deals just to be done with it. I'm angry at myself for giving in. I need reminding of why I'm doing this, where I'm going, and what this journey is all about.

"Yeah, I'm on a journey," I say almost sarcastically, "a hell of a journey."

"No, you're on a spiritual journey," Chuck reminds me, but I immediately wonder what that means.

Is he some kind of religious fanatic? Something in me wants to fight him, wants to oppose everything he says. Something in me wants to throw in the towel and call it quits. Something in me wants to grind this whole thing to a halt and tell him to just shut up. But there's another part of me that knows he's right, that the hysterical feelings arising in me are simply my fears that I can't handle this, when in fact, as he points out: *"You've been handling everything really well."*

When he says this, I'm forced to step back from the panic and take a long look at where I am and how I've gotten here. From this different, calmer perspective I can admit that, yeah, I've been handling everything really well. I'm actually pretty proud of myself. I'm able to admit all of this and, as we end our conversation, I take a deep breath, more determined than ever to plunge right back into the fray and keep going.

"Hang in there," he says.

"Yes, I'm at least doing that."

August 17, 2001

It's clear that we must confront some sensitive issues within the family as my husband and I attempt to live together civilly, focused on keeping the kids feeling safe and protected, presenting them with changes in tiny increments that they can handle.

We made plans for a vacation in New Hampshire months ago, already aware that it would be a challenge for us. But it will be our last trip together with the kids, a yearly family gathering of sorts, as we've joined my brother and his family for the past several years on this same trip. In spite of everything, we decide to go ahead with it.

I have a session with Chuck, back from his journey, before we head out. He's upbeat and optimistic, his wife's tumors literally gone, removed by some kind of alternative herbal treatment that did exactly what they'd hoped.

"Now," he says, "it's time for her to regain strength."

As we talk about my process it becomes clear that the issues surrounding the divorce are of paramount importance now, while the old stuff, the memories of the games I played with my strange little friend have disappeared for the most part, placed into a new memory bank, one that I have access to. I'm driven to ponder myself in relationships, knowing that I'll most likely be confronted with feelings and questions during the week away.

"I wonder why I've always been so restless in my relationships, why I always seem to need something else," I say. "No matter what relationship I've been in, there's always something else that presses on me, telling me that I'm missing something. Why do I always need something more, and just what is it? Why can I never settle where I am?"

Chuck listens to me as I shoot out these questions, suggesting that perhaps there's something I haven't discovered about myself yet, that perhaps the inner restlessness that keeps me moving isn't related specifically to the person I'm with. Perhaps it's not something that will be resolved in a relationship either.

"It may not be about relationships at all," he suggests.

I admit that a lot of women would be fine in this kind of relationship, this kind of marriage; they would be satisfied. I feel almost cruel as I consider why I'm turning away from it, because I'm not really sure why I have to end this relationship at this time, except that I'm dying and I will die sooner rather than later if I stay in it. This is all I know for sure. The fact that I feel death breathing down my neck is enough of a reason for me to make this change, but Chuck may be right that it's not specifically the relationship but something inside myself. My decisions are based on a deep desire to keep an inner fire alive, to fan the flames of a dying inner fire, allowing it to burn brighter with new life.

"Do I ask for too much? Am I odd or overly demanding?" I ask. "Is it unusual to want more in life? Am I unrealistic in thinking more can be had? Am I wishing for something that doesn't exist?"

"There's only one way to find out, to keep going, to keep finding out what life has in store for you, in whatever way works for you," says Chuck.

As the session draws to a close, I tell Chuck that I'll come back to see him one more time and then I'll terminate. I see no reason to keep coming. Money is tight and I feel that I've gotten a good amount of support and inner stability from my sessions with him, but that I can handle things from here on out on my own. He looks somewhat taken aback when I say this, but agrees that a follow up session after the vacation might be an appropriate ending. Whatever I want to do is fine with him, so we arrange for one final visit in two weeks' time.

August 18, 2001

I get up early and pack the van and by nine o'clock we're on the road. My son's best friend comes along as he has done in past years; my daughter will have her cousin to hang out with for the week. I feel the pressure of pretending that all is well with us, even though my brother and his wife are aware of our current situation. It's the kids I'm thinking about as we head off on the long seven-hour drive.

August 22, 2001

In spite of everything, we're having a fairly relaxing time. The cabin is situated on a small lake with a private swimming beach, a dock to fish off of and a canoe to paddle around in. I have a whole day to myself while everyone else goes off to spend a day at a nearby water and amusement park. After a swim and a paddle around the lake in the canoe, I shower and sit on the deck overlooking the lake.

The weather is beautiful. I hear the splash of water birds, the cry of the loon, and the chattering of red squirrels in the trees. It's the middle of the week and quiet, the surrounding cabins hidden from view by the thick evergreen forest. The weekenders are gone, and I have not only our private beach to myself but the entire deserted enclave.

I sit back in a big old-fashioned Adirondack chair; a cup of coffee, my journal and pens, and a stack of books on the wide armrest. In a calm mood I consider the situation I'm in with my marriage ending—the decision to end a long relationship affecting more than just the two people who began it sixteen years ago.

I feel what it means to be cruel and I acknowledge that yes, divorcing another person, admitting that you don't want to be with them anymore, telling them you don't like their companionship anymore, is a cruel thing to do to anyone. It's especially cruel to do this to a person you've loved, have children with, and have gone through many years of life with, good times and bad. I feel tenderness for this man I'm leaving in this way, but at the same time I don't think it's selfish to pay attention to a deep inner need to take another path, to change, to admit that life together isn't fulfilling anymore. In fact, to ignore those truths would be equally cruel.

Something is constantly calling to me and, even though I still have yet to figure out what it is, I know I must pay heed to its incessant cry. When I moved my art studio out of the house I paid attention, and I knew, when I made that move, that I would be called to respond to its cry again and again. I just needed to take the first step, letting the far off caller know that I was ready. Now I hear that voice calling again, louder than ever, urging me to go the next step in figuring out what it is that won't let me rest.

Now my discontent is no longer private, no longer just inside myself. The calls I've been hearing from within are ringing out loud, sending echoes of personal sorrow and pain, reverberating through the canyons of my soul and out into the open air, announcing to everyone that things are changing.

I'm changing my world, and I fully accept responsibility for changing everyone else's too. The ripples created by my little pebble of discontent, my little atom bomb, thrown into my little puddle of water, effect everything else in the world. I know this. It seems like such a tiny thing to send out into the universe, and yet, as my inner thoughts take form in the words I've finally uttered, I disrupt so many contented lives.

Why is it so important to be in a relationship anyway? I'm better alone, happier by myself. I like finding the lost me, and the recapitulation process feels like enough of a commitment right now. I don't want a relationship; I don't want a man in my life. When I'm alone I'm not as needy, not wanting so much.

As I sit in my chair on the deck, the sun dappling through the pines, I begin relaxing, letting tension go with these thoughts, allowing myself to feel that I'm finally healing something on this warm summer day. I let the quietness of the world on this calm day enter my body until I'm feeling like me again, such a well-known person, though she's been gone for so long.

"What more do I need?" I wonder. "Why is this process of change so important to me? Where am I going and why do I have to go there? What is it that draws me? How do I know that this is right?"

Over the past couple of months, in working with Chuck, my childhood came back so clearly and I could look at it, understand it, and move on. Maybe Chuck is right, as he mentioned when I last saw him, that perhaps I've gone beyond the childhood memories now. Maybe it *is* time to truly leave them, to finally detach from them, to let them go and move onto something else without any ties to anything. But, without the past to hang onto, the future is a little scary, so unknown, nothing to look back and hold onto, nothing familiar to anchor myself to. If the memories are done, if they have indeed lost their grip, do they no longer have value or importance? If they no longer have anything to offer, do they still really exist?

It feels almost as if, in releasing them, that I'm just dropping them by the wayside, like Hansel and Gretel dropping breadcrumbs on the path as they go into the woods, hoping to use them to orient themselves later, so they can find their way back out, but the crumbs get snapped up by birds, and when they turn back they find the path empty. With no markers showing the path they took, they are completely lost. In finally looking back at the past and freeing myself from the hold it once had on me, will I find myself lost like Hansel and Gretel? Will there just be emptiness as I look back now? Will it be as if nothing were ever there, everything having disappeared, like those breadcrumbs, without a trace? Or is there still some mystery as yet uncovered? Am I truly done?

I'm a little sad at the thought of leaving Chuck too, though I found it to be such a bizarre situation at first, opening up to another person like that, a stranger. I've trusted him like I've never been able to trust anyone. I even started to nervously look forward to that special indulgent time each week, in spite of the painful things that came out. His insight and always-pertinent reflections offered something to take away and mull over, even on those occasions when I felt so distant and unfocused that I could hardly look at him or speak. Just knowing that someone cared, that someone was there to guide me, to point me in a direction, to help me know myself, is such a gift. And he did it all so quietly, so expertly dragging me out of the darkness.

Now I sit here and feel that I've connected to the long lost inner me again, the part of myself that's been sitting so quietly and patiently, waiting for me to come back and find her again. As I sit in the warm air of this New Hampshire summer day, I feel what it feels like to be me again. I feel what it will mean to heal.

For the moment I am at peace.

August 24, 2001

The week goes well, better than expected. Other people are good buffers and the testiness normally present in our personal interactions dissipates, leaving things somewhat calmer. From this more observant position, I realize how sad and scared my husband has been and how it may take him a little longer to fathom it all. I can't force him to move along as quickly as I have. The whole process must take the time it takes, but eventually it will resolve. I trust the process and know that I must not be afraid, not let his pain overpower my conviction to take this new journey that I see looming ahead, unclear though it is.

I may need to go beyond and wait for him to catch up, to get to a place of resolution about us, that we are indeed meant to move on now, although in truth I've already taken years to get to this point myself. I too dragged my sadness out for a long time, even though I kept it hidden, unspoken for the most part. Although it may appear as if I'm healing from this collapse of our marriage faster than he is, it's really been a most slow and painful process.

Midway through the week I suddenly felt so helpless, fearful that I wouldn't last, that I would physically collapse from the stress of putting on a good show, but with that day to myself something anchored more firmly within. After that day of renewed resolution to forge ahead and stay more firmly connected to my inner path, I've allowed the last few days to pass quietly, telling myself to just be present, to just do and be.

Now, as we prepare to return home, I feel cleansed and ready to forge ahead, lighter, looking forward to unhampered progress. I savor the time we've spent here, the end of an era.

August 25, 2004

The old tensions reappear as soon as we return home. Back on our familiar battleground they rise to the surface like bubbles in a glass of seltzer water and escape into the air where they bristle and crackle without a single word even being spoken.

The hot summer air is oppressive today, mirroring the truth of our position. I know that although the vacation went well it was just a staying of the inevitable, unreal almost in its pleasantness.

August 26, 2001

I realize just how deeply depressed I've been all summer. No energy, no desire to do anything even though I've had so much going on with my business, my art, at home, and inside myself.

For some reason, a watercolor painting I once did comes to mind: a picture of a house on fire. It was a beautiful yellow gingerbread house with flames leaping out of the windows, the entire two-story structure engulfed in flames. I painted it when I was about to leave my old boyfriend, the man who was so much older than me, after he told me he didn't love me anymore, that he'd "made a mistake," as he put it.

I didn't understand the painting at the time, though I remember how deeply depressed I was when I painted it. It just came out of me, painted from my unconscious, but I found it unsettling and disturbing. Even years later, each time I looked at it something about it bothered me, the meaning of it never quite clear. I kept it hidden, even from myself, afraid that someone might see it and wonder about me, certain that I would be perceived as crazy, until one day I finally destroyed it—just to get rid of it, so *I* didn't have to see it again—but it didn't take the image away.

Now I see that painting again so clearly, all the details, and the sadness I painted into it. In every stroke of my pen and every brush of color lay the pale waning of a relationship; the pale yellow colors of the house contrasted by the fiery reds and oranges devouring my anger and pain as the flames whipped high into the sky. I painted putrid black smoke pouring out of it, and I remember thinking, as I painted, that no one would ever call the fire department to save this beautiful house—it was destined to burn to the ground.

I mourned that relationship in the fury of that fire. Even as I see that painting again so clearly in my mind's eye, I also see the road I painted, the empty driveway winding away from the burning house, going off into the distant woods. I see the red rose I painted hidden behind the flames, depicting my past love for that man, soon to be devoured by flames, while the future lay clearly accessible in the distance. It was just a matter of walking away, going down the driveway without turning to look back, without regrets, an end of an era.

Even then I knew I would keep going. And, indeed, I did walk away. However, the resolution of that relationship took years, though I began the process of releasing myself from it in the execution of that painting. But, in truth, I carried pain, regret, and many resentments for years after I had completed the painting. Every time I looked at it, it triggered the old feelings and sentiments, until I was finally ready to release them, until I was done. I remember the courage it took to finally tear up that painting, years later. As I recapitulate, I hear again the soft ripping of the thick, expensive watercolor paper as I tore it in half, then quarters, then into smaller and smaller fragments, fully determined to finally release myself. In contrast to the old anger I had felt at the time of painting it, the tearing was nothing but cathartic. By then I had achieved completion.

Now, as I recount the significance of that painting, I more fully understand what I was doing at the time, allowing my unconscious to carry me across a dangerous abyss, as I sought transformation and new life. That time transformation took place over time, over many years in fact. This time, as I'm soon to leave this current relationship, I don't want to walk away holding onto anything. I don't want to go through years of resentment. With all I've learned about myself I feel that I'm being challenged to do it differently now. I have a chance to achieve a new level of personal transformation and this time I want to do it with that goal uppermost in my mind.

While sitting alone on the deck at the cabin in New Hampshire, I knew I could handle anything and now, again, I feel my strength and know I'm ready. After we returned home the other day I felt so depressed, so back in an old place after reaching such a place of peace and resolution that day. I wondered where all that newfound strength had gone, but then I realized that I hadn't run the whole week I was away. Since then I've been out early each day, doing my usual three-mile run. I feel happier, brighter, more like the new, stronger me as I run; my mind at peace, my spirit happy, and I feel healthy again.

I spent the day with the kids today, getting everything together for the new school year. I did some weeding in the garden and a little cleaning and organizing. The kids were happy; things were normal.

August 28, 2001

I meet with Chuck for a last session. I feel the pressure of the old stuff returning even before the appointment and by the time I get to him I have to admit that it still hurts. It's still bothersome, still eating away, picking at me. Jagged flashbacks etch into my soul like broken glass dragged across flesh, cutting deeply, red droplets of blood seep out, cooling me, giving me relief. At least I'm able to feel something, even if only pain. At least I'm not dead yet.

While we talk, Chuck and I ponder again what could have possibly been going on that my strange little friend and I played those games in the woods, with dirt and sticks. Chuck presents the idea that perhaps a Dionysian archetype was in control, that nature was unleashing through us. I understand what he's suggesting and although it's easy to latch onto that deduction I can't quite embrace it—it just doesn't feel right. At the same time I'm too afraid to dig deeper. I don't really want to think about it anymore. I want this recapitulation process to be over so I can go off in peace, work through the year of separation, get divorced, and move on to a new life.

Chuck asks if I know anything about my strange little friend. Did I know if she ever got any help? I can't answer, because I haven't had contact with her for most of my adult life.

"If she hasn't dealt with it," he suggests, "she's most likely a very disturbed individual."

I cringe when I hear him say. Am I also "a very disturbed individual?" Is that how he thinks of me? But I don't ask him to elaborate. I'm too frightened to hear the truth. I simply reiterate that I see no reason to continue our work. I'm confident that should anything arise I'll be able to handle it, but at the same time, deep inside, I know I'm not done.

I understand that Chuck is perhaps very gently implying that I still have more work to do too, though he really says nothing along those lines. Even so, I know I can't face it right now. I can only face what's coming next. I must face my husband and work out our separation, and I must turn my attention to my two children who I feel such deep sadness for, knowing that I'm the one causing them pain, pain that they aren't even aware of yet.

"The door is always open," says Chuck. "You can come back any time, even if just for a brush-up session."

I'm grateful when I hear him say this, because I don't know how this world of therapy and shamanic healing works. I don't know the protocol, but I do know that in this little office I have met a wizard. A most gentle man sits here dispensing magic, wisdom, and insight, conjured out of nothing except the air around him, as far as I can see.

August 29, 2001

I already feel as if I've lost something, and I'm just on my first day alone without the supports that Chuck offered. I have the studio to myself for a few days after spending the past couple of days out working on a big job. I've had little time here except to drop off and pick up equipment and attend to phone calls. Now I have some quiet time alone.

With no pressing engagements or assignments, I feel the luxury of some creative solitude in which to work. But, wouldn't you know, I find myself quite fixated on the old stuff, the memories. They still haunt me.

I recognize that there's still so much buried, so much still to be unearthed and I also realize that if I don't tackle it soon I'll be forced to bury it again. But I've already spent my whole life doing that, my spirit dying in the process, and it would be pretty sad if that's what I were to choose to do now, after all I've gone through over the past few months. That would be choosing death and I can't see that happening.

August 30, 2001
The old stuff reappears, as if called, steadily seeping in. Growing increasingly pronounced, it seems to know I have no pressing engagements, no busy work to keep it away. It won't leave me alone. The lump in my throat is returning, swelling, large and uncomfortable again.

What am I going to do?

Chapter Six

I Want to Live

September 7, 2001

Soul in pain, mind in torment, in quiet moments the old stuff comes to haunt. I know I won't be able to handle the onslaught of it alone and I wonder how long I can keep it at bay. It pushes at me, prodding for attention. I wish I knew where it all came from. Whatever it is that haunts me sits heavily inside, in hidden places, not where I can see, not where I want to go. It lets me know it's there, showing me images of ugliness, painfully deep, like glimpses of old icons painted in excruciating detail or ancient rounded Mycenaean forms solidly built to stand erect for centuries, guarding. They wait for me to turn to them, for they hold the secrets. I see big-eyed Etruscans peering out from deep within, looking for daylight, begging to be let out, heavy stone sculptures, weighing on my soul, numbing my thoughts. A lump of stone catches in my throat. No forklift big enough to remove it, I carry its weight always within, barely able to breathe, to speak, to swallow.

What *do* I remember?

I meditate. I go back and back and deeper and deeper into myself, until I'm traveling backwards, skimming through the many phases of my life remembering who I've been, where I've been, and what I've done. Suddenly, I'm so far back inside myself that I turn inside out, and I'm no longer who I think I am. I'm nothing. I'm nowhere. I discover that I wasn't in my body in the past. I was totally absent. No one was inside me because I'd been lost a long time before that, before I even knew who I was. Now I exist, but I'm all grown up. Me, almost fifty years old, half done, and I missed all of it.

I come out of the meditation and realize that for almost fifty years I haven't lived a true and happy life. I've been waiting and wondering when it would happen.

"When will I finally feel safe in this life, fully present in this world? When I'm twenty-two? Thirty-two?" I've asked myself that question repeatedly; always sure that one of those years ending in a number two would be my time of salvation from the pain I've never understood. By the time I turned forty-two I'd hoped I would finally be present, but I'm still not fully here.

I thought it was just a myth that life could be rewarding, that calmness and contentment would ever come. They've never even felt close. The closest I've ever come was that moment on the deck in New Hampshire, when I felt what it might mean to finally be a peace in my body, when I had a glimpse of what it might mean to heal. Life was and continues to be something that is full of turmoil, sadness, fear, and more fear.

Life goes on, on the outside, but, as my meditation revealed to me: *inside it stopped long ago, before I was even conscious of it.*

Who was I, and where was I, for all those years?

In the past, I never felt fully present, never fully a participant in life. Life was always something going on *out there*, outside of my body, in another realm so distant from where I normally resided. Peering closely at the world, I appeared observant, as I watched, noted, and took in what was going on around me. Inside, I was trying to figure out some big mystery, always wondering, wanting, wishing for something I could never quite get a handle on. I just knew there was something out there that I needed and I yearned constantly for it, whatever it was.

Now I'm beginning to break through that distant, absent self that I never quite understood either. She still exists, reminding me that she's still important, that she still holds the answers. She's also reminding me that there's still comfort in the old self. It's not so easy to let her go.

What will happen to her if I release her, and where is this new me coming from? What if I don't like this new me? What if she's not nice? What if she's the monster behind the old frightened me? What if she's the one who's been keeping me so rigidly silent and stiff all these years?

What if she's the one who instigated those strange games in the woods?

September 9, 2001

Many things come to haunt, nothing specific, but all of it together looms over every minute of every day, and then sounds or smells, or light or dark, or just thoughts can set me off and I'm lost back there again; lost in that old world, lost in the woods playing Operation, naked nymphs playing curious games. I try to escape its horrors, shifting away and shutting it out, but seem to only succeed in tightening up.

The lump in my throat is growing larger, hurting again. Lethargic and slightly depressed, I'm lost for days at a time in a strange and murky world where nothing makes sense and nothing is clearly defined, where I dance reluctantly, taking part in obscene activities that I don't want to be involved in—that much I know.

September 12, 2001

Whenever two or more people come together the talk is immediately about the terrorist attacks. Yesterday, terrorists using passenger airplanes, which they had hi-jacked, attacked the World Trade Towers. New York City is so close; we all know people who were there when it happened, but even from afar the horror is still palpable. The hole it has left in the city skyline reaches into every heart; we all have a gaping wound. The constant replay on television shows the buildings exploding into smoke and flames, and then crumbling into heaps, gone, totally and permanently removed from the New York City skyline. Stories of horror and heroism abound. The evil energy that could systematically plan, over months or years, to carry this out is horrific to fathom.

September 15, 2001

As the days go on the scenes of disaster replay continuously on television, but now also in everyone's mind. It's so easy to see it all again, those crumbling towers, the burning hole in the Pentagon, and the deep gash of the aircraft that crashed in Pennsylvania; the scattered, shattered lives; people jumping over the edge of the abyss, leaping into the unknown, stock traders trading one death for another, electing how they will spend their last moments on earth. The significance of the collapse of the biggest financial center in the world is certainly meaningful—this event, occurring in the midst of our over-consuming society, perhaps showing us something important—but I'm too distraught to even ponder it, for I cannot feel anything. *I'm dead inside.* I can't shed a tear or feel an emotion. I'm hard, unfeeling, cold steel.

I am a monster.

As I watch the towers fall again and again I fall into a hole too, a big, gaping hole, the immensity of it sucking and pulling me down into its depths, somewhere in the middle of my insides, where I'm lost, choking in the chalky gloom. There are still so many rules to uphold: *no crying allowed, no tears, no talk, no shouts, no sounds whatsoever may be uttered.*

I'm winding up tight again, hiding inside that deep hole alongside the memories still buried there under the showers of powdery debris. I try to hold down what lies so unsettled inside me, though my body wants to spew it out, to be rid of all the terrors that fill me. This is the reality I wake up to every day now—this is what I know I must hold back—my own pain reawakened by this world-shattering event.

I sometimes feel that my own problems are insignificant in comparison, but then again, if I can't make my own little world a better and happier place, how can I be a part of a better and happier larger world? I tell myself again and again that I'm important and that it's still okay to work on my own stuff. It's okay to spend only part of the day remembering all those thousands dead, only some of my focus on the terrorists and the uncertain future. It's still important to work on everyday tasks, which include my own personal problems.

September 16, 2001
What lies inside keeps eating away at me, chomping away, nagging at me until my insides are as raw as chapped lips, as painful as cracked and blistered hands. No one sees the pain, the bloody mess of memories I hold inside, like buckets of afterbirth torn and ripped from my body, leaving pain and cramps in a place no one can go. Even I can barely reach that far down to soothe and comfort the wounds that fester inside me.

I don't know what I'm going to do with it. I don't remember enough, though so much stuff nags at me. I can't seem to let it go and I can't get past it either. No matter how hard I try to push it away, it won't let me ignore it. There are too many things bringing back memories.

Visual images flash like lightning and in a split second I'm lost in the woods again. A sigh, a profile, the nape of a neck, and suddenly a flash of pain stabs through my heart, my gut, and something deep inside is torn out of me and thrown to the ground where it lies kicked and bruised and yet I cannot bear to tend to it, except to stuff it back inside, to push its bloody mass back inside.

September 17, 2001

Taking a walk, I don't dare go into the woods. I'm afraid of the woods now. If I'm with someone else it's okay, but when I'm alone I fear the awakening memories.

As I hike along the periphery of the woods, I notice a dark scent hanging in the shade of the trees, a heavy pungent smell, mixing with the slowly decaying leaves: *my strange little friend's smell, her breath.* I see her instructions inscribed on the bark of the trees, her implements of operation perfectly laid out waiting to greet me if I step into the woods. As I walk, keeping to the fields, away from the dark woods that both draw and repulse me, questions race through my head, revving up to such an intensity that they become like racecars on a circular track, unable to stop once the momentum has built up.

Why did I do it? Why did I do it? Why did I do it?

I hear the racecar tires squealing as they take the turns, screeching: *why, why, why,* and I remember again that I was not at all happy about playing the game, that I didn't like it, wanted to get away, wanted it to stop, but I didn't have the power to stop it once it began. Once the momentum of the game took over, the numbness took over too, and the only thing I could hold onto was that I knew it would end, that the game had its natural course and it would eventually be over, and that was enough to get me through it. But now I cannot help but wonder, again and again: *what was really going on behind that strange game.*

September 18, 2001

Earlier in the summer, it seemed I was confronting the old stuff on a daily basis, but then other things interfered. Life and its many duties and complications took over, and the intensity of it receded. When I thought about the old stuff back then, it seemed easier to deal with than the way I experience it now. From the perspective of a busy life its intensity diminished and the pain was shared, transferred to marriage difficulties for a time. But now that everything else in my life has cooled somewhat, the old stuff, at a mere suggestion, resurfaces with vividly painful intensity.

The last time I met with Chuck, even as I was saying goodbye, I was also wondering how long it would take before I would be back in his office again, sitting hunched over in front of him, bearing the pain of these memories that will not sit quietly any longer. This is not dinnertime conversation to engage in with my children and soon to be ex-husband, or light banter with someone I might bump into in the grocery store, not something I can lightly refer to as I pick out bananas and apples.

"Oh by the way, I'm dying to know what happened to me as a child. I played such strange sexually-oriented games. What do you think *that's* all about?"

I've had so much buried, so deeply repressed for so long that it's absolutely mind-boggling. I'm aware of this now and I know I need to go back there, to find out about it, to really look, to go through myself with a fine-toothed comb or I'll never be free of it. I must find a way to enter the woods again, but I need help, a guide, someone who knows what it means to enter a world that no longer exists in one reality, but totally exists in another.

I find, once again, that I have no other listener than Chuck Ketchel, no other outlet for expressing the strange and unsettling memories that have been emerging, captivating me with their increasingly intense approaches, their sensory stimulations that I cannot eliminate from the atmosphere. There is no air freshener capable of diffusing the hauntingly pungent smells, the bodily odors of my strange little friend that permeate the very air I breathe. I know I must go back to Chuck and back into the woods, and take up where I left off at the end of the summer.

I wrestle with this awareness, with the truth that I won't be free until I recapitulate everything that I hold hidden inside me. And yet I struggle with making the call to set up an appointment with Chuck because, as it becomes clear that I did indeed repress the memories that have so far emerged, I fear that more lie behind them. I feel deep-seated, painfully raw anguish beginning to emerge along with the first hint of new memories, laced with a visceral, gritty awareness that it will not be a pleasant journey.

I don't know how to handle these fears. The only right thing to do is to confront them—that I'm sure of—but I'm so ambivalent. Afraid to live with the past stuffed down inside me forever, I'm also afraid of what I must confront, for it's such a mystery. But, maybe the worst part is over. These past few inwardly focused weeks have been so difficult. Maybe just getting to this point is the hardest part. Maybe the rest of this recapitulation will be easier.

I contemplate this while also admitting that I need help because I have no idea how to handle any of it, except to resort to the old ways of doing things, to totally shut down again, to stay this numb forever, this silent and full of anguish. But that's too hard to do again. Something won't allow it anymore. Part of me knows that I'll die if I do it that way, that even the divorce will not improve the health of my spirit if I refuse this inward journey.

There's another part of me that just wants to feel, *any thing*, just for the temporary release I get. The worst days are when I can't feel at all. And then there are other days when I'm in so much pain, yet I can't cry because I don't know how. On those days, I can't even feel sorry enough for the child I was to shed a tear for her, and so the tension just continues to mount. Sometimes running helps— *usually* running helps—running until I hurt, until I feel nauseous, until I can't go any further, until I feel punished almost. But why would I need to punish myself? I'm just trying to feel.

I spend the day at the studio, reflecting on the process of recapitulation. Chuck always spoke so informatively about it as the means to resolve the mysteries of the self, to arrive at a new place fully cleared of all the old stuff that has been so burdensome, freed at last. As I consider beginning where I left off, I'm confronted with the reality of my situation: *I can't stop the memories.* I can't hold back the onslaughts of thoughts and fears that chase after me, that tackle me and wrestle me down, choking me and holding my tongue. But something still makes me hesitate and I don't call Chuck, though I want to.

Near the end of the day I get a phone call from a client and line up another job, which takes me out of the doldrums and I feel better, lighter, aware that good things do happen.

September 19, 2001
The pain of *knowing* has finally hit. Up until now, I've mostly been experiencing the *realization* that something was drastically wrong in my past, each new memory sending me reeling as I understood, for the first time, that something had happened to me as a child. But now, as each memory surfaces, I *know* that

something happened to me when I was a child because I'm *feeling* it in my body.

At first it was all in my head, as I tried to grasp, to figure out just how it could have happened, as I tried to get my head around the incredible disbelief of it. But now it's settled in my body, in my stomach, a deeply buried, barely reachable pain of truth. And now I understand what Chuck meant when he told me that I didn't need to go searching for the memories, that they would come of their own accord, when I was ready.

Now that I feel stronger about the divorce, certain of life after it working out just fine—knowing I can handle it and life in general—the memories are resurfacing of their own accord. They sense an opening and they take it. I know I can't undergo this process on my own anymore; I need help.

With this admission, and with the past knocking the door down, I force myself to pick up the phone and, with my heart in my hands, I call Chuck and make an appointment. He receives my call with such gentleness that I know I don't have to fear for my aching heart. I don't have to say more than a few words and he knows what I'm trying to convey, almost as if he's been waiting for my call.

"Let's see," he says, "how about next week?"

"That's fine," I say.

We set up a time and I hang up the phone, shaking, filled with trepidation and a curious sense of exhilaration, because I know by making that call that I'm choosing to live. I've made the final distress call; I've reached out for help. I've made the decision to work on myself because I can no longer stand the stench of the past inside me, haunting and killing me, decaying from the inside out.

I want to live.

September 20, 2001

I wait for the week to pass until the appointment, apprehensively holding tight, keeping it all in.

Can I do it? Can I take this journey? Can I really open up and begin talking about it again? I don't want to keep it inside me anymore, my deep dark secret. I don't even fully know what it is, though it sits there, a shadowy fear, heavy with foreboding.

I need to let it go, but the idea of letting go is so frightening that just the thought gives me vertigo. I can't imagine ever letting go of anything. I can't imagine letting go of this control, which has been my strength, the one thing that's kept me going, the tight hold over everything that's been locked inside me for almost fifty years. Control is my power and I'm addicted to it!

September 21, 2001
So, where *did* the games come from?

In our last session, Chuck had suggested that perhaps a Dionysian archetype was in control. The ritual setting up of the game—the sticks, rocks, and earth—suggesting that perhaps some ancient initiation rites were being enacted, nature itself unleashing, channeling through two little girls. At the time, it sounded somewhat feasible to me, though not quite right. But it was much better than confronting the more horrific thought that my strange little friend was being abused. At the time we also discussed the fact that the name of the game was Operation, wondering just what operation might have sparked the acting out.

I wondered if she could have mistaken the word stitches for sticks. But I also remember that when Chuck used the term Dionysian regarding the crude acting out between my strange little friend and I, I knew it would be a lie if I accepted that explanation, though I didn't know how I knew this. Underneath I just knew, with an inexplicable certainty, that it was not that at all. And I knew Chuck knew it too. This certainty, I believe, was the true beginning of the unraveling of everything that I had lived by, of all that I had constructed and controlled in order to grow up, to be present in the world, to block out what was really behind the sexually deviant activities of two little girls playing in the woods. *I knew I could no longer lie to myself.*

I had a sense that Chuck was being careful, not implying anything, yet fully acknowledging that I was leading the investigation, so to speak. He was acting responsibly, letting me find out what I needed to find out on my own, letting it come out of me when the time was right. And somehow he did know that it would come out of me, the same way he knew that the memories would come of their own accord, that we didn't need to decide anything, that the process itself would show us where to go next, that what was inside me would guide us.

Without having said a word he knew we would be meeting again too, and I knew the same. It was just a matter of time, for even before I left his office that day I was already wondering just how long I could hold out before I returned to face the journey that was waiting.

My meeting with my personal destiny is inevitable. I just have to dare myself to begin by taking the first tiny step that will set me on the path again. *I have to open up to another human being.* That is step one. I know that by opening up to working again with Chuck I'm opening up to a blast of truth from the past, specifically this childhood past that has come to greet me again after so many years in hiding.

I also know that I'm about to take the next step on a journey that I had a glimpse of on the night of a full moon eclipse several years ago, when—very much like the scenes of my past playing out before me in that tiny television screen at the end of that dark tunnel on the kitchen floor—I saw my future. That time, as I stared at the full moon and called out to it, asking it to show me what I needed to do to change, to shift out of my ever-present discontent, I was granted a vision. As the shadow of the earth slowly covered the moon, I shifted my gaze slightly to the left of it and saw my future laid out, every tiny detail of it.

I knew I was being challenged. Could I disrupt what appeared on the outside to be so fine? Could I go with what I learned that night? Would I dare to pay attention to my spirit calling me once again?

Though I could not hold onto all that I was shown in that glimpse of future, I knew I had to *choose* to grow. Just as I had once experienced a similar moment when I was living in Sweden, here I was again being presented with a choice. Which way would I go? Would I choose the unknown over the known? In the end, I heeded my spirit's call that time too. It was the only way to go. I saw in that burst of vision that it would mean a lot of hard work, especially in the area of confronting my fears, but that if I chose to do so, I could have a life worth living.

This is that future. I'm living it now. I saw Chuck in that vision, an unknown man who would show me the way to open up to life, and to everything else.

In that last session with Chuck, almost a month ago, he wondered what I was coming away with from those childhood memories. What did I see most clearly from that time in my life?

As he asked those questions, I experienced a profound sense of loss. I sat quietly for a moment and pondered the memories that we had explored, eventually arriving at the conclusion that my childhood was totally lost, then and now. I saw only a huge black hole when I looked back and a sense that I had missed out on something extremely important because of my fears. I couldn't hold onto one good memory of my childhood, for those bad memories totally usurped the other childhood that I'd always remembered.

All I saw was my frozen child self, paralyzed with fright, unable to enjoy a single moment of life. As I looked back, I saw my strange little friend flitting about, teasing me, bossy as ever, not showing any outward signs of abuse. She was extraverted, outgoing in many ways, though she had violent temper tantrums if I didn't play according to her plans. I, on the other hand, shyly introverted, was afraid of people, afraid of my own body, afraid to move.

When Chuck asked me those questions, I immediately wanted to fix things, to put them back in some kind of nice neat order and, rather than come away with that sense of loss, I wanted to believe, in the end, that I did in fact have a good childhood.

"I would like to believe," I told Chuck, "that there were other times, another life that was good and, in spite of it all, that it didn't ruin everything for me."

September 22, 2001

I wake from a most disturbing dream. I'm paralyzed for some reason that's not clear; perhaps I've had an accident. I'm lying in a small hospital examining room where I've been laid on a table by a physical therapist. I can't move on my own. The male physical therapist lays me on my side, "to manipulate" my back, he says. He removes the blankets that cover me and takes off my hospital gown. He gets onto the table behind me and I feel his penis bumping up against my buttocks. I try to scream but no sound comes out. I scream and scream and scream, my mouth stretched open as wide as possible, my throat straining to shout, but still no sound escapes. Suddenly I hear voices and the sounds of people running down the hall and I know they're coming to rescue me. I wake up with a start and find myself sitting straight up in bed, my mouth stretched wide open, desperately straining to scream.

During the day a hard lump embeds itself in my throat. I feel miserable. I can't wait for this waiting time to be over.

I want to feel more comfortable talking about the past when I meet with Chuck, so I practice saying the words that are so extremely difficult to speak: *labia, vagina, sticks, poking, hurting, I hurt, I'm sad, I'm so sad.* I whisper these words to myself, knowing that I need to get comfortable with them, knowing that I need to attach them to those deep dark secrets that I've never spoken of. I need to find a way to explain, to convey what it did to me—how a strange game turned a shy, quiet, creative little girl into a withdrawn, painfully frightened child.

September 23, 2001

I return to the old memories, allowing myself to investigate them once again, preparing for meeting with Chuck, allowing myself to feel uncomfortable. Old familiar tensions arise as soon as I let those old scenes play out. I watch closely, taking in the details, letting the truth of what we did to each other come through more clearly. As I watch, I see that it really was a game; we *were* playing a game. And even though I clearly recall that she was the one who made it up, I did participate in it, and sometimes I enjoyed it. I fully admit that sometimes I actually enjoyed the sexual play.

It's hard to reconcile this with the Catholic upbringing I had, with the demands of the strict nuns at the school I attended and the expectations of my parents. My father, a deeply sensitive and fearful man, went off to work before dawn. I remember him as fairly passive at home where my mother dominated. As I recapitulate, I see her finger in front of my face, like a gun pointing directly at me. I see her angry face and hear the hated phrase, oft repeated throughout my childhood, spewing out of her tightly drawn lips: "You should have known better! You should have known better!" The echoing clang of those words reverberate inside my head once again, hammering any words of retort into a pulp of stunned silence, as they did when I was a child, when it was expected that I know everything.

I could never figure out how I was supposed to know so much, how I was supposed to know what it means to act like a mature adult at the age of three or four. Many times, when my mother hissed those words in my face, I knew she was right: I was guilty, I did know better, but I chose to do the wrong thing anyway. Sometimes I would let myself enjoy a mixed moment of sin and pleasure. But at other times, I just didn't know how to assert my own power and get myself out of a situation that my mother would not have approved of, an experience that I knew I had to keep secret.

Not much was ever explained in the world I grew up in. During the nineteen-fifties the important thing was to create the illusion of happiness and contentment, to hide the truth so the illusion could take root. After all, the war was over. Americans were asked to cultivate a false sense of security and prosperity, much like what's happening now. With the downing of the World Trade Towers we're told to go about our lives, to carry on. Get back to enjoying life, or at least make believe that you are, which was also the message of the nineteen-fifties when I was born. These same rules applied in my family. We were not to talk about ourselves, *ever*. We were expected to uphold the illusion of the perfect family, to never show an emotion and to never, *ever* embarrass the family.

The hard and bitter truths of reality became forbidden subjects never to be broached; they didn't fit into the illusion created by the boom of good feelings. Go have lots of babies, buy houses, spend money on cars, live the American Dream. And it was just a dream, an economic dream of prosperity and contentment. The consumer society was born as we turned outward and bought into that false dream, but in reality we purchased a nightmare.

The world I suppressed suggests that nightmare on a very basic level. What could not be spoken of had to find life elsewhere. Unpleasant topics spoiled the illusion of a perfect society, so anything that did not uphold the illusion was suppressed, and there were many topics that were off limits, sex being only one of them. It was never talked about. This was especially true in my family, where my mother's rules were *the law* and you had better abide by them or else! Anything to do with sexuality, sexual curiosity, natural or otherwise, was a closed topic. Even the opportunity to explain to a daughter that boys have penises and girls have vaginas was never broached. *Nothing* was talked about.

September 25, 2001

The day has finally arrived! I gear myself up for the session as I drive up to Chuck's office. I feel ready to finally begin again, everything sitting on the tip of my tongue, ready to spew out. When

I arrive, however, I go through an excruciating moment of intense shyness and fear. But Chuck knows me by now; he doesn't waste any time. We sit down and he simply says: "Talk."

I fumble through the first few minutes of the session, wringing my hands, silently moaning at my inability to articulate, but then I take a deep breath, open my mouth and begin talking about the game of Operation. I describe the scenes, the memories I've revisited over the past few weeks on my own. As I speak I hear my voice, like a frightened child's voice, spilling out the details of the games, one after the other.

I'm on the bathroom floor, lying on my back, I tell him, as I go back in time. My pants are down around my ankles and my knees are opened wide, exposing my genitals. I'm little, five or six. My strange little friend is using hair curlers and bobby pins, sticking wire curlers into my vagina. I'm hurting. The bobby pins are clipped onto my labia, so it looks like a giant ugly spider has attached itself to me.

I don't tell her I'm hurting because pain is part of the game and we don't speak while playing. That's one of the rules: we have to be able to withstand the pain. I want her to hurry and get it over with. Afterwards it hurts down there, I'm sore and there's an uncomfortable burning sensation when I pee. I like it better when we play the game outside; no one intrudes. When we're in the house, her little brother sometimes walks in to use the toilet or hides in the cupboard under the sink and watches us.

Each time she suggests we play this game—just for a little while, that it won't take long—I drag my feet, walking slowly behind her. I don't really want to play this game, but I go along with her, thinking it will be over soon and then we can play other, more normal games.

She gets bossy, telling me what I have to do to her. She likes the pain, sighs with pleasure. She adjusts the sticks or bobby pins if they don't feel right so they give her more pleasure. I can smell her vagina. She has white pus coming out of it.

When we play the game outside, she makes obstacle courses in the woods, setting it up for us to play there, rubbing on sticks, rocks, branches. Sometimes it feels good and I can't stop rubbing my genitals against things, it's like an itch that won't stop. Then I feel guilty.

She's mean sometimes and locks me in the chicken coop, makes me fetch the eggs from underneath the hens sitting on the nests. The hens peck and shriek at me, flapping their wings because I'm scared and don't know what I'm doing. But she yells at me through the locked door.

"You can't come out until you get an egg!"

I hear her laughing hysterically because she knows I can't move. I'm standing frozen in the middle of the small coop with the chickens milling about, pecking at my feet and ankles, flying at my head as they flutter down from their perches. I don't want to be there and they don't want me there either.

After what seems like an eternity my strange little friend finally unlocks the door and comes into the coop. Much exasperated by my stupidity she takes the egg basket from my clenched hands and grabbing my arm drags me over to a large hen sitting on a nest. She shoves my hand under the hen and when she pulls it out with nothing in it she gets furious.

"Grab an egg, you idiot!"

She pushes my hand back under the hen even though it's beginning to cluck loudly. I'm afraid of the pointy beak and sharp claws, but I quickly fumble for an egg this time. As I pull my arm out from under the ruffled hen I see that I'm holding a warm white egg and I'm immediately filled with a sense of exhilaration; the fear gone. Mission accomplished, this time. I'm allowed to leave the chicken coop.

When I'm done reiterating these memories, Chuck asks me to go back again and look at them from now, with my adult perspective.

"What do you come away with now?" he asks.

"When I go back, I immediately feel that sense of loss that I felt before," I say, "but I realize it wasn't all that bad, it wasn't everything. I went with it, played the games, and that's okay. They were just experiences. Even though they were hurtful and damaging, and even though I know they were bad—not normal— they were, in the end, just experiences I had." I feel empty when I say this, as if I've finally let something go.

"Yes, they were experiences," says Chuck.

Afterwards, I can barely pull myself together and I stand up a little unsteadily. Chuck asks me if I'm okay.

"I'm okay."

"If you weren't okay, would you tell me?"

"Probably not."

"Why?"

"I don't know," I say, "except maybe that's just another part of the taboo, not being allowed to indulge in self-analysis. Just get over it, and be strong. Part of my strength is in keeping my feelings to myself. I don't think anyone has asked me in a long time how I'm feeling, so I'm not used to saying how I really feel. I've been automatically saying that I'm okay, for years. To stay strong and in control I'm always fine. Maybe hiding it all inside makes it easier to cope, so I don't have to admit anything to myself either. I can just appear calm and strong all the time and believe that it's true."

Around lunchtime, exhaustion strikes and I know it's from being so tightly wound up for the past few weeks. I'm shaky and sore inside and out, constricted by a tight hollow ache. I always needed to protect myself and this is how I did it, by keeping silent, by physically keeping everything in, under strict control. If I had talked about it, what would my parents have thought of me? I would have been blamed. It would have been my fault. I should know better.

September 28, 2001
I can't stop shaking. I shake all morning, afternoon, and into the evening, feeling sad and unbelievably tight in my whole body. I can't concentrate, can't do anything except shake. But the shaking loosens something and a memory begins pouring out, disjointed and unclear, but perfectly recognizable nonetheless.

I'm under the stone bridge on the property of my strange little friend's family; a stream runs through it. We're there in the wintertime, two little girls playing the game of Operation. I feel icicles between my legs. I hear the sound of water running through the stream and dripping down the inside walls of the bridge. It's dark and damp, the walls slimy. There are stone ledges wide enough to lie on along both inner walls of the bridge. It's musty with the smell of earth. The snow outside is melting.

Chapter Seven

The Man in the Woods

October 1, 2001

Too many memories, some clear, some hazy, are trying to make themselves known, but I can't shake the blurriness from my eyes to get the whole picture. It's like trying to peer through a black scrim or screen, like squinting at that tiny television set at the end of that long dark tunnel.

Often I'm in the woods, haunting woods filled with dread, doom, and fear. Then I step out from the woods into light and sunshine, leaving all the bad stuff behind. In just a few small steps I go from intense fear and come out into goodness and light, shedding fear like an old snakeskin. But something stays behind in the damp cool woods. There's a shadow sitting on the dirt-packed ground among the leaves and odor of decay.

As I go deeper into this memory of dark and light, I find that I'm able to turn around and look back at the woods once I've emerged into the light, but I cannot go *into* them. I'm only able to walk out into the sunlight, over and over again. I'm carrying something in my hand. I bend over, step into it and pull it on—a diaper! Then I splash in the stream in the sunlight. Someone said I could go into the stream. Naked on top, I sit and play quietly in the water. Muddy and cool it seeps into and weighs down the diaper until it's saturated and heavy.

I'm aware of a shadow lurking, then and forever after, dimly in my memory. It's naggingly familiar. I've been waiting for it to either leave or reveal itself to me my entire life, this I know for sure, because I recognize its gloomy heaviness. Far-reaching in length, it has followed me everywhere. I've been waiting forever for this shadow to lift so my true life could begin.

From the time I was a small child I've wondered: When will I finally feel at home in this world? When will I be happy? What is it that I'm so afraid of? What is it that overshadows every aspect of my life? Now I see that it's in the woods, but I still can't quite see what it is. I wish I could clear the cobwebs from my eyes and see into the darkness, see what I can't quite capture. I like details; I like to know things. I won't be happy until I finally know what's in there. Something is in there. Something still sits in the woods and waits.

October 2, 2001

I turn and go back into the woods. I dare myself to enter the shade and face the memory. I can't go in the water yet, not until something else happens. The water is my reward, then I can play, but first something... I'm almost there... I'm in the woods... standing in front of someone sitting on the ground.

Am I alone with this person? Is that another child in the shadows over there? Do I know this person? Where's my mother? What am I doing by the stream? It's not deep, just a babbling brook, and I'm a very capable child, but who am I with? Someone I trust? Someone I know, and someone who knows me? Has someone taken me to see the stream, or am I with her, my strange little friend? Who is in the woods? *Who is in the woods?*

October 3, 2001

I go back into the dark woods.

Someone took me there. Someone told me to wash in the stream. Someone is telling me to do things. Someone is sitting on the bank, telling me to do things.

I pull out of the memory abruptly, come rushing back to the present knowing I still need to go there, to more clearly see what's happening in the woods. I must push aside the veils that cover this moment from my past, so I can figure it out, see it clearly and finally relive it. I don't think I can get on with things until I've finally confronted whatever it is that's been lurking there, whoever is sitting there, even if I don't recognize the person. Is my strange little friend with me? Are we with someone she knows?

I've seen this place before in memories, dipping in and out of it, off and on throughout my whole life. I've caught glimpses of this spot in the woods, this stream, and this shadowy figure. I've been here before, taken quick looks, but I haven't been able to grasp the deeper significance. The only thing I know for sure is that afterwards, in the act of stepping out into the light, I experience a tremendous sense of relief. Even now, as I relive the moment, as soon as I step into the light, something heavy and dark is shed, though I feel it lurking still behind me in the shadowy woods.

I need to know what it is. This may be where it all began.

October 4, 2001

I'm dreaming. A giant praying mantis is picking away at my skin, digging its sharp claws into the back of my skull. I'm also bleeding profusely down my leg. Blood is pouring out of a huge wound, a deep gash in my hip. Paramedics are trying to staunch the bleeding from the hip wound, but all my attention is focused on the mantis that is clawing so insistently at the back of my head. I barely notice the gaping wound and the blood pouring out of it.

"Is that big bug off my head? Is that big bug off my head?" I keep asking.

I bolt upright in bed, waking out of this dream, frantically swiping at the back of my head. My only thought is to get the praying mantis off me. I still feel its tentacles digging into my skin.

Sitting with my legs drawn up, I massage the back of my aching skull as a wave of anxiety, loneliness, and fear sweeps over me. Familiar feelings that belong to the memory in the woods are trying so hard to emerge. I know it's imperative that I reenter those woods. I must allow the memory to engulf me. As I sit on my bed, that long ago familiar sensation of sinking and shrinking deeply into myself takes over and before I know it I'm disappearing.

Hunched over, I go back as far as I can into myself, into the tunnel of myself, until I'm looking out a tiny pinhole. Everything inside me feels very large. When I touch my lips with my fingers, they feel enormous. When I look at my hands, I see the swirls on each fingertip blown up a million times. My vision is magnified, my sense of proportion totally distorted.

Suddenly, I blow up like a balloon. I puff up into an enormously fat pink girl. Round and buoyant, I float upward, and then, just as quickly, I pop! I get sucked back inside myself, swirling faster and faster, spinning down a vortex until I'm gone. Then I hear a calming voice, saying: "Leave it all alone, don't go near it right now." I slowly return to find myself still sitting up in bed, the back of my head still aching.

The feelings of the memory won't go away. I carry them with me throughout the day. Like messengers bearing hastily jotted notes from the praying mantis that came in the night, they tell me to go deeper into myself. While working at the studio I suddenly and clearly perceive that I'm supposed to look at my old drawings in order to understand that I've always carried the dark woods within me. I've always drawn the woods: detailed pen and ink drawings comprised of strange creatures with arms reaching out, mysterious things lurking in the shadows.

I pull out my old portfolios and sift through stacks of drawings and paintings; some that are thirty or more years old. There are old black and white drawings of dark forests with hidden faces peering out from between densely packed woods. Little girls in nightgowns run through the trees. Hands reach out; ready to snatch the unsuspecting little fairy girls who have so innocently entered the shady coolness. There's a full moon overhead, heavy with foreboding in one overworked pen and ink drawing. As I look at it again, I remember getting lost in that drawing, going deep into trance, scratching line upon line with a tiny crow quill pen, mechanically dipping it into a jar of black ink over and over again, getting lost in the brooding scene. Was it just my vivid imagination behind those drawings? Where did all the ideas come from? I think I know now.

In later years, the girls in the drawings flew naked through the sky, high over the trees, floating, with smiles on their faces. With the sun shining overhead, they skipped across flower-filled fields with reckless abandon and the pen lines, drawn less tightly, became lighter and more fluid, and color was added. But still the disturbing woods lay lurking in the background, clouding even the most delightful of scenes. The hidden faces still peered out, the grasping hands still sought contact, though by then I was putting candles into the hands that reached out, always lit candles. Perhaps my unconscious was preparing me for the day when I would turn back into the woods, this time with light; not to hide things in the darkness, nor to silence dirty secrets, but to seek out what I had once long ago experienced there, to light the way to self-discovery.

Drawing was always a means of escape. Securely encased in a magic bubble, the world closed off, no sounds or other senses entered the space with me, and my physical body disappeared.

Consciousness is the opposite of empty inside that bubble. It's aware, it cooks away, a pot full of ingredients simmering on a stove. First one ingredient and then another bubbles up and spills over the sides of the pot and, in deep trance, I peer closely at the overflow, drawing what I see. The hand works automatically and I'm not aware, most of the time, of what it's drawing; it just does its work. Consciousness, so preoccupied, isn't aware of the hand either and yet the drawing appears. When I sit up and move away from the drawing board, I'm often shocked at what has appeared on the paper.

I recently tried drawing forests like that again and, once again, I entered that old bubble. Silence surrounded me as it used to, and it was the old silence of the trance states of my child self. I wanted to go back to drawing what I had always regarded as fantasy drawings. I wanted to draw and paint again some of those themes that I always found so freeing, because I remembered how they felt, their execution so deeply necessary in some strange way.

In the past, I didn't understand why it was so pressingly important for me to spend hours at a time hunched over my drawing table, to lose myself in that world of inner creation. Now, as I draw those scenes again, as I go back to painting and drawing the woods, I understand that the results will be different because I'm different. I already feel a change, a transformation taking place. My sense of color has changed. My use of paint, my method of handling it has changed. But most important to note is that *I've changed*.

I see it already before me, the new trance artwork that I'll paint as I go through this recapitulation process. In rapid-fire visions, paintings that I have yet to execute appear before me. I already know that I'll go back into those dark woods and paint my way through every dark mystery I meet there. I *see* the work I'll produce.

People would often ask me where I got my ideas, wondering about the significance of the night scenes and the fairies in the woods in my work. I'd simply answer that they came from my imagination, but now I see all the stuff of long ago in those drawings. Most clearly, I see my personal fears depicted and the curious questions being posed. I see depression and withdrawal. What transpired in the darkness of the real woods is reflected in the gloomy, heavy pen work of those early drawings. I see the way it's permeated the years since, remaining deeply embedded in my psyche, my artwork evolving but still heavily influenced by the mysterious past.

I see the connection between then and now, the way I went into the woods in those early drawings and buried everything and how, now, in rediscovery, as I lift the branches of the trees on the edge of the forest, I see more clearly what I was attempting to bury back then. It's only now that it may come forth full force, because I'm ready for it, because I can handle it now. I'm strong enough now. I'm also definitely curious now, but I'm also scared.

This is about me; this is about what happened to me. This is what shaped me. Whatever it is that I'm going to encounter will mean starting life over with a new idea of myself. Out of the memories I'm going to create a new me.

October 5, 2001

I meet with Chuck for EMDR and immediately, as soon as I put on the headphones and close my eyes, memories begin to emerge, in quick succession, vivid and visceral.

I'm inside the stone bridge under the driveway with its wide ledges running the length of each wall, wide enough to sit and lie on. I hear the stream that runs through it. My strange little friend and I go in there often. It's dark and damp under the bridge and I'm afraid of animals hiding in there, of bugs and spiders. Sometimes I just will myself to not think about them, telling myself to just be brave. We play there in all kinds of weather; rainy spring days, hot summer days, even in winter. We have birthday candles that we light and let the melting wax drip down onto our genitals. We pack small stones into the crevices and folds of our labia and melt candle wax onto them, creating hard-packed walls, blocking entrance to our vaginas.

Now I go downstream from the bridge, following the stream as it runs into the woods, where someone sits waiting for me. I go into the stream and wash myself off. Someone on the bank won't let me play in the stream until I'm tested for cleanliness. I'm a dirty girl, he tells me, I have to wash off in the stream.

At first it's a game. I run into the water and wash off, quickly dipping down so my crotch hits the water, then I toddle out and up to him for inspection. He pokes his finger inside me and tells me to go back and wash again, "you dirty girl." I hear his guttural, choked-back laughter falling through the air, landing with a dull thud at my feet. I turn and go back again to the water, bending my knees, dipping into it, then toddle back to him. He inspects me again with his finger, which is rough and painful every time he sticks it inside me. I'm getting increasingly uncomfortable.

I stop the memory for a minute here, take my attention off the finger that's poking into me and notice that it's nice and shady in the woods. The air is warm; it feels like summer. As I look around, I see that the water in the stream is no longer clear, but murky from all the running in and out. I detect another voice and see another shadowy figure, smaller, another girl, my strange little friend. She stands off to my left and like him, she too is giggling. Perhaps she thinks it's a game, but I'm a little confused because it hurts.

"Who's the man?" Chuck asks. "Can you see his face?"

"No," I say. "I'm afraid to look."

"Do you have an idea?"

"Yeah."

He asks me if I can stay in the memory, look the man in the face and identify him, so I can know for sure. I hem and haw a little, afraid, but then agree. I don't want to leave having solved one mystery but steeped in another.

I go back into the woods. I stand in front of the man again and, as soon as I hear his voice, I know who he is, very clearly. I stumble back out of the memory and sit in stunned silence.

"Did you see his face?"

I don't say anything.

"Can you identify the man in the woods?" Chuck asks.

"Yes," I say. "It's him, her father." I cannot say his name, I only know him as the father of my strange little friend.

"It's her father," I say again.

"Are you sure?"

"Yes, positive."

"Okay. Can you go back again and see what else happens?"

"All right, I'll go back."

And with the EMDR headphones sending bi-lateral sound pulses into my ears, I close my eyes and go back into the woods. I go right back to the same scene where the father of my strange little friend is sitting on the ground facing us. He's reaching out to us and digging his left pointy finger into me and his right pointy finger into her, simultaneously feeling around inside us, telling us that we're still dirty, sending us back to wash off in the stream again.

I see his hand coming toward me, over and over again, slowly and deliberately seeking out that place between my legs, which is sore and very uncomfortable. I don't like what he's doing, but I don't understand it either. Maybe this is what they do all the time, him and his daughter. She seems to like it, so I try to like it too, but each time he sends us back into the water I'm happy to be away from him and his pokey finger.

Finally, he tells us that we're clean enough. He gives us permission to play in the water of the stream. I see my strange little friend sitting upstream from me. She seems to be having fun, splashing and laughing, but although I try to enjoy myself it's just not that much fun.

He says I can go now. I get out of the stream, bend down and pick up my diaper. It's been lying on the ground, the large diaper pins at the sides holding it in the shape of my body. I walk out of the woods, into the sunlight, into a different, lighter world. And that's when I pull my diaper on and step back into the stream, sitting in the murky water in the sunlight now.

I relate all of this to Chuck, slowly revealing the truth of where I've been for the past few minutes and then flip right into another memory. Someone comes upon us in the woods, yelling at us, an old lady.

"Dirty girls, dirty girls!" she screams, and I know it's something really bad.

With the headphones still on, I slip directly into yet another memory, its interconnectedness becoming clearer as it slowly emerges. My vagina is sore. It stings and burns when I pee. When my father gives me a bath and attempts to wash my crotch with his soapy hand, I scream at him.

"Don't! I can do it myself!" I can't explain that the soap is stinging me, that his hand is too intrusive, worlds colliding for an instant. I'm two years old, too young to know how to say that I'm crashing, falling apart, but I do what I must to stay present in the bathtub, my father kneeling beside me. I pull back into myself, going deep inside so I don't spin off into a million confusing pieces.

He's flabbergasted when he hears my vehement protest and calls to my mother.

"What should I do? She won't let me wash her!"

"Let her do it herself, if she wants to," I hear her calling back.

I come tumbling out of these memories, out of the woods and the bathtub, and crash back into the present, but I can't quite figure out where I am. I know that I'm not the same person who walked into this session with Chuck. In fact, *I'm no longer who I always thought I was.* My body, stiff and sore, is barely recognizable and my crotch aches with the memory of being intruded upon.

I gather my things together and hoist myself out of the chair, the time capsule that I've been sitting in for the past hour. Having taken me on a journey into the past it now releases me. I'm free to return to the present, but it's too distant. I know that staying in the past isn't an option and I can't quite get back to the present, but I have to shift myself somehow. I bolt out of Chuck's office and walk quickly to my car. The only thing I can think to do is drive straight to the studio and go to work.

October 6, 2001

It's hard to articulate feelings, hard to know what to say about all of this, even to Chuck, but now I understand how everything is interconnected—voices, sounds, smells, tastes, sights, pains, feelings, flashbacks, even dreams—and how my body reacts to everything too.

Now that I'm not pushing anything away, now that I stand and face the past, one trigger leads to another and then another and I find myself falling into old scenes as the memories become clearer. And then the pattern repeats as the cycle of interconnectedness continues to spin, like the falling of planets onto the wheel of an astrological chart, everything in alignment, everything present, everything important and meaningful.

I watch how it all comes together, as fear breeds more fear, which breeds more triggers, the patterns endlessly repeating as I open up to this process of recapitulation. I see the reverberations of the choices I've made over the past few months, the ripples of my decisions taking me farther and farther away from the place I felt so stuck in for so long. I ride those ripples now, as they take me where I need to go, into memories where the shadows perch. Waiting patiently, they haunt and tease, as I peer at them, trying to figure out who they are and what they want to tell me. I experience a sharp kick in the gut each time they come out of the darkness and materialize, as they tear into consciousness and show themselves, known entities.

Voice patterns, laughter, or the sound of a sigh in a yoga class can suddenly sweep me out of the present, as some horrific, frightening scene unfolds and I get drawn right into it. I hear words, normal everyday words spoken around me, innocently uttered, and yet, in an instant, I can be thrown into darkness, free falling through space, trying to hold onto reality as I hurtle toward some dimly lit memory, barely discernable in the distance.

I struggle with the child's feelings of good and bad, as she tries to make sense of these experiences. I'm a child again when I'm in the memories and I'm confused, unsure of what's happening. I make no judgments, *I don't seem to have the capacity for that yet.* I'm just trying to figure out how to react, trying to figure out what I'm supposed to do as I struggle to follow the instructions I'm given. The cascade of emotions, feelings, and questions that jolt through my body each time I feel the finger poking into me are hard to contend with. Do I laugh or do I cry? I see my strange little friend and she's laughing. Is this fun? Okay, this is fun, but it doesn't feel good.

My adult self sits back, fully present, but stunned at the revelation of this memory, at the shattering of such innocence at the hands of such perversity. My adult self fully accepts the child's ignorance in matters of the world, yet is appalled at the lack of parental awareness and oversight, flabbergasted by the vicious assault on a tiny child's body by a man who apparently had easy access.

As I try to figure out how things stood back then, I allow myself to go with what emerges from my unconscious. As I allow more memories to play out, I simultaneously watch what I always thought was reality begin to unravel and a new reality reveal itself, a totally different one.

I'm having trouble sleeping now. On most nights, memories come creeping into bed with me. They sneak into my room and, slipping under the covers, lie beside me, bringing the pain, the soreness between my legs, and repeated flashbacks of the experiences in the woods. They ask me to look at them again, to not leave them behind until I've investigated every tiny, intricate detail.

October 7, 2001

I'm sitting in the back seat of a car, on the way to a wedding reception in the vicinity of the old neighborhood. Because of a traffic accident on the highway, the driver elects to take a shortcut over a mountaintop and suddenly I'm alert. I recognize the road. We're going to pass by his house, my abuser's house. This is how I'm beginning to refer to him in my mind, as *my abuser*. I sit up, peering out the window, rigidly tense, literally on the edge of my seat.

In a heightened state, barely aware of the conversation among the other passengers in the car, I almost expect something to happen, but what I'm not sure. We round a sharp curve going down a steep hill. His house is on the left, the side I'm sitting on. I almost want to scrunch down in my seat, to hide so he won't see me. I don't even know if he's alive, but I feel like a little girl again, and I'm afraid.

As we near his driveway, however, I begin to anticipate this unexpected opportunity to view his property, to see if my memory is correct after all. I feel like an investigative reporter, keen on finding out as much as possible in the seconds that it will take to pass by. I notice that the woods are different, the dense tangle of trees and undergrowth thinned out. In fact, as we get closer to the driveway I see that the property has been totally transformed, bulldozed, flattened. Nothing is what it used to be! The stream is no longer in existence, the culvert which the stone bridge once spanned has been filled in and replaced by an asphalt driveway. The woods and fields have been leveled, reshaped, smoothed over; even his house, set far back from the road, is different. What I remember is gone, totally removed!

For a second, I experience total freedom from everything—from the knowledge I've gained over the past few months, from the memories I've re-experienced—because nothing exists! For a split second, I'm elated, smiling, totally unburdened, relieved of the pain of the recapitulation process, given a break, because it doesn't exist! Nothing exists! In an instant I'm free, light as a feather, happily sailing by. But then I remember what I've been reliving, what I've been feeling as I recapitulate, and I understand that even if it exists only in memory, that's enough to go on. I've had a taste of just what that means. In the few seconds that it takes to drive past his property, I know that inside me everything that happened is still as real as it once was.

At the wedding I'm stiff, only half present, the past intruding so insistently that I can only half hear, half see. So steeped am I in this recapitulation process that I cannot move during the reception, my frozen body stuck to my seat, as I strive to stay present and focused on what's going on around me. I sit next to an elderly uncle and endeavor to make bright conversation, to focus on him. It helps keep the darkness at bay. Later, when I see photos of myself at the wedding, I notice how my head and neck are bent slightly forward. I seem to be peering at something in front of me, staring very intently at something, though there is nothing there. Only I know that I'm trying to see through the dim shadows into those distant woods.

October 9, 2001

I meet with Chuck and tell him about the impact of riding past my abuser's property, how in one sense I felt a great sigh of relief because everything was changed. I felt sort of safe, released from the past in one fell swoop, but at the same time I felt totally freed to more fully commit to exploring the memories too, for that is the only place where my past still lives.

"As I rode past that property," I say, "I felt myself recommit more deeply to this recapitulation—for myself alone—because, although the memories don't exist in this world, they sure are alive and kicking inside me."

We do EMDR and my abuser is everywhere, haunting every scene of every memory that arises. The memories that have already emerged get clearer each time I go back to them. I hear my abuser's voice, loudly and clearly speaking to me.

"G'wan, do it; yer tern," he commands, his strong country accent riding out of the past on the memories.

I see his massive dirty hands and smell the heavy odor of machine oil on him. I recall how the smell of machine oil once haunted an illness. I couldn't get it out of my nostrils, the taste of it out of my mouth, as I vomited and vomited, unable to rid myself of the odors I now recognize as originating with him. As we do EMDR, I have a strong urge to vomit, the smell of oil filling my nostrils and throat once again. Chuck quickly pushes the plastic wastebasket closer to my feet as I lurch over, gagging.

"This was a whole lot easier when it was only two little girls playing games," I say through my nausea, staying with the odors, letting them carry me back, until I see my abuser walking towards me.

"It's yer turn today," he tells me, as he reaches for my hand.

I have no choice but to take his hand and go with him. Perhaps he'll be nice this time. This is my hope, as I walk across the yard with him.

"He's nice today," my four-year-old self thinks, "maybe it's okay this time." He grips my hand tightly, but he's talking so nicely. It's sunny; I smell the summery smell of sun-dried hay in the field we're walking across. But then it all changes.

I hunch over in fright, instinctively drawing my arms in close, rolling into a ball in the chair in Chuck's office, as if protecting myself, because now I see my abuser leering at me in that way I don't like. Things are turning bad and I know I'm caught again. This is not going to be good. His face comes so close to mine that I can see the stubble of his beard magnified to large black dots, the beads of sweat on his quivering lips standing out in warning. He's too close to me now and I smell his foul breath seeping out through his slightly parted lips, his mouth stuck in that hateful leer. He has something in his mouth, a lump in his cheek and he spits on the ground a lot.

The memory suddenly shifts and we go to the stream again, and again I see his finger coming at me, going in between my legs and I feel it digging into my vagina, into the soreness between my legs.

"Who is it?" Chuck asks. "Can you see his face?"

And under the shade of the trees I look him straight in the face and once again I clearly identify him.

"Yes," I say, "it's him, I'm sure of it."

And then new memories flow out—hazy pictures of past scenes flood out onto the floor in front of my bent over body. I see his bedroom, a barn, and the paddle he used to spank his children with. I focus on the paddle. It has a name carved roughly into the wide flat side of it, big bold letters that spell HONEY.

"If we're not good Honey will get us! Honey will get us!"

I was never actually paddled by Honey, but I was present numerous times when my strange little friend and her brother were disciplined. I heard their screams, horrific in intensity, as they were taken to the basement and whacked across their bare bottoms with the heavy paddle. Whenever I heard their screams I steeled myself, covering my ears and closing my eyes, vowing that I would never scream like that. I imagined myself holding it in, suffering deeply, but never outwardly showing even an ounce of discomfort. I imagined being like a saint tied to a burning stake, stoically withstanding anything that could possibly be done to me, never gratifying the accusers with a cry or plea as the flames licked my body, never letting them see my pain. I wanted to totally transcend the physical. And now, as I recall this, I remember myself imitating the qualities of sainthood that I learned about in Catholic school, never showing an emotion, never letting anyone see me cry.

I come out of the memory and tell Chuck that even though I didn't understand what was happening to me when I was a child there were other times in my life when I should have done something to protect myself. Full of self-loathing, I have no pity for myself, not an ounce of tenderness. I just don't understand why *I just let things happen to me.*

"I was an easy target," I tell Chuck, as I get up to leave, "I was always an easy target."

October 10, 2001

I'm very depressed, feeling edgy, brittle, fragile, like a thin shell on the verge of cracking. But I hold on; I won't crack. I'll hold on like I always do. I'll hold on until it doesn't hurt anymore.

As the day goes on I try to ignore my feelings and emotions, but the memories draw me back and all I want to do is curl up and hide. I allow myself to withdraw for a few minutes, to lie on the couch at the studio and go into inner quiet, to relive the sinking feeling of disappearing inside myself. I remember that I could stay in a dissociative state for a long time. It was safe there. No one could get me.

Once again, transcending the pain, I allow myself to go into that state of sainthood so I don't have to feel, to that place where the flames of pain can't touch me. Going more deeply still, I drop even further inside myself until I disappear, until I feel safe. I go so far back that I feel my body becoming a child's body again and I want to dress like a boy, in jeans and flannel shirts like I did when I was a little child. I want to be a boy and hide behind boy clothing, hoping once again that it will keep me safe from the memories and the pain they carry.

As I relive the safety of retreat in dissociation, I find that I'm becoming increasingly unsociable. I don't want to talk to anyone, go anywhere, or see anyone. I hope the phone doesn't ring, that no one knocks on the door of the studio and that no one calls for a job estimate.

But questions still nag and the praying mantis still wants to know how it all started and I know I can't stay away for long. I can't stay dissociated, in that state of grace, leaving the questions unanswered. Mysteries arise once again, stirring up my curiosity, bringing me back to my body.

Was it presented as just a game, did my abuser make it all seem like a game?

October 13, 2001

When I let myself begin to feel again, the emotions that arise are as real as the physical pain, but for the most part I don't want to believe what the memories are telling me. *I don't want to believe them!*

It's taking time to sink in, but I see the shadowy shapes and clearly hear the words, smell the smells, and the soreness in my crotch persists. Yet, I push it all away in disbelief. And, as usual, I push away feelings I don't want to deal with either. I'd rather keep them buried than acknowledge them. But, as the day passes, it hits me: *the pain is real.* There is nothing I can do to deny that I'm carrying an old childhood soreness between my legs, somatic pain that is almost fifty years old.

Eventually, I realize that every time a new memory begins to surface I also see the televised images of the airplanes smashing into the World Trade Towers playing in my head, over and over again. BAM! BAM! BAM! BAM! Violently impacted, I feel like I'm having my own personal terrorist attacks. I feel like I'm being punched in the gut. The crippling analogy of the September 11th attacks feels like something I can latch onto, the visual images giving me an appropriate outlet for my feelings.

I also realize that having a delayed emotional reaction to the emergence of these memories is helping me deal with the impact of the truths I can't quite assimilate and, for the time being, I'm thankful for the unfeeling, numb part of myself that doesn't want to believe. However, I acquiesce to going back, to taking this journey one step at a time, to moving back slowly but more deliberately now. I'm curious too. I wonder how far back I can actually go.

How many times can I go back, and to how many memories? Can I recapitulate, vividly relive, my entire childhood?

October 14, 2001

Emotionally exhausted and sick with a sinus infection, I stay in bed for half the day. I'm thankful for the excuse because it's the only place I really want to be, all curled up under blankets. Everything becomes so clear while I lie under the covers. I feel the shadowy presence of my abuser in a different way. I *see* him. I *feel* him right next to me, lying in bed with me, his odor and presence real. And I see that it wasn't just a game.

We were being manipulated and controlled, my strange little friend and I. He did disgusting things to us. He did things to me alone too; I see that most clearly now. He's present in every memory, directing every event, partaking in his own perverted and lecherous way. I see that I was very young when it started, in fact when I was still in diapers, as that memory by the stream makes clear. *He was an adult and I was taught to do as adults told me to do.* You did what they asked or you got punished, so when he told me to do things, I did them, no questions asked.

With all this knowledge of the past brewing inside me, I still have to go about my daily life, acting as if everything is normal. I have to go to work and be normal, go home and be normal, go to a wedding and be normal, keeping it hidden, like I always did. So I wonder if I'm really doing anything different.

Yes, I'm talking about it. I'm confronting it head on.

October 16, 2001

I meet with Chuck and go right into memories again. I hear the voice of my abuser telling me that he'll "kiss it and make it better." After he plays Operation with me he kisses the hurt and makes it better. He tells me I'm special.

He's there when his daughter and I play Operation. I see him sitting on the toilet seat in the bathroom, directing her, showing her how to clip bobby pins onto me, how to poke things into me. He watches very intently, making sure she's doing it right, correcting her, suggesting things.

When we play the Tree Branch game, he's there. He watches her directing me, but he's really the one who makes up the games. He's the one telling her what to do, telling her to tell me to lift my dress up higher so he can see, telling her that I did it wrong and I have to do it again. He's the one who tells her to tell me to stop in the middle of the branch and hang upside down by my knees, my dress falling over my face, and then to flip off the branch onto the ground where I land on my feet with a thud, my butt in the air, my dress askew. He watches, but he's in charge.

October 17, 2001
Each day now I confront more memories. They pop out of me along with the voices that scold, the voices that say: *I should know better, that I'm bad, evil, a sinner, that I should be ashamed of myself, and that I let it happen.* Sometimes the same memories play over and over again. Sometimes there are glimpses of ones not yet fully revealed. Once again I hear my abuser telling me that I'm special, something he told me often.

I smell him—the machine oil smell filling my nostrils and throat all week. I can't get the taste out of my mouth and even though I gargle and rinse every chance I get, I can't get rid of his odor. I hear him telling me that he'll kiss it and make it better when he's done. I hear him saying this over and over again until I'm nauseous. I hear him telling me what to do, saying things that play repeatedly in my head, like a record stuck in a track.

"It's yer turn today; yer special," I hear.

"Come on, I have something special to show you."

I am empty of feelings. Everything has spilled out of me. I can't quite examine or pick over all that has come through yet, though I see it lying there in a heap at my feet, my life, spoiled.

October 19, 2001
Keeping it at bay as well as I can, I pamper myself mostly by not going there, by not looking too closely, not asking for it, letting it come of its own accord, not ready for more at the moment. Aloof in all aspects of life now, not just in the face of the memories, I'm too tender to bear much tension. I retreat as often as I can.

"Oh please, don't touch me, don't come near me with your tales of horror," I beg the memories. "I can't do it now, no more memories. Later, just not now; I can't bear anymore for the moment."

October 21, 2001

I dream a strange dream about a bodiless head that rides on a small electronic platform that looks like a large, gray plastic model of an aircraft carrier. The features on the face are metallic, hard and set, the eyes glaring. I've stumbled into a large, empty building, unaware of its presence and apparently I've disturbed it while wandering around in this vast space. The head on the platform bolts out from underneath a pile of debris where it has lived for a long time and skims along the floor, the face mean and angry. It pursues me around the empty building for some unknown reason. I run from it in fear, but eventually turn and face it. I attack it, kicking it right off the platform. The head goes crashing to the floor where it explodes. I'm surprised to see that it's no more than a pile of fluff, nothing but bits of paper and plastic.

In the morning I wake exhausted, tired of feeling so empty, so hollow. The crazy head chasing me doesn't make me feel any better, but it does make me think that perhaps the mantis picking at my head was trying to alert me to something besides just the memories. Perhaps I'm not supposed to go after the head, not supposed to dig through my head for the memories, after all. The head doesn't really hold anything inside, as this dream shows; it's just a lot of stuffing. Where do I look then? Where do I go for the memories if not into my head, into my brain, to the place where memories are supposedly stored?

It doesn't matter at the moment, because right now I don't want to recapitulate any more; no more memories. I want it to be over. I want to stop grinding my teeth. I want to stop feeling those old pains. I want to stop going to sleep thinking about it, waking up thinking about it, and I want to stop dreaming about it. But at the same time, I feel that I must barge ahead, blast through those black shrouds and see what's in those woods, what's down those paths, what's under that bridge.

I should do as my dream suggests. Instead of letting the memories chase me around, glaring at me and scaring me, I should turn and face them and attack with a vengeance. I see that it may be the best way to tackle this process—to not let it have control. I must be in control now.

October 22, 2001

I take my daughter to her morning soccer game and bump into Chuck and his wife Jeanne, whom I've never met. Their daughter plays on the same team. Several years older, she's gentle and patient with the younger girls.

Chuck introduces me to Jeanne. I'm aware that she's been dealing with breast cancer for quite some time. She's exceedingly thin, though her eyes are bright and her voice lively, as she shakes my hand. We make small talk about the chilly morning, the night's frost barely melted. She's dressed in a thick down vest, a small hat on her head. I instantly recognize her as the woman I've seen many times, her look unusual.

From the minute I first saw her, several years ago at a school event, I wondered who she was. She seemed so familiar. The thought that I knew her plagued me every time I noticed her, but I could never quite place her. I've often felt that she looked like me; we could almost have been related. But she always appeared so settled, so flowing and unafraid of the world, extremely comfortable in her body, solidly present in this world, while I barely inhabit my body, I'm barely here.

Just as I once cringed in fear when I saw Chuck's name, when I first saw Jeanne I was struck by her calmness. I was not at all intimidated by her extremely self-assured, capable, confident aire—the opposite of me—just curious about who she was and why she seemed so familiar.

When Chuck introduces us the energy between the two of them is palpable. It's clear that Chuck and Jeanne Ketchel are real partners, that they have something special going on between the two of them. I watch as they slowly stroll along the soccer fields before the game starts, his head bent down to hear what she's saying. They have the appearance of a solidly closed unit that nothing can penetrate.

October 28, 2001

I wonder if I should reacquaint myself with her, my strange little friend, my abuser's daughter. It was about twenty years ago when I last bumped into her. She approached, stood right in front of me and, staring boldly, locked eyes. She said hello, and that was all. I turned away, ashamed, when a vision of us playing Operation flashed through my mind, wondering if that was what she was thinking about too.

I saw her tilt her head, following my gaze, as I looked away, breaking eye contact. I remember I couldn't go there, I couldn't even think about it. I pushed the thought away in horror like I always did, pushed it down inside me, made it disappear, as if it had never happened, though her look disturbed me. Her eyes seemed to follow me around for months after that, staring me down, challenging me, but eventually I conveniently forgot about the incident and the game of Operation too. On occasion, however, I would recall her stare and wonder if she was remembering the things we had done to each other, if she too were recalling the games we'd played.

Now I wonder if she thought I remembered other things too, what her father had done, for instance, though at the time I had no memory whatsoever of his involvement in our play. What he did was so deeply repressed that it only came up occasionally in shadowy disconnected flashbacks that I could never discern, but now understand more clearly.

Do I dare make contact now and see what comes of it? Do I really want to do that?

To be perfectly honest, no, I don't want to do that at all—though perhaps someday it may be appropriate, when and if I'm ready, but not now, not yet.

October 29, 2001

I dream I'm with him, my abuser, in the tunnel under the bridge. I'm lying naked on the ledge, a little girl again. He's mixing something in a vat. I'm scared. Then he fills my vagina with a hot boiling mixture of mud and rocks, pouring it into my mouth too so I can't talk or scream, filling my throat and vagina with cement-like mud. Now I'm furious, full of hatred for him. All I can concentrate on is saving the baby so he doesn't do this to her too.

I wake up with that anger boiling inside me and immediately fall back to sleep, intent on finding the baby. It's imperative that I save the baby from this monster.

I dream again. This time I'm in a huge wooden building, a warehouse under renovation, and I'm looking for the baby. I get lost in long corridors, opening every door I come upon, searching every corner. I have a new job in this building and I'm supposed to be working, but I let everyone know that I can't begin work until I've found the baby; I *must* find the baby first.

Fueled by anger, I hunt through old bathrooms, partially renovated offices, and an endless number of empty rooms in this dusty old building looking for the baby. Finally, I meet another woman who says she'll help me find the baby if I show her to her office. I don't know where her office is, but I don't mention this to her as I take her along. There are other people in the building, but I ignore them completely because nothing else matters; I am totally focused on finding the baby. Eventually, we open a door and see a baby girl sitting on a table.

"There's the baby!" says the woman who is with me, but I see right away that it's not the right one.

"She's Russian," I say, "not the right one."

The baby stands up on the table and I'm shocked to see that something is wrong with her genitals. They are grossly large and adult, with a thick shock of curly dark pubic hair. As the baby begins to topple off the table two women speaking Russian rush over to catch her before she falls onto the floor. The other woman and I continue our search for the baby. Still not having found her, I wake in a dark, smolderingly angry mood.

I wonder about my parents, especially my mother. I recall her distant, unemotional, and rarely affectionate style of mothering. I hear the perfect diction and formal tone of her voice, which rarely softened with tenderness. Ironically, she had a master's degree in early childhood education; her style based, I suspect, upon an archaic school of thought. She taught preschoolers, always totally in charge of what went on in her classroom, following a traditionally strict and orderly model with expectations of obedience and adherence to the rules. She was that same strict presence at home. When she withdrew into her books, reading murder mysteries for the most part, we could not break through the barrier she constructed around herself. I see her curled up in her chair, reading, while the house deteriorates around her, while I attend to my younger siblings, embarrassed to invite friends over to our messy house.

I remember her once proudly and naively describing how her small children roamed the countryside at very early ages, perfectly safe in the idyllic setting of the rural neighborhood we lived in, with cousins and grandparents, aunts and uncles nearby. She knew, she said, that someone else would always feed us a peanut butter and jelly sandwich for lunch if we didn't come home, it was just taken for granted. Sometimes, she said, she had ten children in her kitchen wanting lunch and on other days none at all, everyone off playing, asking another mother to make lunch. This is the illusion she spun and it's the one I accepted. It's the happy childhood I thought I had experienced—until recently. I'm sorry to burst the bubble. It wasn't really like that.

I'm struck by the insight that we cannot really know what is happening to or inside another person. We haven't had their experiences nor do we have the same thoughts weaving stories in our heads. We're all different; each of us living unique and separate lives, each of us experiencing life on our own terms, even if we're in the same family. Even if we're in the same room we're not having the same experience. We're all separate, mysterious beings.

I sat in a roomful of people at that wedding reception recently, but was miles away, years away, being molested by a madman, while the person next to me was jumping up at every opportunity to dance, laughing, clapping along with the music, alive in the moment. That kind of moment has been very rare in my life. My childhood, especially, was mostly lived in a hazy, in-between world where I couldn't see or hear very well. In fact, as a child, it was thought I had a hearing problem because it took me so long to swim up out of the fog of my natural state of dissociation, to focus on the questions being asked, as I tried to figure out if I was being addressed.

"What?" I'd ask, "What did you say?"

And this was not because I was deaf, but simply because I was not fully present in this reality.

October 30, 2001
This time, when I meet with Chuck it feels appropriate to ask for guidance from an outside source. I feel lost, as the world I've always considered real has crumbled and fallen into a heap, as I've crumbled too. I throw the coins, asking the *I Ching* the question that has so troubled me over the past few weeks: "Who am I really?" The answer comes in hexagram 56: *The Wanderer*. I'm

immediately struck at how right this is, for I have indeed been a wanderer my entire life, but especially over the last few months, as I've elected to take this recapitulation journey.

This hexagram represents two separate entities that cannot rest together. The mountain below represents stillness while the flames above leap and move constantly, so even though there is underlying stability there can be no rest.

The *I Ching* states: "Strange lands and separation are the wanderer's lot." This is a clear indication that my recapitulation journey is exactly what I must be doing to discover the answer to my question. I must continue visiting the strange lands of my past, feeling the separation from the self I once knew, and yet I must also keep in mind—while I wander into those woods and experience what I must—that I have the strength of the mountain.

In the reading, I also receive a moving line, nine in the fourth place, further underscoring the process ahead. Here the description is of a wanderer who is simple. This type of wanderer limits outward desires and stays inwardly strong and focused. This wanderer finds a resting place within this core strength and yet at the same time knows that to keep moving is essential. It's also necessary to remain on guard at all times and to carry weapons of self-protection, always aware of being a stranger in a strange land. Indeed, this is how I feel as I elect to take this recapitulation journey, this deep exploration into my self. I fully acknowledge that I'm ready to enter the strange inner land of the past that is at once so mysterious and so familiar. I know I must not get caught there, and yet I also know I must traverse its length and breadth, gathering all the information I need, so I can reunite with my damaged child self, and then move on.

I must use the tools and weapons I have at my disposal, finding places to rest as I wander; doing yoga, breathing, and staying connected to the shamanic teachings and practices that Chuck is introducing me to. As the mountain suggests, I must allow for moments of stillness, even as I allow this process to unfold, as *it* will. I must learn to flow with the energy of the intent of this process, and I must learn to make my dreams work for me too, as Chuck suggests. He is teaching me that I can control what happens in them. In the end, I must learn how to let go of whatever it is that keeps me from moving forward.

"A wanderer takes very little with him," Chuck says. "You must begin to let go, so you can move on, so you can begin to feel."

The future of this hexagram turns into hexagram 52: *Keeping Still, Mountain.* This is the double mountain, both above and below, further underscoring that with perseverance—and doing lots more yoga and meditation—the natural end of the journey will be stillness, peace, and wholeness, totally in alignment with nature, male and female energy in synergy. The images of the mountain continue to suggest that my focus on doing yoga, meditation, and the deep inner work of this recapitulation is indeed in alignment with where I am at the moment, but also where I'm headed.

As I turn away from old ideas of stability and turn toward the continued unfolding of this recapitulation process, which is both devastating and empowering, I take this reading seriously. I know I do have the strength inside me to keep going into those frightening and strange memories, to face the man in the woods again and again. Even though I'm still afraid, I sense the truth of this reading and that, in the end, I will achieve the calmness of heart that I so yearn for. I'm learning already to flow with what life presents, rather than run from it in fear. I'm no longer electing to avoid life as I've done in the past, but pushing myself to more fully embrace it.

When I achieve calmness and egolessness, the *I Ching* suggests, I will be connected to my heart's intent, my struggles will be in balance, and I will act from this place of deep knowing, in harmony with self and nature.

Who am I really? This is what I look forward to discovering. This is why I'm doing this recapitulation.

Chapter Eight

Dream States

November 1, 2001

In a dream, I sit across from Chuck in his office. He asks me how I'm feeling. I look down at my body and then I look up at him.

"I feel like a cow," I say.

I look down at myself again and see that now I'm naked and covered in huge black and white spots.

"A naked, spotted cow," I say, then I start to cry.

For some reason, I wake up from this dream flooded with insight. I realize that all this time I've been pretending that I was not really the bad little girl who was abused. At the time of the abuse I had left her body and escaped somewhere else. I dissociated, completely severing any connection to her pain and experiences, and have been holding onto the memory of myself as a nice girl. The memory of having been this more likeable girl is far clearer, making it easy to leave the abused girl behind; distancing myself from her fate. I've even been doing this while recapitulating her experiences. I just haven't been able to connect with the abused girl, repeating what I did as a child. In fact, I've been reliving *that* part of the memories as well, by identifying with the more likeable girl over the abused girl. I realize that although I've been telling myself that I was not that little abused girl, indeed I was!

This spotted cow dream, although it makes no sense to me, somehow leads to this clarity. And now, as I wake up, I sit here trying to accept the truth that she, the frightened and confused little abused girl, was *actually me!*

Wow! I'm struck that this is the first time I'm putting all this together. Have I really remained that disconnected? Am I still that dissociated? Have I really perceived her as some other little girl, even though I feel her pain and confusion so intensely? Actually, I see that I've been recapitulating the entire experience, including the dissociative aspects, as they occurred.

I see dissociation as the inevitable consequence of the abuse. In the past, I had to somehow find a way to leave that abused little girl in the woods so I could survive. I understand that. But, even as I recapitulate lying on the ground waiting for the game of Operation to be over, I notice how I automatically want to switch over to the other little girl, declaring that: "Hey, wait a minute! There was this other *nice* girl." It's much easier to fondly recall a nice, sensitive, kind, happy little girl, who played with a real best friend, rather than the badly scarred and scared little girl who played those disgusting games in the woods.

Yesterday, I woke up hating myself for what had happened, full of loathing for that little abused girl who was part of it. I realized that I blamed myself—always. Even now, when I acknowledge that I was only a child and not responsible, that *an adult* was responsible, I still feel that same self-loathing and self-blame.

As I ponder all of this, I notice I have a stiff neck and slight headache, the praying mantis still digging away at my skull, letting me know I'm doing good work, but that there's still more to do.

More than anything I want to cry, but I can't.

November 3, 2001

I dream that I'm swimming on a lake with my new best friend and her brothers. The water is getting rough and strong winds are blowing up whitecaps. I swim far out into the lake until I pause over a spot and, looking down into the dark churning waters, I think to myself: "Oh, yes, this is the spot where I drowned!"

I wake up out of this dream, and feel how utterly familiar it is, not only the setting of the lake and the violent storm, but even the thought that I had drowned there. Somehow I know that my dream is taking me there for a reason, but I just can't figure out what it means.

November 4, 2001

I dream. This time I'm walking along a familiar road in the rural neighborhood I grew up in. My daughter, who is about five years old in the dream, is with me. As we round a curve we bump into my abuser who is standing naked in the road. He appears as a sort of trinity: he's an old woman, perhaps seventy years old, while at the same time an old man of the same age, as well as a ghostly spirit. I clearly see this trinity of man, woman, and spirit, three naked entities floating in and out of focus. This strange entity, in the guise of my abuser, wants oral sex from me. I refuse. He perseveres, insisting that I do as he asks. I'm reluctant to engage him. I know it's a bad idea, but for some reason I tell him he can have my daughter instead.

I leave them in a field, telling her to lie down, that it will be okay, to just do as the man says. And then I run away, horrified at what I've done, full of remorse and self-loathing. As I visualize my daughter getting raped by this man, I cannot forgive myself for leaving her with him. I know that I have to go back and save her. As I turn and start running back down the road, I see my daughter standing in the distance. She sees me and waves. She seems okay and I'm greatly relieved to see that she has survived.

At this point in the dream, I wake up because one of my two cats, who sleep at my feet every night, is meowing at the bedroom door to be let out. I let the cat out, get back into bed, and go back to sleep with the intention of fixing what I've just done. I hate the decision I made. I feel like a terrible mother, a monster. I'm determined to go back and somehow fix it.

Now I dream that I'm rewriting the dream, literally. The only problem is that my dream pen is leaking and ink is getting all over me, all over the sheet of paper, and onto the bedspread I'm lying on. My hands are also covered in black ink. I fold up the piece of paper I've written on, thinking that if I can just hide it somewhere everything will be okay, that it won't matter that what I wrote is indecipherable. Just the fact that I've re-written the dream solves the problem, I conclude, making everything all right. At this point, I tear up what I've written into small squares of paper and pile them into a little stack of torn shreds. Just as I'm stuffing them away under some clothing in a dresser drawer, I wake up. I see my hands gesticulating in the air above my head, and I almost expect shreds of paper to fall onto my face.

Once awake, the dream haunts me. I see that I'm being asked to confront my true feelings about my abused self. Did I really loathe and despise that child self? Did I really consider her to be evil? Long suppressed feelings are awoken by the plight of my poor daughter in this dream, as she is clearly the abused self who I so easily walked away from, telling her to just do what the man asked. But this time I just can't leave her. I'm appalled at my cruel decision, which forces me to consider what I've been doing to her all these many years. It does make me feel like a terrible monster.

And yet, I'm not sure how to reconcile the fact that those decisions, to dissociate and leave her behind with my abuser, once kept me alive. I'm not really sure that I resolved anything by rewriting the dream either. In a sense, all I did was cover up what I had just discovered, blurring the truth so it became unreadable. Tearing it up just feels like another attempt to conceal rather than face the truth. The dream didn't resolve anything.

I decide to go for a long, thinking walk and, aware that I must also confront the deeper meaning of that dream, I decide to walk into the woods rather than stay in the light of the fields. I let myself pass right through the dark and seamless, invisible shroud that hangs at the edge of the field, into the dry, quiet autumn woods where squirrels, chipmunks, and birds make the only sounds.

I've passed very few people as I've hiked along and there are even fewer on the path that leads through the woods. Even though I'm very tense I walk deliberately toward a stone bridge that crosses over a small stream. I've been here many times before. It's so like the woods of my abuser that, even though I'm determined, I must urge myself to keep walking, telling myself that nothing will happen. My intention is to conquer my fear of the bridge. I walk right up to it, then veer off the path and down the embankment on the right, heading straight to the dry streambed below. I stop, take a deep breath, bend down, and take a quick look under the small stone bridge. There's nothing there!

"It's not the same bridge," I tell myself. "It's just a bridge."

I walk slowly back along the path, stopping at a bench, feeling the tension go, but also feeling deep sadness. I know I must go back to the bridge; I haven't conquered it yet. All I did was take a quick peek and run away from it.

I go back. This time I stand on top of the bridge, firmly planting myself, intending to stay for as long as it takes. Leaning my elbows on the high stone railing of the bridge, I gaze down into the dry streambed and almost immediately memories come flooding back.

"Yes," I whisper, "the woods are like our woods. The sounds are the same. We made beds in them. We did things to each other. He did things."

As I reminisce, I feel his fingers prodding and poking my body; I hear his voice. I don't know everything, but I know enough—that much I acknowledge without hesitation or dispute.

A jogger passes by as I turn from the bridge and head back up the path. I sit on the bench again, overlooking the woods. The bridge is visible to my right. I think about what it all means—all that it meant then, and all that it means now as the memories reemerge.

"I lived through this, it's about me. This is about me and my childhood experiences," I solemnly state.

I want to hold all the memories of myself in my arms, all those frightened little girls that I was, and all that restlessness and fear that is still bundled inside, and calm it all down. Calm it, so I won't be afraid anymore, so I won't run away anymore. I want to slow down, and let myself be.

"Let me emerge unfettered, free," I ask, as I sit on that bench in the woods and finally allow myself to grieve.

It's a cool, crisp day, the sky alternating between overcast and bright blue. I had left the house feeling restless, like I needed to run. More than anything I had wanted to just skip right past the woods, but as I started to run I realized I needed to go *into* the woods and I couldn't if I was running and, so, I had slowed to a walk. Walking allows me to think, running relieves me of that. Only by walking was I able to approach the woods, slowly and carefully.

Now that I'm in here, I find that I need to stay a little while. I get up off the bench again and stroll slowly back and forth over the bridge three times. I confront it again and again until it no longer disturbs me.

"Now, I want to focus on feelings and emotions, rather than events. I want to focus on healing myself," I decide. "It's time to leave this place."

As I walk out of the woods, the further away I get from the bridge the better I feel. By the time I get back to the house it feels like I've been in a dream. Walking into the woods was like walking through dream curtains, like the veils that led into his world, that other world I used to go into with my abuser. I seemed to float along as if in a dream, my hearing muffled. Every movement seemed to happen without action on my part, only thought. I was magically pulled along, in a dreamlike state, my thoughts directing the experience.

And I noticed that the entire time I spent in the woods not one other person, besides the jogger, interrupted my dreamlike reverie. It was as if the universe cleared a path for me and I was left alone to encounter the memories, the bridge, my child self, and the truth of what the man in the woods did to me so many years ago.

November 5, 2001
Once again I dream that I'm wandering through giant warehouses. I'm in these buildings all night looking for something, seeking long-forgotten treasures in cavernous old buildings. There are only women in these warehouses, no men, until suddenly I come upon a man who is touching my daughter between her legs.

"Don't touch her," I shriek. "You'll destroy her! You'll destroy her!"

The screaming wakes me up, but it's just about time to get the kids up and ready for school anyway; then I meet with Chuck.

As soon as I get to Chuck's office I sit right down and begin discussing the spotted cow dream. I tell him that as soon as I woke up from the dream I understood things that I had no awareness of previously. Gaining insight on how I had split myself into two little girls, one of whom I rejected and the other embraced, suddenly became so clear. I find this fragmented child self strikingly poignant.

"I feel so sorry for the little girl who'd been through those experiences," I say. "I feel so neglectful of her and concerned because I didn't consciously realize I was ignoring her in favor of the creative, dissociated child self."

Chuck sees the dream very clearly; the cow representing docility, in alignment with the *I Ching* reading I had gotten, sitting in acceptance of the truth. The black and white spots represent the opposites, he says, the two girls, the shadowy self and the self that lived in the world, the perceived bad self and the perceived good self.

"It was appropriate that you cry in the dream," he says, "as you were recognizing those disparate, fragmented parts, and their truths."

"Yes, and how deeply severed I've been my whole life. I wanted to be the nice girl, not the abused girl who did all those bad things," I say. "I had another friend in the neighborhood; she was innocent, naïve, and happy, and when I played with her I felt that way too. I could be lighter and innocent around her, though I never forgot that I had a dark side. I knew that this friend was totally unaware of what could happen to little girls and I felt protective of her. I left the bad girl in the woods and let the good girl play happily with this sweet and innocent friend because it felt so much better to be like her."

"In recapitulating, you will bring them together," Chuck says. "You have the opportunity to become whole."

As we begin to process the dream of the trinity—the man, woman, spirit entity—I slip immediately into deep remorse and self-loathing. As I describe the dream to Chuck I cannot help but flagellate myself for my actions.

"I didn't act, I just let things happen! I feel terrible, like a horrible person," I say, as I tell him that my daughter was young in the dream, five years old; an age at which I was being abused.

"In the dream, I was fully aware of what he wanted to do with her, but I also knew that she would live through it, as I once did, that she was strong and capable. As I left her with him, I sent her telepathic commands to access her inner strength, knowing that she had it inside, like I did, but I still cannot reconcile with the decision I made to hand her over to him. It's despicable and cowardly on my part and I'm wracked with guilt over it."

As we go back through the dream in EMDR it becomes more powerfully apparent that I must fight this huge entity, that I must go meet him in a new dream.

"I want to kill him," I say. "I don't want to just fight him, I want to kill him."

"Okay," says Chuck. "How will you do that?"

"I don't know yet. I just need to have enough presence of mind to *take action*, to stab him to death or something."

My homework is to go back and dream a different outcome, to take action.

"Go back, *with intent!*" Chuck says.

November 7, 2001

My intent set, I dream of the trinity. I'm on the same road as in the previous dream, standing before the towering man, woman, spirit entity. As I look up at this tall looming creature, fury ignites inside me. I'm not afraid and, even though I don't seem to have a weapon in my hands, I fight with all my might.

I fly through the air, repeatedly, doing karate kicks and punches, lithely attacking the tall figure. After many leaping attacks, each kick and punch landing soundly, the figure suddenly splits in half and I watch as the man part cracks off and falls to the ground. I shove him off to the side and continue fighting the other half, the woman.

She's laughing and talking the entire time, though I can't decipher what she's saying. Her laughter only fuels my anger. She's not taking me seriously; she doesn't believe that I mean to destroy her. No matter what I say she doesn't take me seriously, and this bothers me no end. She won't pay attention to the truth of this confrontation: that I am here to set things straight, that I have every intention of winning this battle and that, in fact, I have more than enough power to destroy her.

Eventually, I stop fighting and, barely winded, lightly step back from the tall female figure. I take a good look at her, swaying and unsteady, towering above me. As I look up at her, I notice a huge bloody hand print on the shoulder of her white gown. She looks at it in horror and surprise and then down at her hand, which is bleeding profusely. As she extends her bloody hand toward me, I wake in a fright, my heart pounding as she begins to fall in my direction, like a tall tree going down.

It's five in the morning. I know that I've conquered both the man and the woman, but there is still the spirit part to deal with. I fall asleep again with the intent to face this last opponent and immediately a tall figure appears before me. This time it's the spirit entity.

Dressed in white gauze, like a ghostly figure in a long nightgown, it silently floats in the air above me looking hurt, helpless, and sadly pitiful. I sense it's harmlessness, knowing that without the man and woman it can do no damage. I stand my ground, look up at it, and simply say: "Go away!"

November 8, 2001

All night I dream that I'm forming a small mountain out of clay. I keep adding more clay to it, building it up, shaping it, patting the clay with my hands, smoothing the surface until it looks the way I want it. I'm aware that it has something to do with the figure of the trinity; as if I'm building a mountain over the bodies I've annihilated, burying the man, woman, and spirit entity under this small mountain of heavy clay. It also seems to be a monument and a tribute to my warrior self, to both the child self who fought them so long ago and the adult self who challenged them to a final battle. The building of this monument goes on all night. Even though I'm aware of dreaming other dreams, I repeatedly return to working on the mountain. I constantly add more clay, almost tenderly caressing it with my clay-filled hands, methodically forming it into a perfectly shaped conical mountain.

As I wake up, I immediately connect this dream activity to the *I Ching* instruction of going into stillness like a mountain. I've been doing a lot of yoga lately, including mountain pose, *Tadasana*, building a mountain with my body, a strong and centered self, rising from the core of my being. In the dream, I felt that I was finally honoring that core inner strength that had kept me alive, as solid as a heavy mountain of clay. I was engaged in an endless process of honoring and building. It felt right to do so.

I acknowledge the appropriateness of the guidance of the *I Ching* regarding the practice of yoga because yoga has always offered me a physical means of connecting to my deeper self. I gain immeasurably as it continues to offer the stillness I seek, through achieving a sense of deep inner calm. Through meditation I reach a clarity that is often otherwise inaccessible. Yoga also offers the balance and stability I need to keep doing this recapitulation, as I learn how to live in two worlds at once. It also offers the release I need as every day I feel it releasing me a little bit more, giving me permission to do what I need to do next: *feel*.

November 14, 2007

When I meet with Chuck we spend our fifty minutes talking about dream states, about having the awareness of being in a dream state even while awake. I mention the experience of walking into the woods as feeling like walking into a dream, when my hearing became muffled and everything went quiet.

"Yes, that's a sign of dreaming, and you're lucky you can do that on command," he says. "You can make your dreams work for you."

"I felt like I literally walked through a curtain. As I stepped into the woods, out of the sunshine and into the shade, everything went quiet. I could clearly hear every animal sound, but it seemed as if the rest of the world got shut out, like the curtain closed behind me as soon as I stepped through it and only what was inside those woods was real."

"You went into heightened awareness."

"It's the same experience I remember when walking out of the woods in that memory by the stream. As I stepped out through that dark curtain, out of the shade of the woods into the sunlight, everything changed. I was no longer in the dream, or rather the nightmare, as that's what it was like in those woods with my abuser."

"You could also call it a state of *non-ordinary reality*, as the shamans call it, an altered state, as real as any other state," says Chuck. "But the important thing is how you elect to experience it. If you don't dismiss it or rationalize it away, which you obviously haven't done, you allow yourself to have a transformative experience, as you did. You got clarity; another piece of the truth."

"I think I've probably had that kind of experience a lot before, but was just not aware of it at the time. This time I noticed."

"This time you were ready."

There's a similarity between the waking dream state I experienced in the woods and what I used to think of as plain old daydreaming.

As a child I was a frequent daydreamer. In fact, the greater part of my school years was spent in daydreaming. I could take myself anywhere, lift right out of the classroom and sail anywhere in the world. Often, just placing my awareness on the woods that I could see from my desk in the crowded classroom was enough to cause a shift.

I had several favorite daydreams, which I liked to reinvent with different scenarios and outcomes, changing them to suit my mood. I had selected one or two women, whom I admired, thought were nice, beautiful, and even exotic, to become my mothers in those daydreams. They became rescuing mothers, who came and took me away from everything as soon as I called to them; fairy godmother types, who paid attention to me, doted on me, clothed me, and lovingly took care of me. But the main intent of those daydreams was most often to have someone to talk to.

Inside those daydreams, I reinvented myself as a talker, as someone who had no qualms whatsoever about talking about her troubles. The women became my imaginary confidants; I could tell them anything. It seemed to work, especially as I got into my teenage years and grew progressively more silent in the real world. These imaginary daydream worlds offered release and a place to safely express what was so confusing. And, lucky for me, I could go there any time. Only in daydreaming was I brave and daring enough to talk to anyone, about anything. Outside the daydream world I was still the quiet, tongue-tied little girl.

I recognize these dream states as similar to being in a creative zone, a similar kind of trance state where everything on the outside closes off. And, just as when I walked into the woods, in this creative state sounds become muffled. My visual sense is honed, and the world outside disappears. This is the state of *heightened awareness* that Chuck speaks about. In essence, *reality shifts*. It happens too when I read or write. As I ponder all of this, I realize I have the innate ability to easily and successfully block out the world. Perhaps everyone does, but I know I have my creative, dissociative child self to thank for so successfully honing these skills.

Sometimes, as a child, I longed to really escape, to actually be in that perfect world I had created with the perfect mother, the perfect clothes, cared for and loved. And if I had not been there for a long time, if I had not escaped into those altered states for a while, I became desperate for the release they offered. I longed to escape back into that calm world where I controlled everything— similar to the release a child experiences by repeated thumb sucking, hair twirling, or some other compulsion that offers numbing, soothing calmness.

I could do anything I pleased in those other realities, simply by conjuring it in my mind. In those dream worlds, I had no fears, nothing to hide, no secrets, and no worries. Life was perfect.

November 15, 2001

I go for another walk and this time I don't even hesitate; I barge deliberately into the woods. Once again I enter a dream state as soon as I take my first step through the invisible curtain at the edge of the woods. I note the stillness of this world and how conducive it is to my recapitulation. As I walk, the reason I am here becomes apparent.

I've been sensing the shadowy presence of someone watching us as we played the Tree Branch game. Memories of my abuser directing the play have already emerged, but I haven't gained full clarity yet; there's still too much unseen. I pace up and down the length of the trail through the woods, going over the mile long length of it three times from beginning to end before the memory becomes sharp enough for me to grasp in its entirety. I sit on a bench and look out over the woods that are so like the woods of my childhood and I let what has come to me sink in.

As I go into the memory I don't see him, my abuser, at all; I only hear his voice. But once I get into the memory and pause the action—so to speak—I can look around. When I look in the direction of the voice I see my abuser sitting off to the side on an old wooden chair. He's holding a movie camera up to his face and he's filming us. The memory has been taking shape over the past couple of days, beginning with a vague sense of someone else being present when we played the Tree Branch game. I also remember him being in the bathroom with us when we played Operation, but this is different.

This time he tells us to wear party dresses. We change out of our play clothes into some pretty clothes, picking things out of my abuser's daughter's closet. Her clothes are not plain and practical like mine. She's allowed to wear pretty, little girl dresses, pink and fluffy, with lots of lacy petticoats, puffy sleeves, and big bows at the back. He tells us no underpants are allowed, only the dresses.

We run back down to the field in our bare feet, dressed in these fancy little girl dresses and climb out onto the branch with all the knobby, poky parts. He tells us to hang upside down by our knees, our dresses in our faces, our bareness showing. And then he comes over and ties our dresses up out of the way and I hear his voice directing us, telling us what to do: to swing down and up, to poke our legs through our arms and dismount, to climb into the tree like two little monkeys and play on the branch the way we always do.

"Yer turn now. G'wan," I hear his voice insisting whenever I hesitate.

I flash to a memory of crouching behind a big armchair in their living room, frozen in fear. My anxiety steadily mounts as I watch them set up a projector and screen to show home movies. I'm terrified that he's going to show those films of two bad monkey girls. I'm certain that he's going to expose what we'd done to the rest of the family. Cringing on the floor, wanting to disappear, and barely able to breathe or quiet my thundering heart, I hate myself for being there. They laugh at me and tease me for being so shy and fearful, wondering what's wrong with me that I won't sit next to them on the sofa. And then it doesn't happen! The films are of normal things, normal play—the first day of kindergarten, the last birthday party.

The relief is immense!

As I get up off the bench in the woods, I suddenly have another flashback. I see him standing naked before me. Too frightened by the sight and not at all prepared to dwell on it, I turn and walk quickly out of the woods. I've had enough of him for the day, quite enough!

November 18, 2001

I wake the kids at five a.m. and grabbing some sleeping bags we go outside into the cold crisp morning darkness to watch a meteor shower. We lie in the backyard, the three of us tucked up close, as the meteors whip silently, sending long white streaks across the dark night sky. They crisscross here, then there, sometimes right overhead, sometimes sneaking past the corner of the eye like bright little sprites, firing away without a sound. The cool nighttime dew falls on our faces as we watch.

"This is fantastic!" exclaims my son loudly, as he takes in the brilliant show in the sky.

"And did you see that!" says my daughter, snuggling against me, thrilled by the magic taking place overhead, pointing out another white flare and then another and another.

I feel those silent explosions so deeply, as if they are the secrets I keep hidden inside, bursting where no one can see them. As I watch the night sky silently exploding above me, I feel as if I'm part of the whole wide universe—me, a tiny speck down here, silently exploding too. I launch my painful secrets out into dark space, all the memories that I've recapitulated. I send them whirling right into the bursting energy of the meteor shower, letting them ride on each glare that shivers past, throwing this one and that one into the energy of the universe until I'm empty and free of them all.

November 19, 2001

I dream that I'm taking care of a little ten-year-old boy, a child of war, an orphan from the Middle East. He's angry, bitterly angry. He begins yelling at me about loyalty, racism, and love of country, all the rhetoric that's been instilled in him. As I kneel before him to console him, he strikes me in the face, slapping me hard. I try talking to him, try reasoning with him, try calming him with words. He stalks away, sulking, then comes back and hits me again, shouting more of the verbiage from his war years.

He repeats this behavior several times, alternately exploding in anger and then going off into silence, until I finally ask him if he wants a hug. He silently nods yes, and as I hug him for a long time, holding him tightly, he cries and cries. I realize he's just a harmless, frightened little boy and that he just wants to be told that everything will be all right, to be told that he's safe now, that there is no war here.

I dream another dream in a different setting. This time I'm in a big apartment in New York City. It's nighttime and there are no curtains on the large windows. I'm able to look into all the surrounding buildings, their windows similarly curtainless and brightly lit.

I'm taking a bath in an old-fashioned claw-footed bathtub that's set up in the middle of a large empty room with dusty bare wood floors and high ceilings. I realize that I'm in full view of everyone who cares to look in, but I don't care. I'm deliberately taking a bath in this exposed room with the intention of cleansing, relaxing, and releasing myself from old expectations and old fears—those I've placed on myself and those based on the rules and expectations of family and society. At this moment I fear nothing and I have nothing to hide. In fact, exposing myself in this way is extremely liberating and freeing.

I wake from this last dream feeling relieved of some of the burden of secrecy. It feels good to have exposed myself, letting the stodgy old rules of propriety go, not caring at all what others might think. I begin the day feeling lighter and freer, almost happy, but it soon becomes increasingly difficult to stay mentally focused and in the present. The old stuff haunts me, pushing at me to come back to it, to take another look, nagging at me with old feelings, old thoughts, old fears. By the end of the day, I'm numb, desperate to talk, needy, feeling so immensely dependent on Chuck and not sure I like it.

In the evening I go to a yoga and meditation class and achieve a good sense of inner stillness. I really like the anchoring calm and want it to last, so I don't speak or do anything to interrupt it as I exit the class and drive home. I spend a little time with the kids, then say goodnight and shut myself into my room, holding onto the peacefulness for as long as possible.

November 20, 2001

I have a session with Chuck, the final meeting for a few weeks as he soon leaves with his wife for Switzerland, to seek healing at a renowned cancer clinic there. Here he's been helping me, and many others, to heal our broken lives, while being personally involved in a different kind of deep healing work himself.

My first reaction, when he tells me about their trip, is that it feels like such a long shot and I wonder why he doesn't let her die in peace at home. I wonder how he'll even get her there in her weakened state. But then I ask myself to step back and look at who this man is. As I've come to understand him, through my work with him over the past few months, I know this about him: he's unwilling to apply any labels or judgments and he fully opens to all the possibilities that life offers.

As I take in these truths about him, I can fully appreciate the willingness of both of them to outrace this cancer that has been dogging them for so long and so steadily. I can't help but love them for their daring and their commitment to life. He tells me that it's been a long journey and they're hopeful they'll find what they're seeking at the clinic in Switzerland and, simply put, *they must try*.

And so with that, we turn to discussions of the last memories that have been emerging. When it feels as if they've been carefully processed and put to rest, at least for the moment, we turn to practical methods of coping while he's away. I assure him that I'll be able to handle any problems that arise, even though he doesn't know how long he'll be gone.

"I'll be fine. I'll just push it away like I used to, I'm good at that," I say, half laughing.

At the same time, I wonder how long I'll be able to hold on, though I don't say so. My greatest desire is for him to be worry-free, to not have to think about me, to be free to go on this adventure with his wife. I wish them both well, admiring them for their courage and ability to face life, and possibly death, so fiercely, and then I leave.

So, how long can I hold on? Not even a day. Films flip, images spark; quick visual somersaults turn my insides out, until I'm bent over in pain.

"Did I really see that?" I ask, as I watch the memories that come flashing throughout the day, jaggedly lighting up the darkness, ripping apart the curtain of reality for brief split seconds at a time. Believing in them means believing in myself, in my personal experiences, and I know I must find a way to hold onto what is presented, to trust the way this is happening.

"Don't force, don't push, don't accelerate it. It's waiting and will come on its own," Chuck suggested, in a final note of advice before I left the session today.

I acknowledge that it's only right to allow this recapitulation process to unfold by letting it happen on its terms. But I don't like the waiting. I'm not going to just sit around and wait for it to come to me. Instead, I intend to stay busy, hoping to outrun it for a while, to stay one step ahead of it. But it pursues me; it won't go away, not even for a day.

November 21, 2001

I dream that I'm in a yoga class. Chuck and his wife Jeanne come in at the last minute, just when the class is about to begin. I notice how weak and sick Jeanne is. I'm trying to hide, a little shy, not wanting them to come over to my part of the room because I don't want her to see me. I'm feeling so physically healthy and strong that I don't want to make her feel sad or bad about her own state of health.

"Maybe she'll get better, I think, and as soon as I think that thought they come right over to where I'm lying facedown on my mat. As I watch, Jeanne spreads her mat next to mine on the left and lies down on her stomach, arms crossed under her chest. I hear her shallow, raspy breathing and realize that she's extremely weak. I can't imagine how she even got here, climbing the stairs to the second floor classroom. I can't imagine either how she'll do yoga, but I'm aware of her determination and her strong desire to take every opportunity to get better. I watch as Chuck quietly rolls out his mat and lies down on his stomach, stretched out behind us, his head at our feet. We form a sort of triangle, three bodies lying prone, our heads facing in the same direction.

November 22, 2001

Again, I dream that I'm in a yoga class. Chuck and Jeanne come to the class again as well. Since they're leaving for Switzerland, I wonder why they're here. At the same time, I know that it's appropriate for Chuck to be teaching this class—it just seems like the right thing for him to do at this moment, as they set off on their journey. I also know that he's a good teacher, that he holds a lot of knowledge, and that I'll learn a tremendous amount from him. The room is huge and the space is filled with lots of people who are similarly aware of the importance of this teacher. Everyone is present to learn and there is an overall sense of calm well-being, a good feeling that everything will be fine.

I'm struck by the synchronicity of these last two dreams, especially because today *is* the day Chuck and Jeanne are leaving for Switzerland. I wonder just what it is that they're trying to teach me, because it feels like I'm supposed to learn something from these dreams. They leave me with a sense of ease, almost as if assuring me that all I have to do is take the journey that is unfolding, without fear, even as they are taking that journey to Switzerland without fear, going forward with hope.

I allow myself to sit and meditate, to let everything go out of my body, all the tension and worry, and before long I leave even my body behind. I'm up high, sitting in the branches of a leafy green tree. It feels calm and nice up here, but I'm aware that there's something disturbing going on below me.

I peek out through the leaves and look at the ground far beneath me where I see a tiny dark-haired girl, maybe four years old, lying on the leaf-covered earth in dappled shade, beside a shallow brook. Her thin body is naked, her limbs splayed, her hair spread out around her small pretty face, her eyes closed, her delicate long-fingered hands curled. She could be asleep, except that tears are falling from the corners of her eyes. They pool onto the leaves around her head and flow into the brook near her feet. The ground is soaked with them. No sound is heard, no twitter of bird, no rustle of squirrel, no wind, no rattle of leaf, just the girl alone in the woods, crying silent tears.

I want to pick her up, wrap her up in my arms and take her away from there and tell her that everything is okay now, everything is going to be okay from now on; that she's safe; that she's mine, and she's safe.

November 25, 2001

In a dream, I walk into Chuck's office. On the chairs in the waiting room are large pictures of Barbie dolls, like matching game cards, four laid out in a square on each chair and at the bottom of each set of cards is the word: GIRL. I'm just noticing that the pictures are laid out upside down when I hear Chuck coming to the office door to greet me. He's wearing a new beige shirt. Right away he tells me that he's fine, that at first he was very apprehensive, but that now everything is fine. I wake up as he extends his hand toward me to shake mine in greeting.

I fall back to sleep and go right into another dream. Now I'm in a hospital. A little boy child is ill and needs my care, but it's not clear who the child belongs to. My parents are also there and I wonder if the child is theirs. A doctor hands me a large bag of marijuana and writes out a prescription for more. He tells me I'll need it. Then he gives a diagnosis for the state of the child, saying that the first signs of Parkinson's disease are apparent. I'm not happy to hear this. I walk my parents to their car and then turn back to the hospital because I know the child needs me to care for him. It's very clear that no one else can do it.

I wake from these dreams wondering what they mean. Something about the Barbie doll cards strikes me as curious and I wonder if I'm in denial of some part of myself or if this is indicating the absurdity of the games I was taught to play, the upside down pictures in direct contrast to the upright GIRL label. After all, I was just a little girl when I was forced to play games that no little girl should have to play, literally made to hang upside down in pretty little girl clothing while my bare bottom got photographed.

I'm also aware that the child in the hospital is trying to tell me something, and that he's bearing a lot of pain. I'm aware that he needs me, that my parents have nothing to offer, and that only I can help him. The diagnosis is as difficult to believe as the truth of the sexual abuse—and it's frightening. But, at the same time, the doctor is offering relief for the predictable stress yet to come, medical marijuana to ease the anxiety. I see this as similar to doing yoga, offering a calming shift. Perhaps the doctor in the dream is letting me know that I have some difficult and painful times ahead of me, especially with Chuck away.

November 28, 2001

I'm fiercely determined to hold on while Chuck is away by holding everything in. I block out old stuff as it arises, even things that continually flash like lightning—a small picture, a smell, a voice. I send them away, sometimes feeling quite brittle, so ready to break apart, but then I push even that away. I refuse to let go to any pressures. I breathe deeply, reminding myself that I can hold on.

"I can hold out, I can hold on, I can wait," I tell myself again and again.

While working at the studio, the phone rings and I hear Chuck's voice, a worried, tired tone, asking how *I'm* doing!

"You are too, too nice," I say too, too brightly, but I will not let him hear even an ounce of pain from me.

When I ask him how Jeanne is doing, he hesitates before saying that she's holding up, and I know it isn't appropriate for me to know any more than that. I only mean to be polite, so I quickly switch back to assuring him that I'm fine, I'm doing great.

"Don't worry about me," I say before I hang up, wishing him and Jeanne all the luck in the world.

But I must not be doing as well as I think.

"You've been so *disagreeable* lately!" my son says when I call him and his sister to dinner. And later, when I go into my daughter's room to say good night, she tells me that I'm *really boring!*

"Well," I admit to both of them, "I guess I am. I'm both disagreeable and boring, and I apologize."

Exhausted and grouchy, I make my way to my own room after the dinner dishes are cleaned up and everyone is tucked into bed. I throw myself down on my bed and beg for help to just get through this.

I want to be me; the real me who's been hidden inside just waiting to emerge all these years, so determined to get out and live.

I just need to allow for the time it takes to reach in, search around and look for her, hoping all the time that she's really in there.

November 29, 2001

I'm wondering how I'll hold on until Chuck's return. I don't like being this dependent; don't like being needy, but I admit that this old stuff is too hard to deal with alone. I'm missing the stability of our weekly sessions. Without them I have no firm anchoring place, no outlet for dealing with what's emerging. I'm not sure if it's better to continue pushing the recapitulation away or just allow it to unfold as it will. Yesterday I was so firm in my conviction to keep it away at all costs, while today I feel like I'm in a tug of war with it. It pulls so strongly, asking me to just let go of my end of the rope, fall into its open arms, and let it drag me back into the past.

In addition, the stress of not knowing what's going to happen to me from day to day is unnerving. I never know what will come in the night to take me back into forgotten memories or what will arise during the day either. Each night and each day are laden with frightening possibilities. My first inclination is to shut the whole damn recapitulation down, but it's not possible, because I realize I can't stop the momentum of this thing. Whether I'm seeing Chuck or not, there's no way to stop this. I'm on this crazy journey until it ends.

In the meantime, I feel like I'm standing on the ridge of a steep mountain path that drops down into a bottomless abyss on either side. I can't quite get my balance and so I teeter precariously on this parapet, feeling like I'll topple over in one direction, but at the last second I pull back, now feeling like I'll topple over in the opposite direction. I can't move off the precipice and so I stand unsteady and imbalanced, feeling like I'm on a tightrope, eternally off-kilter. Every time something pops up out of the darkness of the abyss, out of the past, I jerk away in fright because I just can't bear the first flash of a scene or image. The initial shock is just too much to handle. Instinctively, I push it away because, if I don't, I'll fall; and who knows what will happen if I actually fall. The thought alone sends chills down my spine.

Chapter Nine

Stranger in a Strange Land

December 5, 2001

Two weeks have gone by now, with no outlet. I remain determined to be all right, to carry on, though in order to do that I must hold everything in. As a result, I'm edgy and brittle.

I try not to think about the memories of being with my abuser and his daughter, but I let other things come forth and I wonder where they fit into the picture.

I let this materialize: I'm two-years-old, wandering in the woods, playing with some boys. We're undressing, investigating each other, just looking. One day, a boy I don't know is there. He wants to look at me. I don't like his look, the tilt of his head, the line of his mouth set in a frightening leer, and I begin screaming. My screams won't end until he goes away. Later, when I'm a teenager, I no longer scream. I cannot lift a hand to protect myself, though inwardly I vibrate with fear and rage whenever anyone touches me without my permission. I shut down. Frozen with fear, I go cold and dead.

I feel like that now, frozen and dead. I know I've been growing consistently colder over the years, withdrawing more and more. Will I always be like this? Chuck would say no, that one day I'll melt into a real person, that I'll be whole, but that it will take some work. Will I still freak out or panic when I'm touched? I don't think I will anymore.

I also realize that as I know myself better, I see other people more clearly as well.

December 7, 2001

I dream of suddenly being homeless, of having to quickly move and find a new place to live because our property has been sold. Our yard is being bulldozed and asphalt is being laid. Our house will be rebuilt into an apartment complex and parking spaces are needed. I try to shield the kids from seeing what's happening, but there's really nothing I can do, it's obvious that things are changing. I decide to go apartment hunting in New York City.

There's an apartment on East 76th Street that I hear is for rent, but the landlady won't let me see it. I have to take it sight unseen if I want it. I agree, but as soon as I do I feel that I've made a big mistake. Distraught over the possibility that I've perhaps rented a terrible apartment, I sneak into the building and, much as I expect, it really is a wreck. It has rotten floors, holes in the walls, and the sky is visible in some of the rooms because they have no ceilings. The main stairwell, that all the tenants in the building must use, runs right through the middle of the apartment, so I'll have people traipsing through my place day and night.

I feel stupid for having fallen for such a bad deal. I'm worried that I'll be judged incompetent, proving everyone's contention that I won't make it, that I can't survive on my own, and that I make only bad decisions. The only thing I can imagine doing is fixing it up, somehow making it less pathetic. A carpenter friend comes to take a look.

"Well, at least it's cheap!" he says, after pointing out all the drawbacks and the amount of work the place will need to make it even passably livable.

"It doesn't matter, there are other good features," I say, as I point out a nearby park where the kids can play, as well as all the other amenities of the neighborhood. There's only silence in response as I try to cover up the obvious mistake I've made.

Rather than feeling desperate and depressed after this dream, I feel centered and determined, quite satisfied that I can handle anything. I'm sure I'll be able to handle any problems that arise, no matter how insurmountable they at first appear. And I'm determined that, no matter what others think of me, I will do what I need to do. I like this new feeling of self-confidence as it begins to slowly emerge, take root, and grow stronger throughout the day.

At the studio, I'm in a great mood, bubbling with lots of new ideas, sure that I can accomplish anything I put my mind to. This high energy and confidence lasts all day, until I go home. As soon as I step in the door I feel the tension, the deteriorating energy of a decaying marriage now permeating the whole house, and I'm confronted with the truth of my situation.

This house feels very much like the ramshackle apartment in my dream and I feel my spirits dampen. My first inclination is to curl into a ball and roll under my bed to hide, licking my wounds until morning. Instead, I remind myself that I am indeed good, brave, confident, and talented, and that I can handle anything that comes along. I promise myself that I'll follow through with what's right—not to prove anything to anyone else, but just because I must do what I must do.

Ever the optimist, I'm determined to create a happy life, a new world of my own making, with my own rules, my own positive energy as the main driving force.

December 8, 2001

I dream that all the land phone lines in the house have been connected to the Internet. They no longer function as telephones, so that when I pick up a phone receiver I automatically get an Internet connection. I'm totally frustrated because I can't call anyone. Unable to make a phone call, I become so angry that I throw the phone receiver onto the floor, smashing it to bits.

After this dream, I realize that my lines of communication have indeed gone dead, as far as my recapitulation is concerned. With Chuck away, I have no one to talk to.

I continue to push things aside as I face the coming weeks alone. I acknowledge what's emerging from inside, but turn to practical matters around the house instead, to packing and sorting through shared belongings, separating out my personal items, as I begin to ponder the future.

December 10, 2001

I wake in confusion, not sure where I am, feeling exhausted, my energy depleted. When I look in the mirror I don't recognize myself. I look like someone else, as if someone has snuck into my body while I slept in the night. I stand in front of the mirror in the bathroom and swipe the sleepiness from my eyes and throw cold water on my face, trying to find some recognizable feature.

I notice that the morning is frosty and white after yesterday's snowfall, almost too beautiful and bright, but it gives me incentive to get over my tiredness, inciting new energy. I must remain connected to my journey, to where I'm headed, even though I have no idea what lies ahead. I decide that the best thing to do is to settle in and focus on just staying the course, putting one foot in front of the other. That's enough for now.

An acquaintance stops in at the studio and tells me that a woman from her neighborhood died yesterday in Switzerland.

"Who?" I ask, my heart pounding.

"Jeanne Ketchel," she says. "Did you know her?"

"Only slightly," I say.

I feel such sadness for Chuck, the long journey they took together now at an end.

December 12, 2001

I feel like a prisoner in my own body and my own world, my frustration turning to depression and sadness. I hurt inside and out as I clench down and hold back what I feel brewing from deep within. With no outlet in sight I can only do what I've always done, but that old method is totally unsatisfying—now that I know there is another way to deal with things.

I've been learning how to talk, but I have to remain silent for a while longer. I try to stay connected to the strong and confident woman I really am, but she seems so far away today.

December 15, 2001

The kids and I go to New York City for the day, taking the train down to attend a family party on the Upper West Side. In the evening we take the subway downtown to Rockefeller Center to see the Christmas tree and the skaters in the ice rink below. The night is clear and crisp. We're all bundled up against the cold, excited to be out in the crowds gathered in Midtown. We buy some hot pretzels and stroll slowly along Fifth Avenue on our way to the train station, enjoying the holiday displays in the department store windows, many of which I remember from when I was a child and my grandmother took me to the holiday show at Radio City Music Hall. No rushing, we're just having fun, the three of us on an outing.

We catch a late train home and when we get out at our stop it's past midnight and the car is covered in a thick layer of ice. I can't get the key into any of the locks. We finally kick enough ice off the hatchback to pry it open and my son crawls in and after a few more well-aimed kicks is able to open the doors from the inside, glad to finally put all that karate training to practical use. We laugh at our predicament, our spirits high.

December 18, 2001

I'm trying to get through the days as best I can, but I'm worried about money, about the kids, the house, and work. As tensions inside my body mount it seems as if my life outside is equally tense and uncertain. All the things that make me who I am right now seem so precarious, but I'm determined to get my business in good shape, to pour my energy into that, the only solid ground I have from which to tackle everything else.

December 20, 2001

My neck is stiff and tight, as if I'm holding back the pressure of a volcano. I fear that if I don't stay tightly clamped and tense, it will burst and I'll explode with it. Frustration has turned to anger, which, having mounted, transforms into explosive energy that now propels me to act, to do things on my behalf, rather than wallow in self-pity and sadness. It gives me energy, yet at the same time I must hold it in check. I try to remain contained, balanced, and innerly focused on the path ahead—as much of it as I can see.

December 26, 2001

The holidays were spent with my family, though with little enthusiasm on my part. Not much in the mood to party or celebrate, I've mostly just maneuvered through the events of the last few days. As I looked around at everyone I felt like a stranger in a strange land. My reality has totally shifted—I don't perceive the world in the same way anymore. I see everyone playacting, the holiday celebration the same play we acted out last year, and the year before, and the year before that, each moment and each event predictable, right down to the Christmas ham.

As I've begun to revision myself as an abused child, I find that everything else about me becomes clearer. My strangeness finds refuge in this new idea, and I don't feel so harsh and judgmental of my child self for her lack of attention to the things of this world. I don't wonder so much anymore about why I was the way I was, because I understand that this world was not her priority. The only world that really mattered was that dark other world, the one I've only just begun to step into again.

There's so much that I see in the shadows of the woods, though not clearly at all, and I wonder what I'll find when I go back again. It's both frightening and intriguing to consider.

December 28, 2001

I dream that I arrive at the studio to find that everything has been sold or stolen; it's not clear which. There are only bare worktables, easels, and shelving left. As I walk into the cavernous room I see a thick black mass of bugs skittering and climbing over everything, streams of huge cockroaches! The sight freaks me out and I wake with a start, wondering what it might mean.

It feels negative at first, a sign that my business will fail, only the cockroaches left to inhabit my dreams, but then I wonder if it means something more positive. I remember once reading that the cockroach is a survivor, that it has inhabited the earth since prehistoric times and I wonder if it might mean something like that about me as well.

I wonder if perhaps the dream is telling me that I'll sell out, that my work will be in high demand and I'll actually have a great future, going out of business because I've done well enough to quit. Either way, it seems to be posing the same end-scenario, that eventually I will leave the studio behind, though I don't actually want to think about it; or perhaps I'm taking it way too literally. In any case, at this point, I elect to not dwell on either possibility, but to work on myself instead.

Over the past week I've been gradually letting go of anger. Often, I find anger advantageous. It gives me just the lift I need to get out of a slump, especially when I've sat on something for a long time. This time, however, something is different: I've felt the accumulation of anger in my *physical body*, that volcanic feeling that I'm going to erupt at any moment.

I've been trying to keep loose and tension-free, reminding myself to relax my shoulders, to stand up straighter, to breathe into the areas of holding and pain. Yoga continues to help in that regard, but I realize that I'm dealing with real physical manifestations of the memories and other related issues that have festered inside my body for decades. With no other outlet they had to settle somewhere and this body became the obvious receptacle for everything, holding not just the memories, but the pain and tension and the fear and terror of those memories as well.

I've carried these things for so long and though they've been deeply buried, forgotten for the most part, my body has compensated for their presence. I slump. My shoulders are hunched. My stomach is tightly clenched all the time. I'm thin, nervous and tense. My teeth and jaws clench and I walk too quickly, tilting slightly forward, always in a hurry, always looking like I have somewhere to go, even if I don't. I can't pause or linger too long. My body holds the memory that something is always after me.

For a while my skin reacted harshly, erupting with acne in my late teens and early college years. It seemed that the further away I got from the actual physical site of the abuse, the more I was able to successfully suppress it, removing it from ordinary conscious awareness. This didn't resolve anything, but it did put off the moment of confrontation, until I was ready for it. At the same time it afforded respite, mentally, and even physically to a great extent. Once I left home—as I tried to relax and get on with life as well as I could—my body reacted to no longer needing to be on constant alert, releasing in the only way it could—through the skin—and pimples flared up. For several years my skin got progressively worse, nothing I did seemed to have any effect and finally I sought medical advice. When the skin cancer I had several years ago appeared I knew immediately that I was not dealing with anything other than something inside of me that needed to be released. I knew that it was not from being in the sun, but from avoiding my hidden darkness. My skin was trying to tell me something. That time I knew it was something I would soon have to investigate, though at the time I felt only dread and fear.

Even though I'm not consciously engaging in recapitulation while Chuck is away, this time of holding back is still very much part of the process. In actuality, I've been recapitulating the old process of suppressing the abuse, while being clearly shown just how controlling I've always had to be to feel safe in the world. This time, however, I've been suppressing by choice and, yes, out of necessity too, though not out of fear, as I did in the past.

December 30, 2001

As the past month unfolded, I often felt as if I were in that dreamworld in the woods again, in an altered reality, neither here nor there, but in some middle world where the shadows of the past overlap the present, a stranger in a strange land.

Since Chuck's been away I've stayed out of the woods in reality, running rather than walking, keeping things at bay in the old way, but at the same time the woods have slowly been encroaching the whole time, as if to keep me in sight. As the muffled world of those woods has crept closer and closer, people appear far away, in the hazy distance, as if they're standing in the gloom on the periphery of the woods. I can't quite hear what anyone's saying when they speak to me. I see their lips move but no sound reaches my ears. I just nod at them and feel somewhat stupid, but it's the best I can do. Most people are used to my quiet nature anyway, so I don't feel that I've raised any suspicions.

When people ask me how I'm doing, I cheerily declare that I'm doing fine, just fine. As usual, I'm fine.

Chapter Ten

Tunnel of Self

January 8, 2002

Chuck is back. I'm a little wary as I approach his office. I wonder how he's doing after the events of the past month, his travels and the death of his wife, dealing with his children and their loss, as well as his own. I gather that he and Jeanne had an unusually good relationship and I anticipate that he's deeply feeling her loss.

We've already spoken on the phone, briefly, and I had left a message of condolence when I heard the news, but I feel almost as if I'm intruding, as if it's too early and I shouldn't be here yet. But obviously he's decided it's time to go back to work, and I must accept that decision.

He appears normal, though thinner than I remember, a little shy perhaps, but says he's fine when I ask how he's doing, almost echoing the dream I had at the end of November, and indeed he's wearing a *beige* tweed sweater.

"Really, I'm doing well," he says, and then, with barely a pause, we jump right back to work.

"How are *you* feeling?" he asks, and before I know it I'm back in that awkward, barely able to speak mode, clenching my hands and trying to figure out the answer to his question.

Why is it so hard to answer? Why does that question always stump me? Why can't I answer it?

I have no answer for him. Instead I talk about a book I've been reading, *Tales of a Female Nomad*, by Rita Golden Gelman, a middle-aged woman who decided, after her divorce and after her kids grew up, to no longer maintain a permanent address but to keep moving. She talks about how she's always frightened before she leaves on the next leg of a journey, sometimes with little money and no connections, but something always draws her forth. Something keeps her adventurous spirit open to the possibilities that she knows will come to greet her as soon as she sets out. She knows this because of her experiences in the past and yet it doesn't matter that she has traveled over the globe for years, meeting incredible people and having incredible experiences, her fear still rises. Nothing matters at the moment before take-off except the fear. She still has to break through it and she knows she can only do that by taking the first step on her journey.

"That part really got to me. It actually made me cry. In fact, I wept," I say.

"Really, you actually cried?"

"Yes, I did! The woman who can't shed a tear for herself actually wept because what the author wrote felt so personally true. In that moment, I felt totally alone in the world, absolutely and stunningly alone, as if I were the last person alive on earth, adrift in a tiny rowboat, without oars, on a stormy ocean. It was a terrifyingly lonely moment."

I totally identify with the fear that arises at the moment of taking the first step on a new journey. I experience it every time I'm about to start on a new project. It doesn't matter how many books I've illustrated, or murals I've painted, or how many articles I've written, I still quake with fear before I start a new job. When I stand in front of a blank wall, or sit before a clean white canvas or sheet of paper, or face a blank computer screen, I wonder at my sanity, if I'm crazy for taking the job, for thinking I have any talent, for imagining I have anything new to say or express. And I always have to face the same whimpering question as the scared baby inside inevitably asks: "Why can't I just have a nice simple little job that would be so much easier than this?"

But then, as soon as I start, as soon as I challenge myself to take that first step, I'm fine. This is exactly where I stand now in my life. Even though I'm an adult and I know I'll be fine and that everything will work out perfectly in the end, at this very moment I'm terrified about the next part of my journey.

At the end of our time, I tell Chuck that I'm ready to continue my work with him, but that I need a few weeks to save some money. I tell him I'll call when I'm ready to make an appointment, but that in the meantime I'll continue working through things on my own.

After the session, I realize that even though I don't know where this journey is taking me it doesn't matter. I don't need to know the destination because I've already decided that I'm going where the energy takes me. My intention is to stop fighting at every step and to go with the flow of it, because I know that I'll end up in the same place anyway and I'd rather go with openness and awareness than with fear and trembling. It doesn't mean I won't be full of fear, quaking every moment, but it does mean I'm declaring that I'm ready now.

And so, I intend that this journey be my ultimate transformation and I ask for guidance as I face my fears.

January 9, 2002

I dream that I'm back in the old neighborhood where I grew up, on the steep hill outside my abuser's property. I see the stone bridge leading over the stream. I'm aware of its proximity throughout the dream, glancing at it often, keeping it always in sight.

There is some kind of street fair or bazaar going on and I'm busy doing all kinds of things. For a while I help people rake leaves, then I sit at a table and do a book signing because I've just published a new book. People from my past, from all ages and stages, are there.

I run up and down the hilly street helping people, always aware of the bridge nearby and aware also that I must keep moving at all times. I must keep busy. I cannot stop or something bad will happen.

I wake up in fear and it follows me around all day, as if something is lurking in the shadows. I'm disturbingly aware of its presence. For most of the day I feel like I'm still in my dream, one eye always on the stone bridge.

While I'm aware of this fear, I'm also finally realizing, after so many years of low self-esteem and deep self-doubt, that I have plenty of good qualities and attributes. However, I've had to unearth them from deep within myself where they've lain dormant. And, on top of that, I've had to push aside other people's expectations. Over the past year I've done a lot of deep work, dragging myself back from the dead, becoming reacquainted with my deeply personal truths, one small step at a time.

Now I'm at the point where I can actually say that I'm okay, that I feel I can handle life on my own without support from another, financial or otherwise. But the current main fear, apart from fear of the journey ahead—both the recapitulation journey and the solo mother-with-two-kids journey—is that I will not be able to sustain a strong financial base from which to launch.

Most of the time I think this financial fear is being projected onto me by others, perhaps meant as well-meaning concern, but nonetheless pretty disheartening to someone who's struggling to become assertive and independent. Overall, I'd like some positive outside energy, rather than other people's fears being handed to me as if they belonged to me. It's been hard enough to detach from my own self-destructive thoughts without having to battle what other's project will befall me. I just don't have the energy to fight such negative energy, though I admit I've taken on that money fear, because it's definitely of concern. I'm determined to not let it get in the way of progress or my decision to move forward. It won't stop me from taking the journeys that lie ahead.

As usual, the old fear I always have before any new project is present. I know it well and how it works, but, just like the author of *Tales of a Female Nomad,* I must acknowledge its exceedingly familiar presence and then move beyond it. I also know, as I mentioned to Chuck yesterday, that it will dissipate as soon as I begin the process.

I'm certain that everything will work out, though right now I'm dealing with steadily mounting anxiety. All of my women friends who have gone through a divorce keep telling me I'll be fine.

"Don't worry," they say, "you're a woman. Women can do anything!"

January 10, 2002

I'm constantly seeking equilibrium and balance in the midst of everything that's going on. Yoga, running, and meditation are still my favorite methods of coping and centering.

The separation agreement is slowly being hammered out. It's been agreed that I'll remain in the house for the coming year while I look for a place to live with the kids. The financial future still proves to be the scariest part of this leg of the journey—the "what ifs" coming up all over the place—but I'm as determined as ever.

January 12, 2002

Now that I've opened up to Chuck again and am allowing myself to return to the old stuff, I find that I'm desperate again for my next visit, but at the same time I'm strapped for cash, as I told him.

The financial issue is of real concern and it nags at me incessantly. I wonder if I'll be able to afford my sessions with him after all, but, after having held everything back for so long, I can't imagine closing the door again just when I've reopened it. And I can't stop this shamanic recapitulation, even if I wanted to—I know that. *It has a life of its own!*

I'm beginning to understand that by opening up to the recapitulation process, one thing leads to another. In every facet of my life, the process itself is quite magically leading the way. So, in light of that, I've decided to just take it week by week, to not close any doors but to stay open and positive.

I know, from experience, that if I intend something I'm usually granted the means to afford what I need. So, I'm determined that the money for this shamanic work will be there, somehow—one week at a time, or even one day at a time, if that's how it has to be— but I cannot halt this process.

January 15, 2002

Today, I'm steeped in incredible loneliness—my lifelong companion—smothered by it, barely aware of being human. Deeply depressed, I sit inside a dark hole, cut off from the outside world. I'm certain that no one else will understand what I'm suffering because I can barely understand it myself. I feel such deep loss, but of what I don't know, for I can relate to no specific thing as my own personal loss. I just know that I'm lost and incredibly alone, even when surrounded by others. I'm aware, however, that something is different this time, even though I'm experiencing a very old feeling, a very deep wounding. It's instantly recognizable, as it comes over me as strongly today as it did in the old days. I can finally acknowledge that it stems from what happened under that bridge and in those woods—that much I've learned. I'm able to take the first step toward saying: "Yes, this old feeling is related to what happened to that little girl who was abused, to what happened to me. This is how it felt to be her. This is what it felt like to be so confused, to be so deeply depressed at the age of four that I could not hear what was happening around me in the real world."

How do I reach back and help that little girl who still lives in that silent world of ancient torment? How do I make her, and myself, feel better? How do I get rid of this feeling of deep isolation that is so overwhelming that I can barely function today?

January 16, 2002

I've been trying to sort out my feelings all week, wondering why I won't, don't, and can't feel anything for myself? Why am I so willing to help other people and not myself? Why is it so hard to care about myself?

I'm getting involved in too many things right now, giving of my time and energy to others and acting as if everything is fine with me when, in reality, I'm suffering immensely. But I hold it to myself. No one is allowed to know. *I must stay in control.*

That feeling of loneliness hasn't gone away either and I very much doubt that it will go easily, or of its own accord. It's always been there, creeping alongside that dark mysterious shadow in the woods. Constant companions, they've dogged me forever, lurking in the background of my life, just waiting for the moment to jump me.

Well, I guess this is the moment because at least I have an idea of what it's all about now; at least I finally have something to relate it to. But it's still hard to accept that I have such deep issues of pain and loneliness, that there is indeed something wrong inside me.

While I struggle with this inner process of opening up to the past, I'm also going through the next stage of divorce and, at this moment, I must be strong. I cannot appear weak or vulnerable. I've spoken of my determination to work everything out, to be a strong provider for the kids, to forge ahead with all the fierceness I can muster, so I don't dare show even the slightest weakness.

I've always been this strict and hard on myself, in control of every emotion, never letting anyone see me in pain or as needy. It's a sin to be weak and needy, to be whiny or whimpering about life's injustices. I refuse to be—or be perceived as—a victim. I must be as strong on the outside as I've always been on the inside. I must be like steel, never revealing even a hint of a crack in the façade.

Lately though, I've let myself relax a little, in the privacy of my own space. I've been pointedly, with intent, doing things totally for myself. Besides taking time for lots of running, yoga, and meditation, I've even allowed myself to begin taking baths again, after perhaps twenty years of denying myself even that little bit of luxury, always too hard on myself.

Even though it feels almost sinful to state that I'm taking a bath, that I'm not to be disturbed during the time I'm in the tub, I declare this time as my own. I'm totally inaccessible, telling the kids to go to their father if they need anything, to pretend that I'm not at home. It's taken some time for me to get over my guilt about this and for them to get used to the fact that I won't answer them when they come to the door. I actually tell them to go away. For those few moments I exist for myself alone.

When I shut the bathroom door and begin running the bath water, I disappear from the world, from all expectations, even from the expectations I've placed on myself. In so doing, I offer myself a real attempt at breaking through the hard mold, slowly sloughing off everything as I steep in the hot water, trying to melt my old stiff self into something malleable and flowing.

I'm actually doing something nice for myself.

This is the end of my first little journal, the diary I bought myself over a year ago when I knew I would soon be embarking on a strange and fantastic journey, when I saw that fox in the road, when I knew I had to muster all my desires and face my fears. I kept this little journal hidden for months, not even daring to write in it, but taking it out occasionally to feel the soft leather cover, knowing that soon, soon I would begin writing, knowing that once I did it would be the end of everything. And so it has come to pass, everything has changed.

This has been such a crucial time for me, such a powerful life-wrenching period, filled with discoveries and decisions, filled with this journey, the beginning of my personal recapitulation and the search for who I really am.

As soon as I crack open the cover of a new diary, images begin exploding, automatically and without hesitation taking the moment of turning to the first page as the impetus to further churn up the old stuff. Finally, after holding back for so long, the flashbacks come again, firing anew with their shocking revelations, their disturbing and wrenching truths that I can barely take in. Now I let them flow again after so long. They unravel, a long string of disconnected, yet, at the same time, interconnected images: a dog, my abuser and his pick-up truck, making a tent under my strange little friend's bedcovers and playing the game of Operation, hiding in her closet and mixing a soupy paste of talcum powder and water and eating it.

It's late. I'm tired now and half asleep as these images spark brief memories, taking on their rightful meaning in my life, little by little coming alive. As they come forth more clearly, I begin to vibrate with the old feeling of imminent annihilation and I know they are real, that they happened to me.

As I vibrate, my face feels like it's going to crack, to shatter like a hard ceramic mask, into a thousand tiny shards. I pull back from this crumbling sensation and as I do I see my face actually breaking apart, exploding into a thousand bits of earth colored clay, angry red. It's as if I'm looking into a mirror, watching as my face cracks and splinters apart. I don't want to look so I pull back again, in horror, as the unglazed shards of clay fall into my hands, onto the pages of this book, and all over my bed as I startle awake.

Immediately I reach for my face. Is it still there? Am I still me?

And then I realize I've been somewhere else. I left my bedroom and went back to that ancient place of loneliness and loss. But I also realize that it will be okay to crumble, that I will get through it, that I can let go and still be okay, because here I still sit.

January 17, 2002

I've been pondering why I hold so tightly to everything, even the bad stuff. Is it because I've held it all in for so long, because it's become habit, and because I don't know how to let it go? I recall getting through all the games I played with my abuser's daughter by telling myself that it would be over soon. I hear my child self speaking in whispers, soothing me once again: "It's okay, you can make it. Just a little more, then it will all be over."

The games always ended, and I counted on that. Now, as I recall these long buried memories, I find that I barely feel anything. I'm still that little girl dissociating from the pain and discomfort, from the humiliation and guilt, comforting myself by saying: "You will get through this; it will all be over soon."

Sometimes, when memories begin to emerge, I feel myself starting to disappear, slipping into the numbing zone of protection that the dissociative state offers. At the first inkling that something is turning bad that shrinking feeling starts, as that old instinct to seek protection from shattering annihilation takes over. It scares me. I know it's part of the memory, the part that is perhaps easiest to recapitulate because it's a master move on the part of my child self to survive, but it still frightens me because there's a sense of death about it too.

Intending to study the process, I physically endure a moment of dissociative annihilation, with awareness, allowing the numbing feeling to take over. As it comes sweeping into my body I'm aware of an intense need to curl up inside myself, into the tiniest ball possible. So I do that. With the intention of remaining in two places at once, I allow myself to go into the experience while also focusing on what's happening physically. I want to understand what was really occurring as I left my body in the hands of my abuser when I was a little girl.

I notice that my breathing slows way down and I feel myself literally turning inward, shrinking, rolling down the tunnel inside me as it yawns widely open, welcoming me. Before I know it I've tumbled as far down as I can go. In the cave at the bottom of the tunnel I am rewarded with numbness, with a high frequency vibration that makes me feel safe and distant from what's happening outside of me. The world is barely visible at the far end of the tunnel, only a pinprick of light suggesting that it even exists. It's quiet in here. It's safe in here. But it's also very lonely in here.

As I repeat this experience again and again, like a scientist conducting an experiment, I become better at stopping myself midway through the process. I stop and write down what's happening physically, examining it from a different perspective now. Although it was, at one time, what saved me, I now understand that it may not be that beneficial to keep repeating, though I love the intensity of it and the distance I gain as I go deeply into that tunnel, so far from all that bothers me. I know I must give up this state of dissociation, though it still draws me so intensely. I also understand that it must be fully recapitulated as a true experience of my childhood but not reattached to. It must be relived for what it tells me about my child self, but I must evolve beyond it, comforting though it remains.

Every time I go into that deep tunnel, I must also confront the discomfort of the loneliness, as well as the truth that my person and body were being invaded. And I must work through the painful truth that *I did not matter at all*, for this is the other truth that arises as soon as I enter that habitual state of numbness. Like a scientist, I must dissect the ugliness and loneliness of nullification.

And finally, I must collect and piece together this wounded, fragmented self.

When I couldn't sleep last night, I gave myself permission to think about my abuser's daughter again. I tossed and turned for a long time and the images of playing the games immediately started, each toss and each turn sending me back to the woods, to the bathroom, to her closet; to the dark woods by the stream with my abuser and his hard pokey fingers again too. I thought I was done with all that and I tried to push the images and the feelings away but then I realized I'm not done yet. There is still more to learn, more to experience, even in those memories that have already surfaced, that I've already so boldly faced. I know I must return to them again and again and see what else they're trying to tell me, but I also need to be careful. This is terrifying territory and I think the memory of dissociation is popping up so often these days to remind me to be cautious as I go back there on my own.

Until I can afford to see Chuck again I must tread only briefly in the past. I must save the fuller truth for when I see him again. So, I will continue to hold on, let the images float freely in and out of my awareness, let them show me what they will, write down what I remember, but leave them mostly in the shadows for now.

January 19, 2002
I dream that I'm visiting a friend whose property is adjacent to that of Eudora Welty, the author. I gaze at Eudora's house from afar, leaning against a fence, looking out over golden wheat fields as I imagine her inside, walking from room to room. Later, an opportunity arises for me to attend a dinner party there. As soon as I'm inside Eudora's house, I recall that I've been in it many times in previous dreams. It's very familiar, both the inside layout and the view looking out the windows. I sit at the dining table with all the other guests. Eudora is late and we are waiting for her to appear. A place has been saved for her, next to her assistant. She finally arrives, making a small joke about sitting where she pleases, but there is only one place vacant, so she must of course take that place, but she accepts it as if it were indeed the place of her choosing.

I'm sitting across from Eudora and her assistant. We strike up a conversation. Eudora tells me to proceed very slowly, that I have already been hurt too often. I tell her I will indeed go very slowly and that I'll make no mistakes about men again.

When I leave the dining room I gather up things that have been left behind by others. I take them with me to the room where I'll be sleeping in Eudora's house. I get into bed and go right to sleep. I dream this dream of being in Eudora's house all over again. When I wake up in the morning (still in the dream) I reach for my journal inside my backpack, on a chair next to the bed, so I can write it down. For some reason the house is very noisy, most of the other dinner guests have stayed the night as well, and there's a lot of morning activity. I wander around the house with my notebook looking for a quiet place to sit and write but every room is occupied and I'm getting more and more frustrated. Not wanting to forget the dream, I wake up for real and immediately reach for the same journal that was in my dream and write this down.

As I ponder the dream, I'm mostly struck by Eudora's insistence that the place at the table was exactly the one she wanted, as well as the fact that she doesn't demand anything special, even though she's famous and the lady of the house as well. It was her party, but since she was late, she simply accepted what was presented, saying that it was as it should be. This idea seems to relate to this recapitulation journey I'm on—everything is as it should be. I too must take my place, the one that is pointed out to me each day as I face what comes next, learning to navigate by what is presented, rather than by trying to control and keep everything in its place. I must now be more flowing, accepting what comes as appropriate and right. This is also reflected in Eudora's advice to me, to take it slowly, to let it unfold, rather than trying to force anything.

I realize that I have a tremendous capacity to withhold things from myself—feelings, images, information—that old instinctive ability to block out that which is disturbing. In letting go, little by little, in loosening the memories, the feelings, and even the tightness in the body, I see how everything is coming together, showing me the process and how to acquiesce to it.

As the images of the old stuff began popping up out of nowhere, I really did think, at first, that I could still have a modicum of control over them, as I'd once had. I could push them back into the darkness, but I've since learned that such action offers only temporary respite. Ever since Chuck told me that the memories would come when they were ready, and in the form that would capture my attention, I've been confronting my old tendency to want to be in control at all times. As the months have gone on and the memories have continued to emerge, freed from an old grip, I too have had to loosen my grip.

I understand that by learning to let go and to release control, I've been granted a different kind of respite. Slowly, as I've allowed this recapitulation to unfold, I've learned to temper my initial response, no longer reacting as strongly as I once did— immediately pushing everything away. I know that, once unearthed, what is trying to surface will come into clarity at its own pace. In other words, I can't stop it. *How I want to handle the inevitable onslaught is the only decision to make.*

I already accept that it will come and sometimes it comes, indeed, in a big rush. But more often than not, it comes in slow bits and pieces that I can handle, that I can pick up, examine, and wonder about, as I figure out how this tiny piece and that tiny piece fit into the bigger picture of my past, as if I were working on a gigantic jigsaw puzzle.

If I so choose, I may study this process with some degree of detachment, as a keen observer, as the memories and feelings come over me. I'm free to grab a pen and write down what's emerging. This edge of detachment offers a small respite, tempering the intensity of recapitulating, while I also accept the inevitable truth of what I'm being shown, knowing that when the time is right I'll go more deeply into it. So I end up, in a sense, having some amount of control, however small, even as I let go of the old means of absolute control. In essence, I have become like Eudora Welty in my dream, saying that I will sit where I please, while acquiescing to the place that appears because it is indeed just right.

I'm making it known to the universe that I'm ready to continue this recapitulation journey, that I'm open to taking all that comes, in stride, having accepted the bigger intent that it unfold as it will. This is exactly where I *need* to be at this moment. Can I also say, like Eudora in my dream, that it's exactly where I *want* to be?

As I go for a run, I ponder the blips of memory that are presently sitting on the edge of awareness. I let myself accept the bigger picture of the abuse *as fact*. I also allow myself to go slightly into the details of the memories and take hold of a little control by trying to figure out how old I was, what I was wearing, where I was, and who was with me. Eventually, I know I must finally allow myself to go into feelings; that this is the next stage of the process.

I make the decision to slow down and walk the rest of the way. I shut off the counting in my head, the rhythmic jogging pace and the controlled breathing that keep things at bay, and allow the release of what has been steadily brewing for weeks. As I walk the last mile home I allow memories to reveal themselves. I don't dwell on them, but I accept what comes.

I'm free to note that the feelings that arise with the memories, that fill my body, are strikingly familiar. I allow these memories— with their disturbing, throat-gripping images—to deliver a hint of the intense physical sensations and emotional feelings that are deeply embedded in each memory. I allow myself to briefly recall the pain and fear, the anger and the ever-present frustrating desire that the abuse be over, as soon as possible.

I hear my abuser's daughter giggling. I hear that a lot, her giggles haunting many of the memories and I feel my own child self struggling, deeply confused. I wonder if perhaps my abuser's daughter dealt with the abuse by giggling, on one level, while on another level by acting out the abuse with me and perhaps other girls as well. I remember her rating people as either nice or not, depending on how open they were to her games.

Later in the day, while standing on line at the bank, images come flooding back, sharp and brutally clear. Again, I don't dwell on them. I stand quietly in line, perfectly in control, while they flicker in front of me, slide after slide of old stuff, showing me what I have yet to face. The smell of dirt, perhaps a crawl space; a closet, and an image of my abuser's bedroom, all fly by so fleetingly, like scenes glimpsed out the window of a speeding train. So familiar, I recognize these things immediately, but then they're gone as the train speeds onward. And although I can't call them back to mind at the moment, I know they're there, waiting.

I'll save it all until I can see Chuck again. I hear his voice telling me to go ahead and acknowledge what comes, to write it all down and then to let it go for now. Those memories won't go anywhere; they're waiting in the wings, waiting for the right moment. At the same time that I've adopted this pragmatic and detached outlook about the recapitulation, I also feel the stressful intensity of this time in my life. I wonder if I'm using these memories as an escape from the difficulties of the divorce. I can so easily lose myself in them, in this recapitulation process, and I can ignore everything else. Perhaps it's just coincidental, though I don't really believe in coincidence—I'm convinced that everything is significant and meaningful.

I've always had a tremendous capacity to cope, but the skills I'd previously cultivated seem to be outmoded at this point or perhaps are just unable to stand up to the intent I've set for this leg of the recapitulation journey: *to learn how to let go of control*. I'm learning what it means to let go and I'm having experiences as I do.

I can only hold out for so long now before I find myself slipping, going into that place of loss and loneliness, falling into the old stuff. As I fall, that deep sense of loneliness triggers the old dissociative state and I begin tumbling down the tunnel. I realize I'm still recapitulating that dissociative process, being shown that this was what happened to me when I couldn't handle the feelings and the overwhelming fear. When faced with annihilation this dissociative coping skill kicked in and I was able to rely on it, but it's scary. It scared me when I was a child, and it scares me now.

I feel almost like a packrat, taking all this information that's coming to me, writing it down, compartmentalizing and storing it away for later, rather than tackling it head on. But I do intend to take these memories out of their compartments when I meet with Chuck again and work on them in the safe and supportive environment he offers. Until then, I feel lucky that I can store some things away. I'm in no way rejecting the process; I'm just finding the means to handle it as best I can, and I think that's pretty darn good.

Now that I'm consciously allowing myself to let the old stuff flow more freely, I find that I'm increasingly tense, and that becomes a new thing to take care of: *my physical body*. I have to slow down, breathe, try to relax; and constantly remind myself that everything will be okay.

January 20, 2002

I dream that I'm a child again, at school. I'm entering a music contest, but I can't find the right room. I search up and down long corridors, going in and out of many rooms inside the enormous school building, but for the longest time I can't find where I'm supposed to be. Eventually, I come upon a line of people and I get on the end of it and wait to be interviewed. This seems to be the right place. I'm not afraid, but full of confidence and poise, not at all like the real child I once was, who was afraid to open her mouth and sing and couldn't play any musical instrument.

I elect to stay in my bedroom all day, a snowy Sunday, the day after a big snowfall. The white snow on the branches glistens brightly against the clear blue sky. I just need to be quiet, so I stay in bed, reading a book, happy to be lost in someone else's troubles.

January 21, 2002

Again I dream. This time I'm inside a house that's been newly renovated. The walls are freshly sheet-rocked and primed, the floors covered with paper and construction dust. There are small piles of swept debris lying in each room. I realize that it's my house, standing almost ready, the work just about complete—just some last minute cleanup is needed.

My dreams of houses continue. I've gone from homelessness, to searching for a home, to now renovating one. I seem to be living out some of my anxieties in these dreams and I wake up with a sense of calm certainty that, in the end, things will work out just fine.

I feel peaceful today.

January 22, 2002

In a dream I'm preparing to hike over a steep mountaintop. A winter storm is coming. I refuse assistance, a ride, or any help whatsoever. People at the bottom of the mountain warn me that it's a treacherous pass and that there's a perfectly fine road that I can take. I can either walk or accept one of the many offers for a ride. They point out that I could be driven up in comfort, but I stubbornly refuse to either walk up the road or accept a ride in a car. Instead, I stick to hiking the mountain path because that's what I've decided to do. I must do it my way, as previously planned.

As I hike, I'm confronted with all the challenges of climbing a steep mountain trail. I drag myself over huge boulders, slip on rocky paths, and teeter on the edges of narrow cliffs with steep drops into the valley below, but I'm determined to go it alone, as usual, without any help. The road is right nearby and people continually stop their cars and ask me if I'd like a ride, but I stubbornly refuse any help.

"No thanks," I say. "I'm fine."

But halfway up the mountaintop it begins to snow heavily and suddenly I'm aware that I'm in grave danger. I can't see in front of me anymore and I can't see the path at my feet. The snow accumulates quickly and it's now impossible to move any further.

Cars stop again, and people call to me through the blizzard, asking me if I need help, but I refuse all offers, though I'm aware that I'll die if I don't accept help. Rather than say, yes, that I do indeed need help, I elect to hunker down in the snow and wait for death to come. I'm completely aware that I can ask for help at any time, but still I don't. I'm insistent that I must adhere to my original decision to go it alone, that I must not ask for help nor admit to fear. I refuse to feel my needs. All offers of help are flatly refused. I sit down next to a boulder and wait to die.

Last night, before falling asleep, I thought about the last question that Chuck asks me at the end of every session, without fail.

"How are you feeling?"

That question always takes me by surprise, and it hurts, but I can't figure out why. It's such a real question. It asks me to speak the truth, but every time I hear it I feel as if I'm being stabbed in the heart, and I can't answer.

"I don't know," I always say. "I don't know how I feel."

The question goes directly to a very vulnerable place inside me. I know it's asking me to admit things to myself, to say that I'm scared, that I'm worried, and, yes, that I need help.

I can't sleep. I toss and turn. How are you feeling? Why does it hurt so much to be asked that? Once again these two questions rattle around in my head and down into my body as memories try to attach, until my little girl self inhabits my body and my bed, and I reach an epiphany.

I'm a little girl again, four-years-old and lying in my bed, curled up in a ball, hiding under the covers. I feel the mattress beneath me sink into the shape of a small nest and protectively wrap around me, as my mattress once did in my childhood bed. Now I'm in that bed again, in a hole formed by my habit of sleeping curled up in a fetal position. I'm hurting, inside and outside. I'm rolled into a ball of confusion and pain. I only want peace and distance from the threat of annihilation. My mother is sitting on the side of the bed.

"How are you feeling?" she asks, and I can't tell her.

I can't tell her anything. She thinks I'm sick, but I'm not really that kind of sick, not her kind of sick. I'm my own kind of sick and I don't want to speak to her. I pretend I'm asleep. I wait for her to go away so I can be alone. I just want to be alone, safe in my bed.

I fall asleep in the midst of this recapitulation, curled up in a ball, a four-year-old child again. I dream of fighting in a ragtag rebel group comprised of children of all nationalities, guerrilla warfare taking place in jungle-covered mountains. I fight all night long, running along mountain trails, hiding from the enemy, shooting a gun, and fighting hand-to-hand.

January 23, 2002

It's early in the morning when I wake up. I'm immediately desperate to talk with Chuck, last night's recapitulation still fresh. I agonize over not being able to afford the work I so badly need to do with him. It seems like such a cruel twist. Here I am daring to open up to this transformational process and yet I cannot fully avail myself of it.

Do I buy groceries or do I go see Chuck? Part of me feels terribly guilty, selfishly guilty that I need to do this work for myself, but I also accept that it's just where I am right now.

January 24, 2002

I dream that I have a new studio in a renovated Victorian house. I'm sharing it with an artist friend. A gallery owner who often shows my work comes for a visit. He wants to see what I've been working on lately. I show him a collapsible hexagon that I've recently made out of wooden popsicle sticks. It stretches like a tensegrity toy. I'm quite satisfied with it.

"Very brilliant," he says, "quite good."

I'm very relaxed, lying on a sofa, much more relaxed than normal, as he looks it over. He spends a long time trying to figure out how I made it, playing with it, collapsing it and watching it spring back as the tension releases. Then he starts poking around the room looking at some of my other artwork, making comments and asking questions. At one point, he lifts the lid off a box and a monkey, dressed in clothes and with a little hat on its head, like an organ grinder's monkey, pops out and starts running around the room.

"Is that still here?" I ask the other artist, incredulously. "I thought you took that home a long time ago?"

"Oh my God! I forgot all about it!" she says with some embarrassment, as it becomes clear that the monkey has been inside the box for weeks.

"Apparently you forgot about this too," I say, picking up a huge graying slab of meat.

"It's the monkey's food," I explain to the gallery owner. My artist friend promises to take the monkey home with her and get rid of the decaying meat as well.

I'm totally stumped by this dream. It makes no sense to me. The tensegrity toy was quite complex and it felt as if I had indeed really made it. The only thing I can relate it to is the tension in my hips, which is intense right now. How do I let it go? Is it really as easy as collapsing and releasing, as simple and yet as complex as the toy I made in my dream?

The physical tension was much better the week I went to see Chuck at the beginning of the month, but it's been building again ever since. The pain wakes me up at night, with the same intense burning in my legs and hips as when I had shingles a few years ago. It must be all the holding in and holding back I'm doing as I force myself to keep everything inside, while I wait to meet with Chuck.

January 26, 2002

I wake up early again, coming out of dreams I can't remember. The symptoms of holding back are returning, the sleeplessness, the pain ripping through my hips, the clenching in my jaw, the grinding of my teeth.

While Chuck was away in Switzerland, I was able to sleep pretty well, after a few weeks of struggle, as I consciously worked at suppressing the memories that were beginning to take shape. I shifted away from the intensity of the recapitulation and was more present, spending time with the kids and reading. I felt physically better, with more energy for other things besides this inner work. Now that Chuck is back, things have begun to percolate again, memories are bubbling up to the surface, stirring up all the old symptoms and stresses and, once again, I can't sleep.

I tossed and turned all night, and even now, as I sit in bed in the early morning, the memory that haunted me all night long rushes through me again. My body goes into full recapitulation mode as I go rigid and stiff. My legs cramp painfully and I'm a little girl again, my entire body clamped tightly shut.

My abuser is kneeling in front of me. I'm lying on the ground in the woods, thinking that if I can just keep my legs together he won't get me. I'm squeezing them so tightly together that my knees and ankles lock. I clamp my hands against my crotch, as I go rigid and fight against his hands trying to pry me open. I hear his voice.

"Spread your legs; open your legs!" he says impatiently.

I see his left hand coming at me, reaching for my crotch. I can't stop his hands. I can only keep my legs clamped together as long as possible and now, as I recapitulate, my hips tightly clench and my thighs clamp shut. I fight with all my might to stay closed; my arms locked stiff, my hands stuck between my legs. I will not release them. I will not bend my legs. I will not let him get me this time. I'm as stiff as a board, and the only thing that moves is a tight knot of tension that creeps up and settles in my throat. With my jaw determinedly clenched, I fight against his prying hands with everything I have.

Movement is painful as I come back to find myself in my bed. I cannot unclench my legs. They remain clamped shut, two boards that will not bend. My body is stuck in this position, locked in the memory. Finally, I squirm over to the edge of the bed and ease my stiff legs over the side. When my feet touch the floor I'm able to hoist myself up to a standing position and break the intensity of the memory. Stiffly and awkwardly, I stand next to my bed fighting the cramps that suddenly grab at my hips and thighs, reminding me, reminding me of what used to happen to me. Tense and jittery,

I also notice that my shoulders and elbows are sore and that my hips and thighs feel bruised and battered. I look to see if anything is wrong, if I am in fact covered in bruises, but there's nothing physically amiss. It's only a memory, but I know I can't deal with it alone anymore. With that knot of pain stuck in my throat, I pick up the phone and call Chuck for an appointment.

January 27, 2002

I wake up totally clenched and immediately flash to the memory of lying on the ground in the woods again. My elbows dig into the dirt, my hips are wrenched wide, as a painful burn sears through my entire body. I can't stay with the memory, but I acknowledge why I ache, why my hips and arms hurt, why I'm cramping up. I know where it comes from, and I know what to do about it.

I try to relax as I admit to this. I try to release the pain that's stuck in my body, but I'm completely blocked. I realize I've been blocked and tense my whole life. I'm good at holding things in, bad at letting things out, bad at talking. This is what I must deal with for the moment, but I *am* going to start talking about it again. I just have to hold out for one more day.

"Relax," I tell myself. "Relax. Relax. Relax."

I go for an early morning run, needing the breathing, the loosening, the expanding, the letting go, the emptying that the physical activity affords me. When I get back I do some yoga and meditation. I take a shower and then, feeling like I need to be held, wanting to be held, I turn off the shower and turn on the bath instead. I sit in the tub and take a long hot bath, the heat holding me together, comforting and soothing me. I feel almost calm afterwards, the intent of this Sunday to get myself to a place of relaxation. I'm hopeful that if I can accomplish even a little bit of release every day throughout the week maybe I'll stay loose, though I still carry the hurt inside and out. My throat is sore from the nugget of pain stuck there, my legs and hips still bruised with memory.

Yesterday, at my son's band concert, I lost twenty minutes. As I sat and listened to the band playing, I remember looking over the program and noting that there were still two more pieces to be played. All of a sudden the audience was standing up, cheering and clapping, the conductor bowing, the band rising to their feet and bowing too, and I sat there stunned, thinking: "It can't be over, what about the last two pieces?"

It *was* over!

I was so totally lost that I couldn't even remember where I'd been or what was going on in my mind, because I wasn't even there for those twenty minutes; I was *gone*. I know it was about the old stuff. I was out-of-body, so gone that I wasn't present when the conductor introduced the last two pieces to the audience, nor did I hear the music. When it dawned on me that it was over and I became aware that I had lost time—been totally absent—I found myself slightly embarrassed, worried that I may have spoken out loud or done something strange, but no one even looked at me or seemed aware of me. I knew I hadn't been asleep because I didn't wake up, per se, but simply returned. I found myself still sitting straight up, as if I'd been totally present, paying attention to the concert the entire time.

I have no idea where I went.

January 28, 2002
In a dream, I'm lying on the floor of a waiting room in a strange office, tightly rolled into a ball of pain. My legs are hurting and I can't move. People keep coming over to me, asking me what's wrong.

"I'm waiting," I say.

"Are you okay?"

"I'm waiting for someone."

Finally a woman clears a space for me to sit on a sofa. I slowly get up and hobble over to the sofa and sit down and try to talk. As I try to talk, the pain builds in intensity. Excruciating pains shoot up and down my legs, spreading into my hips and torso until my entire body is tightly clenched.

I wake up to find myself in this tightly clenched state, rigidly stiff and in excruciating pain, and suddenly I know that something was stolen from me a long time go and I want it back. *I want it back.*

I meet with Chuck and after only a moment's hesitation I begin speaking, getting right to the point. Blurting right through the solid nugget of pain in my throat, I describe a memory that has been emerging.

"My abuser had a red pickup truck. He puts me up onto the hood of it, sitting next to his daughter. We have no clothes on and I can feel the heat of the hood beneath my buttocks. I keep my legs clenched tightly closed because I don't want him to touch me down there. I see his hand coming toward me and I try to push it away, to hold it back. But then I hear his daughter giggle, like she always does, and I'm not sure how to feel. I try to laugh too, but I still don't like his hand touching me. I can't keep it away."

"Afterwards we play with the garden hose on the side of the house. We wash our crotches with the hose. When I squirt my abuser's daughter she hops and squeals, laughing, holding her labia apart. She likes it when I aim the stream of water at her crotch."

"How old are you?"

"Three."

January 29, 2002

I dream all night of moving large pieces of furniture, my body aching the whole time and yet I cannot allow anyone to help. I wake in such pain that, try as I might, I just can't release.

I know I have to acknowledge and accept what my abuser did to me. In the past I dealt with the abuse by cutting off the part of me that was hurting, numbing it and forgetting about it, cutting off my feelings too so they didn't alert me to the pain that truly existed inside me. It's like I cut off part of my body back then, my arm for instance. It's like finding, at this point in my life, that it's still there, that it's been hanging useless, unused all these years and I never even knew it was there. My feelings lie equally dead and unused inside me, undiscovered as of yet. I must excavate them, rejuvenate them, and bring them into life.

When I couldn't stop my abuser by keeping my legs together, or by blocking his hands, or by saying no, I had to stop him somehow. My body had all the answers back then, as did my psyche, and in consort they saved the day. I successfully blocked out the experience, dissociating on demand. In addition, I was able to keep my soul, the deepest part of me, safely locked away, far from his reach.

In truth, he never really got me, not the heart of me, though he tried to own as much of me as he could. I kept myself so protected that it was impossible. This was one of the pacts my body, psyche, and spirit made together. We decided that though he could do whatever he wanted, *he was never going to own us.*

In the end, however, he did control a good deal, stifling who I potentially could have been as a child and who I became in adulthood. In reality, I stayed locked in his embrace long after the abuse was over. He didn't physically or mentally destroy me—I wasn't going to allow for that—but he ploughed under valuable assets of personality and spirit. With no regard for the body and soul of a child, he took what he wanted.

His actions raked through me, leaving my sense of trust, my innocence, and the ability to truly feel, in shreds. The only thing I could do at the time was to gather up those tattered shreds and take them down into the bottom of my soul, down into the tunnel where I escaped so often, and bury them there. The longer I kept those shreds of self buried at the bottom of that tunnel the more difficult it became to access them. As a consequence, in order to survive, I became a solid brick of hard determination, innerly defiant. I would let no one in. No one would ever get that deeply inside me. No one would ever touch those tattered shreds of potential, too battered and tender even for me to visit. This was another pact I made with myself.

I tried to tell my mother, but it didn't come out right. I wasn't understood. I was too young and didn't have the right words, and she was too unavailable. With my feelings so painfully hurt already, even attempting to ask for help meant I had to scrape some sense of self up off the bottom of that tunnel floor and actually present it to my parents. But with little practice in asking them for anything, and with little receptivity from them, even a simple hesitation on their part would send me spinning deeply back down inside myself.

They were not bad parents; they just didn't have a clue as to how to communicate, and so I decided I would never be rejected again. I simply wouldn't ask for help again. Instead, like in my dream of climbing the mountaintop, I would just go it alone. I would bear the cross and carry on alone. I was determined. I didn't want to have to fight off my parent's disbelief while struggling with my own sense of imminent annihilation. Far better to just keep it buried. I knew how to do that, how it worked, and besides I had my abuser's daughter to work things out with. We had our games that brought us relief. We had our pact together, and it was more solid than any pact I had with my parents.

Memories intrude and I'm a child again. He makes it very clear that he's in charge. He hurts me. I can't keep my legs closed. I can't keep his hands off me, his mouth off me, his smell off me. He hurts me. I can't make him stop. I can't do anything about it. He always gets me. I'm lost. I'm so lost. I disappear. I disappear forever.

How could he do that? How could anyone do that to babies? Why did he need to? I'm disgusted! I'm angry! Why did he do that to me?!

I know I couldn't stop him. I know it wasn't my fault, even though I knew it was wrong, even though I was supposed to know better, even though I was the responsible one—the big sister who took care of everyone else in the family, the one all my friends' parents trusted.

"If she's going, you can go too," the mother of a friend said once, looking pointedly at me, as some friends and I negotiated taking a trip together when we were teenagers. "I know she'll take good care of you."

I stood there, accepting the charge, knowing she was right. I would indeed take good care of everyone, yet I also bore the anger of always being the responsible one, carrying the expectations of my friends' parents with me wherever I went. One friend called me "Little Mother Hen—always taking care of her brood." I was the ultimate caring and protective adult, the one who never allowed friends or siblings to get into trouble when in her care, the one who guarded them all.

Oh God, I was the one who needed guarding! I was the one who needed someone protecting me.

January 30, 2002

I dream that I'm walking in woods and find a dead woman's naked body lying on the ground, under some bushes. She's partially covered with leaves and moss. I poke at her with a stick.

Pulling aside some branches I see her bloated, decaying body. As I pull back in horror I see fossilized creatures, animals frozen in rock crystal, tumble out of her carcass, emerging from deep within her. As I watch, they come to life, fly through the air, and land on the headboard of my bed. They perch there in a row over my head: an owl, snakes, squirrels, frogs, small creatures and insects, all lined up. I know that more are going to keep emerging from their frozen states and I'm concerned they won't have enough room to sit on the headboard. Tilting my head, I look up at them above me. The owl, on the left, barely has room to perch, one of its feet slipping off the edge. I watch with apprehension as it attempts to readjust itself.

"Move over so the owl has room," I say to the others.

I'm only able to settle back to sleep when I see that the animals and insects have made enough room for the owl to comfortably perch, when there is plenty of room for a few more critters, who I am certain are soon to emerge.

When I wake up, I'm aware that the dead woman in the dream is me, the adult me, long buried, feeling emotionally dead under all the decaying debris of the abusive past. The animals are the frozen parts of myself yet to emerge: feelings, emotions, and memories of a forgotten past. I see the owl as thoughtful wisdom, as I continue to work through this recapitulation intelligently—in dreams, memories, flashbacks—knowing I have more work to do. I'm asking for more room to let it happen, to give it more space. I also know that I have so much more inside me that will emerge over time. I am confident of this.

January 31, 2002
The dead woman in my dream is the dead, frozen, numb me, but she's also the feminine side seeking to become known. In the dream, I uncovered her a little, poked at her with the stick, and then discovered the crystallized animals, which took my attention off the figure of the woman. The animals represent feelings and hidden aspects of myself as of yet unused, unexercised, which I've been focused on awakening lately, as I've attempted to break the old pacts I made with myself.

It's appropriate that I turn to these fossilized aspects of myself in the dream, as my intent has been to access them. And they did, after all, present themselves as quite attractive in the dream, their intricate crystal shapes quite noticeable. It was almost as if they sought to draw my attention away from the figure, saying, "Look at us," wanting me to stay focused on figuring out what I really hold frozen inside and how I feel about it. But the feminine side is also of utmost importance, so I must acknowledge and uncover this other long-buried part of myself too.

I've always preferred to cover my femininity, barely been able to acknowledge that I'm a woman at all. I tend to think of myself only as a person, rarely as a woman. Most of my life I've preferred dressing in boyish styles, covering my breasts and body, slouching, hiding my face and figure, not interested in curves but only in presenting a thin, flat appearance from every angle.

I'd cut my hair in short boyish haircuts when I felt a need to be especially harsh toward myself, for whatever reason, and it gave me a sense of being in control of how I appeared. It was too difficult to be pretty. I didn't want to be a girl, to be perceived as a girl, as attractive. Look what happened to me because I was a girl! Why would I want to grow up and be a woman!

The maternal aspect of being a woman was, however, very acceptable to me. I could nurture others, appreciate the beauty in others, but I was not able to be kind, nurturing, or accepting of my own beauty. Animals and small children, especially infants, brought out the gentlest of qualities in me. A tenderness I couldn't feel for myself escaped when I was in charge of those innocent others. At one time I had thought about becoming a veterinarian since I communicated so well with animals. It was always far easier to speak to my pets or the wild creatures I'd nurture back to health than to communicate with humans. It's still easier to care more about others than myself, to nurture others, to cry for others.

Why can't I do it for myself now? Who's stopping me, except me? I always felt so ancient and battered, and being quiet and unnoticed was always more comfortable. I admit, the old pacts I made with myself as a child take a lot of energy. Constantly upholding them, adhering to the old strict code of silence, has exhausted me.

I also grew up having learned that selfishness was a big sin. There were so many rules to follow both at school and at home. We were expected to be perfect examples of Catholic goodness out in public, while at home we were expected to quietly go about our lives, disturbing our parents as little as possible. There was little nurturance in either school or home and I didn't have the skills to understand what was happening to me outside of those two strict environments, where the rules were clearly defined and punishment delivered when deemed necessary. My most sensitive self, injured early on, accepted those rules of conduct, finding it much easier to lock up what was happening, retreat into the tunnel, and pretend that everything was as it should be.

I *pretended* to be normal.

I was so young when the abuse began that I couldn't have had even an inkling that it was harmful. Yes, it hurt physically, but if you don't understand that you're being harmed, how do you go the next step to saying that it hurts emotionally too? To begin with, how does a two year old child even know what an emotion is? I don't think I could ever have articulated any of what was happening to me at such a young age.

Although judged to be an extremely shy child, perhaps the abuse, starting at such a young age, coincided with my emerging personality, creating this withdrawn child self, leaving little room for a true child self to evolve. In the end, shyness became my most apparent personality trait. My painfully withdrawn self emerged and became my accepted identity in the world.

As I recapitulate, I see how the abuse became a normal part of my life too. It happened in another world and, although it seemed wrong within the perfection-demanding worlds of home and school, it was *real*, taking its place within the context of my existence. Simply put, it became a normal fact of life though enacted in a different reality.

I lived in two separate and distinct realities and, just like the normal world, the world of the sexual predator was another world I had no control over. Already well-trained to be quiet and obedient, I was faced with the challenge of developing the means to survive what happened in that strange world. Coping skills learned and utilized there became efficient means of survival, though they ended up doing more harm than good as I carried them into adulthood. They were no longer pertinent once I left the world of the sexual predator, but I didn't know this. Now however, I see how they've kept me bound in fear and despair, my physical body carrying everything, my spirit dying as a result. If I hadn't begun this recapitulation journey, if I hadn't paid attention to the signs of the fox, I believe I would have succumbed to death within a very short time—death of the spirit leading very quickly to death of the physical body.

So now I understand that I need to take care of that tender side, the side that went away somewhere and hid, that didn't like what was happening and disappeared down that tunnel. The fact that the tunnel keeps reappearing is showing me just how significant it is in this process. It was the first thing I saw when I fell to the floor the night I was making cookies. It opened before me and showed me what was buried there, but at the time I didn't understand that I was the one who had buried the visions I saw that night as I lay crouching on the kitchen floor. I didn't understand that the tunnel was inside me, that the tunnel *is* me. But now I see that it was mine from the start, used for protection in more ways than one. That tunnel saved my life, but it also saved all the secrets I couldn't share, that I had no outlet for. It became a place to store everything that hurt, confused, and frightened. And it's all still stored away there, along with my precious, vulnerable, innocent little girl self.

As I recapitulate more deeply, the tunnel continues to show me things that I remember as soon as I see them. Far away though they feel, I know they belong to me—in some way utterly familiar. It reveals its secrets, this long narrow tunnel of self, over and over again, as I continue plodding along the winding path of this recapitulation.

Now I must find a way to nurture and be kind to my little girl self. She's still somewhere inside that tunnel, still waiting to be found. I must find a way to connect with her, the pretty, delicate, gentle little girl who rolled into a ball and hid away at the bottom of that tunnel.

I need to keep digging. Eventually, I'll find her.

Chapter Eleven

They're Real

February 2, 2002

I dream that I'm taking a bus trip. A man in a white trench coat wants something from me; he keeps trying to get my attention. We stop for food at a buffet restaurant. I put some bread and butter on a tray. There doesn't seem to be much else available. I get a large plastic cup full of red wine. Then I'm walking fast down a narrow cobblestoned street, carrying my tray, trying not to spill the wine. I'm looking for a quiet place to relax—I want to be alone. I notice that the man in the white trench coat is following me again, still trying to get my attention. I sip a little of the wine as I run away from him. I'm not afraid, just annoyed.

The man in the white trench coat in this dream is very similar to the tall white-clothed, menacing trinity figure from a dream I had several months ago when I let my daughter be molested in my stead. In a follow-up dream I killed him off, so why is he back now? I'm aware that he wants something from me in this dream. He's after me for a reason. He's trying to get my attention, but I don't want to engage him in any way, even though he doesn't appear threatening. I only want peace and quiet. My immediate reaction in the dream is to ignore him and run away.

I wonder at the bread and wine; bread, as the staff of life, with the addition of wine implying the ritual of the Catholic mass, the body and blood of Jesus Christ, leading me to consider that it indicates something sacred. Life is sacred and all I want to do is be alone, enjoying the sacrament of sacred life. I want to be left in peace.

February 3, 2002

I meditate, sitting in a lotus position. My awareness actively begins to shift into an out-of-body experience, as I feel myself curl down and roll into a tight ball until I can see into my vagina. In reality, I could never do this, but in the state I find myself in I'm quite amazed when I reach out and pry my vagina open until it yawns wide like a cave. With a flashlight in one hand, I dig with the other, cleaning, excavating, tossing out all the twisted, rusted hunks of old stuff, all the debris of a lifetime of confusion and abuse. I curse angrily, my temper flaring, as I dig and scrape, allowing my frantic and distraught emotions to escape, allowing myself to feel what I've held pent up inside me for so long. When I'm done there's a huge pile of twisted metal, wood, and debris strewn on the floor around me. I close my vagina back up to normal size and uncurl back into my body still sitting quietly in meditation. With my awareness back, I find that I'm extremely calm and empty, the quiet I've been seeking now sitting firmly inside me.

I sit in the bathtub afterwards, the hot water pressing against my body allowing me to relax. When I feel the urge to curl up and be held I generally sit in the tub, a womblike hug substitute. It's what I always liked about swimming as a child; not only was there total freedom in the water, but there was also the caressing quality of the weight of the water, attentive arms holding me in the embrace of no attachment.

My abuser's family didn't belong to the community pool where I spent much of my time during the summer months, in fact they rarely left their own property, so it was one place where I could feel fairly safe. I excelled at swimming and could never get enough of it. However, one day, a man sat on the side of the pool, his feet dangling in the water, staring intently at me while I swam back and forth, until I became so uncomfortable I had to get out of the water. I was about fourteen at the time.

This happened again about a year later, in another pool. I was with friends who noticed a man staring intently at me.

"That man is watching you," one of my friends said. "Do you know him?"

"No, not at all," I said, realizing I'd been feeling his piercing stare for quite some time.

"It's really creepy," the other girl declared, and indeed it was.

This strange man sat on the side of the pool, staring at me with the same trancelike intensity that had so unnerved me at the other pool. I got out of the water and sat on a chair with a large towel over me, covering my girlish bikini-clad body until my friends were ready to leave. It was almost as if those men knew me, recognized me. They sat mesmerized, peering right through me, unable to shift their eyes away, their expressions deadly serious, and yes, very creepy.

As I lie in the tub, I think about my innocent feminine side, the side that got hurt right from the very beginning, and the side that continued to feel injured as I grew up and had relationships and adult encounters with men. I see how the repercussions of the early abuse reverberated throughout my life, unbeknownst to me and to my partners, but a part of our interactions nonetheless. I see how I sought to protect myself further by instinctively shutting down the innocent feminine side whenever I felt her being hurt or rejected, on those rare occasions when I thought it might be okay to present her in a relationship. Often it was more important to be in control, to be the dominant partner so that I was never hurt, but this only resulted in my feminine innocence being further pushed into oblivion, far from even my reach.

The area where the abuse happened is the most tender of places on the female body. It's also where I've stored all the pain. It's where the memories emerge from. They come tearing out of my most tender, female self in painful recapitulation.

Today, in my meditation, I felt as if I was extricating everything that had been done to that part of my body, ridding myself of the memories. And yet I know I must keep digging for those distant feelings and for that innocence that I lost somewhere along the way. It feels like an endless process, an exhaustive search.

I've been protective of my tender feminine side, and especially my innocence. I've kept them locked away while I've acquiesced to the other, more masculine side, which is stronger and can take all kinds of abuse.

Some yoga postures are feminine and some are masculine in intent. I find that I'm most happy doing the masculine sun salutation, *Surya Namaskara*, rather than the feminine moon salutation, *Chandra Namaskara*. I could do sun salutation every day, all day, and be perfectly happy, but when I do moon I'm confronted with having to shift out of and push beyond my comfort zone, as I strain against the unawakened feminine self. I know it's good for me to challenge myself to go beyond the known, but it's such a struggle. I still want some of my old comforts to hang onto. They've become my family, caressing relatives who never reject me, always offering their loving comforts no matter what I do or say. They keep me from falling into the abyss of nothingness where there are no comforts whatsoever.

Running has become a very comfortable cover that I pull over myself any time I begin to feel too much. If I run until my body hurts, I can attach to the real physical pain produced by the run, rather than suffer the phantom somatic pain of feelings, such as loss or rejection or inadequacy. In so doing, I can assign pain to decisions made and actions taken.

"Okay, you feel pain because you overdid it," I can say—and it's certainly the truth—while at the same time it gives me the perfect alibi for ignoring what's really at issue. I understand that in so doing I simply perpetuate an already avoidant behavior and just continue to cover over what's truly wrong at my core, but I need the relief I get from this little trick I play on myself.

I do know that the real reason I'm doing this recapitulation is because something inside me is crying out to be noticed, asking for those stale but comfy covers to be removed, swept off, as I continue searching for all the truths. In the meantime, I'll use whatever works so I can get through the tough times that arise now each day.

February 4, 2002

I'm in my bedroom meditating again, sitting cross-legged in a lotus position, my hands resting on my feet. Immediately, I grow huge and puffy. My arms and hands become soft and fat, blown up like marshmallows, although the one foot that my hands rest on stays small, feeling like a child's foot beneath my huge hands. I'm trying to figure out what's happening, and whether it feels good or not. I decide to just stay with it as long as possible, to see where it takes me.

My daughter knocks on the door and comes into the room. I tell her that I'm meditating but find that I'm able to stay with the puffy feeling while I talk with her. I keep my eyes closed while we speak for a few minutes. She doesn't seem to notice that I'm puffed up into a huge pillow. I stay with the sensation after she leaves, recognizing it as that old feeling of trying to escape, of dissociation, of ballooning up and then shrinking fast into the depths of the tunnel. But this time only part of me shrinks and grows small while the rest of me remains suspended in space.

I float, hanging in the air like a balloon, wondering what I'm supposed to learn. I feel an urgency to remember something, aware that I'm on the brink of a memory. I stay in this place of mystery until I'm unable to sustain it any longer. The balloon pops and I come tumbling back into my body.

It wasn't totally unpleasant, I decide, not unpleasant at all, in fact.

I meet with Chuck and I'm a little miffed when he starts singing a Bobby McFerrin song to me during the session:

Don't worry, be happy
In every life we have some trouble
When you worry you make it double
Don't worry, be happy...

I've just unloaded a lot of the painful stuff that came up over the past week, and I'm feeling pretty down, grimly unhappy, not smiling at all. I realize that perhaps he's just trying to send a little spark of life in my direction, but it just pisses me off.

He says he spent the weekend in California at a *Tensegrity* workshop and it really affected him, helped shift him, but I can't take his energy. I feel it throughout the entire session, *way too happy*.

I snarl at him as I leave, but I can't get the words of the song out of my head either. They rattle around in there all day. And maybe, by the end of the day, I am a little happier, the heavy veil of worry about everything ever so slightly lifted.

February 6, 2002

I dream that the house is on fire and I'm trying to get everyone out. It's engulfed in a fireball of destruction that rolled in from somewhere else, outside of us. I'm aware that the entire world is burning, but the kids and I are safe. I'm aware that my soon to be ex-husband is also safe, though he's not at home. I know that I don't have to worry about him anymore. Chuck is dressed as a firefighter, directing the water hose at the flames.

"Don't worry, everything will be okay," he says, turning to me.

I'm very calm as I stand next to Chuck and watch the flames burning, engulfing everything. I'm aware that what Chuck says is true, that indeed everything will be okay. In spite of the destructive fire, I am serenely calm.

February 8, 2002

You lose your sense of self during the long years of a slowly deteriorating marriage. With little or no interaction between you and your partner you eventually forget who you are. With nothing celebrated anymore, no personal notes of kindness, no loving attention, and no nice words spoken between the two of you, you begin to lose even the good feelings you once had about yourself. You become a drudge. You look like a drudge, act like a drudge, feel like a drudge. The only escape from my drudge self has been in reading, art, writing, and my work. But now, as I open up to a different life of my own choosing, I find that people like and respect me, and I begin to accept that I'm worth more than nothing. I'm discovering that I matter.

With the emergence of the memories and as I distance myself from the repercussions of the ending of the marriage, gaining personal space and identity, my feelings about myself are beginning to change too. I'm somewhat surprised but also gladdened by this, as I slowly begin to care about myself again, as I see other people also caring about me.

In the spot where love and joy should sit, in my heart center, I feel only thumping hurt at the moment, but I know it won't always be there. I know I must find a way to resolve this pain. I must release it and replace it with something good, something healing, something wonderful and fulfilling. I carry the hope that this recapitulation, difficult and mysterious as it is, will get me there.

February 9, 2002

I couldn't sleep last night. I thought the old stuff was over. Really, I thought I had gotten through all there was. I just couldn't imagine there would be more memories, but then, as I tossed and turned, BOOM, out of nowhere, BOOM!

Now I lie in bed as memories flood over me again, suffocating me. I don't want to believe what's happening, old stuff enshrouding me in stale air from the past, but I know it's real because my body acts out the memories as they emerge.

Now I'm curled in a ball in my bed, panting and whimpering, trying to hold my sweater out of the way so he won't get his 'stuff' on it. I'm burning, my vagina on fire. Why is he shaking me? I can't keep my legs twisted tight enough...if I can only keep my legs together.

"Stop it, stop it, stop it!" I mutter through clenched teeth. "Stop it, stop it, stop it!"

Then I remember: It *will* stop; it *will* be over soon. It will all be over soon.

February 12, 2002

I meet with Chuck. I'm devastated. Over the past few days, as memories have been flashing and firing away, I've realized that the abuse happened throughout my high school years. I know this because of the age I am in the memories as they emerge. I see my body, my clothing, my bedroom.

I see myself walking along mountain roads and hiking through fields as a teenager, bumping into him, my abuser. The abuse probably happened right up until I left to go to college. I can barely hold onto this idea though, and, in actuality, I have no concrete memories to substantiate this thought. The only thing I have to go on are the tidbits of memories that have been emerging, bombarding me in the middle of the night, as I toss and turn, trying to sleep.

I turn one way and I'm hit with one memory, so I turn over to my other side and get hit with a different memory; glimpses of things that I know are true as soon as I see them because they are so viscerally familiar. I taste, smell, and hear what's happening in those brief dips into the past. I see everything so clearly when I go back that I have no doubt as to the truth of those memories.

We do EMDR and I go into the memory that has been plaguing me: being on fire. I don't know how I got there, standing in front of my abuser, but as soon as I see him I know he's going to get me. It doesn't matter what I do. I can't stop him. I try, but I can't keep my legs together, even if I twist them tightly. I just can't keep them closed. He's shaking me. Everything hurts. I try to move, to switch away, but my teeth are chattering, my jaws clacking. I can't breathe.

"I gave up. I just gave up. I couldn't keep my legs together," I say, without emotion, as I come out of the memory.

Chuck asks me if I can go back into the memory again and see if there's anything else. I go back, but this time it's to a different memory.

I'm with my abuser in his truck. A rifle lies across his lap, the butt pointing out the window as we drive far into the local orchard. He stops, facing a row of white painted beehives, and tells me to get out of the truck, pointing the gun at me, telling me to walk in front of him, to get in front of the truck.

I glance back at him and then I have to hurry up because he's slowly inching the truck forward, the gun pointing out the window in my direction, the bumper inches away from me, nudging me along toward the beehives. The ground is rough. When I stumble I'm afraid he'll run me over if I fall. I have no choice but to do as he says. He stops the truck when I'm pressed up against the beehives, squeezed between the bumper of his truck and the row of wooden beehives, the bees buzzing around me.

Frightened, I stand numbly petrified, holding my breath, until he backs away and tells me to get back into the truck. He turns toward me, points the gun at me, and tells me that if I ever tell anyone about what he does to me, he'll bring me back to the hives and let the bees have me. The bees will kill me, he says. He won't have to do a thing.

I sit as far away from him as possible as we drive out of the orchard.

I hate him.

February 13, 2002

I'm back in the past, feeling ragged and raw. The channels are fully open, memories flooding, and I can't stop the infusion of sadness, anger, and the empty hopelessness of my childhood, now so palpable again. The feelings are real. They drag me back until I'm a little girl once again.

"Such a pretty girl. Why so glum?" is a question I heard often and I wonder if people really think that being pretty is something good, if they think being pretty is all that's necessary for a happy life.

"Why so serious? You look prettier when you smile."

So I cover myself over to make myself not so pretty; cutting my hair, wearing baggy clothes, thinking that maybe if I'm not pretty, things will be okay; that I won't be noticed or touched.

I want to curl up. I want to go away for a while. I'm so unhappy. Instinctively, I roll over, away from the memories that are emerging and find myself lying in bed. It's early morning. I've had a restless night.

The memories won't rest and so I can't rest. But truthfully, I really don't want them to rest. There's so much confusion in them that I'm determined to figure out what really happened. Although I'm coming from an adult perspective, after a lifetime of experiences, the old hurts and confusions of my child self are still sitting inside me, waiting. That lost little girl is still in there too, and she's still in pain.

I'm finally beginning to understand why I suffered such agonizing inner turmoil and why I felt so lost and helpless as a child. *The big bad wolf got me.* I was always trying to hide, purposely trying to be invisible, and in so doing I wandered off on my own, feeling safe in my aloneness. But as I wandered I walked right into his trap, his territory, and once trapped I had no choice in the matter—I was hopelessly caught.

There was no way I was going to be able to get away once he'd gotten hold of me. I was his from the moment he spied me. I couldn't save myself, I couldn't stop him, I couldn't fight him. I just couldn't get away. He had too much power and I knew, deep down, that he would always get me. I always felt his presence, lurking in the shadows of my childhood. I still feel him. That's why it's so hard to let go. If I let go, he'll get me. If I let down my guard, or relax, he'll get me. If I go down that path, he's there waiting for me.

The old fears are all sitting there in the old loneliness, the old hopelessness, the old confusion, shame, and self-hatred. I know now that it wasn't my fault, but back then it must have been because I was supposed to know better. I was supposed to be a good girl, supposed to know how to behave and act, in every situation. Goodness and right action were always expected, and to be in compliance with those moral codes of conduct was a given.

I was supposed to be perfect. Being bad and doing bad things were sins. As a good Catholic girl, I was supposed to *only* be good, and I tried. I agonized over it. I tried going to church, I tried praying, I tried confessing. I tried to be what they expected.

It's tough reliving the past, steeped in those old feelings while trying to deal with the present. Flashbacks, full of confusion and sadness, keep firing. Even with adult knowing, even having gained access to the shamanic process of recapitulation, the flashbacks still feel like bombs going off. I see how deeply confused I was as a child, how haunted by fear of the thing that could always get me, the thing that followed me around my entire life. It's time to kill it off, to confront it and tell it to go away.

Leave me alone, I don't want or need you anymore! I hate you! I don't want you in my life!

I finally dig my way up out of the tunnel where I've spent most of the day deeply, deeply lost. I reach for the phone and call Chuck, leaving him the message that I'm sinking, that I'm lost and I can't find my way back.

"Stay in the moment," he says, firmly, when he calls back. "Don't spend hours alone."

"I want to figure it all out, to stay there, to feel what it felt like back then, but I think I'm getting stuck," I say, as I feel one big tear roll down my cheek.

"Get out; change the routine. Do something to shift."

So darkly wrapped in the past and thinking that I will never even make it through the day if I stay at work, I immediately leave the studio and the heavy backward looking tunnel as well. I go out into sunlight, home to my children, into the real world where people want and need me for perfectly good reasons.

February 14, 2002

Apparently, I have too much solitude at the studio these days and not enough protection from my old obsessive behaviors because even being extremely busy is not enough to quell the intensity of the onslaughts from the past.

I go to a yoga class with the intention of breaking the stranglehold of this process that I have so willingly undertaken but find a bit too intrusive at times. I'm able to stay focused throughout the class, staying in the moment, successful at pushing aside anything that tries to intrude. But during the quiet *shavasana* at the end of class, I can't still the thoughts and images that come rushing over me, marching right back into my brain the moment I slow down.

Without physical activity to keep me safe, I am once again at the mercy of my most pressing intent: to do this recapitulation. Memories continually emerge from out of the depths, looking for a place to land. It's as if, having been loosened, they have nowhere else to go, except to perch like heavy clay figures on my shoulders. I'm able to shove them off long enough to chair a meeting at the artist's gallery in the evening.

The meeting goes well and I forget, for a little while, that I have other business to attend to. But as soon as I'm back in the car, on my way home, my shoulders hunch up and the heavy clay figures come thudding right back down on top of me again. Their solid weight digs into my already sore flesh and by the time I arrive home I feel bruised, inside and out.

It's been a hard day.

February 15, 2002

The impact of the memories is intense. I feel them physically as they come cruising out of nowhere, suddenly landing in my body and my awareness, encasing me in overwhelming fear, dread, and self-loathing. In spite of my desperate attempts to figure things out the memories lie muffled in mystery, surrounded by veils of confusion.

I'm having partial flashbacks of these things: shaving my pubic hair; being manipulated mentally, physically, emotionally; wanting to die, drowning in the lake, waking up in the garage with the car running; feelings of despair, just wanting it to end because then it would all be over. I remember sleepwalking, doing ritual masturbation, peeing in a jar in my bedroom.

These quick glimpses into my childhood are enough to activate fuller memories that come tumbling out of the muddle of confusion. Out of the darkness of the tunnel they come back to me in living color, so to speak, as I once again become a child reliving what happened.

And then I remember my pants around my legs, my abuser's hand moving between my legs, my body jerking. He's electrifying me. I don't understand it; some kind of jolt of electricity, lightning striking, my little body jerking and twisting—his power, I think. He enters me and continues the bone-jarring jolting, thrusting, pushing; my head aching as my teeth clatter uncontrollably. I, clenching jaws tightly shut, try to keep from hurting so much, to keep from disintegrating into just teeth and bits of bone scattered on the ground.

His stuff gets on me. He rubs it on my legs, between my buttocks. His stuff gets on me! He wipes me off afterwards with snow, like a baby. I feel sick, sick! His tobacco smell mixes with machine oil smell and I throw up and again he wipes me off with snow. I am no more than eight or nine years old in this memory.

I shave my pubic hair as it starts to grow so I won't be a big girl. Ouch! Cutting myself with scissors in the process, the uncomfortable feeling of the hair growing back, itching, trying to get rid of the short curly clippings. I store them in an envelope for a while. Later, I try flushing them down the toilet, ashamed of the dark pubic hair swirling in the bowl. No matter how many times I flush they won't disappear down the drain. I'm ashamed of breasts, covering, hiding, crouching and hunching so they wouldn't show, wanting to be a boy. I'm cutting my hair, keeping it boy short.

"Cut it short, like a boy!" I say when I go to the hairdresser. Boy, girl, boy, girl, boy, girl, boy, girl, boy, girl, boy.

My mother brings up the subject of the pubic hair in the toilet bowl at dinner one night. She doesn't actually call it pubic hair, but she quite pointedly looks me straight in the eye, as she addresses the entire family, gathered around the dinner table.

"Don't put that hair in the toilet anymore. It doesn't flush and it's bad for the septic."

"It's not m...m...mine," I stammer.

Thinking quickly, I say that it belongs to my little sister's curly-haired doll, that she cut the hair off her doll.

"I threw it in the toilet bowl thinking it would flush, but obviously I got it wrong."

My four-year-old sister looks confused when I say this, but I don't care.

"Uh-huh," my mother says blandly, not at all convinced. "Don't do it again."

When I got pregnant with my first child I was so afraid I would have a girl, fearful of what girls had to endure. My first child was a boy, but I was so happy when I did finally have a daughter. I could handle it. She would be different. She wouldn't be me. She would be her own strong person, and she definitely is.

I wonder if I would have been more like her, if I had been afforded a different life. Based on simply never meeting my abuser, who would I have become? Who would I be instead of me? I'm not allowed to stay pondering the what ifs—that which was not meant to be—because the memories jerk me back to the truth of who I was and what my life was like as a child, taking me back to that strange little girl.

As a teenager I walked and talked in my sleep. Sometimes I woke up far from my bed, in the room of a sibling, in the basement, in the garage, outside in the yard, muttering that I was looking for something, always looking for something I'd lost. I roamed the house at night looking for my shoes, my boots, my blanket. I was steered back to bed, night after night, by my parents who woke to find me poking around their room, looking behind furniture, under the bed they were sleeping in, bumping into closed doors, always searching for something.

I recapitulate. When I'm a teenager I masturbate, laying out objects in a row on the floor of my room. Dressing in a short skirt I masturbate with each object and then finally pee in a jar that I've placed at the end of the row. I must do everything in order. The ritual of laying out the objects and enacting the masturbation is as intensely focused and necessary as the strange game of Operation I played with my abuser's daughter, but this time I'm in charge. It's my game and only I play it.

I'm not allowed to hurry. I must do it properly, counting the amount of time I masturbate with each object so that none of them is used for even a second longer or shorter than the next. And even though I long for the relief of peeing, even though I see the jar at the end of the long line of objects, I'm not allowed to jump ahead to use it. I must follow the rules I have prescribed.

The relief of completing the ritual and finally peeing in the jar lasts me for months, until the tension builds up again and I must do it again. I store the pee in my closet, almost tenderly and lovingly wrapping the urine-warmed jar in a piece of clothing. I keep it tucked away until it goes cold and then I sneak it to the toilet and dump it out.

I feel something being pulled out of me when I do this ritual. When I masturbate and sit on the mouth of the jar something is happening to me physically, though I don't know what it is or how to explain it. And in saving the pee and then throwing it out later, something else is released, something unseen that is stuck there. These are the only ways I can get them out of me.

The objects I lay out to masturbate with range from pencils and rulers, to twine, shoestrings, belts and scarves, wooden blocks, and some sticks, about a dozen items in all. I lock my door, methodically lay these items out in a row, and in a trancelike, altered state, in some other world, I enact this secret game. When I'm done I pack the objects away in my closet with the jar of pee, change into blue jeans and literally shake myself back into the good Catholic girl, the big sister, the quiet one. I unlock my door, walk down the stairs, and go back to being what is expected.

Some of the memories, like this one, come with sexual arousal and I imagine it must be built into the memory. Deep shame is also built into each memory, riding in on its moment of clarity, along with feelings of helplessness, dread, powerlessness, and the sense of imminent loss of control.

A shroud of doom falls over me when I hear my abuser's voice commanding me at the beginning of each abusive episode and it doesn't lift until I hear it again at the end, when he's done with me, when he shouts at me.

"Now Git! Git!" Like a rabid dog barking, he angrily and viciously snarls at me to get out of his sight.

I remember reading *I Never Promised You a Rose Garden* by Joanne Greenberg when I was a young teenager. This story of a young girl who spends time in a mental institution struck a note of resonance. I knew how fragile my own hold on sanity really was. I felt that if I let go, even the tiniest bit, I would end up like her. If I even uttered a word, my world and everything in it would crumble. My mental state would shatter and I would go tumbling into the abyss, and into the deeper oblivion I knew existed at the bottom of that abyss. I knew that if that happened, I would be stuck in a worse state of confusion than the one I normally existed in. I knew that mental shattering, as in that girl's story, only led to another, deeper kind of numbness from which it would be impossible to emerge. It was safer to remain silent; to never speak, to bear the tension of whatever it was that bothered me.

I knew that something was direly wrong with me personally. I wasn't normal, but I just could never get a handle on why I was so miserable, I just was. And although I kept tight control over my feelings, emotions, thoughts, and the inexplicable misery that permeated my life, there were those nights of sleepwalking that I could not control. Feeling the cold dew on the lawn under my bare feet had awoken me more times than I like to recall. Finding myself standing on the front lawn looking up at the stars, I'd wonder why I was so crazy.

One night, when I was a teenager, something else happened. Perhaps my unconscious was setting me up to confront something, in a way I would not have consciously planned. I allow myself to go fully into a memory that has been emerging.

I'm fifteen or sixteen and find myself sitting in my father's little Volkswagen beetle, parked in the closed garage. I don't know how I got here. It's the middle of the night, snowing heavily, and I think of listening to the radio with the idea that school might be canceled in the morning. I turn the key in the ignition, thinking that if I listen to the radio with the car off I could run the battery down and then my father would be angry.

As I turn the key, I'm aware of a vague thought that I could end it all. I could make it stop. It would be over, though what it is I want to stop I'm not aware of—I just know I'm miserable all the time. I don't know how long I sit; I have no sense of time passing. One minute I'm listening to the *Beatles* singing on the radio and the next my father is pulling me out of the car, grabbing my arm, hurting me, dragging me out into the snow, into the cold air, standing there all wobbly in his pajamas and bare feet, screaming at me.

"What are you doing! What are you doing!"

I barely hear what he's saying. The only thing I can hear is a loud zinging sound, the vibrating springs of the garage door that he's just flung open.

"Go to bed! Go to bed! Just go to bed!" Yelling, he shoves me into the house.

At the time, I interpreted his anger as utter disgust, but I realize now how frightened he must have been. The incident was never spoken of, not in *any* sense. No questions were asked, no conversation around whether or not it was an accident or intentional, whether I was just stupid or if I have ulterior motives. I didn't have an answer myself and whenever I recalled this incident it was with great embarrassment and shame. But as I recapitulate, and in light of what I know about my childhood now, I clearly remember the underlying intent was to end my miserable existence. The idea emerged as if spoken outside of myself, almost as if an outside voice was suggesting it to me, or perhaps it was my own true voice, trying to alert me to the truth. The fact that my life didn't end that night is a sure sign that I had other things ahead of me, that it was not my time to die.

I remember standing in the snow, shaking and lightheaded, while my father's anger and disappointment seethed out into the cold night air and hung there suspended between us, heavy blocks of ice forming on his words, sealing them in. I turned from him and looked up into the silent dark night, the falling snow hitting my face, quite a few inches on the ground, thinking that at least there won't be school tomorrow.

My father was on the mental health board, shouldn't he have been aware? The sleepwalking, could he not have consulted someone? He too kept everything hidden. I took my cue from him, as closed as my mother. Their silence warning me: *You don't talk about anything. Keep everything to yourself, and don't ever let people know there's anything wrong with you.*

Another memory is strong now, of the swim in the lake, originally sparked by the dream I had in early November when I dreamed that I was swimming in a lake with my new best friend and her brothers. As the dream progressed the water got rough, with strong winds blowing up whitecaps. I was far from shore and paused over a spot to look down into the depths of the lake. "Oh, yes, this is the spot where I drowned!" I said.

Ever since that dream, I've felt the stirrings of a memory beginning to emerge from my unconscious, as if it's been calling to me from the bottom of that lake all these years, as if the experience did indeed lay drowned there, calling and calling, until I was ready to go back there and relive it. I'm ready now.

I remember the long bike ride, probably fifty miles that day, with two friends, my best friend and another girl. We were teenagers, about seventeen years old. It was August, I believe. My best friend became my best friend after she moved into the neighborhood when I was nine. She offered respite from my abuser's daughter and the strange games I played with her. This new best friend was different in every way, and so I too became different when I was with her. It was light in her world, the opposite of the darkness that I was forced to enter in the world of my abuser and his daughter.

On that day in August, the three of us set out early in the morning, off on an adventure, directionless and free, intending only to see where we might end up. Traveling through the rolling mountains of the countryside over remote dirt roads, we stopped at country stores to buy snacks and drinks, winding our way southward until we realized we were fairly near the cabin on a lake owned by my best friend's family. When we arrived we found the cabin locked, closed up tight, no one using it in the middle of the week, but we really only wanted to swim in the lake after our long, hot bike ride.

A storm was brewing, wind whipping our hair into our faces; the water churning dark green, boiling and white-capped; the blue sky suddenly hidden by low dark clouds; the trees bending from the gusts of wind. But all we wanted to do was jump into the water. We took off our clothes and, naked, leaped in from the dock, hooting and hollering as we hit the cool water. The other girl immediately got out, scrambling back up onto the dock, while my best friend and I swam out a bit. We were both strong swimmers, but suddenly we were fighting the wind and the choppy waves and we called to each other that we should go back.

I struggled. Fatigued after the long bike ride, I no longer had enough strength or energy to swim back to shore. Exhaustion overtook and I dipped under the water, once, twice, a third time. Out of the corner of my eye I saw my best friend swimming, her long arms lifting out of the water in struggling stroke after struggling stroke as she made her way toward the dock.

All of a sudden the waves were too big, the water too rough, and it was beginning to rain. I could no longer hold my head above the surface. A wave came along and washed over me and I went under the water, thinking that I would go down for a while and rest. I let myself relax in the water—calmer down there than on the surface, no hint of a storm. After a while, I noticed that I stopped needing to hold my breath. I was floating in a new world where breathing wasn't necessary. Thrilled by this discovery I felt myself go with the sensation and, as I did, all connection to life above the surface of the lake disappeared. In an instant, every action of my life, everything I had done, right or wrong, passed by me, and I had no sense of needing it anymore. It didn't matter. It all floated away into the lake, and I felt perfectly safe.

I was deep in the water now, with the most incredible peacefulness enveloping me, carrying me even deeper. I looked down at my body and saw myself floating in the yellowish light that surrounded me; my nakedness luminously white. I no longer felt the weight of my physical body. And then, from a perspective outside my body, I looked over and saw my body floating, hanging suspended in a bubble of strangely glowing light.

I sensed that I could stay there forever, that everything could be over now. I was surprised that I felt no fear, no pain, but only a deep sense of peace. Again I noticed that I wasn't holding my breath or struggling to breathe. I simply did not need to breathe. I was like a mermaid, floating in the light, deciding if I should stay.

There was a definite decision to be made. I knew this, and more than anything I wanted to stay. The incredible peacefulness was like nothing I had ever experienced, so easily acceptable. But then a voice spoke to me; a compassionate voice filled with such loving kindness, as if it knew that it must disturb my beautiful, peaceful state of grace.

"Not yet, not yet," it said very gently.

I heard the voice very clearly and knew it was speaking the truth, that I had to go back, that I had to go back and finish the journey. It wasn't time for my life to be over. I knew this, and yet it was so enticingly peaceful and loving in the water. I knew I'd be perfectly contented to float there forever, but I also knew I had other things to do.

With a tremendous sense of regret at having to leave, but knowing that it wasn't right to stay, I felt myself being propelled upward. Without doing anything, as if in a dream, I sped back up through the dark water. I crashed through the surface of the lake, coughing and vomiting, as a huge wave smacked me in the face. I was back in my body, heavy again, so heavy, though I was floating in water and though I weighed barely a hundred pounds. Struggling now to find breath, I turned my face away from the waves, fighting to keep my head above the water. I heard my best friend frantically calling my name. I saw the other girl pacing back and forth on the dock and then I heard her shout and saw her pointing in my direction.

"There she is, there she is!"

"Are you okay? Are you okay? You scared me!" I heard my best friend shouting, near me now, as she too struggled to stay afloat in the rough water.

I couldn't speak. I only had the strength to nod. I barely had enough energy to swim to the dock—it took all my effort. It took great concentration to pull that heavy body out of the water and plop onto the dock. Shaking with exhaustion, coughing and gasping for air, I couldn't believe how heavy it was, like a dead weight.

I was stunned, probably in shock, and even so I was embarrassed, embarrassed to be seen like that. Thankful for the cover of pouring rain, I crawled on my hands and knees along the dock, barely pausing for a second. I couldn't feel my body, but I finally stumbled upright, trying to get back into familiar feelings, shifting immediately into survivor mode, pretending that nothing was wrong, saying that everything was okay, I was fine, but I'm certain the truth was plain to see.

Lurching like a drunkard, I headed toward the boathouse where we had left our clothes. Forcing my body to move, I put one leg in front of the other.

"Just do it! Just walk, breath, you can do it," I urged myself, the need to be in control at all times overtaking the frightened girl inside.

The girls told me that I had disappeared, that they both stood on the dock looking for me, my best friend jumping back in when she realized that I was not right behind her.

Barely in my body and barely able to speak, I somehow communicated that I was all right. My lungs would not fill with air, as if the wind had been knocked out of me, though inside I was silently screaming that something happened down there.

"Something happened! I drowned, I think I drowned," I wanted to say, but no words to that affect came out.

Drying off as well as we could with our summer clothes, we pulled them on and sat on an old picnic table in the boathouse. By now the storm was in full swing and I was shaking uncontrollably. My best friend found a dusty, torn sail lying in a heap of old boating equipment and even though I thought about the spiders and bugs crawling inside it, I let her wrap it around my shoulders and hold me while I shook. I still could not talk. We stayed like that, the other girl nervously staring at us, frightened, while the storm raged around us, growing increasingly intense.

Lightning struck the water, thunder clapped, tree branches fell to the ground, waves flew out of the lake threatening to wash over us as the aged boathouse creaked and groaned under the pounding rain and wind. I sat there cloaked in the experience of the underwater world, the beauty of it, trying to hold onto the peacefulness I had experienced. But at the same time, the shock of returning to life overpowered me, as I struggled to re-inhabit my body and quell its shivering, each breath a painful, shuddering gasp for air. Not wanting to reveal the truth of my condition, either my physical or mental state, and both unwilling and unable to talk about what had happened to me, I was the first to suggest that we head back as the storm subsided.

We started the long ride, intending to take a more direct though busier route back, but after a few miles we were so exhausted we called for a ride, doing something we had promised we would never do: wimp out. My best friend's father came to get us in the family station wagon, big enough to carry our three bikes and us. When we described the long mountainous roads we'd ridden that day, he exclaimed in amazement.

"That's at least fifty miles, probably more!"

He assumed we'd been on our bikes during the storm. With trees downed and the power knocked out, he couldn't believe we'd survived out in the open. We laughed at that, but then revealed, to his great relief, that we'd actually been safe in the boathouse through the worst of the storm. We didn't reveal, however, that we'd gone into the lake.

The three of us never talked of that day. Even I, who had experienced that profound event in the water kept it to myself. I eventually forgot about it, too traumatic to assimilate, blocking both the beauty and terror of that near-death experience from memory.

February 16, 2002

So many memories of a mixed up little girl are emerging now that I'm often not aware of where I am, what world I'm in, the dividing line between the past and the present blurred now.

As I'm driving I repeatedly, absentmindedly, put the blinker on. I'm not aware of doing this, but then I notice that it's on because all of a sudden I tune into reality and hear it ticking away. So I turn it off and then, a few minutes later, I find it on again, with no recollection of having turned it on.

This morning, I did a scary thing while coming back from the hardware store across the river. Just after I'd driven over the bridge and was heading down the arrow-straight road that leads away from the river, I saw the stoplight ahead turn red and I automatically stopped. Then I saw the light change to green, but it seemed so far away—at the end of a long tunnel. It took me a minute to realize that I'd stopped dead in the middle of the long stretch of straight road, a quarter of a mile from the light! Stunned by my lack of attention, and more than a little freaked out, I checked in the rear view mirror and noted, with a sigh of relief, that no traffic was backed up behind me. No one was leaning on their horn, though I noticed one or two cars coming from the opposite direction, the drivers peering at me strangely as they passed. I quickly accelerated, realizing that my perception was off, *way off.*

When I'd seen the light turn red I was so lost in the past, being raped, that I completely lost track of where I was and what I was doing. I sat in the middle of that empty road gazing down a long tunnel, where I could see the light and react as it changed, but far from present in this world, not aware that I was in the car and driving. Totally gone, immersed in that other world, I'd sat there with my hands gripping the wheel, my mouth hanging open, staring straight ahead, as I experienced something that took place almost fifty years ago. My unconscious had already been sending warnings, with the absentminded blinkering, signaling that I was about to enter another world; a warning to watch out, crazy driver behind the wheel. She's about to drive right into another reality!

As I resumed driving, I forced myself to focus on staying present, keeping my eyes alert to what was around me, remembering the old driving instruction to never let your eyes rest on any object for more than two seconds. The whole incident was extremely disconcerting, though I couldn't help but laugh my head off as I sped away from my standstill position in the middle of the road, trying to make it through the light before it turned red again.

I note the memories now emerging, hoping that by writing them down I'll release their fixation, freeing my awareness to be more attentive. This is what was emerging while I was driving that so took my attention: my abuser was stabbing me, causing me to bleed. At least that's what I thought was happening. He was, in fact, raping me. I thought he was stabbing me with a knife he kept in his pocket.

As I write this down a memory emerges of my mother confronting me because she finds a spot of blood on my pajama pants.

"What's this?" she asks bluntly, in her usual manner.

"I don't know," I say, and it's the truth because I don't know where the blood came from.

She holds the pajama pants out so I can see that there is one perfectly round drop of red blood, the size of a dime, in the crotch of my white summer pajamas. I don't have a clue as to how it got there. Did I see it and try to hide it among the dirty laundry, hoping it wouldn't be noticed? I don't know for sure, except that she found it in the laundry tub when she was doing the laundry. She's standing in the downstairs half-bath, trying to get the bloodstain out, rubbing the fabric under cold water when she calls to me.

I'm immediately afraid that I've done something wrong and the sight of the blood frightens me. The idea that it came out of me is disgusting and I wonder if my abuser's daughter and her foster sister where right all those years ago, when they told me I would have blood coming out of that place between my legs.

I'm ten years old when my mother shows me the blood on my pants. I clearly remember those pajamas, how old I was when I wore them. I was still small, not yet a teenager, and in my memory I didn't get my period until I was turning twelve, but maybe I got it when I was ten. I do remember that when I did get my period for the first time I denied it, vaguely thinking the blood was because of what he did to me, the two worlds momentarily overlapping, offering logical explanations for things I could not fully comprehend.

I go over the pubic hair memory again. I review how I cut it off with scissors and then shaved it with my father's razor because I needed to look and be like a little girl again, though I'm not clear why this was so important. I suspect it had something to do with being raped.

I go through the memory of the ritual masturbation process again too and I begin to see how it's connected to the games I played with my abuser's daughter, the methodical laying out of objects, the sticks, the need for everything to be controlled. I was acting out what was happening to me in another world, though I had no recollection of that world in my everyday life. In my own bedroom I could not recall what happened in the world of my abuser and his daughter, but a part of me was desperately trying to figure it out.

I begin to fathom how interconnected everything was. I see that this ritual transpired—not because I developed some strange masturbating habits out of thin air or because I was bad, as I always suspected—but because of what was happening to me in another reality. I thought I had an evil side, a deviant personality, kept hidden and controlled most of the time, though now I see that I was actually more confused than I ever suspected. I see that I wasn't at all conscious of the abuse, though it made itself known in the most curious of obsessive behaviors, manifesting in this masturbatory act, as I sought relief, while subconsciously I was searching for some explanation, some means of assimilating the two worlds I lived in.

I go through the memory of cutting my hair again, pixie short, boyish, not wanting to be pretty, while at the same time wanting to be beautiful, inside and out. Inside I felt bad, ugly, because I was ashamed, dirty, sinful, lost and confused. On the outside, I didn't want to draw attention to myself, didn't want *that* kind of attention, though I longed to be beautiful, pretty and easy going, unafraid. I longed to be so carefree that nothing bothered me.

I remember again that my abuser made me achieve orgasm and that I didn't understand what it was. I thought it was some kind of shock he was giving me, the jerking and jolting intensity of it like an electrical charge. I thought he was stabbing me with something, a knife, and electrocuting me somehow. I had no idea about any of it, no knowledge of sex, sexual arousal or sexual feelings, and certainly not of orgasm.

I've been shaking and cold all week. My stomach aches, my eyes hurt, my neck is stiff and all I want to do is roll up into a ball, pull the covers over my head, and be alone. As the memories come with their somatic experiences, I fight the urge to retreat into the comfort of this old habit and instead make myself do things to forget. I plan my day around forgetting. Keeping busy, I clean the studio, do my taxes, and concentrate on learning how to live in the moment, so I don't have any more of those freaky driving episodes and so I don't crawl into bed and hide.

I've succeeded in staying present through most of the day, but now, as the night approaches, so does he. My abuser comes crawling into bed with me. I hear the sound of his breathing, smell his smell, see his staring eyes, feel his hurtful hands. His face looms large and real, right in front of me.

February 19, 2002

I meet with Chuck and tell him about what's been happening lately, about the memories that are emerging and the clarity I'm getting around the duration and severity of the abuse. I have no illusions, but it's too hard to fully take in. I'm full of shame, feeling like a bad person; the badness of the little girl I once felt myself to be quite palpable and real. I cannot escape it.

Chuck listens quietly as I tell him about the ritual masturbation, the suicide attempt, the near drowning, nodding and letting me talk, as I stumble through what I've recalled.

I realize how angry I am at the woman who was my mother. When she informed me of the 'facts of life,' as they were called, she slipped a small pink booklet under my closed door one day, rather than actually talking to me. As I read it, I couldn't quite figure out what it was referring to. It was so vaguely worded, not about getting a period—that was pretty clear—but about sexual intercourse. It was difficult to understand the insinuations made through metaphor, with no pictures and no identifying terms, like penis and vagina.

I found that little booklet totally incomprehensible. I'd take it out again and again, reading it from cover to cover, trying to make sense of it. It was tiny, could fit into the palm of my hand and was only about fifteen pages in all; life's mysteries explained in so few words, it floored me.

"There must be more than just this," I thought, while at the same time I already knew everything there was to know about sex, though I didn't know how I knew, I just did. But what I knew was nowhere to be found in that little pink book.

"Why all this secrecy? Why can't anyone be straight?"

The little pink booklet left me wondering if there was something I was missing after all. Even though I was more confused than ever, there was no way I could ask my mother. A little while after she'd slipped that pink booklet under my door she left a box of Kotex pads in my bedroom, accompanying it with a strange belt-like contraption. I had to figure out how to wear it following the page of instructions that came with it.

I thought it was such a crock of shit that girls had to go through all of this, because I knew boys got off easy. I was jealous of my brothers. They didn't have to deal with blood pouring out between their legs for several days each month. I couldn't imagine them being able to handle such a thing, but I knew I could. *I could handle anything.*

February 20, 2002

The memories fall into place, a picture of a life emerging, *my life*, as I begin to understand just what happened to me as a child, how I dealt with it, and where it took me as I matured.

I must have felt safe at one time with the man who abused me, as a very young child just out of infancy perhaps, safe enough to trust him. What happened with him, however, took place in such a different world from the one I lived in with my family. When I go back into the memory of being in the woods with him by the stream, I experience profound confusion. Something isn't right about what's happening to me there. My abuser's pokey finger is painful, but there are other events that suggest normality—the giggling of his daughter and my struggle to figure out if it's fun or not—combined with a feeling of familiarity, of having been around the two of them in similar situations.

In the long run, those experiences taught me never to trust anyone; to keep everything tucked deeply inside, protecting my innocence by never letting anyone in, never letting anyone get too close. I made so many pacts with myself, vowing to never ask for help, to go it alone. I was so extremely sensitive that being turned down just once—another person not living up to my expectations just once—was devastating enough that I closed down for good. I can feel now how I used to shut myself in; closing a door to the outside world and vowing to never let that part of me get hurt again, to never expose myself in that way again.

I found the pact of marriage a safe haven, doable, because I had already vowed—long before I was even out of elementary school—to never reveal my true self because of fears of being hurt, rejected, abandoned, or abused. I've been able to maneuver through all of my relationships by maintaining my strict inner pacts, reminding myself of them when necessary, reasserting their valued presence, drawing on their availability. These pacts were old friends I could count on when there was nothing else to rely on. But I've discovered that playing it safe, closing off my feeling self, and being in control, aren't enough. Keeping myself hidden and protected isn't fulfilling, though I have no idea what it means to be truly fulfilled. I just know that there has to be more to life.

I see Chuck's kind face in front of me as I write these words, as I recapitulate the decisions made by my child self, and as I struggle to figure out why I was the way I was.

"Well, you were abused, that's why," I hear him saying, in response to my puzzlement. And yes, that's the truth, the painful explanation that is now so apparent. But even those truthful words can't penetrate all those solidly closed doors.

I've been reading about the grooming process, how sexual predators groom their victims over time and I understand how I was groomed by my abuser, over many, many years, one step at a time.

Early on, he would touch me, but I mostly see him watching, observing, and directing in those early memories, as he instructed his daughter and I to do things to each other. Maybe he got more physically involved when he thought I was sufficiently groomed. I just don't have clarity on the progression of the abuse, though it's obvious that at some point he began to get more aggressive, if my memories are anything to go on.

When I first began dating the boyfriend who was twenty years older, I saw him as some kind of savior. I felt liberated by him from the blackness of the past to more fully live, but really it was just an opportunity for something from my unconscious to come to light. I fell right back into an old pattern, the grooming of the adult me almost as easy as the grooming of the child me had been, maybe more so, because I was so willing and offered almost no resistance. This was followed by a deeply cutting rejection that thoroughly devastated me at the time, as my vulnerable self retreated, as it had always done in childhood, in actuality, repeating yet another old dynamic. A deeply numbing depression appeared like an old friend at that time, come to wrap me up and take me back into the familiar tunnel of my childhood where I could feel safe again.

That tunnel was never far away. But what happened out in the world, in my relationships, and how I reacted to the vicissitudes in life, suggested that there was always something else that preceded the retreat to the tunnel, though it was strictly blocked from memory—what I am only now making sense of—a childhood of sexual abuse. I now understand my relationship with this older man as familiar territory. I immediately fell back into the patterns that had once played so strangely in my childhood. Perhaps it was an attempt on the part of my psyche to wake me up, as Chuck would say, but at the time I just wasn't ready. It would take until now for me to awaken to the fact that I was indeed repeating old behaviors, and be ready to find out where they had originated from and why I still needed them.

I've been reading that deviant behavior isn't curable but only controllable. It makes me wonder—am I not curable either? Am I only salvageable in some ways, never to be fully healed? I want to be healed, I want to be whole, I want to be fulfilled in this life; it's all I've ever yearned for. Will I ever be able to trust, love, accept and give fully, both physically and emotionally? Will I ever feel complete and at peace, as I so yearn to be?

I don't understand why I can't feel sorry for myself as I go through this process, even a little bit empathetic, but I just don't have any feelings when I speak about the memories. No emotions arise whatsoever when I go into the memories in EMDR. I take in all the details and my body acts out, replays what happened in the past as I twist and turn, kick, clench, tremble, gag, and scrunch into a ball. I feel pain in my physical body but otherwise I'm without emotional response when I relate the memories to Chuck. Each time he stops the EMDR machine and asks me what's happening, I pull myself out of the intensity of the past and speak in a deadpan monotone without a hint of emotion. When I hear my voice I note that I'm like an observer, a narrator; distant, detached and cool as a cucumber. It's almost as if someone else is speaking. And then, in embarrassment almost, I mention that I can't emotionally *feel* anything. Perhaps it's a symptom of dissociation or that I just haven't reached the deeper emotional component yet.

I do understand that, as a child, I wasn't able to fully trust or depend on another person, or feel that anyone was truly there for me. I had only myself to depend on. As a result, I needed to remain strong and detached, invulnerable, to protect the vulnerable child self who hid inside the tunnel. If I started to feel, who would protect me then? I always needed to be hard on myself and perhaps I'm still being too hard on myself. Perhaps I just won't let myself feel anything because I don't believe I'm deserving of compassion or empathy.

I never identified myself as having low self-esteem because I never understood what it was, nor would I have applied a label or drawn attention to myself by declaring that I was one way or another. With little awareness of myself and no idea of how to assess myself, I had no inkling if I was intelligent, no knowledge of my virtues, no sense of self-worth. Such things were totally inaccessible to me, and so I never entertained any positive feelings about myself. I feared the wrath of a punitive God and was equally afraid of unleashing the anger of the nuns and my mother by bringing attention to myself in any way—a grave sin indeed. Now, however, it's clear that I suffered from extremely low self-esteem.

I didn't like other people complimenting me or noticing me. Any direct look or attention sent me reeling into a self-immolation of sorts, set afire by a hot blush rising up my entire body until my face burned feverishly red. Once, a girl in high school asked me why I wasn't going to the prom.

"A cute, petite girl like you?"

"Oh, no," I said, immediately embarrassed, blushing hotly.

"You would look so cute all dolled-up in a beautiful dress."

"No, no, I wouldn't," I protested, growing more embarrassed, beginning to sweat, unable to breathe.

"You could do your hair in curls, you'd look like a little angel."

"No," I still insisted, shaking my head. "No."

"Okay you wouldn't," she said, angrily, finally giving up. "Jeez! What's a matter with you?"

At other times, other girls, spreading rumors that boys liked me and thought I was pretty, sent me deeper into denial.

"No, I'm not; I'm not pretty."

"I'm not cute, no, no, no."

But I could accept the same kinds of comments coming from teachers, which I seemed to get a lot of in those days, from both male and female teachers. The compliments were never about my schoolwork, which rarely warranted any attention, except my poetry and writing, or my presence in the art rooms where I was genuinely appreciated.

When my father would return from parent's night at school, from meeting our teachers, I would ask what they had to say about me.

"They said I have a beautiful daughter!" he would say each year, smiling broadly.

He was clearly pleased with that response, though it angered me no end, the idea that beauty was all that mattered for a girl. Though, I admit, I graciously accepted the compliments I received from those teachers—with a smile—some part of me craving recognition. I had a German language teacher who, each day, as I sat at my desk, would say something to me, without fail.

"You look lovely today, *Fräulein*! That's a nice dress, nice hairdo, etc," he'd say, while I stumbled through his class, barely passing, speechless when it came time to go into the back room with him for the oral exams each semester.

"Well, only one of you failed the oral part of the exam. Let's hope you do better on the written test," I remember him boldly stating one day, stepping into the classroom where we all sat nervously awaiting the results of the just-completed oral exam. My face burned hot and red as I sweated in my pretty outfit, crossing my legs tightly, scrunching down as far as I could in my seat, trying to disappear. Of course I didn't have to hide, everyone knew it was me, since I never opened my mouth in class if I didn't have to. I was always the one failure, though the other students were always gentle with me afterwards, saying how hard the oral test had been, yet again.

I took four years of high school German and by the time I was a senior I slept with my German language book under my pillow, hoping it might seep into my brain while I slept. I began dreaming in German, night after night, waking up with German words in my head, the taste of them on my tongue, for I was fluent in my dreams. I attempted reading Goethe's *Faust*, seeking something in the original language that I found lacking in translation. My years of high school German, no matter how stumbling and inept, helped me immensely when I later moved to Sweden and learned to speak Swedish fluently, in a matter of months.

I go into a memory in the girl's locker room at school. I'm back in high school again, changing out of my blue gym suit in the last section of the rows of lockers after a gym class. I'm the only one with a locker in this section, no one else is near me and I like it that way. A girl peeks around the corner. I'm aware of her looking at me, a cheerleader, but I act as if I don't notice.

"I didn't even know anyone was back there," I hear her say to a few other girls.

"Who is it?" someone asks. I hear the cheerleader say my name. I didn't even think she knew who I was.

"Don't you think she's cute?" I hear her ask the other girls.

"Oh God, yes!" I hear someone say.

"And the clothes, she wears such nice clothes."

"So quiet."

"But she's really nice."

"And she's such a good artist!"

I finish dressing and then I have to walk past them, embarrassed now, embarrassed that I overheard them, embarrassed at what they said. I have to walk out and see them all combing their hair before the big mirror, fixing their makeup, girls who are able to look at themselves like that, admiringly, able to primp so confidently in front of others, not embarrassed to be attractive. I slip past, stiffly, acting as if I haven't heard them, acknowledging them, the popular girls, in my usual shy way with a quick hello and a smile. They smile at me in return, say hello, and I feel a great sense of relief as I pass by, much lighter in my heart. I leave feeling that they spoke truthfully about me, offering me a small tidbit of kindness to hold onto and mull over.

As I left the locker room that day, I admired the ability of those girls to preen in front of the mirror, to like or dismiss their looks in front of all those other girls. Perhaps a quick glance to see if my slip was showing, or to make sure I didn't have anything on my face, was all I could ever muster; a quick I-don't-care look. But really it was my fear of the old doctrine that kept me from looking at myself too closely: *the voice that said it was sinful to admire the self, in any way, especially in front of others—to show off.* This doctrine has ruled my entire life, though now I see this inability to acknowledge my own looks as a deep lack of self-esteem, including the fact that I could not bear to look at the fragile girl I really was, fearful of what she might tell me if I peered too closely into her eyes.

Even though I could blame the old voices of my upbringing, there was another reason I knew it was folly to admire my looks. I knew that things could happen to take good feelings away. It wasn't safe to feel too good about yourself because, suddenly and unexpectedly, in the most impersonal manner, everything could shatter, leaving you wallowing in bottomless emptiness where even good looks couldn't save you.

February 21, 2002

I dream that I'm stepping into and pulling on a pair of men's baggy khaki pants. At first, I can't find the belt and the pants are slipping off. Finally I discover it hanging off the back of the pants, a cloth belt with a shiny buckle. I grab it, push it through the belt loops and buckle it in front. I'm preparing to go on a long bike ride, which I know I'll finish. I'm certain of this, though not many people finish the ride because it's a long and strenuous journey, which only the fittest and most determined complete.

Suddenly I'm sitting at a desk in a classroom. The bike ride has been successfully completed, as previously determined. A little girl is sitting under the desk, between my legs, staring at my belt buckle, peering into it, looking at her reflection. There's something familiar about that belt buckle; it seems significant.

I wonder at the meaning of the shiny belt buckle, but questions of trust and reliance pulse through me more insistently, and the little girl under the desk bothers me too. Once again I feel utterly alone and I wake up knowing that I have only myself to trust and rely on. With this dream the anxiety kicks back in, revving up after a few days of relative calm.

I wonder why my old boyfriend had made me feel so safe. At almost fifty years old, he had a lot of practiced charm, but he was also well-versed in a kind of mature romance that I hadn't experienced before. He held me a lot, was physically attentive with a lot of touching and hugging. I seemed to need it. In fact, I craved it.

Although I'd been married before I met him and had had a good, physically connected relationship with my first husband, I desperately wanted to be held and touched by this man. It was almost as if he had some magnetic attraction because I was strangely and intensely drawn to him and his style of intimacy. I let myself go to him. He would hold me in his big arms and I would feel completely safe, but then, as soon as he deceived me, his embrace was no longer safe. His arms were no longer protective, or loving, after they suddenly and rather cruelly, I felt, dropped me.

I turned my anger on myself, however, for my stupidity in falling for him, for allowing myself to be so naively deceived, believing we had a monogamous relationship. At the time, I felt that my innocence, so trustingly exposed and so purely open to partnering with him, had been taken for granted, deeply violated, and left abandoned.

As I recapitulate my feelings for this man the innocent child self creeps out, still wanting to be held in a tender embrace, asking me to once again feel what it felt like. That childlike innocence wants to crawl up onto my lap. It wants to be held by loving arms; wants to be told that it's okay, that everything is okay. It wants to feel safe. That innocence asks to be reckoned with, re-awoken after all these years by these memories of having once been in the world, of having once lived, even if only briefly.

I feel that innocence again so strongly and yet I know that, in actuality, I can't do what it asks. It's too hard. I can only continue to do as I've always done and staunchly protect myself by keeping in all my feelings and blocking out anything that might interfere with my need to remain strictly in control. I must keep everything in balance, as I've always done. I'll continue to guard it in the old way, the way that's always worked so well, by pushing it down and keeping it down. I know it's inside me, safe under my terms, and it has to stay that way because I just can't make it feel safe any other way. I just can't love that part of myself either; it's impossible. It's too hard.

Perhaps I hate myself too much. Perhaps I don't think I deserve to feel safe or to be innocent, though I would not say the same thing about my own children. Their innocence is so readily acceptable to me, their safety paramount. They need my love, they deserve to feel safe in my arms, and when I hold them and tell them they're safe, calming their fears, I believe it for them, because I know I will never let them down. I will never reject them or their innocence, but I can't offer the same kind of security to myself.

I feel only fearful as I think about releasing my innocent self into the world. I have a staunchly guarding sentinel inside me, constantly standing at attention, keeping things in and keeping things out. I reject what comes from outside because I fear rejection above all else, better to keep everything as is. And though I may be rejecting my own innocence in the process, I know it's better to stay closed off and let the status quo prevail: don't let anyone in, and don't even dare flirt with the danger of letting the innocent self out. It's too painful. I fear the pain of rejection more than I fear loneliness and a loveless life. Love doesn't last anyway; I already know that.

I'm better at taking care of others than I am at taking care of my own needs; I see that now. I essentially don't believe that I matter as much, so I turn toward others and away from myself. I've also already proven to myself, over and over again, that there's no one else to trust, except myself. And yet the thought of being totally alone in the world is frightening; anxiety builds just thinking about it.

In truth, I don't want to be alone, and even though I know that people care about me, I still don't think I can ask for anything from them, not just because I've always done it that way, but because I don't trust that my requests will be granted. Perhaps I also fear that my requests will be misunderstood, or that I'll owe something in return and even that debt might be misconstrued and I'll just get hurt again. Perhaps this is why I'm so afraid to reveal that I have worries and anxiety; why I'm so afraid to acknowledge that I actually have feelings; why I can't admit that I'm hurting, that everything really isn't okay. I'm always saying I'm fine and I'm great, in spite of the truth, which is the complete opposite of that.

I also think this is why my own sense of responsibility toward others is so great. I find it very hard to disappoint. I just cannot let others down, even if I must go into personal crisis and debt to uphold their trust. I want people to be able to rely on me, so they won't have to suffer the disappointments that have been so prevalent in my own life, the disappointments that come from not being able to rely on others. I find it very hard to say no.

It wasn't my fault! It wasn't my fault! It wasn't my fault! It wasn't my fault! It wasn't my fault! It wasn't my fault! It wasn't my fault!

The abuse is not my fault; I get that. But why is there that deep-seated feeling that I *am* at fault; that no matter how often I'm told that it's not my fault, I still feel so bad about it? I can intellectualize and rationalize about it until the cows come home: that I was a child; that I was manipulated and groomed; that no matter what I did or said it would happen anyway because I had no power to stop it; that I was not really involved, but merely available.

I think the fact that I was not involved is at the root of solving this problem of not being at fault. Not only was I not involved in the planning; I was not even involved in the execution. I was merely a thing, an object, and deep down I knew I didn't matter and I still don't matter. My feelings don't and never did matter. The pain inflicted on my physical body and my emotional and mental health didn't matter. No one cared about me, no one helped me, no one protected me. I was absolutely alone when I entered my abuser's world and when I left it again too, because nothing about *me* mattered, either when I was with him or when I left his world and went back to being normal. So even knowing that it was not my fault doesn't really matter. *I don't matter.*

I don't exist the minute I enter my abuser's world. As I recapitulate stepping into his world the personal is buried, hidden, kept from him. It has to disappear in order to be protected, in order for me to survive. I've learned this. It doesn't matter that it isn't my fault because I'm so totally removed, in an impersonal state of non-being, not mattering to him or to anyone or anything in the great wide world while I'm with him. And I come out of his world having absolutely no feelings about myself, except perhaps thankfulness for the blissful state of numbness I'm in, everything losing its intensity, soon to be forgotten.

I quickly learn that when I'm numb and without feelings I won't be so hurt, so I learn to trust dissociation as the only thing I can count on. I become numb and dumb when I'm with this adult who disregards all human kindness and respect for another being, showing me, in the basest way possible, that I mean absolutely nothing.

In his world, the fact that you hurt physically doesn't matter, that you hurt emotionally doesn't matter either. That you say no doesn't matter. That you don't want to play his games doesn't matter. That you are crying or screaming doesn't matter. You are nothing, and the only way to get beyond the moment is to accept this as fact; to accept the fact that it doesn't matter that you feel bad, like an evil person. That you blame yourself doesn't matter. That you don't understand doesn't matter. That you can't get away doesn't matter. Nothing matters! Nothing!

In this totally impersonal reality you do not really exist. You are nothing. As such, you are offered the means to survive, if you so choose.

This total loss of personal importance and significance, this state of egolessness, Chuck tells me, is a valued shamanic ability. It offers the means of transcendence from ordinary reality, which is what I learned as a child. It allowed me to survive, but Chuck also points out that I gained valuable knowledge. I learned how to go out-of-body and I learned things in that state that most people never discover. He tells me that I can learn to use that ability volitionally, to my advantage, both as I do my recapitulation and as I go on into new life.

I get what he means, but I'm not really sure how to use it, how to gain control over it, because right now it comes out of the memories, as part of them, and I don't feel that I have any particular mastery of it.

I start to dissociate in yoga class as the inner work I'm doing aligns with my outer world, showing me again how it happened, how I was truly able to survive what happened to me. But, as usual, the dissociative spell is filled with flashbacks.

I'm hanging monkey-style in a tree, upside down by my knees, my abuser's face appearing over and over again between my legs. In another flashback there's a knotted rope that he rubs against me as I hang suspended from a tree branch, the big knots hurting my genitals. In another, I feel his hands on my buttocks.

I try to block the scenes out as I sit through the meditation period that winds up the yoga class, but I can't stop my hands from growing huge and swollen, puffy like marshmallows. My foot, under my now huge hands, feels tiny, like a child's foot. I feel so protective of this tiny child's foot; the sensation reminding me of the other time I meditated recently and felt this tiny limb beneath my hands.

I try to come out of the dissociative state by opening my eyes, but the feelings in my hands and foot remain. I sit paralyzed and unmoving for a few moments after the meditation ends until I'm finally able to break out of it. I come back into the present. I stand up, gather my things, and quietly leave, needing to figure out the meaning of the flashbacks that continually fire away, alerting me that I still have more to recapitulate.

February 22, 2002

I suffered excruciatingly yesterday through flashbacks, pain, and deep seated feelings of aloneness and loss. I experienced the depths of damage done to my child self as she popped up throughout the day. She's still inside me, holding it all together. There's still a brave little girl in there, in pain, not able to cry. I can't seem to get her to let go either—her grip is tight and fierce, her determination as unflappable as my own.

Today I've been experiencing intermittent pulsing pains high in my ribcage, as if I'm being held down, some great weight pressing me, choking me so I can't breathe, and then—out of nowhere it seems because I can't actually feel them—one or two tears fall. Maybe something is loosening; maybe it'll start to come out now. Maybe whatever is stuck inside will release and flow out of me in a river of tears.

Even as I sit quietly and jot down these thoughts, flashbacks intrude, coming in sharp jabs too quick to hold onto. I feel stretched to the limit, tense and jittery, as these splinters of memory reveal themselves. It's as if I've had too much coffee, my adrenalin pumping with barely a moment's rest. Old phrases scroll through my head now, wiping out all other thoughts, as they repeat their dire messages.

"Spread your legs, so I can open you up. Spread your legs, so I can open you up! Spread your legs, so I can open you up!"

"No, no, not that today, not that today!"

"It will all be over," I hear myself say. "Don't worry, it will all be over soon."

Will I ever be free of all this? It feels like such a crucially important time, as if something is finally coming together, about to make sense, as it all comes crashing in on me, with multiple experiences, flashbacks, words, and feelings tumbling out of me, but also tumbling on top of me. But still, I can't feel any empathy for myself, or for my child self either.

After reading the book Chuck lent me, *Transforming Trauma* by Anna C. Salter, I understand so much more. I see myself so clearly in the classic description of an abused person: the empathic victim; the one who still feels so bad; who feels empathy for others, but not for herself; who maniacally works, going and going non-stop, running and running; who needs to keep busy, to keep moving; who always takes on another task, another challenge.

Constantly caring for others keeps the focus off me. I'm relieved of dwelling on myself because I'm too busy dwelling on the needs of others. I lost touch with myself at a very young age, taking care of the needs of my siblings, being the responsible one, pushing my own needs away in the process, not really knowing how to take care of myself, but always knowing, instinctively, what others needed. Now I'm learning how to stop the maniacal activity and take some time for myself. I've improved greatly in that area over the past year.

I'm beginning to turn inward to that child inside me now, as I soften toward myself. I recognize her great need for comfort, her desire to be held, her search for reciprocal trust. At the same time I struggle along with her, finding it so difficult to turn to another person and expect to be treated decently, kindly, compassionately. Even with Chuck, I still have to work myself up to a place of trust. Before each session, as I sit in his waiting room, I tell myself, over and over again, that it's okay to be there.

"He's great, he understands, he's a professional, he won't hurt us," I say, attempting to temper my nervousness and fears.

"You need to talk," I say, speaking to both the adult self and the frightened child within. "Please, talk to him."

And if I don't get those few minutes alone outside the door of his office, I have a harder start once we sit down and face one another. Speechless and lost, I don't know where to begin.

I live in two worlds now, just as I did as a child. The old stuff doesn't leave me. One minute I'm being dragged into his world, the world of the sexual predator, by some trigger and then, in the next, I have to pull myself back out to the present. I have to talk business, negotiate a deal, work, teach a class, drive the kids somewhere, be a mother, when mostly I just want to get in bed, crawl under the covers and stay there. I'm drawn to the oblivion and safety offered by those bedcovers, to the relief they offer, needing the comfort they provide as incredible feelings of sadness sweep over me. I want to be told that it's okay to stay there, but I know it isn't really appropriate.

Today, I had to drag myself out to do a job estimate. I literally forced myself to shift back into this world by putting myself behind the wheel of my car. I made myself drive to the client's house—*with awareness*. I barely stayed present in my body while I looked over her project, while I talked business, techniques, paint, supplies, and time frame. By the time I got back into my car I was exhausted.

Even though I find it difficult to be here at the moment, *I must stay present*—a mature adult woman who has duties and responsibilities. Even so, I'm aware that I'm not functioning very well, only fifty to sixty percent capacity, as part of me is constantly being pulled back into the woods, by the flashbacks, and by the little girl who's still there, feeling hurt and abused.

I flash back to when I am eleven years old. Summer. A rash has developed in my armpit. I'm so ashamed of it. I keep it hidden, holding my arm down tight against my side when I'm wearing sleeveless tops or dresses. It worsens, oozing yellow pus. Skin cracks and bleeds. Scabs form; thick dark scabs. At night I soothe it with a damp handkerchief, which I soak in cold water and then fold up and tuck into my armpit, falling asleep hoping it will be gone in the morning. I don't know what causes it, poison ivy or maybe the deodorant I'm using, but I do know that my armpit is a shameful part of my body. I don't want anyone to see it, either the armpit or the rash. Once, while swimming with a friend, she sees it.

"What's that under your arm?" she asks in horror, as I climb up the ladder out of the deep end of the pool ahead of her.

"Nothing," I say, as I clamp my arm tightly against my side, embarrassed at my momentary lack of attention, for I have been careful, for weeks now, not to lift my arm in public.

Eventually the rash goes away, but it takes weeks, maybe months. I never show it to anyone or tell anyone about it. I can't admit that I'm in pain, discomfort, or even speak a simple statement like, "Look, I have a rash," because I don't know how to do that and because my armpit is a dirty place. I have such bad feelings about it. I think the rash appeared because I did something wrong. I think it's punishment that I deserve, so I silently bear it. I must suffer.

This memory leads me to recapitulate another experience. My mother comes into my bedroom. She's acting like an actress in a television commercial, as if I don't know her and she doesn't know me, as if I'm not her daughter and we're not really standing awkwardly on opposite sides of my bedroom.

She never comes into my room. We never have conversations. The only communication between us is when she scolds me for my mistakes or bad grades, for not doing chores or when she asks me to take care of my siblings. I don't understand why she's here. Then I get it. She pulls a bottle of deodorant out from behind her back, the kind for women, not the smelly spray my brothers use that stinks up the bathroom, but a roll-on just for girls. She holds it up between her two outstretched hands, displaying it, as if she were trying to sell me this product.

Posing with it, she tells me, in a totally detached manner, that it's time for me to start using deodorant. She shows me how you roll it on. Lifting her arm and pressing the head of the bottle against the armpit of her blouse, she makes a circular motion, as if I might not already know that this is where it goes, as if I haven't already snuck into her bathroom and used her deodorant on occasion. She tells me that it's not something you leave out in public view, that it's personal, and she hides it behind the mirror that sits on the top of my dresser.

"Here," she says as she tucks it out of sight. "Keep it here. It's hidden then."

I'm both repulsed and saddened by her attempts to communicate with me. I have no feelings for her, except a slight rush of fear as she turns and leaves my room. I take the pink bottle out of its hiding place, take off the lid, smell it, and then rub some under my arms. I wonder why my deodorant is so secret, why it has to be hidden, while my brothers are allowed to leave theirs lying on the bathroom counter for all to see. I put it back in the hiding place and it stays there, until one day a friend sees it and asks me why it's behind my mirror.

"What a weird place to keep it," she says.

"I don't know," I say, shrugging, "my mother put it there."

But after that I stop hiding it, resentful of my mother and her strange ideas of propriety, daring her to come into my room and see that I just don't care what she thinks.

For some reason this memory leads me to recall my mother telling me, long ago, that I compulsively pulled out my eyelashes when I was very young, sitting in my stroller, nervously plucking at them until I had none left. She'd hated that I did it and I hear her scolding me again, telling me to stop.

At night, in my bed, I was free from all rules. I could do as I pleased, as long as I stayed under the covers, as long as I didn't let even one toe stray out into the darkness where the bad men under the bed could grab me.

February 23, 2002

I go back to a memory of having sex as an adult, completely void of feelings, nothing, no arousal, no interest.

"Rub my back," I say, in an attempt to feel something, to awaken sensation.

Afterwards, I roll over into darkness, into loneliness. I curl up on my side, sliding down into gaping black nothingness, wondering why I always feel this way afterwards. No longer craving touch or closeness, I slowly withdraw into the tunnel; until I'm completely removed, not present, not in my body. Loss of self—the feeling that there is no me, that I just do not exist—arises as this memory, repeated just about every time I had sex, re-enters my body. Once again I withdraw and detach, not only from my surroundings, but from my physical body as well.

I've read about the inability of the traumatized, sexually abused adult to achieve success, which has plagued me throughout my career. I'd get to a certain point and be afraid to take the next big step. I just could not trust success and, even though I had so many opportunities, I continually turned them down as I ran for cover, back into the safety of depression and unhappiness.

My first children's book, published when I was twenty-one, was extremely successful. Even before I had graduated from art college I was doing the publicity circuit, giving talks and doing book signings, visiting book stores, classrooms, libraries, and colleges. I was terrified of where the process might take me in the long run as I began experiencing what it meant to step out of the comfort zone of nothingness. Suddenly I was pressured with having to be in the world, feeling, reacting, interacting, being real and alive when I could not, for the life of me, connect with anything even remotely real inside myself.

I didn't much like change back then. It was far easier to be that teenage girl who couldn't look in the mirror and acknowledge herself, far easier to ignore her talents, her abilities, to deny that she had anything to offer. It was so much easier to be that self-deprecating and fearful girl, to turn away from what the world had to offer, to close off rather than open up to it.

Immediately following the first book, another, equally successful, was published, but still I couldn't accept even the thrill of it. I tried to feel happy about it, but even that went by in a few quickly fleeting moments. I remained detached, unable to allow the pleasure of my achievements to hit home, though it was the career I'd always envisioned for myself. Here it was unfolding in reality, mine for the taking, and yet I couldn't embrace it. Too scared, avoidant of the publicity and afraid to feel good about myself, I found other things to do once my obligations were met. I literally ran from success while it chased after me, encouraging me to accept what was blossoming at my feet, but I just could not do it.

It wasn't until I began to run from my fears that I consciously embraced the defensive side of change. I discovered that it could offer escape, the opportunity to constantly shift away from whatever bothered me. I ran and ran and ran; simultaneously fearful of the world that was opening up before me and of what I knew was lurking in the background. For yes, I knew there was something hiding in the shadows, always waiting for me to slip up, to get too uppity, waiting for me to feel too secure and safe.

I knew that feeling good never lasted. I knew that it just wasn't worth it, that it was folly to feel good because something bad was always one step behind you, coming to get you, to knock you back into the darkness. So why even bother, why get all excited about something that would only leave you looking like a self-indulgent fool?

This is the way I thought back then, coming out of college in my early twenties, always looking over my shoulder for the inevitable whack over the head. There was always a heavy hunk of wood, a thick two-by-four, held by invisible hands, just about to swing out of nowhere and knock me straight back into the old feelings, which was where I really belonged. Back then, all I could do was run, even from the career of my dreams, already in the palm of my hands.

The old voice is so clear. It used to tell me that I couldn't; that I was not capable; that I would be a failure; that I wasn't good enough, brave enough, smart enough, pretty enough, strong enough.

"What a jerk! Do you really think you can ever be happy?" it said.

"How dare you feel good, you stupid person?"

"Who the heck do you think you are anyway?"

That old critical inner voice, constantly putting me down, is probably the biggest obstacle I've faced my entire life, leaving me feeling worthless, with nothing to offer. I hear its haughty laughter and wonder how other people dare to be so bold and actually take on what life presents them with. How do they allow themselves to be so present, to so loudly announce themselves, and to fully accept that everything that comes to them is meant for them? How do they dare to be so powerfully alive, so knowing of what they want and unafraid to go after it? I think they must have something that I don't have. I think they must have bottomless reserves of bravery, confidence, self-assuredness. They must be utterly fearless.

I tend to shrink from confrontations with life, better to just disappear into the wallpaper, into the background and go unnoticed, out of the public eye, out of sight. It's safer living in oblivion. Just watching people actually take on life, being daring and adventuresome, makes me so nervous. I have to turn away sometimes, so painful is it. I just can't stand to watch.

What is it I fear? That they'll fail? That they'll be ridiculed? That they'll be reprimanded for being themselves, for being happy, for being alive and real? Yes, I fear all of those things, for them and for myself. I tend to put myself in their places, projecting my own feelings onto them, feeling my own inability to perform as a full member of society, feeling the consequences of my own deeply embedded fears.

At least now I realize that I have, in fact, plenty of unused potential, hidden resources never accessed. My entire life's focus has been fighting fear and trying to keep those inner voices placated, but I'm not going to listen to them anymore, because I don't believe what they're saying anymore. I understand that this is another part of my recapitulation process. I must not just work at remembering the things that happened to me, but I must constantly turn away from the old voices. I must cover my ears to their old rants while I dare myself to become a new person, totally independent of the past. My challenge now is daring to live a new life on my own terms, freed of the old fears and the old reprisals, in a new world of my own making.

On the one hand, fear of leaving childhood and going out into the world is normal. We must all face our fears at the moment of maturity, when fast approaching adulthood asks us to become responsible for ourselves. However, at the time of my own maturity, I was contending with additional fear, as do many others, directly related to what happened in childhood. And although I had no memory at that time of what had happened to me, so deeply repressed was the abuse, I could not get away from the overarching fear that my unconscious constantly permeated me with. Fear was in my body, in my mental outlook, in my emotional make-up. It ruled me.

The heavy demon sitting on my shoulder has always been there, crouching, digging his claws into my skin, daring me to turn around and acknowledge him. I've pictured him often enough, but I knew if I did turn around and look at him that I'd be lost, that he'd devour me and take me away forever, so I never dared to face him. Instead, I pretended, as best I could, that he wasn't really there by trying to run from him. But no matter how hard or far I ran, even to other parts of the world, he still clung to me. Finally, I could no longer ignore the fact of his presence and that's what got me here, into this process of recapitulation. I've finally turned around. Now I face him. I'm facing the truths he's been poking me with all these years.

I must learn to live with the little girl again too, that confused and lonely little girl who I couldn't wait to leave behind, who I ran from as well. I left her behind with the demon in the woods, though I understand now that neither of them ever really left me. She had so many problems and I just wanted to get away from her, as fast as possible. As I ran away, I kept waiting for the moment of release, but it never came, and it still hasn't come. It won't come until I face her too, until I find out everything about her, everything I suppressed and hid from myself, until I free us both of the demon and his energy.

February 24, 2002

He sits in his red truck, one hand on the steering wheel, stopped to talk to me. I see his tight, trim body in his khaki clothes, the shiny gold belt buckle. He grins, says hi, slowly drawing out the syllable of my name. I see his sidekick, a man who worked with him, sitting beside him. Those khaki clothes were always ironed and neat, his hair slicked back. He looked friendly enough. I knew him; I talked to him. He had a big grin that made his eyes crinkle up and disappear into slits, a strong jaw. He was very tanned and muscular. I remember once seeing him swing himself lightly onto the seat of a big farm tractor. He was a man to be admired for his physical prowess, though he was small and wiry too. This is my abuser.

I was listening to the radio the other day when I thought I heard his name being announced. A wave of panic ripped through me, until I realized it wasn't his name at all, but the shock of it remained.

I run and walk for an hour. It's Saturday and everyone is still sleeping when I return, so I go back to bed, feeling heavy and sad. Last week, I told Chuck that I was so glad it was me, and not my best friend that he abused, because she was so fragile. She would have been totally destroyed.

"Don't you feel destroyed?" he asked.

"No, I don't," I said at the time.

But now, as I return to bed and pull the covers up, I allow myself to acknowledge that yes, I do feel somewhat destroyed, though some small part of me staunchly refused to be affected. Some tiny iota of strength was not going to give in, no matter what, and it's what still keeps me going. It still won't give in.

I only felt safe when I was in my room or off alone somewhere, but I also realize that need for aloneness made me vulnerable. I often wandered around the countryside and right into his path, Goldilocks meeting the big bad wolf. I'd be going along by myself, perfectly happy, feeling secure in my aloneness and then BOOM! There he'd be, waiting, grinning. The peaceful solitude I'd been enjoying a moment before immediately shattered, as sudden darkness overshadowed everything. The sight of him triggered frozen numbness, as the world outside went silent and slowly dissipated, as I stood at the entrance to a dark tunnel.

Caught in mesmeric gloom, paralyzed and unable to hear, except for the rush of blood in my ears, indicating that I had already entered a different reality, I immediately lost all ability to react. Saliva formed in the corners of my mouth as I focused intently on the dark silhouette of the figure at the other end of the tunnel. My ears were covered by hands not my own, which held my head in a fixed position, as I observed his slow and steady approach.

At the same time that I stood transfixed by inertia, the shadow of doom creeping closer and closer, I also held onto a small vestige of hope that this time would be different, he'd be different, he'd be nice now. Between this juxtaposition of ideas, between the fragile uncertainty of hope and the opposite learned certainty of doom, arose the moment of collision, the imminent disintegration of one reality and the certain entry into another world, his world: the world of the sexual predator.

I notice that my emotions, even as I recount this experience, are totally dead. I am dead. In the impersonal world of sexual abuse, where nothing mattered, I became nothing in response to what was happening to me. It was how I survived.

February 25, 2002
Meeting Chuck in the grocery store, I swim up out of a memory, shaky, tightly wound. I emerge from the darkness and croak out a hello. I'm disconcerted by the sound of his voice. We're in the wrong place, the encounter uncomfortable, and for a moment I can't figure out where I am. I want only to hide. We stand on line at the deli counter and I pull myself together enough to say: "I like your hat."

It's the only thing I can focus on and he picks up on it and tells me a story about having given the hat away to someone once, though it was his favorite hat. He'd always regretted having been so impetuous, though one day, to his great surprise, he got it back. The story is enough to cover the awkwardness of the situation, keeping me grounded in the moment, while at the same time I totally forget why I came to the store. I take the package of turkey that's already been sliced for me, saying I don't need anything else and, with a quick good-bye to Chuck, I walk away. I can't focus, can barely walk, but I need to keep moving, to get out of the store, but also out of my head.

I need to get my mind off things. This has been my struggle all week, as I fight against the demons that come repeatedly, attempting to drag me back. I don't want them to get me. I want to keep them away from that last little shred of myself, save the last pieces for me. But the memories persist, repeatedly playing out.

Over and over again, I see my abuser's lap and the shiny belt buckle. I'm standing next to the door of his truck, climbing in over him, seeing the buckle. There's another man in the truck. Then there's the other memory of getting out of the truck, standing on the side of the road, watching him drive away, feeling dead, no feelings, just emptiness and deadness as I watch the truck drive away. But there's a glitch in the story, because I don't know what happened in between getting into the truck and then getting out of the truck. But when he drops me off, I'm a different girl. I'm not the same girl who got into the truck. This is where I was when I met Chuck at the grocery store. When I stood on the deli line and saw him coming toward me, I was staring after that red pick-up truck as it drove away from me, as I stood there feeling dead.

I feel like I need to cry, but it's extremely hard to do so. I still need to have that little bit of control week to week, holding on and holding in. I feel like I'll barely make it until I meet with Chuck in the morning.

Sometimes I feel that this recapitulation process and my past are only important to me, that I can't tell anyone else about it because it might bore them or make them think I'm making it up, or that I want attention. How could anyone possibly be interested in what I have to say?

February 26, 2002
I'm heavy with the burdens of these unpleasant, frightening memories, nervous, sad and edgy when I meet with Chuck at eight in the morning.

I tell him that I was wearing my abuser's khaki pants and shiny belt in the dream I had last week, the belt buckle so familiar, though I couldn't place it at the time. Now I can place it exactly, but I just cannot go into the memory, the big one that has been forming all week. It's been following me around, biting at me to remember, remember, remember.

Though it torments me, I'm only able to talk about some aspects of it, the beginning and the ending of it. So I sit with the tension of it, looking at the floor through most of the session, struggling to find a way to both accept the truth of the memory and to talk about it, but I just can't get there.

I leave steeped in bad feelings about my inability to speak the truth, angry at myself for failing to talk and, in so doing, release the anxiety that is steadily mounting. I know I won't be able to handle the pressure, which is physically disabling, unbearable, like a volcano cooking inside me, so I call Chuck at noon.

"I can't do it," I say. "I can't hold it in. I have to talk again. Can you fit me in this afternoon?"

I go back to see him again at three. Haltingly, full of shame and sadness, I tell him about the truck and the two men.

"I've tried to pretend that I didn't know what happened between getting into the truck and getting out of the truck," I say, "but the truth is that they took me to a barn and hung me up, my hands tied, they suspended me from a beam and then they..."

We sit for a moment in the tortured silence of the unspoken word before I'm able to speak again.

"I can't say it," I whisper. "I can't say it. I just can't say the word."

Chuck doesn't pressure me. I can hold that word in. He let's me keep it to myself, the final blow, the final spewing of the volcano. I get to keep a little of it down.

"I feel like crying, but I can't—it feels wrong, not allowed."

"Crying," Chuck says, "is not indulgent. It's a form of release of tension, of sorrow, of everything that's pent up."

We work at it with EMDR and as much as I want to, I just can't release the gigantic lump in my throat, but just telling the story makes me feel as if a great burden has been lifted. I feel incredibly light by the end of the session.

"I'm alive! I'm alive!" I say.

I feel the invigorating energy of life coursing through me as I leave the office, knowing that just talking about that horrific stuff is enough for now. But by evening I'm worn out again, feeling the tired weight of the past, exhausted by holding it in. My whole body clenches tight and shakes with the tension of the memories, even lying in my own bed under five blankets.

I really did try to release something today, but I just can't seem to let what has been my strength for so long go so easily. Even though I know I don't need this level of control anymore, I just can't let it go. But today Chuck let me know that I won't always be like this.

"One day," he told me, "you will let it go. With time you'll be able to."

February 27, 2002

My abuser called me Pretty; he called his own daughter Pussy. No wonder I could never stand it when someone said I was pretty. It made me simultaneously furious and fearful, sending me inward, as I ran to hide in the tunnel.

Suddenly, I'm recapitulating. I hear my abuser's voice, asking me if I'm going to be a good girl. I can't figure out what he means when he asks me this.

"You gonna be a good girl? You gonna be a good girl?"

If I tell him that I promise to be a good girl, I think it means he'll stop, because he must be doing this because I'm not being a good girl. Why else would someone do this to me? I must have done something really bad. I must be really bad to have this punishment. If you do something bad, you get punished. What did I do to deserve this?

"Yes, I'll be a good girl, yes," I say, thinking he'll stop.

But to him it means I'll stop screaming, fighting, and struggling. To him it means: proceed, she's giving permission.

It happened. It really, really happened.

I'm recapitulating getting into the truck again. It's different from other times because the other man is there. There's tension in the cab. I can feel it and smell it, and I feel my own fear rising, suffocating me. I need to get out.

I sit in the middle, between the two men, plotting how I can possibly reach over the man next to me and open the door and leap out, but it's impossible. We arrive somewhere. The truck stops. I try to get away. I scream and fight, twist and kick. They drag me by my hands and feet, still kicking and screaming, into a dark barn full of hay bales around the edges and crossbeams in the ceiling. I can see back through the door where the red pickup truck is parked outside in the sunlight. Someone hits me hard, a shattering blow to the back of the head. I'm crouching on the ground, dizzy. He's yelling at me.

"You gonna be good, you gonna be a good girl?"

I think he means he'll let me go now, but what he means is cooperation. My head hurts, my ears ringing, as one of them holds my arms and the other takes my clothes off. They tie my hands with something, pick me up and tie me to something above my head, though my feet are still touching the ground. I'm kicking again. He grabs me hard by the ankles, forcing my legs up in the air. I fear that my head is going to hit the ground; it throbs so heavily as I swing back and down. The other man, standing behind, grabs me under the arms... Ahhhhhhhhhhhhhhhhhhhhhhhhhh!

I must have done something really, really bad to be punished like this. I crawl inside myself. I go away, deep inside. I hide in there.

I don't remember the actual act. I remember my legs being held, his hands around my ankles, being jerked up, fright and fear tumbling inside me; his face, his body as he moves.

Afterwards, I'm lying on the floor of the barn. They're sitting on a log just outside the doorway. The sunlight is streaming down on them. They're talking, drinking, and smoking. I'm so far inside I can't get out. I just lie there, lost. I'm lost and dead inside, curled up inside myself, feeling dead. Nothing's there, no feeling at all. I'm gone.

Later, I get out of the truck. The other man isn't there. I watch the truck drive away. I stand on the side of the road, perfectly calm, with that same deadness inside.

"He's gone. There he goes. He's gone now. It's okay now; he's gone."

February 28, 2002

"Please help me! Please help me!"

I'm tied to a stump in a desolate landscape, being raped. I struggle out of this dream at the sound of my own shouting, as I cry for help in the middle of the night. I awaken groggy and full of fear, not sure where I am, suffering with intense vaginal and anal pain.

I lie in the darkness, grappling with the pain, throbbing with the incredible debilitating terror of it when an overwhelming sense of goodness floods over me and I feel embraced by what I can only describe as an angel lightly descending over me. Utter calmness flows through me, coming from this entity, as it lies directly over me, as light as a feather, filling me with its energy.

I feel pure white light flowing into my entire body from the bottom of my feet to the top of my head. I feel the pain and sadness and everything that is troublesome being cleansed, washed away by this radiance, as it fills me with a sense of perfect well being. At the same time, I'm made aware that I was and always have been a good person. In an instant, I know that it wasn't my fault, that it's never been my fault, that I'm pure and good. I have never felt this calm in my entire life.

I fall back to sleep, comforted, knowing I am loved.

During the day, I get pulled back into the memory that's been emerging. Once again, I recapitulate being in the barn.

I lie curled up into myself, barely breathing, looking out, as if through a long dark tunnel. I see things outside of myself, out there, as if looking through binoculars, not quite able to clearly see or hear what's going on because I'm not out there. I'm only in here, where it's dark and quiet, with no feelings, yet full of feelings. I'm dead and unable to move, frozen in time and space, but at the same time overwhelmed with pain, loneliness, and sadness.

I'm hurting, lying on the ground, rolled into a ball, not crying, just steeped in incredible silence, looking out. From deep inside myself I see the men sitting at the door; talking, drinking beer, smoking; their backs to me.

Once again I get into the red truck. The smell of motor oil overwhelms, as does the incredible fear of knowing that this situation with two men is worse than normal. This is a really bad situation. There must have been other times just like this, because somehow I know this is not going to be good. I must have had other experiences with him and other men that I haven't recapitulated yet.

This time, I'm desperately planning how I can get out of the truck. I see that I'm wearing turquoise petal pushers and now I know that I'm nine years old in this memory. I clearly remember those pants.

The rest of the memory returns again too: the blow to the head, a tremendous whack and then I'm hanging by my hands in the barn, him pulling up my legs, my head hurting, not because it would strike the ground as I feared, but because of the blow I'd suffered, and it felt worse as blood rushed into my head.

One man behind me, one in front, they swing me back and forth, one entering in front, one entering behind. I am raped front and back. Their rough hands are tight around my hips, around my legs, around my arms. My hands are heavy unfeeling lumps. My arms feel like they're going to be pulled out of their sockets.

I hate those pants, those turquoise pants. I don't like them. I never want to wear them again. They stay in my dresser, even when I have no other clean clothes. I never take them out or wear them again.

I'm nauseous as I recapitulate; head hurting and throbbing. There's intense pain in my hips, vagina, and anus. I'm pulling in, disappearing, folding down into a tight, faraway ball where no one can get in; not even me. The pain in my hips, the flashbacks in yoga class, the feelings of withdrawal and dissociation, the memories, dreams, and somatic experiences are all coming together now, telling me the truth: *they're real.*

Chapter Twelve

Never Again

March 1, 2002

I dream again that my hands are tied to a stump in a blackened, desolate landscape that has been scorched and burned. I've been raped and left alone to die. Then I shift into another dream of being with Chuck in his office. He's telling me that it's okay to talk, that it's good for me to talk. His wife Jeanne is there too, standing to my right, telling me that Chuck is safe, that I can work with him. She urges me to trust him. I hesitate at first, but then I nod.

"Yes, yes," I say, "but it's so hard to talk about this stuff."

Suddenly, I bolt upright in bed, wide-awake, in the throes of a recapitulation experience, nauseous, my stomach cramping, my anus throbbing painfully. I'm in that barn again where two men are taking turns raping me, swinging me back and forth. My hands, tied to a beam, are heavy, cold and numb, the blood drained from them long ago. I'm a nine-year-old child again, in the throes of a rape.

My hips cramp in pain as I try to close my body, as I clamp down as hard as I can, but I can't stop what's happening. I'm being ripped apart! Tossing violently, I fall out of bed and land on all fours with a hard plunk, my knees slamming into the wood floor. Doubled over, my vagina burning now as well, I crawl into the bathroom. I'm going to throw up! Slumped on the floor in the darkness, retching into the toilet bowl, my stomach muscles ripple uncontrollably, though nothing comes up.

Try as I might I can't get control over the experience—I can't stop it. Dizzy and whimpering, I press my hands, prickly with pins and needles, between my legs to soothe the searing pain when suddenly Chuck's dead wife appears in the bathroom in front of me. Young and alive, she glows with a brightness that seems to radiate from inside her. The entire room goes from dark to light as she tells me that I'm safe with Chuck, that I can trust him, that he's safe to work with.

"Trust me, and trust Chuck too. You can trust him," she says.

And with that she gestures to her left and Chuck appears next to her, glowing with the same ethereal light, both of them looking down on me with such tenderness.

"Trust him, you can trust him," she says again, nodding.

Chuck smiles and nods along with her as she says this, their eyes deep pools of kindness, like nothing I've ever experienced. I stare up at them, stunned. I can't figure out how they got here, beamed into my bathroom at three o'clock in the morning. Suddenly appearing like holographic images, they seem to vibrate—made up of some kind of misty vapor that solidifies, pixel by pixel, into two luminous beings.

Hunched over on the cold floor, still gripping the toilet, I wonder if I'm going crazy, hallucinating, when the same exquisite calmness of the night before washes over me. And in that moment, I know it was Jeanne who came to me last night, who laid on top of me and calmed me. I immediately recognize her energy, the same vibrancy, the same calmness flowing through me.

"Trust him," I hear again, as the two figures dissipate, evaporating into the darkness of the night. I reach out toward their disappearing images, wanting them to stay a little longer, wanting to figure out what's happening, but my hands go right through the last vestiges of mist and they're gone before I can ask them anything.

After a few minutes, with the pain considerably lessened, I'm able to get up off the floor. Feeling much calmer, I crawl stiffly back to bed, still doubled over, but definitely in a better place. Something has shifted.

In a state of wonderment, knowing that I've just had an experience of mystical proportions, I lie in bed with my hands tucked hard between my legs. My stomach muscles ripple, spasm, and clench, though I feel no pain whatsoever in that area. It's as if my body is taking this opportunity to release something that's been held back for too long, something it no longer wants to store. My body automatically goes into recapitulation, while I lie shivering uncontrollably for a long time. I acquiesce, allowing this memory of rape to unravel, knowing I can't stop it.

When I wake in the morning I'm still slightly shaky, my body empty, purged by the events of the night, which are still vividly real and, yet, I can barely believe they happened. I go into the bathroom to see if there are any remnants of what happened there in the night and to see if I can get Jeanne to come back.

I sit on the toilet seat and face the spot where she stood, where Chuck stood, and although I sit there for a long time, gazing softly into the morning light, she doesn't reappear. I pray to her to guide me through this recapitulation, so I can find my way to that calmness on my own, and so I can learn to trust Chuck.

"Okay," I say, "I'll trust him. I promise I'll find a way."

I have no choice but to do so, because I understand that as soon as I elected to take this recapitulation journey there was no stopping it. Once I said, "Yes, I'm ready," off I went, everything happening on its own, everything part of the process. I must acquiesce more fully to trusting the unfolding of this journey, to trusting Chuck, and now Jeanne too. And I must not be so afraid every step of the way because—afraid or not—I'm taking this journey. Already well into it, there's no stopping me either.

As I sit in the bathroom watching the morning sun creep onto the walls, I'm able to re-experience, quite easily, the tender love and compassion that flooded out of Jeanne and Chuck during the night. It flows quite easily into my body and feeling it again leaves no doubt as to the realness of my nighttime visitors. The vision of the two of them standing in my bathroom in the middle of the night was as real as the memories that come to me in the middle of the night too, as real as any experience I've had in the real world.

As I conjure up the vision of their presence, I hear Jeanne's voice again—the same voice I heard in the night. She tells me that I have a three-year journey to complete, that I've already made a good start, and that at the end of that time I'll understand everything. I must stay focused on this recapitulation journey she tells me, without being distracted by other things.

"Let everything else go for now," she tells me. "Don't worry about anything. Life will unfold as it should and all that is right will come to pass as you take this journey. Stay focused. It's crucial that nothing distract you from this most important task. This is your work now."

The mysterious quality of this communication and the wonder of the experience in the night stay with me, though doubt also creeps in. Fear that I'm going insane creeps in. Fear that I can never talk about any of this, to anyone, creeps in too. I don't know how to explain it to myself much less anyone else and yet I'm able to hold onto the gift of knowing that I'm being lovingly watched over. I take it and hold it in my place of secrets, where it comforts me the way the tunnel once did when I was small.

I was always looking for a safe place in the world, a place where I could feel at home. Now I know I have to find that place within myself; that it's up to me alone to provide it. At the moment, I feel that it may take some time, as Jeanne says, but I know I'll eventually achieve the sense of security I've always yearned for. I'm certain of that now. After the experiences with Jeanne over the past two nights, of being filled with the light of utter calmness, I know that I'll one day find that peacefulness within. She showed me that I have goodness inside myself; that everyone else does too. It's just waiting to be accessed and experienced.

As I continue to recapitulate, I know that I'll be able to empty my body of the old memories and the demon energy that inhabits me. Even as I allowed it to ripple and spasm out of me last night, I know I must continue to allow it to leave, so it can be replaced with my own energy, as calm and peaceful as Jeanne's.

During the day I can't stop the flashbacks to the smell of motor oil and to being in the red pickup truck, desperate to get out. They come upon me repeatedly, asking me to look and look again, asking me to take in everything that was happening, to not let any detail slide by unrecapitulated. What comes across most intensely is that urge to jump out of the moving truck—I recognize it as something I still carry in me, something I've always had to fight. It happens when I'm a passenger in the front seat, the urge sometimes so strong that I must cling to the seat so I don't fling the door open and jump out.

Now I flash to when I was a child, perhaps nine or ten years old, riding in the car with my father. I'm sitting in the front seat next to him when I'm overcome with a frantic need to get out of the car. I have my hand on the door handle and the next thing I know I've pulled it, unlatching the door, opening it slightly, the sound of the motor louder now, the street rushing by like a grey river. As we round a curve I push the door open. It swings wide and I'm just about to leap out when my father grabs me.

"What are you doing!" he screams.

Stunned and speechless, and totally unaware of why I'm doing what I'm doing, I sit back in the seat and stare out the front windshield, unsure of what just happened. It's as if I've just awoken from a dream, the jolt of my father's hand on my arm waking me up. As much as he probes, I can't tell my father why I just opened the car door. I have no answer to give him. The incident leaves both of us baffled and frightened and, adding to my great embarrassment, he tells my mother about it when we get home.

Though the incident scared and puzzled me, I could never figure out why it was so pressingly necessary to jump out of the car, nor why I've felt that same frantic urge off and on my entire life—but now I sure do!

I'm afraid right now! Everything is crumbling. Everything I thought I was, I now find, was built on nothing. I find no comfort in the world I grew up in. It just doesn't hold up for me as I continue confronting the lies and illusions it was predicated on.

Chuck tells me that the shamans say that the world of everyday life is a consensus reality, constructed according to certain agreements. From the moment of birth we're taught how this everyday reality works and the longer we're in it the more accepting we are of it, the more we trust it, and the more we want it to stay exactly the same. In fact, we count on it always being the same. That world is real as long as we remain in it, but once we step outside of it and enter a different world we discover that what we were taught to believe just doesn't hold up. And what do we fall back on then?

In the shaman's world, which is really any experience outside of the ordinary and the known—such as my experience with Chuck and Jeanne in my bathroom, as well as the many experiences of my childhood—we're forced to confront the fact that the rules of normal reality, that consensus reality, just don't explain the experiences we're having.

In order to survive in those other realities, and be available to experience the mystical and frightening events we might encounter in them, new techniques must be learned and honed. We must learn *fluidity*, so we can traverse those other worlds and return unscathed. We must be able to withstand the impact of our experiences if we are to truly gain new knowledge, insight, and clarity that will benefit us as we go deeper into the mysteries of self and life. We must not return steeped in fear but instead steeped in *awe.* In order to do that we must accept other perceptions and interpretations as meaningful and truthful. We must, as well, accept our other-worldly abilities, perhaps tapping into our innate *shape shifting* skills, as I did as a young child. Though I had no conscious awareness of this skill at the time, I automatically dissociated and went into the tunnel or shifted totally out-of-body, out of *human form,* upon traumatic impact.

"Trauma," Chuck explains, "offers us the unique opportunity to break through one reality and enter another, as we are forced out of our normal state of being, far from everything we've been taught. The trick, of course, is to hold onto our awareness and yet allow ourselves to have the experience."

In a sense, we must become like infants again, learning about the workings of a new world, the rules and expectations all different, which is exactly what happened to me as I entered my abuser's world. During this recapitulation, I'm afforded the opportunity to relive what happened to me in the world of the sexual predator and, rather than get stuck there feeling sorry for myself, to revision my childhood from a totally different perspective, from a healing, empowering perspective. As I recapitulate, I'm also confronted with the secrets, lies, pacts, and rules taught to me and forced upon me by others, both in the world of my abuser and within the consensus reality, the social world that encompassed family, school, and church.

So which world was real? They were equally real, separate and real at the same time, and while I was in one world the other didn't exist—it couldn't. Now I must dismantle the secrets and lies of both of those worlds in order to understand what really happened to my child self. From the strong position of my adult self—better able to handle the impact of the truth than my child self ever could—I must find a way for my awareness to interpret and my psyche to integrate my experiences differently this time around, as I face the truth of each emerging memory.

In re-experiencing everything again I'm also learning how trauma, and the stories we live by, keep us confined and fearful, impacting every aspect of our lives. In reality we're living out an illusion, whether predicated upon us by others, by our own experiences, or by our desperate need to keep our world comfortable, reliable and safe. We repeatedly tell ourselves stories to remain in control, fearful of the moment of annihilation, of death, always one step behind us. In addition, in my memory of attempting to leap out of the car when I was a child, I was being shown how past trauma stays present, even though highly disguised. The truth of that moment is that I was in the throes of a shamanic recapitulation as two worlds collided while driving with my father.

I was simultaneously in the car with him, but I was also back in that red pickup truck desperate to jump out, to escape the heavy sense of dread that was so palpable as I drove off with those two men. I was about to enact what I had so desperately wanted to do in the real moment of being in that truck. I was being given a second opportunity to save myself, in essence fixing what I had failed to do the first time around, but I was also being reminded, very powerfully, of a traumatic, repressed event. But I was jerked out of recapitulating that moment in the truck—literally pulled back into the reality of being in the car—by my father grabbing my arm at the last second.

All of these events are shamanic in proportion, if one chooses to view them that way. I'm learning this now, as I engage in recapitulation with Chuck as my guide. Rather than getting stuck in thinking that I was a fucked up, crazy little girl, I'm being offered a different perspective—a very healing one. I'm also learning that reality is multidimensional and that all of the dimensions are available to us all the time, if we're ready and willing to perceive and experience them.

I'd only learned a few rules and received only bits of guidance about how life worked when I first entered my abuser's world at the age of two. I had little else to rely on, but I somehow managed to understand his rules, learned how to play his games, and instinctively grasped how to behave in order to protect myself and survive. What I learned in his world hardly made sense back in the normal world of childhood, so the confusion I felt is clearly understandable. Somehow I was able to keep the worlds totally separate, able to pass back and forth between those two realities with my wits and sanity in tact.

Now, in order to fully grasp the details and greater meaning of the journey my child self took, I must shed the rules and behaviors of both worlds by dismantling the judgments, criticisms, thoughts and ideas placed on me by self and others. It's only by achieving a different perspective that I'll be able to free myself of PTSD and the triggers that set off the constant replays of trauma. Those triggers also trigger the same old patterns of self-soothing behavior. I'll never get beyond either if I don't break the lifelong attachments to an old world structure. It's only in gaining a new perspective that I'll be able to break through the strict rules I've placed on myself in my stalwart attempts to remain whole. It's only now, in embracing these new perspectives that I'll finally achieve true wholeness, fully integrated, all my fragmented, frightened parts freed of their duties of watchfulness. It's only then that I'll also achieve that inner calm that I now know is waiting for me as well.

The old voices constantly bombard me with the terms of the pacts made long ago, reminding me of the secrets kept sacred for so long, asking me to keep up my end of the bargain. But that's an old world to me now and I know that upholding those pacts will only continue to lead to stagnant compromise and debilitating defeat. They're part of the problem and must be dismantled. And, as I recapitulate and deconstruct myself, I'm given the second task of constructing a safe new foundation, personally relevant and meaningful, upon which I can stand as I discover who I am. I must rebuild a new world for myself with the correct materials, with new voices of clarity speaking of new awareness, based on interpreting my experiences in alignment with my inner truths, with my inner spirit, with my innocence regained. I'm certain to find all the right ingredients inside myself and, with some help and healing, I'll be fine.

The first project is to tackle this pile of rubble at my feet, which grows daily, as the old world tumbles down in heavy chunks, old illusions that burst apart as they hit the ground. I have to sift through the debris of this recapitulation, extracting only what's necessary for the journey ahead. As I move on, I must learn how to let go of the hurt, release the old tensions and the desperate need to control everything. I must let it all go and fully discover just why I don't want it or need it anymore.

March 4, 2002

In a flashback, I'm hiking with friends. I'm about sixteen or seventeen years old. We come upon an old barn in the woods. We all go inside, but I immediately feel nauseous. Fear overtakes me as I stumble around in the gloomy atmosphere unable to focus. It feels evil here. I have a strong sense of foreboding. Something bad happened here. I can't stay. I feel dizzy.

I stumble outside, leaving the others to explore without me. I wait for them in the sunlight, feeling like I'm in a dream, in a hazy dreamworld filled with physical pain and sickness. I know the barn; I've been in it before. I'm also aware that I've felt like this at other places, at other times.

I realize that my body stored all the memories for me. It's been telling me for a long time now that it's time to let them go, *by actually revisiting them*. The pain in my hips, shoulders, neck, head, vagina and anus, must be fully recapitulated. The burning, cramping, nausea and stomach spasms are all telling me the abuse happened.

It did happen!

Letting myself believe it is one of the first steps to healing.

March 5, 2002

I can't tell Chuck what happened the other night. I argue with myself over telling him about Jeanne coming to me as I drive up to meet with him.

How do I tell him that he too visited me in some out-of-body state? How do I explain what happened without coming across sounding psychotic, as someone who is having hallucinations and hearing voices, or wanting to be special in some way? How do I tell him that his dead wife comes to me, that she comforts me and tells me things; that I communicate with her?

The truth is too risky. I fear rejection, that he may send me to a mental hospital, that he may not want to hear anything about her. I don't know anything about their relationship really and he might find my experiences too disturbing, perhaps even frightening. After much inner turmoil, I decide I'll tell him that Jeanne comes to me in dreams. One day I'll tell him the truth, but not yet. That feels safe.

And so that's what I intend to do, in essence giving myself permission to keep this new secret to myself, to carry it around inside me for a while; to not share it. I need to explore what it means to me personally, to find out why she's coming to me specifically and what it might mean in the context of my recapitulation. I sense that I must be open and without fear toward her, that I must be very careful not to dismiss or doubt her presence in my life in any way. I sense that I must also protect Jeanne in this new form, until the time is right to share my experiences with Chuck.

And so I tell him that Jeanne comes to me in dreams; that she calms me and tells me that I must learn how to trust him so I can do this recapitulation work. I see that he's intrigued by this. He grunts a little and cocks his head to one side as if to hear better. And he smiles when I tell him that she looks glowingly beautiful, bathed in an ethereal light, that she embodies total loving kindness and compassion. I take note of his smile. Perhaps he is open, and perhaps I can indeed talk about my mystical experiences of his dead wife—but not now. *I'm not ready.*

Having determined that, I plunge into the memories that have been emerging. I tell Chuck about the somatic experiences that wake me up in the middle of the night, about the incident in the barn with the two men, and this time I speak the whole truth of it. I don't hesitate at all as we do EMDR around what happened. I even say the word rape.

"They raped me."

Everything becomes clearer, and more of the details come to light as we process the entire memory.

"I thought I was being punished." I say. "I thought I had done something really bad. I must have, it was the only explanation that made any sense to me at the time."

March 6, 2002
My anxiety is high today, my emotions fluctuating wildly. As soon as I feel the familiar stirrings I realize that this recapitulation may not be over yet, that there may still be more memories stored in my body and, as Jeanne says, that I do indeed have a few more years to go before I'm done. Each night I pray that I'll wake up in the morning free of this torment, that I'll be done with this recapitulation, and yet every day I wake up still stuck in the same place, still holding so much in.

I'm scared of what's been revealed and shown to me so far, afraid of what may still come. I don't know if I can handle any more, but I guess if I was able to handle it back then, when I was just a young child who didn't understand what was happening, then I ought to be able to handle it now. After all, I'm an adult and nothing should really shock me at my age, but the feelings, as they come over me, are intense!

I try to keep busy, to keep from crying, to keep from even wanting to cry. I'm not even thinking about running away from the truth of my past anymore because I know there's no longer any possibility of that, but I must keep it from intruding during the workday as much as possible. I ask it to wait until I'm home, preferably in bed.

"Wait until tonight," I whisper, as if I'm speaking to my lover.

March 8, 2002
A heavy stone of emptiness lies in my stomach, the clutch of tears won't release, nor the pain in my shoulders. I'm holding on with the last reserve of self-preservation, feeling like I must protect myself even as I slowly acquiesce to this journey.

The only method I've ever had of taking care of myself, by clutching the horrors and storing them deep inside, is being taken from me. Blocking them from becoming known has been a means of control, as well as protection. Now, to release all that I carry inside is a major challenge. I'm partially reluctant to do so, while at the same time I know that I no longer truly have any control. I know that this slow process is the undoing of me, the person I've always been. I'm half sad to see that woman go and half frightened to see what happens as my fingers are pried open and my hands pulled away from all that they've held onto all these years, the secrets I've been keeping my whole life, just as I was taught to do.

As the secrets fall out of me, I fear that I'll have nothing left inside to shore me up. Without the pain I'll be empty and alone because the pain too is part of me, giving me weight and presence, grounding me in this reality. I won't know myself without it and the world won't recognize me either, or I it. And where will I go then? There's also a desperate, lonely idea that if I let go of control that I'll disappear, that I only exist because of it, its firmness my only solidity. I worry that if I let go of these things that have anchored me in this life—fear, pain, control—that I'll completely disintegrate; my dignity and the impressions people have of me shattering along with them and I'll be lost. I won't be able to show my face again. I'll have to leave this solid world, sliding into the morass along with the ugly past. I predict that life in the real world will be too much to cope with if I am to carry my ugliness on the outside now.

I'm a box filled with lots of tiny boxes; everything closed and locked down tight. I've been holding myself together this way for so long. As each box bursts open and the memories fly out, I'm horrified, disgusted at what I've been carrying around inside me all these years. I want to snap the lids back down, close the boxes and pretend that the awful stuff spewing out of them didn't come out of me. But at the same time I know that closing everything back up again isn't going to work for me anymore. Keeping the horrors all boxed up will only continue this mental, emotional, and physical agony. Those secret boxes, stored so deeply out of sight, have been my protection from the nightmares of truth. But what will protect me now, as I face those ugly truths?

Chuck tells me that I'm strong enough to handle the onslaughts of memory and truth now. That's why they're coming forth so quickly, eager to expose themselves to me, emerging into the light of day after so many years in the darkness. I understand that I may be ready, but I'm still afraid, afraid that more horrific memories will come and I'll crumble under the terrifying weight of them, that I'll never be able to bear them.

I just can't risk breaking down now. I can't risk annihilation. I can't risk rejection. I need to be strong right now, my children need me. I need me.

March 12, 2002

I dream that I'm in a warehouse full of boxes. Chuck is there too, wearing a white coat, with a clipboard in his hands. We're doing an inventory, carefully going through each box. I open a box, peek inside, and tell him what I see. He writes everything down and we go on to the next box. I'm getting bored with the process.

"I don't want to be here, doing this," I tell him.

When I wake up there's a hand clutching my belly, twisting it in a tight grip. I'm in such pain, feeling sad, lonely, and desperately anxious. My ankles, waist and hips, my shoulders, vagina and head, are aching. I feel fragile, physically unbalanced, incapable of even walking. It's as if I've been wounded in the night while sleeping, battered and pummeled, deep gashes cut into me, and on top of that I still can't release. I can't cry or complain, though I need to, though I feel so much. I'm so stuck on holding everything in, keeping it close and secret still, though it feels like the death of me. Even so, it's much easier than the death of letting go.

"Did he comfort you?" Chuck asks.

"NO!" I say loudly. "A resounding: NO! He tortured me, then he kissed it to make it better and then he did it again. He raped me using a screwdriver handle, the handle of a hammer. He stuffed a rope inside me. He tied me down."

March 13, 2002

"Wear a dress," my abuser says one day. So I wear a minidress, with blue, red, and yellow stripes. It smells bad afterwards, my fear and his smells. I wash it by hand, scrubbing hard to get the odors out. When I wear the dress to school I feel sick all day, the smell of him on my skin, in my nose. I'm fourteen in this memory.

In another memory, he ejaculates on the white sweater I wore to my First Holy Communion. And then other memories emerge, years overlapping, one minute I'm five and the next I'm fifteen. He swears, yells, and hits me hard on the back of the head. He smells like motor oil and the ever-present petroleum smell makes me nauseous. His tools are hard and cold. He pushes or hammers them into me and makes me parade around in front of him while he laughs uproariously. The sound of his laughter sickens me.

He makes my vagina hurt by poking a stick into me. It's supposed to hurt. Then his mouth is on me, making me come to orgasm. Then he takes the stick out and does it with his penis, telling me that I fucking like it—I fucking like it! I'm eleven years old in this memory.

In another memory my wrists are painfully chafed. As I recapitulate, I look down at my ankles and see skinny little-girl ankles, raw and chafed. Then an old daydream comes to me and I remember how I used to fantasize that I was a slave girl, my hands and feet tied and bound, but it was really only a cover for the truth because in another memory, my hands and feet *are* tied to stakes and I'm being raped, an experience buried so deeply as to seem a lifetime away.

March 14, 2002

I barely make it through the onslaught of memories, the flashbacks intense and constant. I ease the shock by jotting them down and moving away from them, by studying what's happening in my body as they emerge from my unconscious. My emotions, recently so inaccessible, seem to be emerging now more acutely with each memory. They arise like tidal waves, threatening to drown me until I'm able to get control over them, holding them back, letting them seep out in tiny increments.

I notice the unpleasant patterns of severe restlessness and anxiety that precede the moment of sinking deep into the tunnel, even before there is a hint of memory, before the flashbacks begin firing. I feel a strong urge to go home to bed as that restlessness and anxiety begin their irrepressible march. I need to lie down, pull up the blankets and just roll into a ball as they come stomping over me. I yearn for bedtime, for the time when everyone else is tucked in at night, so I too can go into my room, shut the door and curl up with the memories, the same way I used to curl up to hide from them. They seem to be lurking under the covers. I go there to find them. Going to bed used to be my escape. As a child I always wanted to get there as early as possible because it was a safe place. Now I want to go there to find out what happened to me.

I recapitulate being a teenager again, so lost and unhappy, living in the world but not part of it, barely present. I don't belong anywhere, except in my own room. Once I step out of it I'm lost, gone, not me, a different person. I pretend I'm alive, that I really do exist, but everything is slightly off-kilter, blurry, distant. Sometimes I communicate with my friends, sometimes not. It's impossible to talk to adults, even if I want to. I don't trust them. I don't need them. I don't want them. I want a new mother.

In my imagination I pick the perfect one. She's happy. I imagine her being my mother. I imagine curling up against her, being held by her, being called "Sweetheart." I daydream this fantasy often. It helps.

I'm angry and sad as a teenager and sometimes I don't talk for weeks. I hide out in my room, writing poetry about climbing to the mountaintop and standing on a precipice crying and shedding tears where no one can see and hear. I write about sprouting wings and flying, disappearing into the clouds. I write about the loss of innocence, gone forever; about my world crashing down on top of me like a stone wall collapsing, me lying buried beneath its heavy rocks.

I sit in my room and draw dark pictures, pouring my feelings into them, one tiny ink stroke at a time. In deep depression, I scratch out pen and ink drawings of poor little girls, ragged and curled up, small lumps under tattered blankets that no one notices. The girls I draw are hiding in dark alleys, trying to disappear from the world, though in reality there is no escape, no hiding. High walls, impossible to scale, surround them. They are tiny girls in pain, hiding deep wounds under their rags that no one sees except me. I draw their wounds first and then I cover them with blackened rags.

On the inside, I'm the poor little girl that I so expertly draw. On the outside I'm quiet, shy, neatly dressed, and pretty.

TAP! TAP! TAP!

Oh God! He's pounding something into my rear end!

TAP! TAP! TAP!

TAP! TAP! TAP!

TAP! TAP! TAP!

I hear the rapping of wood on wood. I feel *pounding, pounding, pounding* in my entire body. I feel pushing, painful scraping intruding and jarring my bones. Drooling and grinding my teeth, my body fights against it.

TAP! TAP! TAP!

I can't stand it anymore! I pull out of the memory, shaking and gasping for breath.

I'm bent over his knees as this painful flashback momentarily returns and then suddenly I shift into another memory.

Now I'm in a house, visiting people my parents know. I peek into a room at the top of the stairs that I'm not supposed to go into. It's dark in there, a dark room. I'm aware that someone is in there, an old man, a mean and grumpy old man.

"Stay away! Don't disturb him," someone told us.

But the other girl, the one who lives in the house, goes into the room and shuts the door. I can't believe she dares to disobey!

Later, I'm standing at the bottom of the long staircase, looking up. I see the girl coming out of the room at the top of the stairs. She has no pants on and she's holding a jar of petroleum jelly in her hands. I see her trying to put some of it on her bottom. She's crying. I know that someone is doing it to her too. *Someone is doing it to her.*

I feel very old and very sad as I look up at her, but I'm only three or four years old. Her crying is louder now, turning to hysteria. She's asking me to help her, but I can't move. I'm standing there at the bottom of the stairs, frozen, looking up at her. Her mother comes and picks her up, scolds her, and takes her away.

Now I'm with this family again. It's summertime. My family has come to visit them at their cottage near the ocean for the weekend. I'm in a bunk bed with the girl. My brothers and her brothers share the other bunk beds lining the dark little room we're in. I'm still a little girl, about four years old. The boys have already gotten up, but the girl and I are not yet out of bed. We've been sitting on our top bunk playing with paper dolls. A big boy comes into our room. Standing next to the bunk he reaches under my nightgown and pushes his finger into my vagina. He mumbles as he does it. I hear my mother's voice, calling from another room that it's time for us to get up and put our bathing suits on to go to the beach.

"Oh good, she'll come in, she'll save me!" I think when I hear her voice. But the big boy calls out that he's getting us up. I see that he's doing the same thing to the other girl and we sit there for a moment in stunned silence with his fingers poking inside us. Then the big boy leaves.

I put my bathing suit on and go outside. I won't go back into that house or that room. I won't even go into the kitchen to eat breakfast. The adults try to entice me inside to eat, but I refuse. I stay outside in the hot sun, clutching my beach towel, waiting to go to the beach, standing on hot sand among scrubby dune grass, confused, on the verge of shattering. I just cannot figure out what's happening, but I stubbornly refuse to budge, even though I'm hungry. I will not go into that house where that big boy is.

"Who's that big boy? How long are we staying here? Do we have to sleep here again? Who's that big boy? Is he staying here too?"

I ask these questions over and over again as we drive to the beach, trying to figure out if I'll have to encounter him again. My mother tells me that he's the other girl's uncle and that he'll be leaving soon. He's not going to the beach with us and he'll be gone by the time we get back.

It still doesn't matter. I don't feel safe here.

I flash to a memory of seeing a jar of petroleum jelly and it freaks me out, makes me gag and want to scream. I'm nauseous at the sight of it, the yellowy color of it, the blue and white label.

"Get it out of my face! Get it out of the house! I never want to see it again. Don't you ever, *ever*, bring that stuff into my house!"

Why did I react like that? I must be crazy. I've never bought a jar of petroleum jelly in my life. For some reason the thought of it sickens and frightens me.

The toolbox! It flashes into memory: tools with smoothed wooden handles, screwdrivers, rope, a yellow carpenter ruler that folds out—click, clack, click—*a jar of petroleum jelly*.

I'm ten years old, sitting on my bed with my knees pulled up, resting my chin on them. I carefully pull down my white socks to reveal reddened, rope-burned ankles. I put my hands over the painful swelling, soothing them. I'm not sure how they got that way, so I tell myself a story.

"It's long, long ago and I'm a beautiful slave girl," I whisper. "My feet are bound and shackled. I'm dressed in lovely flowing genie clothes, purple silk pants and embroidered vest, with golden bangles and jewelry. My hair is piled high on my head, with curls falling around my face. I'm graceful and beautiful and I bend down on my knees with such grace and poise that all the other slave owners want to own me, but only the king can own me."

I very gently pull my socks back up over my wounded ankles, lie down on my bed, and forget.

Next I flash to a memory of having intercourse for the first time as an adult. The feeling of penetration and sitting on top of my lover is so familiar.

"I've done this before," I say to myself.

It's so clearly true in the moment, but then I find myself briefly and mysteriously dipping into a black pit where nothing is visible.

"But how could that be?" I ask myself, quickly pulling out of the darkness and back into the present moment. "I'm a virgin."

"In another life," I say, answering my own question. "It was a long time ago, in another life that I did this. In another life."

March 16, 2002

My abuser does everything to me, in every orifice, with any object. His sweaty lips stretch into a half smile that quickly turns into a quivering, ugly leer. He pants heavily as his sexual arousal heightens. His intensely focused eyes are peering intently at what he's doing to me. His face is mask-like, except for the half smile always on his face, now creepily distorted. He's so focused on what he's doing that I don't really exist. I'm just a body part. I have no say in the matter.

I cut my body in half. I cut off what's happening and leave that part of me down there with him.

He's taking me for a walk into the woods; he wants to show me something, just me. I'm the special one today. We arrive at the natural spring in the woods where his water comes from. There's a thick black hose going down into a dark hole in the ground. He grabs my arms and forces me to bend over the black hole where I see a shimmer of water far below. Then he picks me up and holds me upside down, head first over the hole. I smell the earth and the bright green grass surrounding the spring, my head dipping into the hole, just enough to scare me into stiff silence.

"It's bottomless," he says, "and if you go in there, if you force me to put you in there, you'll disappear forever! You'll never be found. No one will ever find you!"

Then he rapes me, my head on the edge of the dark hole, the darkness creeping into me, settling in as big black fear. There's water down there, in a bottomless hole in the ground. If you didn't know it was there you might fall into it and disappear forever.

Memories continue to emerge, all scrambled up. I can't make sense of them, snippets of abuse as of yet not fully realized.

We play Doggie. I sit in his lap. I hang from a tree, upside down. I lie over a log. I lie on an old patchwork quilt. I sit in the rough bottom of his pickup truck. I smell dirt and leaves. It's cold, damp, and musty under the bridge. I go into his bedroom, into his basement, a shed, that barn. He gets me, simply because he wants to. I fight him until I can't anymore and then I get out of there. I get out of that body. I get away from what's happening until I no longer know what he's doing.

I have no power. The only power I have is to get out of that body.

He hurts me until I beg him to stop and then he's makes it better. This is the ritual that we do over and over again. He does what he wants and then makes it better with his mouth. I know about oral sex and objects in the vagina and anus. I know about kinky weird sex, but I'm just a little kid. He's grooming me to be his sex slave. He has a lot of time and he's very patient, but once he has a plan it's impossible to stop him or get him to change his mind. Then he's mean, cruel, focused, in that bad-breath-panting way. He gets what he wants, no matter what I say.

When I look at my ankles I see pale white scars there. There's always been something mysterious about those ankles.

As a child I'm deeply confused. I need to go off by myself a great deal. I want to be totally alone. I'm always looking for the perfect spot where I can hide from the world. I hide out in my daydreams when there's nowhere else to go, creating such a happy life that I escape into them whenever I can. One day I'm sitting at my desk in the sixth grade, deeply immersed in another world.

"Look at that little dullard in the fifth row, staring out the window with her mouth open. See? She doesn't even know I'm talking about her," I hear the nun say, and before I know it she's beside me, landing a huge whack on the back of my head.

"Wake up!" she shouts. "Wake up!"

This was the same nun who once made us kneel on our chairs facing the back of the classroom while she walked around and looked at the bottoms of our shoes. We didn't know this was what she was doing until after the fact, when she told us she did that to every class of students because she could see by our shoes who was poor. I cringed when she said that because one of my loafers had a big hole in the sole and I knew she'd marked me that day. I was poor and I was a dullard.

That nun sent me to the principal's office the day I daydreamed so openly. Not caring if I was caught, I brazenly stared out the window, aware that I was going into another world, not even attempting to pull myself back into the reality of the classroom. The nun's cruel remark, calling me a dullard, barely penetrated the veils I was sequestered behind, but the whack on the head brought me fully back. The kindly old principal let me sit quietly for a few minutes in her office before sending me back to the classroom. I was thankful for that, fearing that my mother might be called.

As I recapitulate these events, it strikes me that no one ever asked if I was all right. No one seemed to notice anything unusual.

I'm a good artist and I hear the adults talking, saying that I should be in a gifted program, but there isn't one in the school district. I hate school and I'm not sure what a gifted program is, but I don't want to go to another school. I'm fine where I am. At least everything is predictable in the Catholic school with the harsh nuns. Later, when I'm in public high school I hide out in the art rooms. The art rooms are my sanctuary. Every free period I go to work on some project. I carve driftwood and draw with oil pastels. I know I need to do this to survive, because if I don't get to do art I might die. I can only breathe and think and be present when I'm doing my art. By the kindness of my art teacher I survive. He lets me sneak into an empty classroom and quietly do my own thing any time I want.

March 17, 2002

I recapitulate, putting together bits and pieces of recent flashbacks into a solid memory.

We're playing the Doggie game. He's the daddy dog and I'm the mommy dog.

First, he makes me do a bowel movement in a hole in the ground. He watches closely, praising me, then he pees on top of it, like a dog does, and we cover it over together. We crawl around on our hands and knees and say hello to each other by sniffing and licking, like dogs do. I lick his penis.

Tap! Tap! Tap!

He isn't so nice anymore.

Tap! Tap! Tap!

He gives me a tail.

Tap! Tap! Tap!

I lie across his knees as he hammers an old wooden handle into my anus. He pushes me around, holding onto my tail; making sure it stays in; making me walk on all fours. Every time the tail slips out he hammers it back in again.

Tap! Tap! Tap!

Now he's mean. I'm a bad doggie. He fucks the bad, bad doggie with the stick.

"Fuck the dog!" he says, growling like an angry dog.

He takes the stick out and shoves his penis into me, fucking the bad doggie in the rear end. This is what daddy doggies do to bad mommy doggies, he tells me. Then the bad, bad doggie—me—goes home.

More memories come rushing out of me. I watch them playing out on the television screen at the end of that long tunnel. I recognize them as the same movies I saw the night I made cookies, but now they play slowly. I see them more clearly, the details readily apparent. I'm both watching them and I'm in them.

I'm with my abuser in the woods. He takes off his clothes and lays them neatly over a bush. I do the same. We're in synch, methodically doing things as if we've done them a million times. There's no need to speak. He has a toolbox. It has a big jar of petroleum jelly in it and other things too. He takes things out of the toolbox and stuffs them inside me, into my vagina, and I crawl around with them there while he watches. He hammers a stick into my rear end and makes me crawl around some more. He puts a rope around my neck and walks me like a dog.

In another memory, he knots rope around my ankles and wrists and ties me down on the dirt packed ground and pulls stuff out of my vagina. I see that there is some string and a necklace coming out of me. He puts other things inside me too, tools to open me up. I see screwdrivers, hammers, and funny-shaped wooden things.

Now I'm lying over a log; the bark is digging into my back and buttocks. He spreads my legs wide and ties them down. He uses things in his toolbox to open me up. He hurts me, but it's important to open me up, he says. He likes to open me up.

I don't understand how he can make me feel so good too, because he's shocking me with electricity and I know that electricity can kill you, but it still feels good—at first—kind of tickly pleasant, but then he doesn't stop. He's punishing me for being bad and for feeling good, I imagine. I'm trying to figure out how he has electricity in his fingers and penis, how he does that thing that feels so good. But now I understand how electricity can kill you because now it hurts. Enjoying it was bad because now he's killing me for it.

Bad doggie needs to be punished. Fuck the bad dog! Fuck the bad girl! I try so hard to be good, but I'm never good enough.

I don't believe in God anymore. God does not come to help me in my time of greatest need. I know he doesn't even exist, that it's all a lie. Now I'm even worse than bad, because I don't believe in God. I'm evil. I have the devil in me and I'm being punished for my sins.

When my daughter is little I make her a cat costume, but I don't make a tail. The idea of a girl with a tail is disgusting to me.

"You didn't put a tail on," she says, obviously disappointed.

I gag when she asks me to sew a tail on. I'm nauseous because all I can envision is a wooden tail sticking out of a child's rear end and it makes me sick. Why do I see that? I can't figure it out, but I feel like I have a stick up my ass, my anus throbbing painfully, as I get the materials to make a tail for my daughter.

I push the vision and the feelings away and make my daughter a soft, fluffy tail for her costume.

March 19, 2002

Stomach tightly clenched, I talk about the memories, sorting through them piece by piece. I tell Chuck about the Doggie game and the strong odor of petroleum jelly, the haunting smell of it. I tell him about the stick getting hammered into my anus, about being tied down, about the rope tied around my neck and being walked like a dog. I hear my five-year-old self telling the story of the game, my voice the voice of a child.

Saying the words—*anus, stick, vagina, tied me down, rape, bad doggie, fuck, bad girl, orgasm*—getting them out, makes all the difference. A ten-ton lead cloak has lifted, but I'm still haunted by those memories and others. I'm haunted by my abuser's voice.

"I'm going to open you up. I'm going to split you open."

Open you up—split you open—open you up—split you open—open you up—split you open!

I wonder if the memories are coming in some sort of order and if the next one will be a bad one. I see how one memory triggers others. I also see the pattern of abuse, how my abuser groomed me to be his playmate and how the games we played together were often of the same intensely mesmerizing quality as the games I played with his daughter. I also see how the methodical masturbation I did as a teenager reenacted the abuse, the tools I laid out so like his tools.

I look at my ankles now and see the palest sort of pucker of white scar, right where I have the memory of swollen and chafed skin. Am I seeing it because of the memory of being tied down, or is it really there?

Could Chuck see it? Would I want him to?

I'm too afraid to show him.

March 20, 2002

My body remains tightly clenched. I'm unable to relax. As soon as something comes up—a memory, a flashback, a feeling—I'm caught in its grip. I automatically tighten, warding off evil. My shoulders curl now in the very old but familiar posture of my thirteen-year-old self. I have to consciously force them down and hold them down, which is very hard to maintain, much easier to let them protectively hunch.

My grandmother, concerned about my slouching posture, once told me to walk around with a book on my head until I could stand up straight and proud.

March 21, 2002
There's a dark little voice inside me that speaks in a sinister tone.

"You don't deserve such kindness," it says.

Just as I begin to feel that block of ice inside start to melt, as I begin to have a modicum of good feeling about myself, that sinister voice speaks up and I freeze over again.

Why don't I deserve anything? Why can't I let someone be nice to me? Why can't I let someone else into my world?

I can be kind, loving, generous, and nurturing to others, but I'm hard and mean to myself. I'm trying to change; learning how to be kinder to myself, but deep down there is that mean old voice telling me that I don't deserve any of it.

As I recapitulate, I discover that I couldn't understand why my abuser was treating me so badly, why he was doing the things he did to me. After a while I stopped questioning, knowing that my thoughts and protests had no affect on him. He was going to do what he was going to do and so I sought coping skills instead. I protected myself by going silent and by blocking off access to any feelings, constructing protective boxes, walls, barriers of steel and ice, in order to survive. I was also determined to be the perfect daughter that my parents expected and so I carried those protective measures into that world as well. The perfect daughter never disappointed and she certainly didn't bring home stories of sexual abuse. I became silent and rigidly tense at home too. I had too much to hide and I was alone with it, so the best way to survive and get on with life was to block out the experiences and everything related to them, including feelings. It was important that there be no possibility of a crack in the facade.

I had no confidence as a child and rarely spoke about myself. Now, as I sit each week with Chuck, I'm learning how to talk. I'm trying to find a way to break through the still tight defenses and find the right words to describe the memories as they come. To describe what was happening back then is like trying to speak a foreign language, having to form unusual words in a mouth that will barely open. I feel as if I haven't spoken a word in a hundred years. It's as if I can barely remember how to move my lips and force sound through them.

I'm also trying to accept that it's okay to need things, but I don't like being needy—it's hard to deal with. I'm almost fifty years old, why should I need anything? On the other hand, I acknowledge that there's a large gaping hole inside me that has never been filled with anything positive. I want to fill it only with good now. I want to believe that I deserve to be treated kindly, like everyone else, but even a hug is too hard to accept. And the old feelings of being bad, inadequate, and undeserving still sit on my hunched shoulders, those heavy demons waiting for me to slip up, waiting to get me. As old as they are, they still hold on with an iron grip.

I'm standing in the shower. There's pain in my vaginal area, a stinging feeling for no reason that I can think of and suddenly I flash into a memory.

He's peeing on me. My abuser is peeing on the bad doggie whose legs are stretched wide and tied down. He's done with 'opening me up' and 'splitting me open,' though I'm not sure what those things mean. I'm sore and bruised and his pee on me is hot and stinging. The water from the shower triggers the memory even as it brings me back to now, where I stand with the hot spray running down my legs and the sensation of stinging on my genitals.

Steeped in the past again, as more memories stir inside me, I wonder how I'm going to get through this recapitulation. I almost wish the memories would come rushing out of me and be over with in one fell swoop, but I realize the process will take its own sweet time. The physical and emotional pains associated with the memories weigh me down, but on the positive side I'm gaining access to the bigger picture of what happened. Clearly, negative feelings and attitudes that I've always carried stem from the abuse: the need to be so hard on myself, to constantly punish myself, as well as the withdrawn, empty shadow of a girl who suffered from such low self-esteem. These negative feelings were countered by a fierce determination to survive, to prove to the world that I was somebody to be reckoned with. I was driven to achieve, to excel, to keep moving, to go forward at all costs. This was the fuel that kept me going for so long. It's what kept me present in this world.

Another memory emerges.

I'm playing in the sandbox with his daughter on their back patio. We see him coming out of the house. The rest of the world slows down to a grinding halt and freezes. The only thing moving is him, walking towards us, shimmering in the light. I'm no longer breathing. The only sound is the loud rush of blood in my ears, drowning out the sunlight sending me into darkness and silence. The day disappears as the dark curtain opens, revealing the entrance to his world.

It's my turn today.

I look at his daughter as she slowly turns her head away, fear and sadness etched on her face. She looks down at her hands in the sand, silently stares at them, knowing what I will be confronting. I get up and take the hand he offers me. We walk across a field. He's friendly, joking and funny.

"Maybe it will be different this time," I hope, "maybe it will be different."

 But now, as we enter the woods, I know I'm wrong. I've been tricked again. The curtain falls behind me with a loud clang as I step reluctantly through it.

I come out of the memory, but I still see him coming toward me. The scene plays over and over again and each time it does I freeze immediately. I become a zombie, a robot, a little girl without feelings, without hope. I give up. This scene plays repeatedly in my mind and in my body; a horror movie clip that I can't turn off.

March 22, 2002

I go to bed each night and wake up each morning with such bad feelings about myself, just as I did as a child. I know I'm caught again, back in the old feelings of despair. Still existing deep inside, they come to visit me. I'm worthless and lonely. I'm not loved or cared about. I'm lost, frightened, depressed and sad. No one understands me. No one sees that I'm so totally alone in the world. I function, but I'm not totally present or involved in living. Part of me is stashed away, hiding out, fearful and alert, while zombie girl pretends to live.

I know my parents loved me, but from a great distance.

"Isn't she beautiful and talented? Isn't she eccentric? Isn't she shy?" they would remark whenever they caught a glimpse of zombie girl.

They rarely talked about themselves, or expressed any feelings or emotions. There was no touching, no physical contact whatsoever; no hugs or kisses, no tucking into bed at night.

"Your mother put herself to bed every night," my mother once chided my own children, as I put them to bed in the manner that felt right, sitting beside them, reading, connecting and conversing with them, rubbing their backs, soothing them as they went into the night.

I didn't *want* to put myself to bed as a child—it was the only option.

I'm hard on myself. No one can possibly have a kind thought about me. I think Chuck forgets about me as soon as I leave his office. I must always make sure that he knows I'll be coming back.

"Next week, right?" I say, needing to be assured at the end of every session that he'll be expecting me again.

I'm worried that he won't remember that I exist. I'm afraid that I'll be sitting in his waiting room on the next Tuesday morning desperate to talk to him and he won't be there. I worry that he'll forget what I've already told him and that I'll have to start all over again.

Emotionally fragile, I'm ready to break.

March 23, 2002

How do the memories start? How do they progress and develop into full-fledged memories?

I notice physical sensations first: pain, numbness, stinging, cramping, clenching, gagging, nausea, and an overwhelming desire to withdraw, to retreat from the world into the old numbing tunnel. Sight, smell, taste, and sound are memory triggers as well. Then the emotions kick in, smoldering and building to the point of bursting; the need to cry triggering additional anxiety and fear. Adrenalin pumps and I shake and jitter as if I've had too much coffee.

Then there are the visuals, either in quick flashbacks too bright to take in or those dimly lit movies too distant to clearly decipher. The flashbacks—starkly vivid scenes—crack the world open, the curtains of everyday reality rip apart and, in the grip of heart pounding drama, I'm thrust into another reality where something is revealed in a split second before the curtain drops back into place and the world returns to normal again. Sometimes cobwebby pictures swim up out of murky memories, like old movies flickering in starts and jerks, slowly emerging as if from dirty pond water or thick fog. I can barely make out what they're trying to show me.

I may see many different views of a memory before the entire picture is finally revealed. Sometimes emotions don't arise until after the visuals begin to appear, sometimes the reverse is true, but often visuals are accompanied by physical or emotional reactions as well—most often shock, horror, and fear.

Eventually, the flashbacks and foggy visuals begin to merge with whatever physical sensations and emotional feelings have been plaguing me. And then, almost suddenly it seems, the fog begins to clear and the pieces fall together into a cohesive scene, finally interlocking—clarity achieved at last.

"Oh, that's what happened!" I say, surprised by the process alone as much as by the revelation, and then I know something new about my past.

The final step is being able to accept the truth of what I'm being asked to remember, to make sense of the memories, to assimilate them and learn from them, to thoughtfully fit them into the context of my life and, finally, to give them meaning and significance.

Why did these things happen to me? This is the question that ultimately arises. There must be a reason.

In trying to piece together the memories, I'm trying to figure out the past, but the future as well. As the memories appear, I must look at each one closely; feel each detail—mentally, physically, emotionally—and give it a place in the past while moving forward with the truths that are being shown. I must be patient as I go through each step of the recapitulation led by what emerges out of my body and psyche, accepting the process as it unfolds. I have little control over it, but, as Chuck keeps reminding me, I must be ready for it. And, indeed, I must constantly remember that I've already firmly set my intent to take this shamanic journey.

As I seek a deeper understanding of my place in the world—in the predator's world of the past, but in the world I'm in now as well—I must bravely face what's presented each day so I can continue taking this journey that I'm beginning to see *is* meant to be.

When a memory does me the honor of finally emerging, I must be prepared to meet it, to tackle the whole picture, in whatever sense that may mean. I must be ready to address the deeper emotions, the misunderstandings, and the feelings of both the child self and the adult self so that, eventually, I may merge into a whole person, my separate parts integrated. That is the ultimate goal, as Chuck tells me: *to become whole.*

In yoga class, I'm uncomfortable when lying on my back. I must constantly adjust my head because of intense pain at the back of my skull. Even though I'm lying with a mat and a blanket under my head the pain penetrates, like a sharp dagger stabbing through the floor. It even hurts if I press against it with my fingers, a raw, bruised spot that I can find no explanation for. It feels like I'm lying on a bumpy surface, a sharp rock under my head.

March 24, 2002
It's coming, bit by bit, the next memory, the 'open you up' and 'split you open' memory. It hurts so badly. No longer a fuzzy old movie, the pieces are starting to coalesce, dropping into place, creating a picture. It feels as if it's happening now! It's hard to handle as it begins coming through more clearly. I'm reluctant to go more deeply into it, while at the same time I know that it's waiting for me.

I acquiesce. I let myself go. I let the memory unfold, as it will.

I begin spinning, shrinking, rushing down the tunnel. I literally feel as if I'm hurtling back through time. I go beyond the moment when my abuser was peeing on my sore and swollen genitals, go back to the beginning where I'm lying on the ground in the secret place in the woods. He takes a folding yellow wooden carpenter's ruler out of his toolbox and measures my insides with it. He measures himself too, his penis.

"I need to open you up," he says, rather gaily.

He takes tools out of his toolbox and pushes and turns them inside me, trying to widen my vagina. My stomach grabs and clenches and I feel nauseous as the memory unfolds. His penis is standing up straight, blue-veined, ugly—ugly and dangerous. Something is being pulled out of my vagina, long and ropelike. I can't see what it is. My legs are spread wide, tied down, my hands pegged to the ground. I can't move at all. I'm desperately anxious as I feel something rising inside me, ready to burst out. Fear, it's fear!

I see his penis coming out of me, withdrawing, long and blue; it feels like sandpaper being rubbed against my dry insides. Then he pees on me. It seems like an afterthought, though everything else seems calculated and planned.

I dare myself to go deeper into the memory.

I try to see what he's doing. Something is being used to pry my labia apart, something is holding me open. Hard things are going in and out; he twirls and pushes them inside me and then pulls them out. My stomach is clenched tightly. I listen to the sounds in the woods. I hear the birds and the rustle of leaves in the trees. I smell the earth and feel the warm air.

"Is he talking to me?"

"Now, I'm going to split you open," I hear him say.

My back and head slide along the ground as his penis shoves inside me. I'm dragged back and forth as he fucks me. My hair twists into a hard knot at the back of my head, rubbing against the ground, raw and painful.

More memories emerge.

He takes tent stakes and rope out of his toolbox. I lie down and he ties me to the stakes, pulling me wide, pegging me to the ground. Time to open me up. He stands over me for a long time, looking down at me, his clothes on. He doesn't take them off. He looks like a workman with his toolbox. Then I see him from up above. I'm up in the trees looking at that little girl down there. I see her lying down there, limbs spread wide, and him bending over her.

Sometimes I'm up above; sometimes I'm on the ground. When I'm up above, I see that it's the same spot where we played the Doggie game. I see the same bushes and trees. It's deep inside the woods, bushes all around, well-hidden, secret. A sense of dread hangs heavily in the atmosphere of these woods.

I go back to the beginning of the memory. I know this is going to be one of those bad times. I know that I won't be able to stop him. As soon as I go with him, I know something bad is going to happen and I can't do anything about it—I know that. Filling with anxiety and fear, I desperately seek a way of escape, but I also accept the truth that it's inevitable. There's no escaping what he has planned. Resignation is mixed with an overriding sense of impending doom. I accept the truth that I personally have no control.

"Here we go again. I'm caught, and I can't get away," I say to myself. "He's going to do something really bad."

As these scenes unfold they sometimes feel like pieces of different memories, then they seem to be the same memory, out of order but finally falling together, piece-by-piece. I recognize each part as it emerges, even being in the trees above looking down on the scene below. I'm totally out-of-body, out of harm's way, looking down on a little girl I feel no connection to. I don't recognize her. As I recapitulate, I realize that this was often the case when I looked down on what was happening on the ground below. I saw a poor little girl whom I felt bad for, though I didn't see her as myself. It wasn't until afterward, when I had to go back into her body, that I felt some connection to her, often only in the role of her rescuer.

The feelings that emerge with this memory have been with me forever, lifelong reminders of the traumas of my childhood. I now understand how we really do hold everything inside us. It's also clear to me that our feelings are trying to tell us certain things. They're guiding us to challenge their presence, to find out why we are the way we are. This has been the question I've been struggling with my whole life. It's been circling in my head forever.

Why am I like this, what is so wrong with me?

This memory underscores the reason for the presence of the intense anxiety and fear that have accompanied me throughout life. The clenched stomach and the feelings of dread and doom are old friends. I see how they've been showing me, all along, what I needed to do: *go back into the woods of my abuser.* Now they lead me from one painful experience to another, giving me the opportunity to confront the past and free myself of it, to gain clarity on so many aspects of my life. I now know that these things didn't happen because I made them happen or wanted them to happen. These things happened to me because someone else was in control and I had no power to stop him.

I learned very quickly that I had no choice in the matter, except choosing survival. I learned how to dissociate and how to leave my body. I learned to abandon the poor little girl on the ground so I could go back to her after he left, pick her up and get us out of his woods. Those were the decisions I made, as I faced the man in the woods.

March 27, 2002

I never had words to describe what he was doing to me. I didn't equate the experiences with anything except the terms he used: *fuck the dog, open you up, split you open.* I didn't really know what it was all about. Even when I was older, I now realize as I recapitulate that time in my life, I never thought of what I did with him in the woods in any way, except his way. I had no explanation and attached no meaning to what happened. It just happened.

I recapitulate another memory.

I'm sleeping over, lying in the double bed in his daughter's room. I'm fifteen or sixteen. She's sound asleep. I wake up feeling a shadow in the room, sensing his presence.

"She ain't gonna wake up."

I'm crouching over the pillow, trying to disappear, pushing my face into it, hoping I'll suffocate. She ain't gonna wake up, she ain't gonna wake up? How does he know that? He grabs my legs and pulls me down and around until I'm lying on my back. His daughter and I have been sleeping naked. He puts his hand over my mouth and whispers harshly through gritted teeth.

"You gonna be good? You gonna be a good girl?"

His hands are all over me now, inside me. I see his daughter lying on her side, turned away, sleeping heavily, almost as if drugged. He pulls me off the bed and, forcing my legs up, bends over me. Then I watch from above as he pulls me to a kneeling position and pushes into me from behind. Afterwards, when I'm back inside myself, aching and dully sad, he presses my forehead into the bare wood floor, threatening me before he leaves the room.

"Keep it to yerself! You hear! Keep it to yerself!"

I desperately want to leave. I stand gazing out the window for a long time, wondering if I can jump out the second story window or leap onto the little sloping roof over the kitchen doorway below. My bicycle is down there. I could ride home by the light of the full summer moon. I could sneak up the stairs to my bedroom without anyone hearing me. Eventually, I get back into bed next to his daughter, deciding it's over, that he won't come back.

I promise myself I'll never come back again, but do I remember that promise?

March 28, 2002

I'm having a black day. I walk fast, trying to walk away from the past. I walk into the woods, but no ghostly memories can haunt me this time because I'm too lost in despair. The further I walk the further I push the old memories away, but feelings of worthlessness stay with me. The feeling of not mattering seeps out of the past and accompanies me as I walk, an adult woman who is certain that she does not matter to anyone.

"Except my children," I whisper, "to them I know I matter."

I stand on a ledge overlooking the river and the railroad tracks below, feeling so lost. Aside from my children, I can't connect to feelings about anyone or anything, including myself. I hear a train coming and immediately I imagine running down the embankment and leaping onto the tracks, just a blur of red; my red fleece vest flitting like a small red cardinal in front of the train. And then it will all be over. One hundred and two pounds of fragile human flesh meeting steel tonnage at ninety miles per hour. I'd disintegrate. I'd hold my arms out wide and meet it head on, eyes open, just a little bird meeting its death. It would only hurt for the briefest of seconds, and then nothingness, peaceful nothingness.

I imagine doing this as the train speeds past. Suddenly, exhaustion hits and, frightened by the thought, I collapse on a nearby bench. I realize I'd never do it. My children matter too much to me. Even if I don't matter, they do. As I gaze out over the river, I begin to shake violently.

I need to talk to Chuck. He's been on vacation and we haven't met since the nineteenth. It's been a long and difficult time since I last saw him, days filled with bad memories, laced with almost debilitating depression. I can't stop the ancient voices inside, still chanting their poison. No matter how far away from those really bad years I've come, those voices of oppression are still strong and real. They keep me numb and dumb, gripping my throat so I can't ask for help. They tell me I'm not worthy or deserving of anything. They stop me from asking Chuck for help.

"Why would he care about you?" they ask. "Why should anyone care about you? Don't bother him; he's on vacation. He doesn't want you bothering him now. Wait your turn. He doesn't care. He's got better things to occupy himself with."

I get up and walk quickly away from the river and the train tracks, my need to outdistance the oppressive voices eclipsing everything else. I begin running to get away from the feelings that run right after me. I'm not just afraid of my abuser, *I'm afraid of myself now too.*

I drive back to the studio where I'd been working when I felt the need to get out and walk. Totally lost and disconnected, as if I'm driving through a tunnel, I barely see the world around me. I numb myself again so I don't have to feel anything. Feeling hurts too much, I decide. It's better to just stay numb and sad. I fight with myself all the way back, because I want to call Chuck, certain that I'll only be able to release the grip of this day if I share the tension.

A friend stops in when I get back to the studio and inadvertently helps me get out of the dark hole I've fallen into. She thinks I'm handling everything so well. Aware only that I'm dealing with the issues of divorce she admires the fact that I appear so in control. On the outside I still uphold my usual armor of calm steadiness, never revealing what is really going on inside.

"I'd be a frantic mess," she says.

I wonder if maybe that would be better than being in such control. But this is the way I cope, steeling myself to handle one thing at a time, sorting everything into little compartments, organizing, so I know exactly what I have to deal with. And then I only deal with what I can handle.

I feel a little better after she leaves and to take my mind off what happened by the river, I sit quietly and visualize myself and the kids living together in a happy little home, a future home that I don't have yet. I envision everything being perfectly okay. I hold this vision in my heart and decide that I'll just keep tackling one thing at a time. As I sit and contemplate my situation, I admit that although I automatically go numb to block out what is most unpleasant, reverting to old techniques from the past, they aren't really working anymore.

I also understand that I must find ways to refuse the old habits as they come seeking me out, as used to me as I am of them. I must cope differently with the stresses that ride in on the memories. I must swim up out of the fuzzy numbness and use the adult self now to tackle what arises during this recapitulation process. I must break the grip of the old numbness, get out of the tunnel, and allow the new me to take over. She needs some practice, so until I see Chuck again, she has to take over.

I realize I can set the memories aside while I take a breather without fear of losing touch with them, without them receding back into the darkness. I can ask them to hold off, to give me some time to collect myself, to be gentle with me while I get my bearings. Now that they've been unearthed they won't disappear. *I'll never forget them again.*

I think it's okay that I had those gruesome thoughts about the train today; that I allowed myself to go through that process of killing myself. I have too much to keep me here and would never kill myself, but in a sense I confronted death, not really intent on suicide but only in killing off the old me. I find that I have plenty of reason to live—I'm needed and wanted. But in order to truly live differently now, the old me *must* die.

I must begin constructing a new me. A firm-talker must come forth and tackle those dark voices as they emerge from the past. A stronger-voiced self must chant them back down into the gloom. Even though they may be loud and powerful, I can be louder and more powerful.

March 30, 2002
The voice of the fifteen-year-old girl inside me is strong and determined. She's the one so full of despair, so sad and hopeless. She's the one telling me that I'm worthless, that no ones cares, that even I don't care about myself. I must constantly contend with these extremely potent, ancient feelings as they emerge from the past.

It was the fifteen-year-old girl who felt so low when I went for a walk the other day. She was the one who felt the need to end it all, to jump in front of the train. She's the one who keeps me from calling Chuck when I feel so desperate. She's constantly belittling me, saying that even he doesn't care.

"You just walked in to his office one day and started talking. Do you think he *really* cares?" she says. "You're just another client. He wants you to hurry up and get done. Every time he mentions how long it's taking, how slowly everything is emerging, he's really telling you it's time to move on and get out. He's tired of you. He has nothing more for you. Don't call him, you're just bothering him."

She's the one who's stuck, with her tight hold on the secrets of the past. But, in all honesty, it's been her method of coping and I have to respect what she was able to do back then. However, as a result, she can't trust anyone and she doesn't know any other way of being. She can't, for the life of her, let go of the old habits. She's been so deeply lost inside me for so many years that she can't find a positive way to express herself.

The fifteen-year-old girl takes over when the memories emerge, the scared and damaged teenager who can't speak, who holds everything locked in silence. Otherwise, I'm amazed at my own real voice, so strong and confident when I need to be. But when a memory sweeps over me I'm lost, with no voice again.

She won't let me trust anyone, even though I want to. She won't let me care about myself, even though I want to. She wants me to stay in the tunnel with her where it's always been safe, hiding out, avoiding, keeping it all in. I don't know how to quell her fears or get rid of her, though perhaps I just need to change her way of thinking. Perhaps I just need to tell her that we're going to do it another way now. I'll tell her that things need to change and that it's okay now, we're safe now.

Do I really feel safe now?

Sometimes I do. In Chuck's office I do, but where else?

Nowhere—not yet.

Even though that fifteen-year-old girl won't let me care about myself, she will let me care about others. It's a need we both have, to protect and guide others, to give what we can't give to ourselves.

Why?

Because we don't deserve anything, we don't matter. That feeling dominates. Stuck inside me, it sits like a heavy boulder in my heart, blocking everything. I don't matter; even to myself. No one really cares about me, least of all me. Why should I? Look at all the horrible, disgusting things I've done. Look at the secrets I'm hiding, the thoughts, the words, the deeds I've got stored away in my little boxes. Look at all the feelings, all the emptiness. Why should I, or anyone, really care?

The fifteen-year-old has been dominant for so long. Taking over a long time ago, she dealt with getting on in life in the best way she knew how, but it meant giving up everything to stay safe. It meant hiding, wrapped up in all that fear and despair. And that's where I am once again: wrapped up in that old despair, crouching under that heavy lead cloak, in the darkness of an alley, in despair; thinking that no one cares, not even me.

I'm bad. I did bad things. I'm a bad girl. I don't matter. I'm evil.

I don't know how to stop her thoughts, how to stop her feelings, how to stop her sadness. She's living inside me, pulling me down. I'm curling up into a ball with her, and she's holding me so tightly. Her voice is so loud it drowns out the mature adult me.

She won't let me go.

March 31, 2002

"She's afraid and she trusts no one," Chuck says. "You have to, very firmly and empathically, tell her no! She's not making the decisions."

She's afraid and she trusts no one.

Well, that's me to a tee. Even if I'm making headway, those feelings are still inside and ruling me. *I am that lost little girl*, so I can't just tell her to go away. I can't just throw her out of my life. I have to deal with all the stuff she's holding.

"She's hiding, she's afraid of life," Chuck says. "You are choosing life and she's afraid of it."

I know this. I recognize the fear of being in the world. And, yes, I admit I've been hiding out with her most of my adulthood; it's safer there. Sometimes it feels like the only place to be. Rather than confront someone or get angry about something it's always been much easier to slip away and hide, to go back to that fifteen-year-old self who figured out a long time ago how to cope.

When I feel hurt or vulnerable I hide even deeper than normal, retreating inside where only she goes, keeping her company in that very familiar tunnel where no one can get me. This is a lifelong habit.

As I recapitulate and change the way I've always done things, I must also challenge the fifteen-year-old self to come out of hiding. We must confront our fears together, the old habitual ones that have kept us safe and protected, as well as new ones that arise as we step out into the world. In truth, they all seem to be the same fears just getting recycled and until I dismantle them, Chuck says, they will continue to rule me.

As I work through this stage, with the intent of breaking through my abandoned and lonely fifteen-year-old self, I once again feel helpless, worthless, and afraid. I know that if I don't confront these old feelings now, they will just continue to haunt me. I need to end the stalemate. I know what I have to do. It's just a matter of barging ahead, "for growth and life," as Chuck says.

It's the fear that something bad will happen that has always kept me from fully living. I get to a certain point in my life and that fear slips in and takes over. If I feel too good about myself something bad will happen. If I feel even slightly happy, I expect to rocket back into sadness. Don't get too happy, don't get too contented, and most of all: *trust no one.*

Good feelings never last and in the end, I'll be alone again, hiding out in fear, with no one to confide in, no one to trust. I now know, however, that if I don't change my ways the old scenario will remain the status quo.

It's up to me.

I *want* to trust Chuck. I'm trying to learn how to trust him. I need his help as I clear the decks of the old me, as I start over directing my own life, everybody else out of the picture. There is no place for the old stuff anymore. I don't want it to be in control, though I still have to contend with it when it does arise and attempts a takeover. I need to keep shifting away from its attacks while I find closure, while I resolve the traumas of the past in a new way, in a way that totally clears it from body memory and mind memory, totally freeing my spirit.

I accept the memories as they emerge out of the darkness, out of the depths of me, but I still have to go deeper into this recapitulation process. I must understand what happened to me on a deeper spiritual level. I must find out why I had this kind of past, what it meant then, what it means now, and what it will mean in the future.

This recapitulation process is how I will change my life so that the past will no longer find a foothold, a handhold, or any other familiar place inside my body. I must release everything, completely, but in order to do that I must look at it in a different light. I must take it out of the darkness, pluck away the fear surrounding it, hold it up, and see it in the clear light of day from a new perspective. Only then will I be able to file it away, not to hide it, but having thoroughly explored it and understood it.

I must not avoid what I have inside myself; I must face it. I must go there now. I must learn to know myself on the deepest level or I will never be free.

Sometimes I am absolutely overwhelmed by what comes out of me. Every day, in some way, I confront my traumatized self. I realize I always have, though for the most part I've been largely unaware of its existence as anything other than an annoyance. But, after the last few days of darkness and being with that fifteen-year-old self again, I realize I've been carrying the burden of acute trauma my entire life. Now the most important thing I can do for myself is find out why. In order to do that I must change the old ways of coping, because that fifteen-year-old self can't stay in control—it's too debilitating and frightening being her. I must bring her with me out into the light of the present and find a way for both of us to trust that we can change how we feel, how we react, and how we choose to live.

I must get back to taking care of myself, in this moment, even while I take care of that poor little girl inside. I must consciously *choose* to be nice to myself. I must decide if it feels right to run or not run. I must choose to do yoga and meditation because it offers me what I need and not out of some old notion that I must be strict with myself. I must choose to be pretty and feel good about myself too. What happens, however, is that as soon as I start to think I look pretty I immediately want to go and chop off my hair, but I'm not going to do that this time! I'm going to deal with the pretty me and the buried, abused me too. We're going to confront this stuff together.

With Chuck's help we'll see the light at the other end of that tunnel where we've been hiding all these years.

Even while I write this I feel so terribly damaged and sad for the girl I was back then. I want to dig her out of the muck of the past, clean her off, bathe her gently, wrap her in a big towel and hold her and tell her it won't happen, ever again.

"It's not going to happen anymore—*never again!* We're safe. Life is good. Don't be afraid. We can go on from here. We can be happy and successful. There's nothing to fear. There's nothing that's going to get us. We might feel hurt every now and then; we might backslide a little; we might want to still hide sometimes, but in the end, we can do it. We can come out and be part of life. We can have our own safe and exciting life."

That's what I'd tell her.

Chapter Thirteen

Slave Girl

April 1, 2002

I turn away from confrontational situations and hide inside myself instead, because I learned a long time ago that confrontation never works. It didn't help at all in the world of my abuser and, in fact, it sometimes made the situation worse. Rather than fighting or sticking up for myself, I go diving headlong into the tunnel. At this point, however, I realize that although it's a place to hide, it doesn't really offer a safe respite because I take all the sadness and hurt with me. It's what I've always done, in every confrontational moment in every relationship, and I'm still doing it. I take the pain of the moment into hiding, where I curl around it and feel bad. I can hide out, shut down, and not talk or engage for weeks or months on end while there, but I can't escape the pain. It's really a thoroughly depressing place to be.

When I walked the other day and the voice suggested that the train could end it all, I was deep inside, as far as I could go inside that tunnel, curled up with that depressed fifteen-year-old self. That time, however, I answered her back and she didn't like it. I was challenging the way things were normally done. I separated myself from her, and in so doing did something out of the ordinary. I reacted differently, which was totally unexpected.

She would like things to stay the same. She'd be perfectly happy if we just hid out for the rest of our lives, not telling anyone about what happened, just staying closed inside where no one can get us. But I can't do that anymore, and I can't let other people get to me in the same way anymore either. I don't want to spend the rest of my life inside that tunnel, but I admit, I'm still frightened and I still don't trust anyone—even Chuck. I desperately want to, since he's the only person I *can* trust with any of this, but still the old voice pulls me back.

"He doesn't care! Nobody cares!" taunts that scared fifteen-year-old girl. "You think you deserve his kindness, his caring?"

I know she's just frightened, trying to hold herself together, but after her battery of old reminders I end up feeling completely alone again, thinking that even Chuck will forget about me. I attach to her negativity and despair, worrying that he'll put someone else in my time slot, or that he won't show up. I'd be devastated if anything like that actually happened after I've bared my insides to him, after I've let him in, someone who presented himself as a trustworthy confidant. If I were to discover that I had actually opened up to someone who wasn't what he professed to be, I'd sink right back into the tunnel. Fooled again, I'd never be able to rise above my stupidity for falling for the likes of a conman and I'd feel rightly punished for my disregard of the old rules that have stood by me so well and for so long.

I realize this is my lost child self who has these feelings. I know she's the one who expresses such distrust, but at the same time I, the adult, have stepped out of the way so she can speak now and I must let her express her feelings, no matter what they are. Even if she speaks words of fear, it's a good sign because it means there's hope we'll get through this recapitulation and onto something better.

April 2, 2002
When I meet with Chuck the depressed fifteen-year-old self accompanies me. I have with me a statement she wrote. I know I must read it to him. It's the only way to express her feelings properly, to speak the words she uses. I pull out the few sheets of folded paper and say that I have something to read, that it's often much easier to write than to speak. Chuck nods and I begin to read from the pages in my hand.

I am Slave Girl. Slave Girl is always tied up. Ankles and wrists bound, a rope around my neck, I'm splayed out, tied to stakes, to racks, to barn posts, to rafters, to ramps. My legs and hips cramp from being tied apart for so long. My ankles and wrists are bruised and blistered, ugly. Why are my ankles so ugly? Slave Girl, because I'm Slave Girl.

He talks, he raves, he nervously paces as he sets everything up, as he prepares everything for me. He does it for me, only me. He says I'm special. No one else is so special and beautiful to him.

No one else is his beautiful Slave Girl. No one else gets special attention the way Slave Girl does.

He ties me down so I can watch as he prepares, so I can see everything he is doing especially for me. He comes to prepare me, to open me up, to get me ready for everything he's planned. He's maniacally talking, muttering, clearly getting aroused in his sick way. I can feel that mounting arousal spreading to me—it and fear fuel the whole thing.

He makes me want to be hurt. He makes me desire everything he's going to do. He makes me feel disgusting and cruel to myself, as cruel as he is, so I will feel as much pain as possible, so I will be properly punished. Punishment and pain are the only way to get through it. If I feel the pain and disgust and remorse then I have accomplished what he set out to do with me.

Once again we're in the barn. I'm older now, fifteen or sixteen. I have sexual arousal and climax. I have knowledge of what is going on to a certain extent. I hate him, but at the same time I'm caught in his game. I become his Slave Girl. I become exactly what he wants. I become his fantasy.

I punish myself for being there, for being his sick fantasy. He touches me, he does whatever he wants and although I'm tied up and helpless I want him to hurt me because I need to feel vindicated. I need to feel punished for being there. I need the pain.

I am bad and he is punishing me. He tells me this over and over again. I'm bad and I need to be punished. I'm a bad Slave Girl and he is rightfully punishing me. His beautiful Slave Girl is bad and he's giving her what she deserves. Even in the midst of the pain I know I deserve it too.

It's silent in the room when I finish reading. Chuck doesn't say anything. He looks stunned. He looks like he's just seen a ghost. I automatically begin to apologize, but he very gently cuts me off.

"No," he says, "no, there's nothing to apologize for. Thank you for reading that to me. Thank you."

April 3, 2002

I dream that I'm in a yoga class and suddenly I can't hold it together anymore; I feel as if I'm heading for a complete breakdown. Erupting from inside out, waves of release go rippling through me and I can't stop or hold them back. My entire body is breaking apart, my muscles spasming, my skin crumbling, my teeth chattering, my head buzzing and heart pounding. I wake up in a complete panic sure that I must be dying.

I struggle to sit up in bed, to shake it off, but I can't stop the vibrations. My physical and emotional damn, long held back, crumbles and gives way, threatening to overflow as my whole body shakes as if possessed. Gasping for breath, I roll into a ball, wrap my arms tightly around myself and, holding back the flood, talk myself down from the edge of disintegration into a calmer state, acknowledging that I can't really hold this back for much longer.

At some point, I'm going to have to, literally, let myself go through this moment of annihilation. At some point, I'm going to have to, in a sense, *really* die—the old me is going to have to completely let go of life as I've always known it and totally shed the past. I realize that for the time being I'm merely preparing for that big moment. In doing this recapitulation I'm preparing for the big moment of breakthrough to new life. I know that.

The old me just isn't ready to die yet.

The stress is getting to me. I've lost another two pounds this week, down to a hundred now. I have to start running again to work off some of this stress though I know it's related to more old memories brewing. I can feel that something is preparing to emerge, the dream of annihilation perhaps paving the way for a memory of fearing imminent death. Anxiety is building, the edgy tension rising, and it's beginning to show. Yesterday, while talking to Chuck, I felt so fragile, so unsure of everything and he noticed.

"Are you all right?" he asked.

"I don't know—maybe," I said. "The hurt fifteen-year-old girl inside is pulling me down to her old numbing state, trying to convince me that she has all the answers, but my body is reacting, not wanting to do it that way any more. But I'm not sure how to do it differently, except to shift away from her when she tugs at me, and then I feel bad for deserting her again."

I don't know if I'm all right today either, but I'm determined to get through this. I just have to keep pushing on, staying focused on good things to come. Ever the optimist, I remain confident of my own abilities, connected to the surety of all things getting better, both as I take this strange recapitulation journey and as I push ahead with the divorce. I'm already certain that everything will be much improved in the future.

In the meantime, I need to keep my sanity and my wits about me, as I plod along working out the details of the divorce and as I trundle ever deeper in my inner work too. I can certainly remain focused on a better future, even while everything feels so huge, demanding, and pressing. I know that if I stay where I am now, nothing will ever happen; nothing will change. But I also know, from experience, that if I make a move to change, I'll be setting a chain reaction in motion. Soon other things will move too, as one thing will lead to another.

This is all good. I'm doing it for myself because it's the right time to do so, and I'm not stopping. The divorce is going forward, the business is going forward, dealing with the old past is going forward. I'm not sitting around any longer. The time to act is now.

April 6, 2002

I used to think that no matter how vile an imagination you think you personally have, there's always someone imagining something worse. Perhaps I used that thought to soothe my troubled mind. Now, in light of the revelations of my own case, I'm struck by the thought that Man, as a species, is not only fully capable of imagining horrific atrocities, but fully capable of *committing* them as well. All I can say is: *you better believe what you hear!*

When ugly flashbacks interrupted my normal, creative imagination when I was a child and teenager, and even as an adult, they horrified me. Where did those strange and disgusting images come from? How could I imagine such sexually explicit things at such a young age? I thought those images resided only in my imagination, that I had invented them out of my own quirky inner world, but now I know they came from *my experiences*. This leads me to believe that if you can imagine something being done or happening, then you can bet there's a possibility it has been done or will be done, to you or to someone else. I know this for a fact because this is the kind of evil imagination I met in the woods. If evil has no bounds and imagination has no bounds, then evil imagination has no bounds either.

My penchant for staying late at the studio and working long hours is an old habit that I recognize from previously difficult periods in my life. At such times there's a pressing need to be alone, to sort things out by going innerly. I must set a frenetic pace, remaining busy, so I don't break down, so I don't give in. I must keep a tight hold, hang in there and not let anyone get to me, but just work, work, work. On the bright side, however, there is a great outpouring of creativity.

The energy of fear seems to stir up this creative energy, rousing it from its bed where it's been sleeping buried beneath the covers of endless activity. As I turn inward and work through the issues and memories that arise, I ultimately access this wellspring of creative energy. As I allow my turmoil, my pain, my mysteries to speak through my artwork, expressing what I cannot speak out loud, I experience a breakthrough to an undiscovered self. Even if no one else gets what I'm truly expressing in my work, it doesn't matter. The blissful energy of creative release is in the action of producing—every tiny line and brush stroke flowing out of me, completely in alignment with my inner self. And actually, once the creative process is done and the work is completed, I find that it has little meaning for me.

I created a large hanging sculpture last summer during a lost week. It was a week when I was smothered under a tent of confusion; lost in the past, full of heavy thoughts and anger, as far down as you can go and still function. The week remains lost to me, except for the memory I retain of my busy hands working away while my mind and body dealt with the acknowledgment of what had happened between me and my abuser's daughter, before I even had memories of him.

At that time, I was totally unaware that there was any more to it, though there was a vague feeling of someone else being present. There was a shadowy sense that we were not alone, that we were being directed, encouraged, coached, forced to do what we did to each other. The creativity that emerged out of those memories and brutal truths was intense, as all-consuming as the memories that sparked it.

I keep coming back to this thought: *If you can imagine something, then believe it can possibly happen.* I cannot get away from this truth, in both a positive and a negative sense. If you can imagine something wonderful and positive, then it can happen because *everything is possible*. And if you can imagine something awful or evil, then there certainly could be someone else imagining something worse. This is what I came to last summer as I worked through those early days of my childhood, as my mind shut down to all else except what was emerging from deep inside me and as my busy fingers gave me an avenue of expression and release. It took me a while to wrap my thoughts around the horrible images that were emerging and why certain ones kept popping up over and over again. I thought I was probably a certifiable whacko, or that I had a hidden dark side smoldering inside me, or that I had been some kind of deviant child. I now know that I have so much buried inside, so many secrets, though at the time I simply thought I had a very twisted imagination. I thought I was crazy, sick-crazy, but now I know I was viciously abused, by a most brutal molester. I could never make this stuff up.

For so long now I haven't wanted to believe it myself, to fully accept that these terrible things truly happened to me. It's almost unfathomable, but I know that it's all too true, too true. My body confirms it. I'm beginning to accept that I walked into the territory of a most brazenly daring predator. I'm also more accepting that everything that's flowing up out of my memory is true, and that it wasn't my fault. And yet, even so, I seem to get no relief in such acceptance. Even if I look for relief from the onslaughts of memories in the truth of it all, I get only more memories emerging.

"Yes," the memories seem to say, "and here's another to prove it!"

In truth, I hate this process of returning to the horrors of the past. I find it crippling and I want it to be over as soon as possible, but the past continues to sneak in everywhere. It sneaks into my conscious mind, my body, my feelings. When I'm exhausted it jumps out and grabs me. It wants to devour me, but I won't let it. It wants to bring me back there and leave me in tattered remnants, a heap of bones, but I won't go.

The corners of my mouth are sore now, and have been for several days—numb—and, in addition, I keep gagging.

He got me everywhere else, so why not there?

Now that I accept the fact that I was sexually abused as a child I more fully understand some of the stone-cold reactions I sometimes had during sexual intercourse as an adult. One minute I could be enjoying myself with my partner and in the next completely shut down, gone limp and unresponsive. It's a little hard to fathom that I was so hurt by the abuse as to suffer long-term damage, beyond childhood, long into adulthood. Sometimes I feel maddeningly damaged by it, but at least now I'm gaining some understanding of the dynamics of my body, how my physical self took much of the responsibility for keeping me sane. I used to simply wonder at my faults, blaming myself for how I reacted when I shut down in so many ways, but now, as I go deeper into the past, I better understand the immensity of the damage I suffered as a child.

And now I wonder, where do I go from here? How do I start over knowing these things about myself? What do I want in a partner now? How am I ever going to deal with this in reality? What if I want to get intimate with someone? How will I be able to stand letting someone touch me? Because really, that's all I want, for someone to hold me, and tell me I'll be okay, that everything will be okay.

I haven't had a partner through all of this, nor have I shared any of these personal findings with anyone. I can't even bear thinking about doing that, the mantle of shame still too heavy. Chuck is the only person I've spoken to and I've really felt the lack of a close partner as I've taken this journey, the tremendous lack of a deeply loving person to confide in. I crave physical closeness, but without the sex; I don't have a place for that now. I must settle for being alone with my inner findings, I know that. It's part of the recapitulation process too, and yet it's so hard to hug myself—and not very satisfying either!

New flashbacks are coming up, of being in the same spot in the woods with my abuser again and again. I see more clearly now that the area in the woods is set up in a circle of stations, stations of torture. There is a large boulder. I remember sitting on it, feeling its heat on my bare skin and its hard coldness too. Over there on the left is a bush where he hangs his clothes and beside which he puts down the old quilt or a tarp. That area off to the right side is where the branch is that he makes me hang upside down from, monkey style.

There's something I can't quite see, but he makes me sit on it. He has his hands around my waist, pushing me down, asking me if it's all the way in. He makes me squat over this thing as he opens me up. I feel hollow and bursting at the same time whenever this memory comes up.

In another memory he's lying down and I'm sitting on his erect penis. He moves me up and down and I feel like everything inside me is going to explode, everything pushing up into my chest, my organs jiggled to the point where I feel like I'm shaken, chewed up and spit out. I'm sweet red gelatin, chewed up and spit out, except gelatin doesn't hurt. But this gelatin hurts; this gelatin is everything crammed up inside and no more room left and there is pounding, pounding, pounding, non-stop pounding...

I feel angry.

April 9, 2002

I'm a brittle leaf stepped on and crushed to dust. I don't feel safe anywhere. Keeping my distance and keeping my guard up, I find it hard to trust even Chuck. I have to force myself to interact, to be present in sessions with him and in life in general. I'm so fearful all the time because every situation is full of triggers waiting to go off.

If I let my guard down something bad will happen. This is the truth I have always lived by. I'm afraid to talk because I feel so vulnerable when I do, so exposed—the pain of the truth too much to tolerate.

"Get beyond it!" says the logical adult self.

But that's the way I've always done it. Keeping my guard up, living in fear, is the habitual pattern I'm stuck in at the moment. To indeed get beyond it is the next step in this journey, but only by facing it head on.

April 11, 2002

The other day Chuck proposed that the old cautious voice, the frightened, untrusting voice inside, the fifteen-year-old girl, was probably good for me. Yes, but she also pointed out the train tracks as a means to end it all. She's that voice of deepest despair. She's in the darkest place where no hope exists and with no way out. She's the lost child who had no way of dealing with any of this except to hide. And hiding didn't always work because it's awfully lonely in that tunnel, and the bad stuff is hiding in there too, having followed her into her hiding place. Sometimes the burden of trauma becomes too much and she can't cope anymore, and then those train tracks look inviting.

I continue to be puzzled by visions, or perhaps they are indeed hallucinations, of Jeanne Ketchel. She appears now regularly, in one form or another, sometimes in dreaming, sometimes in waking states. She gestures me towards her; her skin smooth and beautiful; her complexion translucent with a golden glow; her eyes dark pools of incredible love and kindness. Sometimes she points to Chuck, who immediately appears next to her, smiling big.

"It's okay, trust him. You can trust him," she says, quite matter-of-factly.

At other times, in other visions, she just points to her side and Chuck appears and just stands quietly, patiently waiting, looking at me with his big, kind, compassionate eyes. She nudges me towards him. While all of this is going on I feel a little uncertain, not sure how to interpret these visions and although they exude profound feelings of love, they also make me a little anxious. And, although I feel that everything will probably be okay if I go to Chuck with greater trust, I still hesitate. I'm reluctant, but Jeanne doesn't give up on me. She continues to urge me to trust Chuck. Both of them exhibit such tenderness, as I continue to struggle through this recapitulation process.

"Trust him," she says, speaking very clearly, but without words while I sit opposite Chuck in his office. I seem to hear her telepathically, at such times, her words just appearing in my thoughts. Sometimes I see her standing beside him or kneeling next to my chair, urging me to speak, telling me that everything will be okay, that it's a safe place to talk. Sometimes I hear her whispering in my ear.

"It's okay, trust him," she'll say, as if it's the easiest thing in the world.

Chuck did ask me the other day if I still have difficulty trusting him and I admitted that, yes, I still have a hard time trusting, that each time we meet I'm not certain how much I can tell him. I sometimes sit for a long time before I can open my mouth. He waits calmly and patiently while I agonize and battle the old voices, grappling with my old fears until I take a deep breath and force myself to speak, and yet I cannot speak about Jeanne. I still hold her close, afraid of rejection, of losing her to rationality and cold sanity when I so need her in the way she comes to me.

As a visual person I feel so awkward when it comes to speaking. I don't feel that words are always adequate; they don't go far enough for me and so I cling to my magical images of Jeanne and Chuck that are so fulfilling to my inner process. Feelings and words don't go together; they seem such opposites and I find no means of explaining things that I have yet to fully understand myself. In addition, words are so hard, feelings so soft and often when Chuck asks how I feel I cannot express myself. How do you explain what you feel when you feel so raw, so horrified, so ripped open, and utterly sad? Perhaps throwing up would more clearly express what I'm feeling.

"This is how I feel. See?" I could say. "*I feel sick. It makes me sick!*"

Maybe it's the child in me that still doesn't trust. Yet, she *is* me; she's part of me and if she's uncomfortable, then I'm uncomfortable. I feel how far apart we still are. I feel how deep the tunnel is, how sad she is, and how she gave up a long time ago. I have to convince her that it's going to be okay now, that we can trust this process and the people who are helping us. She has to learn that I too am a capable and safe partner, that she can also trust me, or she'll never come out and participate in this journey.

April 12, 2002

I'm in yoga class. We're doing a standing pose, *vrksasana*, tree. I accomplish the pose on the right side, get my balance and hold the pose quite easily. When we switch to the left side I struggle. I'm extremely wobbly, my balance off. I can't keep the pose for even a second, though a minute before I had done fine on the right side. I can't even pull my leg up without toppling over, having to catch myself, until I feel Jeanne Ketchel's presence. I recognize her energy instantly, behind me and to the left. I feel her hand very gently touching my shoulder, utter peacefulness and calmness pouring into me, steadying me. At the same time she points at the wall in front of me, pointing out Chuck, whose face appears on the wall about five or six feet away.

"Trust him, focus on him," she says, and I immediately stop wobbling. In fact, I'm able to hold the pose magnificently, without a flutter, rooted in quiet stillness, hands raised above my head in steeple pose, leg up, focusing on Chuck.

Jeanne's hand stays lightly touching my shoulder, letting me know that I can do this. I realize I need to trust her, as well as Chuck, but mostly I need to trust myself. I have the thought that at long last I have a guardian angel and I feel immense joy and inner peace as she continues to fill me with warmth and love, grounding me on my journey.

I could have stayed in that pose forever.

Physical sensations and numbing soreness are bothering my lips again, though I don't have a memory.

April 14, 2002
"Have you been able to have enjoyable sex, without bad feelings or thoughts intruding?" Chuck wonders, as our conversation centers on feelings that may or may not arise during sexual experiences.

"Yes," I say, "Sex has always been very fulfilling physically, but at the same time I sometimes have to battle numbing coldness that turns me into stone. But am I able to allow myself to have totally abandoned sex, feeling totally free to enjoy? I don't think so."

And I remember more clearly the questions that invariably arose from within during sexual intercourse: Why can't I just enjoy this? Why do I feel so bad? What is wrong with me? Why do I blank out? Why do I suddenly go cold?

April 15, 2002
The weekend is extremely busy. The kids have lots of activities, which I too am involved in, so there is no time to think about anything. But the past simmers on the backburner, making itself known in physical ways. I'm still very anxious and not sleeping well.

Unfortunately, I'm letting worldly worries about money and where to live have their way and, for the moment, it's just easier that way. On the bright side, a deal is being proposed that will allow me to sell my half of the house so that I'll have enough money to move out and get my own place, a little house for me and the kids, my vision becoming a possibility. I see an easing of a few burdens in that, but feel I must forge ahead calmly and pragmatically. So I elect to deal with daily, present day needs and activities, one little thing at a time, trying to proceed without cracking, while the old stuff sits at the pit of my stomach bubbling and churning away.

April 16, 2002

"Why don't you trust me?" Chuck asks.

"I'm afraid. I'm afraid of everything."

I find it incredibly hard to articulate how I'm feeling; to express the turmoil inside, the whirl of feelings that I can't put labels on, the whys that I can't explain, but it's true. *I'm afraid.* I'm afraid of Chuck even though he's the person I trust the most. I'm afraid of everyone, men and women; I'm even afraid of children, whom I find particularly frightening.

I'm afraid in every situation, but I've learned how to cope and how to appear normal. I've spent my entire life teaching myself how best to approach people, how to get by, but I'm still afraid and guarded. In truth I still don't trust anyone. It takes time before I feel at ease around people. I keep my unease well hidden most of the time, with a calm and withdrawn exterior presentation. However, there are still situations, especially in crowds, where I feel the need to escape as quickly as possible, afraid I won't be able to breathe as I feel suffocation coming on. I don't like large gatherings and I must brace myself before entering a crowded room. On the other hand, I must also brace myself before entering an empty room. Even when passing a lone pedestrian on the street I feel a strong urge to turn my face away, cringing as I pass by, avoidant of human contact. I realize this is one of the things my abuser did to me; he made me so afraid, so untrusting.

I just want to roll up into a ball and hide.

I'm pushing away feelings as they come up, the beginnings of some new memory. I don't know what they are or what they mean yet, so I'm just ignoring them for the time being. They feel too big, too hard to handle. Maybe I'm just not ready for them yet.

April 17, 2002

Every encounter with another human being has the potential to turn into a threatening situation. So even though I feel safe with Chuck, I also can't ever let myself feel so secure that I let my guard down, because when I let my guard down that's when the opportunity for something bad to happen will sneak in and, before I know it, I won't be able to stop it. How can I let go of *that* fear? How can I trust so completely that those fear triggers won't impact me any more?

It feels as if every situation has the potential to turn abusive.

A certain kind of intimacy exists in therapy that requires complete trust, but how can I get there? I feel like I can't totally relax, thus I'm tense and cautious. The tension is holding in the fear, and the fear is that something bad will happen because something bad always happens. It's a vicious cycle. I use the tension to hold back the fear and the inner voices back me up with their incessant warnings.

"Don't get too relaxed. Don't feel too safe," they say. "Don't say too much because it will be used against you."

Those are the warning mantras that have guided me all my life; they're all I know. And they work, upholding the world I've needed to be in; avoidance being my primary goal; avoiding intimacy, confidentiality, and conversation. Avoiding life has kept me safe. If I reveal too much of myself I will invariably get hurt. If I put myself in a vulnerable position I'll get hurt. I must avoid intimacy. I must continue holding back.

There are dangers everywhere!

Articulating what I'm feeling is hard work after so many years of shutting down. I'm having a hard time letting go of all the inhibitions that have become so necessary for survival, my closest allies. I *want* to trust Chuck and I imagine I'm *almost* there. If only I could be sure the vulnerable inner me would not suffer. I know I won't be free until that part of me feels safe. I do *want* to evolve and get to a point where I can continue opening up to life, where I can go the next step, unhesitant, without fear of reprisal.

The big ball of emotional pain is sitting deep inside the tunnel with the fifteen-year-old self, popping up at inopportune times.

"It hurts," I hear her saying.

It's really too painful to stand it for very long, so I push it away or it goes away when I ignore it long enough, though it continues to reappear sporadically. I may not be aware of what triggers it, but I know I'm not comfortable handling it yet. I don't feel ready, especially because I don't know how I'll be able to get through the immensity of emotions that surround it. It's such a huge tangled mess of everything I encountered in childhood.

The triggers I still carry produce additional trauma. They lie encased in those sad memories and in the many that are still unknown. So, aside from the physical abuse I suffered, there have always been and continue to be the constant threat of those triggers going off, of them being activated by outside and inside situations. I'm ready to shed them, but first I must encounter them so I can stop being so afraid of everything!

I want to evolve into a person who's comfortable in the world. I want to be able to have intimacy. I want to feel naturally calm and laidback. I want to feel pleasantly at ease in the world, not faking-it out of watchful necessity. I've utilized the guise of calmness for too long, having long ago found it a handy cover-up for my fearful inner self. I've used it as a protective measure, appearing quite together and unaffected by my environment when in actuality I've been on constant heightened alert, aware at all times that something bad is going to happen at any moment. It's been an exhausting lifelong experience.

What will happen now? Why does every situation still feel threatening? Because that's how I've always perceived things, as threatening, and a BIG part of me still believes that every situation is potentially dangerous. That BIG part is that little girl hiding in the tunnel with all that stuff weighing her down. So, yes, I can admit that I still believe that every situation may potentially turn bad and that she is afraid of everyone, which doesn't leave much room for a chance to change things any time soon.

April 18, 2002
In a dream, I'm fighting a man; he's attacking me over and over again. He won't believe me when I tell him that it's over. I scream at him repeatedly, totally frustrated that he just doesn't get it.

"Don't you get it? It's over! It's over!"

"I guess I don't!" he says, laughing right in my face.

I attack him, scratching his face with my nails, physically abusing him, angrily pounding at him with my fists, his childish taunt sending me into a rage.

In a second dream, I'm driving a car over mountain roads. Two little girls are in the back seat. The road is treacherous, with lots of sharp curves and I can't see very well; something is obstructing my view through the windshield. Several times I feel that I may be too close to the edge and risk going over the steep cliffs to the valley below, but I keep driving anyway, somehow able to stay on the road. Finally, I get to where I'm going—to some kind of ranch. The girls take showers. They come out looking so clean, pink and adorable. I leave them at the ranch while I go for a walk. While I'm walking my pants keep falling off. I only have one hand free because I'm carrying something in my other. I'm wearing sweat pants with an elastic waistband and drawstring that is too hard to pull tighter with one hand. No matter what I do, one-handedly hiking them up, I just can't keep my pants up. Finally, I just leave them down as I walk past a schoolyard where there's a girl's track meet going on. I feel very self-conscious and embarrassed as I stumble along with my pants down, but no one seems to even notice me.

I wake up steeped in those feelings of extreme embarrassment and self-consciousness, wondering what this last dream could possibly signify. That I am exposing myself in public seems to be the most logical explanation, if taken literally. But, as I open up to what really happened in the past, I must face the deeper personal challenge of whether or not I can be okay with it.

Can I be okay with breaking the pacts I made with so many people in my life as I grew up? Those pacts included not only the ones I made with my abuser, but also the ones I made with his daughter, my parents, and myself, all equally necessary at the time. Now, as I break them, as I confront the man in the first dream, declaring that it's over, I must face the deeper fears attached to the reasons for those pacts in the first place. On the other hand, my feelings of self-consciousness may only exist inside me because no one else seems to even notice as I walk around with my pants down in the second dream. In one way, I felt somewhat freed as I dreamed, not able to keep things covered up anymore, but in another way totally flustered because I had no control. The challenge is to actually lose control, to let go of my pants, my fears of exposure, and just keep going and be totally okay with it.

The first dream strikes the firm note that I'm letting my abuser know that I'm no longer playing his games, though he just laughs in my face. But I know it's over. I'm moving on, and when I lose my pants it underscores that the old pact is indeed broken; I'm unable to uphold either the past or the pants. Now that I've decided to recapitulate the old stuff I'm forced to accept the consequences of making that decision. I'm forced to acquiesce to whatever comes along to guide me, even if it means losing my pants.

This dream points out the total truth: I've had to accept that this recapitulation is leading me where I need to go, that total exposure of the past is necessary, and that I really have no control.

April 19, 2002

I don't want to get out of bed today. It's too hard to switch from one identity to another. I want to stay under the covers and be sad, the old me, lost and sad.

Out of that damaged childhood I had to construct a functioning human being, someone who could carry me through life, someone to do all the things I felt incapable of doing. I had to invent someone capable of interacting in life, who could go away to college, who could publish her first children's book at the age of twenty-one. I had to create a woman who could have sex, get married, have children, and get divorced. She had to be fearless, not be held back but keep moving, to travel, to explore the world, always searching for greater meaning beyond herself. Out of the rubble I had to pull together a new person who could be a part of the greater world. I had to create a persona capable of walking into a roomful of people and giving a speech. She had to be able to teach a class, get a job, publish books and articles, and illustrate for national magazines and advertising agencies. She had to be someone who people would like, respect, and want to know.

Out of the old stuff, I deliberately set about building a new life. I was not going to let it destroy me, though it still sits deep inside, piles and piles of boxes holding stuff; festering, heating up, ready to explode.

Chuck and I talked about the need to get to the pain, as well as the memories. I do feel pain when the memories come, though only briefly and intensely now, and then it's gone. However, I've noticed that lately the pain automatically switches from down there, as it intensifies in my genital area, to another place on my body, some place that is less traumatized perhaps, to my head, my arms, my hands, or my feet. I ignore or block out what's happening down there. I guess that's what I actually did when the trauma was originally occurring too: I left my body, dissociated, fragmented, blocking the pain that was occurring down there. And I've continued to do it for all these years. However, now that the memories are emerging, I suppose all the pain will emerge too.

Even as I write about pain I notice that the numbness and soreness in my lips continues to plague me, but I still have no clear memories, except a brief glimpse that comes charging up out of the past. In this vivid flashback I'm lying on top of my abuser with my head between his legs, my feet toward his head. My stomach clenches tightly. I feel so incredibly sad and scared and I'm very, very unhappy. It's all I have to go on so far to explain the recurring soreness in my lips and corners of my mouth.

"I don't want to be here!" my child self silently screams. "Why is this happening? What did I do now? Why am I so bad? Why am I such a bad girl? I can stand it. I can stand anything. No matter what he does to me, I can stand it."

These are the thoughts of my five-year-old self in that momentary flashback.

I feel that I've finally gotten to a point where I can function fairly well in the world. I'm not so frightened all the time and I can do normal things fairly easily without having to talk myself into them. Simple things like going to the bank, to the grocery store, going to a gallery opening, or to a movie alone used to be enormously paralyzing endeavors. I'd nervously talk myself through every step I'd be taking, visualizing everything happening in a safe way. At other times, I couldn't even leave the house, too frightened by what I knew not. I couldn't walk, talk, move, let alone function in the world, and so I'd put off my excursion until another day, for perhaps even weeks.

But now, after all these years, I've worked my way to a point of balance and stability, having devised coping skills and tactics to help me move beyond the old paralysis and fear. Most of the time, I function in the world quite adequately now, able to accomplish what I set out to do, though I rarely linger long. Home is still the safest place to be.

I find it ironic that now that I've finally reached a sense of balance, precarious though it may be, I find all this old stuff catching up with me, unseating me, sending me right back where I started from. This time I can't avoid it. This time I have to face it, sift through it all, come to terms with it, understand it, and see what it means.

It has to be meaningful in some way.

Another memory emerges, a long flashback I can't avoid.

I'm standing at eye level to his waistline; perhaps I'm five or six years old. My abuser is holding my head and pushing me into him, his penis thrusting into my mouth. I'm gagging and choking. I'm going to throw up. He'd grabbing and pulling my hair; my head hurts and I'm unable to breathe. I can feel his penis hitting the back of my throat, and I think he's killing me. He's suffocating me—it's impossible to breathe!

"It will end soon, it will end soon, it will end soon, it will end soon, it always ends, just hold on a little longer, it will be over soon. I can do it. I can make it."

I withdraw now into myself, into an old place, as this memory comes through. I remember more about the girl I used to be. I'm painfully, alarmingly withdrawn, but everyone thinks I'm just extremely shy. But the truth is, I'm paralyzed by fear.

I'm in seventh grade and I can barely walk; I can barely talk. I can't let anyone get too close and if someone does come too close I can't breathe, so I stay away from people. When I go to the dentist I constantly pass out in the chair, much to the doctor's dismay. I watch other kids playing, having fun, being carefree, and I ache to join them, but I can't move. I'm stuck to the ground.

I make my plans for how to act at the bus stop each day during my long walk to where about a dozen other kids are gathered, waiting for the school bus. I'm eleven, twelve, thirteen, fourteen, fifteen, sixteen, seventeen when I do this. I must prepare myself each day for being around other children. I plot out each step I will take, each word I will speak.

I have to decide where to stand each day and what I should say if that carefree girl talks to me. Suppose the other kids are playing a game? How will I dare myself to speak and say: "No, I don't want to play?" Or how will I say: "Yes, I'd like to play?"

That carefree girl asks me to play tag one day and I want to play, but I just stand frozen, off to the side, and shake my head no.

"Come on, it's fun!"

She frightens me because she acts as if she doesn't have a care in the world. I'm the complete opposite. *I have to be on my guard.* I have to be scared, alert, ready to flee deep inside where it's safest. But finally, one day, I dare to play when she asks me to join the game of tag.

"Okay," I say, somewhat surprised at myself.

And I force my stiff arms to unfold and I lift my aching legs just enough so I can lurch away from my safe spot. I run stiffly. I try to look happy, my face feeling like it's cracking as I attempt a smile, reshaping its normally guarded and serious expression. I dare to let a moment of light in.

"See it's fun!" the carefree girl chides me gently.

After that day, I play at the bus stop all the time, though I always have an alternate plan, just in case something is different. But most of the time I feel comfortable enough to run and be a little bit free, to laugh even, but not as much as her.

"Remember how you used to just stand over there and watch and never talk? You used to be so shy!" she says to me one day and I do remember.

I remember the hollow, stiff girl I really am, but I'm embarrassed that she also remembers her.

April 20, 2002
In a dream I'm desperately trying to find Chuck because I've decided that I'm finally ready to tell him everything. I can trust him now, but I can't find him. When I get to his house I find that he's away somewhere, but I go inside and sit down to wait anyway. I know it's his house even though there isn't one sign of him anywhere, not even a photo. I look everywhere for him, thinking he's hiding under furniture, in closets, but he isn't to be found. I decide to sit down again and just wait, as patiently as possible, though I'm also extremely anxious.

After a while his family comes in, but not him. They don't seem to think it's strange that I'm sitting there waiting. A woman comes in, but I don't recognize her, it's not Jeanne. She's a different kind of person all together, plump, bossy, distracted and short-tempered. She tells me she doesn't know where Chuck is either and then she turns her back to me and starts rooting through drawers, totally ignoring me. She seems angry, preoccupied with packing and sorting clothes, as if preparing for a trip. Then I think that maybe he was the one who died and not Jeanne, but I know he didn't because he needs to help me—he can't die.

I decide I need to get him a gift so I go to a nearby store; a gourmet food store. I don't know what to get. I see nuts wrapped in fancy bags, but when I pick them up I find that they're dried beans and I know that isn't a good choice. There's a basket of striped candy sticks, so I think I might get him some kind of candy that his kids could eat if he didn't like it. I bundle a bunch of them together, selecting several different flavors, but the bunch immediately turns to a spray of asparagus spears right in my hands. Nothing is right! Frustrated, I go back to his house to wait. I'm sure he'll come, that he'll know I'm waiting, that he'll sense I'm there, that he won't forget about me. But now there are workmen at the house getting ready to do something. I'm totally frustrated because now that I'm at last ready to talk I can't find him anywhere.

I wake up feeling the frustration of this dream; here I am ready to finally trust and I can't find Chuck, and Jeanne is nowhere to be found either. I wonder if she's letting me seek him out on my own because she knows I can do it. Maybe she doesn't need to be here helping me anymore.

April 21, 2002

I still want to trust Chuck, and feel safe doing so, but only the adult me knows it's okay, while the other part—the hurt, abused part—can't let her guard down. She's not safe with men, women, or children. No place is safe. Life is not safe. I'll never be safe. The tension is always there; the need to protect myself is always present. I can't relax, let go, or trust, though hopefully some day I'll get there. But for now I'm still afraid.

April 23, 2002

Today I'm very tense; I sit in Chuck's office all clenched up, shaking uncontrollably. He turns up the heat, which helps, but I can't concentrate. I can barely breathe. He just sits quietly, patiently waiting.

"When you're ready… when you're ready… whenever you're ready," he says soothingly.

We try to do a little EMDR, but I can't stop shaking. Finally I'm able to speak.

"I feel like I'm drowning. I'm in the bottom of a deep well and I'm drowning."

"What do you want to do?"

"Get out."

"Okay, why don't you do that?"

It's easy for me to visualize the well. It's lined in damp rock and when I tilt my head back I can see a disk of blue sky, far above me through the circular opening at the top of the well. I'm standing at the bottom, neck-deep in water, far down in a hole that's as deep and dark as that spring in the ground where my abuser got his water.

While Chuck works the EMDR equipment, stopping occasionally to find out how I'm doing, I slowly begin to shimmy up the stone-lined walls. It's a slow and difficult climb. I find footholds along the walls, moving one hand and then a foot, and then the other hand and the other foot. Slowly and steadily I climb to the top. I pull myself up and over the side of the well and quickly slam shut a wooden lid that I find near the opening. I climb on top of it and jump on it as hard as I can, enough so it won't open again, but that's all I can do.

"That's all I have the strength for today," I tell Chuck when I'm done. Then I sit and shake some more, saying very little, until my time is up.

April 24, 2002

All night I dream that I'm at a large gathering, like a concert or festival. The grounds are packed with lots of young people and families with children. I'm there with a friend from childhood. A man comes over to me, trying to steal my wallet, sticking his hands into my pockets. He comes back again and again and each time he approaches I turn and fight him off. I chase him away, shaking my fists at him and I don't care who sees me—I have lost my self-consciousness. One time he succeeds in getting my wallet, but I grab it right back and scold him, shouting loudly. I'm amazed that I can actually open my mouth and shout out words. One time I fight him physically, punching and kicking him until he goes away. Another time he takes my friend's wallet and I get that back too.

I feel powerful and in control in this dream, determined to protect what is mine, no longer fearful or embarrassed in public.

April 25, 2002

In a dream, I'm inside the house of an acquaintance while he's away. I don't know him very well at all, but for some reason I've entered his house. I sneak into the bathroom to take a shower. I'm careful not to touch his belongings or mess things up. He comes home while I'm still in the shower, which causes much embarrassment on my part. It was not my intention to run into him, but since I'm there he wants to talk. He's asking me questions, but I can't get over my embarrassment. I'm in a hurry to finish showering and get out of there, but he doesn't seem at all surprised or fazed by my presence. He's very accepting and easy going about it, but I just cannot get over that I so blatantly walked into his house and took a shower. I can find no way to explain my actions, either to him or myself. I finish showering, get dressed and, apologizing profusely, leave. I end up going into an old building, a crumbling warehouse across the street. I walk up a flight of stairs that leads to an attic room that has no walls. The room is filled with toys and games from the nineteen fifties and sixties, things I used to have. In fact, I recognize everything as my personal belongings from childhood; a record player and records, a Parcheesi game and stacks of books are among the items. These are my childhood books and toys sprawled out in this tumbledown house, a ghost house, but they seem to belong to someone else now.

April 26, 2002

I'm still trying to figure out why I have such fear of Chuck. Why am I so afraid? Why is it so hard to go there and just talk? I realize that *all* the stuff my abuser did to me still hurts like hell.

April 27, 2002

When I'm in Chuck's office I'm not just a forty-nine-year-old adult sitting there, but I'm also five, nine, eleven, and fifteen years old as well, and I'm full of the fears of those girls. I'm full of panic and nausea and pain and screams of fear long held back. My abuser is there in that office too. His smell is there, his voice is there, his tools are there, and he's there doing things to me.

I can feel everything now, except the pain. For some reason I no longer feel pain as the memories come up. It is as if I'm refusing to feel anything, as if my child self has decided to detach from feeling. I must be recapitulating this move on her part. As I investigate further, I conclude that it's a mystery as to how I'm able to do this, but I know that if my abuser knows I'm hurting then something worse will happen. He'll hit me or do something else if I make a sound, so I refuse to admit to pain. In so doing, I'm obeying him—by not crying out—but I'm also upholding something that's important to myself. I've figured out that if I admit to feeling pain, then he wins. In a sense, if I can block the pain, then I've won because he only gets my body, he never totally gets *me*. I save a small piece of me, in a place where I won't let him go.

I do realize that *I'm* not actually the one who is afraid when I meet with Chuck. I'm a fairly well-functioning adult, able to make important decisions and act on them. I'm able to care for myself, and others. I'm confident and competent, strong and capable, but when I enter his office all that I am melts away, and those frightened little girls walk stiffly over to the chair and sit down.

I can truly say that I, the adult, am not afraid of Chuck. I like him; I enjoy meeting with him. But the others, deep down inside, find him threatening, because he wants them to talk. He wants them to come out and be a part of life. He wants them to heal, but they've been hiding for so long that it's nearly impossible for them to come out and be okay in the world, or even in the world of Chuck's office. They've been solely intent on hiding from the bad guys, just trying to save a little bit of themselves, providing a foundation so that I could grow up.

Part of keeping the pain at bay, of not acknowledging it, is the little bit of control it gave me. Otherwise, I had no control whatsoever over the situations as they occurred. The only thing I could control was how I reacted to them. I could control my own response to the pain, in a very powerful way. I could pretend it didn't hurt in order to keep myself together, to keep from disintegrating. By pretending he didn't hurt me, pretending I was not in pain, I developed a method of controlling an untenable situation.

He's not going to hurt me; he's not getting to me; it will be over soon; he'll never, ever get all of me because he can't hurt me.

I go into a memory.

"You used to like this," I hear my abuser saying to me. "You used to like doing this. What's the matter? Why don't you like this? You used to like doing this."

"No, not that! Don't make me do that, anything but that!" I tell him. "Just don't make me do that! I don't want to do that today!"

He's holding me down by my legs and there's another person holding my shoulders, pushing me down so I can't get away. Hot salty tears fill my throat, choking me. I'm panicking, a huge lump of panic and fear rising in my throat. He's wicked, he does wicked things, and then he tells me I like them, that I like doing them.

He's going to kill me. I'm aware that I could die.

"Why is he trying to kill me? Why does he want to kill me?" I wonder.

Suddenly I'm aware of death as a possibility, whereas before all I knew about was holding on long enough until he was done, until it was over, but now my awareness is different. I'm aware that the violence is capable of killing me. I seriously consider that *he may really be trying to kill me.*

Not crying is part of being in control. Not acknowledging the pain and not crying are two ways of protecting myself, of retaining a part of myself, a raw piece of me that is sacred, in safekeeping for later. Pretending it doesn't hurt, not crying, means that the pain and tears get buried, paired together down there at the pit of me, at the bottom of the tunnel I mostly resided in.

Even now it hurts to cry; it physically hurts to cry. The pain and the crying are connected and I refuse to do both. I refuse to feel the pain and I refuse to cry, that's what I decided back then, and I'm still doing it.

April 28, 2002

I wake up in clenching pain, my legs pressed tightly together. I can't remember any dreams, but my legs are sore and achy from something I encountered as I slept in the night, either in dreams or body memories. The back of my head is hurting again in that spot that rubbed on the ground and the need to cry is back too, stuck in my throat. The fear of pain is stuck and the memories are stuck too.

As I lie in bed I can't help but encounter the deep everyday pain of the divorce and the intruding pain of the old stuff, the two issues that plague me night and day. My stiff legs are caught in a vise grip as painful cramps grab my thighs and my attention. As I toss and turn I can't help but fall into fears over the future, as I face the unknown. I end up getting more and more tangled up in the fears, real or not, as I attempt to shift away from the grip of pain.

As I struggle, I cry out for help and immediately I'm filled with a wave of warmth. Liquid light and utter calmness seep into my body, from the tips of my toes to the crown of my head—and my body relaxes! Full of knowledge, foresight, and deep insight I am flooded with confidence for my journey ahead. I experience deep serenity and I know that everything will be okay.

Jeanne again, I recognize her energy. Wow!

Whenever I think about the sexual abuse I won't let myself feel anything for myself. I won't even let myself acknowledge that my abuser did violence to me. I can't stand the barbarity and cruelty of what he did, but those are just words, not something that I can attach to. Yes, I can say those harsh words: *violent*, *cruel* and *barbaric*, and the things he did were all those things, but to feel anything for myself is so hard. I'm still so frozen, so numb, so cut off from feeling anything that I can't allow myself to feel violated against, because somehow it seems wrong. It seems selfish, like I'm trying to be special.

April 29, 2002
I realize that I handle most incidences in life by going numb. Numbness is a fine weapon against that which is unpleasant, difficult, or frightening. It blocks all feeling. At the moment I'm numb because I've been experiencing sporadic pain 'down there' and I suspect a new memory is brewing, just beginning to come into body awareness.

I'm nervous, anxious, feeling really strung out as the vaginal pain incrementally increases in intensity. Someone is prying me open, opening me. I'm being pried apart.

April 30, 2002

I'm in the throes of intense pain again this evening, around the same time as last night. For some reason it seems an opportune time for memories to approach. I'm not so busy that I can ignore it, yet I'm still fairly present and alert, not yet in the oblivion of the dream state.

I'm experiencing piercing vaginal, anal, and abdominal pain, as if someone is ramming a stick up me. I lie down with cramping and soreness centered deep inside; the whole pelvic floor now throbbing with pain so that I'm bent over and nauseous.

Writing helps ease the pain. The pain lessens with each word I write, though it's already lasted for about an hour.

Chapter Fourteen

Sweeping Breath

May 1, 2002

In a dream, I write my name in large script across my arm with a big black marker. Suddenly I don't know who I am; I feel no connection to the name I'm writing, I don't even recognize it. I don't even recognize my own handwriting. I begin to panic as I enter an impersonal state, aware that *I am nothing*. I have no personality, no individual characteristics that I can identify. I no longer recognize myself because I am nonexistent.

"I don't know who I am," I say, panic rising higher, but then I calm down as I hear Chuck's voice telling me that I can fix my dreams, that I can fix anything.

"It's okay. You'll be fine," he advises. "You are you. Just let yourself be you."

"Just let yourself be you. Just let yourself be you. Just let yourself be you," I tenderly recite to myself, soothing my panic.

I wake up; those words flowing off my tongue.

May 2, 2002

In a morning yoga class we work on opening up the pelvic area and hips. I ache during the entire class, especially in my tight hips, but by the end of the session I feel that I've loosened up considerably. For the rest of the day I notice how unusually loose my hips are—I sway when I walk and I feel pretty good.

At night I lie in bed trying to fall asleep, but I can't, though I'm extremely tired. I curl up under the covers as numbness and blackness creep over me like a blanket being drawn up by invisible hands. I'm lonely, sad, and depressed, lost in the darkness where pain is fleeting but numbness 'down there' is intense. The words 'down there' seem to come from the darkness and I can't feel that part of me, it's totally numb and cut off. It's especially noticeable in contrast to the good opening I got in the yoga class today.

Suddenly I'm losing it, physically vibrating, shattering, disintegrating. I blow up into marshmallow girl, puffy and floating, and then I deflate like a balloon and shrink into a tiny replica of myself, only about an inch tall. With a wisp of sensation, like a puff of smoke, I rise up into my head. I sit inside my head on a little marshmallow pillow where I'm safe, while my body lies totally dead, unfeeling, numb and unmoving way down there, seemingly far below.

The only thing I can feel of my body is the back of my head. It hurts. It feels like the praying mantis of my long ago dream, digging away at the back of my skull, asking me once again to *remember, remember, remember.*

May 3, 2002

I notice the numbness again, early in the morning. I take note but don't pay much attention to it, choosing to ignore it for the time being because I've got a busy day ahead of me and I need to be present. I succeed in forgetting until nighttime when I realize I haven't gone to the bathroom once during the entire day. I haven't even felt like peeing. I figure I'd better go and, when I do, I discover that I'm totally numb 'down there.' I can't feel anything, either the pee coming out or wiping afterwards.

I stab, jab, poke and pinch myself as hard as I can to make sure I'm not imagining this, but nope, it's real. *I'm totally numb!* I realize this is a memory related thing, so I don't automatically jump to the conclusion that I'm having a medical problem. However, there's still a small part of me that wants to call my doctor and say that I have something wrong, to ask for help, to fix me, but I push the thought away because it makes even less sense than what I believe is really happening. I'm confident that this is a somatic experience related to the emergence of a new memory. I recognize it as the same numbness that's been present for a few days. The only thing that's changed is that now *I'm acutely aware of it.*

When I lie down in bed, I realize that I have no feelings at all right down into my toes. As I acknowledge this fact, the numbness creeps up from my legs, spreads over my pelvis, up my torso, and, in a matter of seconds, right into my arms and neck, where it stops. My body is a dead weight now, heavy and totally paralyzed. I can only move my head and eyes. I feel nothing at all from the neck down!

The back of my head against the pillow feels as if I'm lying on concrete, as if I've been lying on cold hard concrete for a long time. Frozen on my back, unable to move my arms or legs, I stare into the darkness, wondering how long the sensations will last. I lie there for a long time, somewhat fascinated by the phenomenon, until I wonder if I can roll over.

"I'll give it a try," I think, and it's as if the thought alone is enough to break the paralysis because I'm surprised at how easy it is to roll over and curl up on my side. However, I'm still numb, my entire body up to my neck swathed in a thick, impenetrable layer of numbness. Intent on falling asleep, I warn myself not to roll onto my back during the night, fearful of falling back into that state of paralysis. I hope the numbness will be gone by the time I wake up in the morning.

During the night I wake up a few times and pinch myself—I'm still numb. By the morning it's mostly gone, although my pelvis, pubic area, hips and thighs still retain some degree of numbness.

May 4, 2002
I realize the exercises in yoga class the other day loosened more than my hips because memories are definitely brewing. I've felt anxious and jittery for days now, the familiar feeling of having too much coffee readily apparent; a sure sign of something getting ready to emerge.

I work until eight-thirty in the evening and take a bath as soon as I get home. I'm hoping the hot water will offer some much needed relaxation, but it doesn't comfort me as it normally does. I look at my ankles in the water and recall that every time I looked at them when the memory of Slave Girl was emerging I saw scars and swelling. Now I can't see anything there. The skin looks perfectly normal. But, as I sit in the tub looking down at myself, my stomach suddenly bloats up before my eyes, and I'm thrown right into a recapitulation.

I'm twelve years old now and my stomach is getting big. I'm sick all the time. Food tastes bad, everything tastes bad, and I can't eat. I can barely drag myself out of bed in the morning and go to school. My uniform doesn't fit right anymore. The belt especially poses a problem. Each day as I dress, I have to decide where to put it, whether to place it high or low over my protruding stomach. I'm so uncomfortable. It feels like something is inside me, and all I want to do is reach down and get it out because it's clawing and eating away at me. If only I could throw up enough I could get it out.

"Who? Who? Who? Who?" yells my father. "Who did it to you? Who did it? Who?"

"Why is he yelling? Why do they yell?"

Something is in there. It's a big black crab. I don't know how it got there, but it's hurting me. I feel sick and rotten, as if I'm rotting from the inside out. I pick at my food, eating very little because I have no appetite and it tastes bad anyway. Milk tastes bad too.

Something is killing me. I'm probably dying. I'm in such pain I can barely drag my body around or stand up straight anymore. I walk hunched over, sucking in the pain, pretending that I'm perfectly fine, but I suffer tremendously for a long time. All I want to do is lie down and die. Something is wrong. Something is in there, draining the life out of me.

At this point there's a big blank in the memory. I'm sick for a long time and then it's over, the big black crab is gone.

I get out of the tub and climb into bed, intent on returning to the memory, wanting to know more, but all I hear is my father yelling and shouting.

"Who, who, who?"

"I don't know what he means. Why is he yelling at me like that? Who what?"

The bad taste of the milk at school is so prominent that I taste it again as I recapitulate. It's so bad that I mention it to the nun every day when she walks down the aisle, tapping her finger on my milk carton.

"Drink your milk, drink your milk," she says.

"It tastes bad," I say every day, until one day she picks up my milk carton and sips the milk through the straw.

"It's fine," she says, putting the carton back down on my desk.

"Is anyone else having a problem with the milk?" she asks turning to the rest of the class.

Everyone else says it's fine too, but to me it tastes metallic.

"Drink your milk," she says firmly.

I try sipping it one tiny drop at a time, wary of the taste. In the end I gulp it down as fast as I can, hoping I won't throw up, hoping the black creature in my stomach won't be angry.

As this memory comes up I ponder what could have been going on. Maybe I was just severely depressed. This was the time when I no longer hung out with my best friend from my younger days. We were in different schools, worlds apart, during those crucial middle school years. My allegiance had shifted to other girls who attended the same Catholic school, girls from other neighborhoods. I was mostly alone, spending time in my room after school. Even my abuser's daughter and I seldom spoke during this time.

These memories come encased in a mood of black depression and hopelessness, but they also carry intense physical pain, issues around eating, and the gnawing feeling of something inside me, clawing away at my stomach.

May 7, 2002

"Yes," Chuck says, "yes, yes, yes, the feelings are related to the memories. Now you have to put all the pieces together. Don't force it, let it come on its own."

He teaches me a shamanic *Magical Pass*, the *recapitulation breath*, to help me deal with the intensity of the memories as they emerge, to help fill in the blanks too, but also to recapture and restore my own energy from those memories. Chuck demonstrates the breathing pass, but it feels impossible to do it in the manner he describes. I tell him that I feel my abuser's energy inside me, controlling and ruling me, taking up space, making me feel ugly and bad. I desperately want it out, but I don't feel that I have any room inside me for my own energy while he's still in residence. At the same time I'm a little apprehensive and not sure what it will feel like to get his energy out of me. Chuck instructs me to let go of my thoughts as I breathe and only stay connected to my intent, which is to incrementally clear the ugly abuser energy from my being and slowly replace it with my own good energy.

With that intent in mind, we sit and practice the breathing pass together for several minutes. We begin by taking in a deep breath as we turn our heads to the left. Then slowly moving our heads to the right, we breathe out completely, expelling my abuser's negative energy. We then turn our heads slowly to the left as we breathe in new fresh energy belonging to me. Then holding our breaths, we move our heads twice, to the right and left, in one continuous sweep, sealing in this new energy.

This *sweeping breath*, as it's called, is multidimensional in intent. It can be useful in scanning through and clarifying memories, while also retrieving personal energy that has been caught in those memories. This magical pass offers a sense of rejuvenation as the energy of others and physical, mental, and spiritual attachments are released. Chuck tells me that it doesn't really matter how I do it, that it's the intent that matters and that I can't really do it wrong.

We do it again and again, following the original intent I've set for this practice, breathing out the bad energy of my abuser, breathing in the good energy that belongs to me, sealing it in. I do it with my eyes open, watching Chuck, keeping up with him until I get it. It's not that hard and it's easier if I give myself a mantra.

"Out with the old stale breath of him, in with the new fresh air of me, seal it in. Out with the old, in with the new, seal it in."

When I've gotten the hang of it we sit and quietly do the pass together for a few more minutes. The breathing and turning of my head become easier and easier, loosening my anxiety as well as my neck muscles, sharpening and clarifying my vision, as I reach a new state of mental release and awareness. I get into a very calm place, as I say: *Out with the old, in with the new, seal it in. Out with him, in with me, seal it in.*

I feel refreshed when I leave, as if I have indeed released some of my abuser's energy and replaced it with some of my own lost energy, before I became that poor confused little girl. I feel her thanking me as I thank Chuck for teaching me this most magical pass.

May 8, 2002

I wake up in the morning and I'm lost again, feeling like I did when I was twelve, caught in the memory of that black crab in my stomach. I can barely drag myself out of bed. I can barely eat. Food is beginning to taste bad and my appetite is dwindling fast, just like it did when I was twelve.

I do the sweeping breath. I go back to what I know and, beginning there, I slowly scan through the scenes of memory that have emerged so far. This time as I fan my head back and forth, a mountain range suddenly appears on the far wall of my room. It stretches out in front of me, looking very much like the mountain range that was visible from the front yard of my childhood mountain home, it's blue silhouette painted across the far distant horizon. I fan my head back and forth, using this mountain range as a focal point. Slowly, bits and pieces of memory begin to appear between me and the mountain range. They hang suspended in space like shards of painted glass, disjointed pieces slowly emerging as if from the distant horizon.

Feelings and pain come to greet me from such a long time ago as I do the recapitulation breath. I breathe in what I can make out, as much of the truth as I am shown. I breathe out what has been getting in the way of discovering the truth. It's almost as if the slow fanning of my head back and forth sweeps away the fog of time, clarifying the details on the shards of glass, as more and more comes into focus.

As I move my head from side to side I feel an intense urge to do this breathing pass all day long, to just settle in and do it until I drop because I love its calming and clarifying effect and because I want the memories to hurry up and come. I want to speed up the recapitulation process and I see this sweeping breath as one way to do that, but I hear Chuck reminding me to go slow, to let the memories come, as they will, in their own time.

I don't know who I am anymore. I stare into the mirror, looking for signs of recognition, but my image changes constantly. The whole person I once was, the whole person I thought I was, no longer exists. Instead, I see the eyes of a hollow shell of a person staring back at me, a young girl who lived a miserable existence for eighteen years and then tried to move on. Until a year ago that is who I was, the person who constantly tried to move on, to distance herself from the past, who tried to get as far away as possible. Now, yes, a new person is emerging and there are signs of new life, but at the same time there is also a lot of death and burial going on as I dismantle and put to rest all the old ideas of myself.

This growing and changing process comes with a certain amount of stunning shock. *I'm not who I thought I was!* That is perhaps the most brutal shock of all, as weekly, sometimes even daily, I lose another part of who I was, as my image of myself changes once again.

I'm not at all who I thought I was.

May 9, 2002
Again, I'm reminded of that terrific inner strength, aware that it came from somewhere deep inside and that I had used it at some point. But, until now, I didn't know why or what it was all about. I

only knew that I had used it many times, though I could not relate it to anything in reality.

I remember watching old films about the Holocaust, watching people being tormented and tortured, and I knew exactly what they were doing in order to not only survive the torture, but *to transcend it*, to not be broken by it. I would whisper words of support to the actors in the movies, encouraging them to hang in there, that it would be over soon, wondering how I knew this, how I knew intimately how to transcend the pain of torture. I never had an answer before, though I certainly do now.

I also remember reading Carlos Castaneda's three early works and knowing exactly what he was talking about when he spoke of learning to become a warrior, a man of knowledge, of entering alternate realities and knowing how to act, how to survive, though I could not relate it to anything personal. I just knew that I had done the same, but could not find within my own life any examples, though I could feel it viscerally. Now, as I find out that I'm not who I thought I was, that I have not lived the life I thought I had lived, I relate to his writings in a different manner. I understand now how you can indeed live several lives simultaneously and not even be aware of it, because I did so.

It strikes me that Chuck has been interested in Castaneda's work for a long time and that I have found my way to him at this time in my life, that I get to immerse myself in this recapitulation with him guiding me. I always knew there was something of great and strange value in what Castaneda wrote, even though I couldn't quite put my finger on it. Only now, as I take this recapitulation journey, a process described and taught by don Juan Matus to Castaneda, do I begin to see why I might have felt such a strong connection to Castaneda's experiences and stories. In addition, I read his books just a few years after leaving for college, not long after leaving the old neighborhood to go live in another state, distancing myself from the past as much as I could at the time. Having already repressed the abuse, I was not in a position to find my way back to it at that time. I wasn't ready.

Now, as I wake up each day and find myself in yet another memory and another world, what Castaneda wrote about begins to make more sense, while at the same time living this way is absolutely disconcerting. Some things that I encountered in my past, that I lived through, are almost unbelievable, so much so that I almost refuse to accept them, but then the memories fill out, little by little becoming clearer and clearer, and then I know they are true.

I'm reliving a nightmare, one that occurred in a different reality from the one I remember, though real nonetheless, an *alternate reality* as I'm learning it's called. Just writing these words about the nightmare world pulls me back into it.

I'm twelve years old again.

Something *is* growing in there, a thing, like a ball or a tumor, but I don't know what a tumor is. Something is growing inside me, a monster, a hurting monster that makes me feel sick so that I can't get up in the morning. It hurts all over—my back, my legs, my pelvic area, my hips—everything hurts with the weight of it, and I'm terribly, deeply sad. I drag myself through the days, walking around in a fog, just wanting to curl up somewhere and hide. I need to disappear, and I need *it*—whatever *it* is that hurts—to disappear and go away too. I know something is very wrong, but I don't know what it is. I walk hunched over, sucking in my stomach muscles to ease the pain and hide the bulging monster as best I can.

I come out of the intensity of the memory and slowly begin the recapitulation sweeping breath. Once again the mountain range appears and as I fan my head back and forth I breathe in the feelings of my twelve-year-old self. Setting the intent that she tell me more, the details begin to clarify. Pretty soon the picture fills in even more, but it's too much to handle. Abruptly, I shut it down and call Chuck in a panic. Barely able to talk, I utter something about pregnancy.

"How do they get a baby out of a twelve-year-old?" I ask, my voice cracking.

I recall knowing that something was physically very wrong at the time, but I never knew what it was. The words pregnant or baby were never used, neither by me nor anyone else.

As this memory begins to emerge it dawns on me that everything that I've retained as conscious memory was a lie, covering over these real memories, this *stuff*. It feels as if all this stuff was real, the rest of my life a total fabrication.

May 11, 2002

I wake up in a state of shock, so agitated that I call Chuck again, needing the contact and the anchoring as the memory slowly cracks open, sending sparks of pain and fear rattling through me.

"I was pregnant, I had an abortion."

I listen for Chuck's calming voice, barely reaching me through a dizzying blur of flashbacks and realizations. I know I have to let the memory come, that I have to access what I was feeling back then, but the feelings stick painfully in my throat, sending me into a deeper depression and I need to talk yet again before the hour is out. By sheer force of will, I vow to face the memory, to let it come, to go through it alone.

I sit and do the sweeping breath. I use it first to calm down, scanning the distant mountain range that once again appears as soon as I begin fanning my head back and forth. My intent is to get into a stable place from which to process the scattered pieces of memory. Almost immediately several flashbacks pop up out of nowhere, shocking in their revelations. They flicker past in the blink of an eye, twirling around in the space between the bed I'm sitting on and the shadowy mountain range on the opposite wall. Eventually, the disjointed flashbacks, flung at me like jagged pieces of broken glass, slow down. They spin more gently, in slow motion for awhile, until suddenly they're little bits of real time dangling in front of me. I'm still not yet sure how they fit together, but the longer I sit and do the sweeping breath, the more I'm able to swipe aside the veils of confusion, horror, and anxiety that block the truth. As I slowly let the memory form on its own, a clearer, fuller picture eventually emerges. Here is what I recapitulate as I continue doing a slow and methodical sweeping breath:

I'm in the car with my father. We arrive at the doctor's office. It's nighttime and dark and there are no lights on. I remark on this.

"It's okay, the door is open," my father says.

We go into the dark waiting room; a light shining into it from the inner office.

"Hello, bring her in."

No one talks to me. I go into the examining room with the doctor's wife—she's his nurse—while the doctor and my father stay in the office and quietly talk. I go behind a screen and take off my clothes. I come out wearing my underpants but she sends me back to take them off too. I get on the table, naked now, and she covers me with a sheet.

No one tells me anything. They strap me across the chest, so my arms are pinned down. My legs are propped up and open. My father is off in the left corner, by the changing screen. I see him standing there.

The doctor doesn't say anything to me. He has a mask on, so does his wife. She's standing at my left, by my head, her hand resting on my shoulder. The doctor pries me open, sending me out-of-body because the next thing I notice is that I'm looking down on the scene from above.

I see my face, looking pale and blank, slightly turned to the right. My adult self who is recapitulating this memory knows it's me, but my out-of-body twelve-year-old self is not identifying with the girl on the table, she's merely observing what's taking place. I see what she sees. I see the doctor's big, shiny bald head and white shoulders, the nurse at my left side, my father off in the corner. My father leaves the room at one point and then stays away. It's just me, the doctor, and the doctor's wife. Quiet—it's intensely quiet.

The memory abruptly jumps to when I leave the doctor's office with something like a wad of towels stuck inside my underpants. And then it stops altogether, no more pictures are appearing, no more shards of flashbacks. I stop the recapitulation breath and contemplate what I've just learned.

I don't feel or remember an actual abortion during this unfolding memory. However, in one of the long periods of pain that I experienced last week it felt like I was being painfully pried open; the pelvic pain intense, and now I wonder if that was related to this abortion memory. It's not apparent if narcotics or any numbing agents are being used, though the memory is far from complete. Perhaps the somatic numbing experience I had not long ago, when I was paralyzed from my neck down, was related to this memory as well.

I'm only present and aware of what's happening in my body up to a certain point, until the doctor begins doing the procedure perhaps. After that, what I recapitulate from my ceiling vantage point is minimal at best, just a few broad strokes setting the scene. No memory of what is actually taking place on the table is available. I can't even see my whole body, only my pale face is visible when I look down on the scene, and then I flip to the moment of leaving with a towel between my legs. I walked out, but little else directly before or after that is coming through right now.

How long was I there; how long did it take? I don't know.

Did they put me out? Did they use a local anesthetic? I don't know.

I can't see or feel the whole picture yet.

May 12, 2002
A friend said: "You need a little break!" So I went out with friends last night, had fun and was very funny myself, all of us joking and laughing. It was good to feel like a normal person again for a few hours.

I've been doing the sweeping recapitulation breath pretty regularly over the past few days for a half hour or longer each time, as often as I can throughout the day. The calming effect is good and the memories are clarifying too, enough so that I can make sense of all the jumbled pieces that have been coming in stark flashbacks and intense somatic experiences. I wonder if the rest of the abortion memory will become accessible as I continue to study what I've so far recalled. Or I wonder if the fact that I left my body inhibits my knowing the entire experience. Anything is possible.

I'm fascinated by the fact that, as I recapitulated this pregnancy memory, my period was delayed, synchronistically aligning with the emerging memory, recalling my twelve-year-old body's true state of being. Now, after having achieved a fuller memory and having also accepted the truth that I was indeed pregnant back then, and that I had an abortion, my period is once again flowing. But it's coming in big clots of dark blood, as if I have indeed just given birth, also in keeping with the memory perhaps. As I said, anything is possible.

I noticed that when Chuck mentioned my abuser the other day, I cringed, as if about to be struck. Just the mention of him in our conversations and just thinking about him hurts. I am gripped with fear and loathing at the thought of him. He still gets me.

May 16, 2002
It's been a terribly difficult week with memories bounding out, in rapid fire. The sweeping breath definitely loosens things up. It clarifies things as I do it, filling in minute details. It actually lifts the veils, the fog that is sometimes so difficult to see through, so that I'm there in the past again, physically reliving the experience in a deeper way, every aspect clearly highlighted.

I notice that each time I begin the sweeping breath, the ghostly mountain range appears on the far wall. It gives me something to focus on as I breathe, and eventually it acts as a backdrop to the scenes that appear and slowly coalesce into fuller memories.

I sit and do the sweeping breath and pretty soon I'm back there again, in the doctor's office. I see the doctor and his wife, their faces highly defined, in exquisite detail. It's intensely quiet in the room, the atmosphere heavy, dark around the edges. It's dimly lit except for the light focused on me lying on the table. As I do the sweeping breath and scan the memory it's as if a light is being shone on what is most important for me to recapitulate, each detail that I'm drawn to suddenly illuminated so that I see very clearly. Now I see the baby, *I see the baby*, brightly lit and starkly white. But to my twelve-year-old self it appears to be only a doll.

"Why do they have a doll here? I'm too old for dolls. I hope they don't think I want it. I don't play with dolls."

It's tiny with delicate features, waxy white, bony, skeletal, no ears, no eyes, lids tightly closed.

"Four or five months," the doctor mutters in answer to a soft question from his wife, as he continues to work between my legs.

Why did they let me see it?

"That is the bravest little girl I have ever met," I hear the doctor say to my father when he goes into the other room.

I'm still lying down as they talk out there in the office. The doctor's wife stays with me. My legs are allowed to go straight again. The pain, the relief of stretching them out is immense, of being able to close my legs tightly together again, no man between them looking at me down there, doing something down there.

I'm clenched so tightly as I recapitulate, my neck and head hurting, my shoulders hunched and tight. I'm shivering, cold—then and now—the thin sheet over me not offering enough warmth. I'm nauseous, then I'm sick, throwing up, bent over the side of the table. The doctor's wife holds my head, her palm cool against my forehead as I vomit onto the floor. As I lie back on the table the thoughts of my twelve-year-old self come through, looking for explanation:

"I just had something wrong with me. That's all it was—I was just sick with something."

My parents sign me up for art lessons over summer vacation. I'm ecstatic and terrified at the same time. The only lessons I've ever taken outside of school were swimming lessons when I was five. The girl I'm afraid of, the carefree one from the bus stop, is in the art class too. We become good friends that summer.

Our watercolor paintings of a local scene get into the county art show, the youngest exhibitors. I'm interviewed by a reporter writing an article in the local newspaper and I'm photographed holding my painting. My work is praised for its expertise of technique and ability to handle the difficult medium. I'm congratulated by the older exhibitors who kindly accept my presence in their show. I'm very nervous, but I get through it. Everything was always something to be gotten through, even something good. I turned thirteen that summer.

I've been thinking about the fact that I never took control during the abuse, not only because I couldn't but also because I didn't know how. As I recapitulate, I experience what it was like to be caught in my abuser's world, so groomed to numbly do exactly as I was told that I never even knew I could react; so groomed I didn't know there was any other option. Fighting had no effect and I'd soon give up. Nor were girls taught to be aggressive when I was growing up. We were still being socialized to become obedient housewives. The only occupations readily available to women aside from raising a family were limited to nursing, teaching, and secretarial work. Here I am now, almost fifty, and finally realizing that life doesn't have to be that way, that I can indeed react, that I can fight back, that I can make things happen differently.

I'm not blaming myself for what happened in the past, but I'm discovering something new, that *I actually have power*. This is mind-blowing to me! If I can make things happen in dreams, then surely I can make things happen in waking life too. I don't have to just go along with someone else's plan. I can have my own plan and I can be in charge of my own life. I see my lack of awareness around personal power as a devastating consequence of the abuse. Being groomed from a very early age to be submissive has led to an almost total lack of active participation in making decisions regarding my own life. I've tended to let things happen, to let fate have its way with me.

I've remained caught in the veils between the two worlds of my childhood, never fully grasping that I was more than just a poor wanderer. I've just blindly, submissively, gone along with what's been presented, most of the time unconsciously participating in life rather than acting in full awareness of my situation. I've been driven more often by fear than by a sense of my own power. In my normal state of numb compliance I'm not actually aware that it's possible to live differently, to live reactively, to protest or take action on my own behalf. I meekly tend to let things happen because I think they're supposed to be that way.

As this new perspective emerges, I realize that when I did react and force a change, I would soon fall back into the old mesmeric gloom of numbness and depression. Fear quickly reasserted itself, overshadowing those fleeting moments of clarity.

This is how I've mostly lived my life; dimly plodding along in a state of depression interspersed with brilliant moments of action. But mostly I thought that whatever was presented was the way it had to be—the way it would always be—so I admonished myself to just accept it, just buckle down and trudge through the muck of it and pretend that everything was okay, as I'd been taught. But now I'm learning that I have the power to take action, in a way that is right and meaningful for me. I don't have to wait around for anger or something catastrophic to be a catalyst. I'm learning that I can actually instigate change because I want it and because it's right and good for me.

I know now that someone took away my power. The groomer, my abuser, took it away from me. He literally trained me like a dog, to obey, to do his bidding, and forever after I've obediently done as people and circumstances have bid me. I could probably be so much more than I am if I had not encountered his dominance, but for some reason my life unfolded as it did. I have to accept and understand that. And I have to remember that fierce inner strength, that strong, yet tiny bit of me that I've kept hidden, protecting it, never letting anyone get too near it. It's been a flame glowing inside me the whole time, just waiting for me to reclaim it. And now, as I do this recapitulation work, I have allowed it to flare up again. And no one is going to put it out, *ever again*.

Chuck tells me that I am indeed taking back my power as I recapitulate, that I'm taking back what rightfully belongs to me, what my abuser usurped a long time ago; that it's been waiting for me to return, recognize it, and reclaim it as mine.

May 17, 2002

I dream long rambling dreams during the night and can't remember a thing when I wake up. I retain only a sense of something complicated being unraveled all night long, as if a tangled string were being patiently unwound. The mystery and wonder of it stay with me as I wake up with pleasant, almost contented feelings, in stark contrast to what is going on during the day as the memories unfold. It seems as if the nightmares are happening during the day, while I'm awake.

Unfortunately, the good feelings don't last and I grow incredibly depressed as the day progresses. I just can't shake the gloomy feelings. Yesterday, I was so lost as I recapitulated what happened in that doctor's office, not wanting to believe what I was seeing, not wanting it to be true. Like all those memories, I don't want them to be true. They're so difficult to accept, but I don't want to bury them again either and I certainly don't want to go back into that old numb state of depression, filled with intermittent horrifying triggers. But I'm getting impatient. I'd like the whole thing to be over and done now. I'd like to move on to a better place.

May 18, 2002

I don't feel anything, nothing. I don't sense any feelings anywhere inside me. But I must have feelings. That's all I am, a bundle of overwhelming feelings, full of anxiety, caught in fear, totally alone and lost in memories.

I recapitulate what it was like being a child.

I'm a young girl again. I know that I have to cope with everything on my own. There's no one I can safely talk to. There's no one to comfort me, no one I can explain anything to. There's no one saying they love me and no one telling me I'm a good girl; except me. I have to figure out a way to explain to myself what's happening.

Now, as an adult, I must find a way to communicate and comfort the distant child self. At the same time I need to more fully grasp what all of these memories are trying to tell me. While I struggle with accepting these recapitulated truths and make attempts to understand my child self, what often happens is that I'm immediately thrown into the next memory with barely a moment to take in the reality of the one that just came before.

When I do have a chance to spend some time investigating the child inside me, I discover that she feels nothing. In her deeply depressive state, she's totally numb and cut off from her feelings. And so I rattle around in her numb world and in my own disjointed reality, trying to figure out what part of me is feeling and what part of me is not feeling. It gets confusing sometimes.

I go to my child self and ask her to remind me of something that I've forgotten, so I can understand her better. In a moment of recapitulation, I go into her world.

I'm a little girl again, terribly depressed, putting myself to bed at night. I lie curled up with all the hurt and the aloneness, trying to make myself feel safe.

"I'm a good girl, I'm a good girl, I'm a good girl, I'm a good girl," I chant softly.

I curl up with all the anxiety and the horror, taking them under the covers with me until they gradually seep away in the darkness under the blankets, until the night takes them. Eventually the night takes the pain too and I forget. My dreams take the fear and the sadness; feelings float off into dreamland so I can forget even more. This is how I comfort myself, by forgetting and by not feeling.

As an adult, I still find that it hurts too much to feel. It's been much easier to navigate through life without access to feeling. When feelings do arise I automatically push them away, the same way I always did. I walk away from them briskly, so practiced am I. But really that old self is caving, slowly accepting that feelings are necessary, meant to be *felt*. In actuality, all I want to do now is sit and cry out the old buried feelings, let them come rushing out into my lap, where I can hold them and accept them. I'm thinking that once I get through this achingly painful step I might feel better. Once that little girl and I get together on *feeling* what really happened we might just be able to heal.

The truth is that I was a sad little girl, but in actuality I was just trying to figure things out, trying to figure out whether or not a situation or a person was safe. Everything was a big question encased in fear. No one was there to explain the world to me, so I invented my own explanations for why things were the way they were.

I still uphold the skewed and yet absolutely necessary perspectives of that fearful child self. Her behaviors and habits, so useful at one time, are still active. But now I understand that nothing was really the way I thought it was back then. I was living a horrible existence, but trying to make it seem normal, trying to find ways to fit my other-worldly experiences into a child's world, creating stories that I could comprehend and understand. In a sense, I created a new world that I could safely live in. But really, what I craved, above all else, was normalcy. Normalcy was what I saw in other, happier children. I wanted to be an adored child, carefree and unafraid, surrounded by people who loved me and expressed that love in a normal, positive way.

My bed still seems like the only safe place in the world, more so now that I'm in the midst of this recapitulation. Since I haven't shared it with anyone else for so long, it feels like my personal place of refuge again, my safe place thankfully returned to me with the return of the memories. I know I need it again; the same way I used to. When I'm under the covers I remember more clearly the feeling of hiding there, trying to get away from everything, glad when it was finally bedtime; happy to crawl in and hide at the end of the day.

Even as a child I never really felt like a child. I didn't feel that I could be a child. I had too many responsibilities and too many anxieties to deal with. I was a good big sister, a good babysitter, and a good chaperone. My parents had a lot of children, which I resented. As the oldest daughter, I spent a great deal of my early years taking care of my parent's children, while they, I felt, were not taking proper care of me. I hated them for not knowing that I needed things from them, that I needed to be held and loved, that I needed to be comforted, that I didn't understand anything about life, that I needed explanations and guidance. But I also know that I appeared so self-sufficient and aloof, so responsible, so quiet; rarely questioning, rarely disobeying or doing anything out of line. I was well trained. Fear of punishment was only a hair's breadth away, wielded like an invisible knife held over my head by my parents, by the Catholic Church, by God. Now, I also understand that the punishment inflicted by my abuser was only a memory away, where he wielded an equally deadly instrument.

Not knowing things is far worse than knowing, because not knowing means you have to make up your own explanations, and a child's perspective on reality is never going to be complete. It can only accommodate as much as the child can fathom and it will only assume as much as the child can handle. Often a child's perspective is not factually based but only based on the child's conscious or unconscious desire to make things right at that moment. In my case, I was capable of telling myself anything in order to bring soothing comfort. I could believe anything was true, simply because it seemed like a good explanation. Whether a lie or a fantasy, it didn't really matter, as long as I could hold back the moment of annihilation, of disintegration and death.

I think about Slave Girl again and how I made up a story to tell myself when I was nine or ten, in effect saving myself from the horrible truth of what was really happening, the truth of what was causing the painful rope burns on my ankles and wrists. The fantasy story of a beautiful slave girl became real. It meant life. Later Slave Girl became an outlet for self-hatred and punishment, just another fairy tale.

Of course, I would never have been able to accept or even consider that I was pregnant at the age of twelve. Why would any twelve-year old want to admit that? Not only is it unthinkable and overwhelming to consider but also, even if I knew what it felt like to be pregnant, I would never have thought that about myself. I didn't equate what was happening to me at the hands of my abuser as sexual acts that would result in pregnancy. It was not at all related to what I'd read about in that tiny pink booklet my mother gave me that so vaguely skirted the truth of becoming a sexual being. Nor could the reality of being a young Catholic girl crack through to the reality of what happened in the world of my abuser either, and vice versa. The two worlds simply did not exist simultaneously and I simply was not capable of fathoming that what I was dealing with was a pregnancy. Instead, I had a big black ball of a crab inside me that hurt as it clawed away at my insides, that spoiled the taste of my food and made me sick. I convinced myself of whatever I needed to comfort myself and, above all else, to simply be a twelve-year-old girl.

When I return to memories of that time it's abundantly clear that I felt totally alone and without support. That I only had myself to turn to was predetermined by what had already gone before. The long pattern of abuse and neglect from earliest childhood had already shown me that there was no other outlet, that no one seemed to care. And the way my parents acted, as if the pregnancy hadn't happened—by never calling it by its true name or ever talking about it with me—pushed those feelings of neglect and abandonment ever deeper. I was left to carry forth the shameful, shocking experience alone, but only as a deeply buried memory, and buried it stayed. So, okay, in that reality the pregnancy *didn't* happen.

There I was, a child needing so much, but they must have thought I was handling everything so well. They must have assumed I was okay and that I would forget. *Children forget everything, so of course she'll forget.* This seemed to be the common assumption back then and I was too well-trained to ever question an adult decision. It was almost guaranteed that I would never make them uncomfortable by bringing it up. Forgetting was convenient for all involved.

As I recapitulate, I discover that, in truth, I was totally turned inward, lonely and unhappy. I knew I had to take care of myself. I had to just go on and do what had to be done. There was no time to pause for feelings or for investigation of the incident. There was only the opportunity, offered by silence on the part of my parents, to move on and, yes, to forget. But deep inside I knew I just needed to wait, that time was on my side. I knew I had to continue living the life I was dealt, that I would encounter my abuser over and over again, in memory and in reality, but that eventually I would grow up and move on. Someday I would get away and I looked forward to that day with bated breath, knowing it would arrive, but fearful of it as well.

While I waited for that moment to arrive, I only lived a half-life. On the outside I lived a sort of robotic, doing-the-motions kind of life, my ego fragile but functioning. On the inside I was bundled up and closed off. Inside I was dead and lonely and afraid. I'm still dead and lonely and afraid, even though I went ahead and had a new life after that dark childhood. I did all the things expected of me. I grew up and created a life for myself, thinking I was happy, thinking I was finally free, but in reality I discovered I'd never really left the past. No matter how far around the world I went, I always carried what happened in the woods inside me.

I've lived many years and yet I'm still waiting for my life to begin. When is it going to start? When is my life really going to begin? Why don't I enjoy anything? Why can't I feel?

These questions have dogged me every step of the way, trundling along beside me, perhaps trying to get my attention. I've wondered why they've stuck by me for so long. Now I know that they've been asking me to go back and find out.

I've resorted to the old habit of pretending I don't have feelings, shutting them down as soon as they arise—synchronistically, it seems—as I continue recapitulating my twelve-year-old self. She had no one to speak to, and I don't have an intimate partner to confide in either. I find myself automatically resorting to what once worked so well: *silence.*

In the family of my childhood, we all went around bottled up, our feelings suppressed, everything quietly put away, pushed down out of the light of day. We were not an expressive clan and if we dared express something—even a few tears—we were soundly ridiculed, made silent by shame, just another shield blocking the truth. So, when Chuck asks me what I'm feeling, I automatically resort to the old numbness. *I feel nothing.*

"I don't have feelings! Feelings are not allowed!" I say, quite emphatically, mimicking my child self.

I admonish myself to do what I've always done, to just get on with things, just put it aside, forget about it, and move on. The old me wants to be hard, but the new, softer me understands now, with insight from Chuck, that I can't successfully leave anything behind if I haven't allowed myself the opportunity to fully explore it. I have to find out what those feelings are; to express them; to let them go through me the way they want to, naturally. Feelings too are part of this recapitulation process.

"Those feelings are sitting there waiting to explode out of you," he says. "Let them come."

May 19, 2002
I talk on the phone with Chuck, once again in the throes of a recapitulation. Severe anxiety, shaking, and nausea accompany a memory that kept me up all night. The feeling of something coming to clarity kept me alert, as it emerged piece by piece throughout the night, in stabbing shards. I knew it was related to what happened when I was twelve, something that must become known. More details appeared as the night went on, coming in slow, painful spurts, clarifying the truth of what happened back then.

This morning, while doing the sweeping recapitulation breath, I was finally able to put it all together, as similarities between that abortion experience at the age of twelve and my experiences at my daughter's birth quite strikingly aligned. I had gotten part of this experience earlier, the feeling of woodenness, of being unable to feel anything, my arms stiff and unable to hold my beautiful new baby when she was born. I go back again to the day of her birth and to the memories that emerged during the night.

It's June 1991, I'm lying on the delivery table; the birthing room cool and very quiet, dark around the edges. A bitter sense of loneliness creeps into me, a feeling of incredible isolation, as I notice that no one is paying attention to me. They're all busy. There'd been a problem with the placenta and I'd been lying on my side for hours in an attempt to keep it out of the way of the cervical opening. They didn't make a big deal about it, but I was aware it wasn't a good situation. I'm lying on my back at this point, in the throes of the last minutes of labor. No one speaks—neither the doctor nor the nurses—all are focused on what the doctor is doing between my legs. Suddenly I realize: "Oh my God, I'm so alone!"

I notice how eerily quiet it is in the room and then I feel myself going numb. The numbness creeps quickly up my body from my toes to my neck until the only things I can move are my head and eyes, the same numbness I recapitulated at the beginning of this month. I start to dissociate, to leave my body, but the doctor yells at me.

"Don't stop now! We're almost there!" he says, almost angrily.

I make a great effort to be present, pulling myself back into my body, focusing on the voice of the head nurse who appears at my left and talks me through the next labor contractions and pushes. Then my daughter arrives, though I can barely feel her being pulled from my body. I lie there distant and numb, my body paralyzed, able to only turn my head. I watch the nurses clean her up, wrap her in a cotton blanket, and print her tiny footprints onto her birth document. They hand her over to me, but I can't feel her in my arms. I'm so afraid I'll drop her on the floor. I ask my husband to take her.

The head nurse comes over and compliments me on how quiet I've been throughout the whole birthing process, but the truth is that I'm struggling with the memory of having felt that numbness and dissociation before.

My daughter's birth, had such a scent of familiarity to it; so similar to something I just could not put my finger on. The quiet intensity of the room and the feeling that no one was paying attention to me, were distinctly familiar yet so far from memory. I couldn't pull up whatever it was that was being triggered, nor could I move or talk immediately after my daughter's birth. I felt as if I was at the bottom of a deep well looking up at the sky above, not sure how to get back up there, similar to the experience I had a few months ago in Chuck's office. Finally, I felt the doctor sewing me up, the sharpness of the needle poking through my skin, the tugging pull of the stitches bringing me back.

"I can feel that!" I said with a mixture of relief and annoyance.

"Almost done, just a few more. Can you stand it?" he asked.

"Sure, I can stand anything," I said, and as I spoke the numbness dissipated. I was ready to hold my daughter.

I returned to a semblance of normalcy, though the strange quality of the experience stayed with me for a long time after that. I realize now that the birth of my daughter triggered a flashback to the earlier experience at the age of twelve. Perhaps it was the serious atmosphere in the room, the same quiet intensity and focus, and the feelings of being completely alone and cut off from everyone, as well as the placement of the people in the room. The doctor between my legs, the nurse at my left, and the two student nurses observing, standing in the corner watching, in the same place in the room where my father had stood on the night of that abortion so long ago. They even moved over to the right side at one point to get a better view, just as my father had moved from his spot to go out the door on the right. Everything was set up for me to remember, but I just could not grasp the underlying significance at the time.

As I lay on that birthing table waiting for my daughter to be born, I remember thinking that this is the way life is: I have to go through things alone—no matter how many people I have around me, I have to go through certain moments alone.

I was chased all night by the anxiety and terror that preceded and accompanied the collision of those two birthing events. It was as if two photographs, taken twenty-seven years apart, had been superimposed over each other. Very little was different.

As I struggled through the night, unable to accept the truth that was so obstinately pursuing me, I did what I always did, what always worked: I dissociated. As the chase went on, I'd duck away from the anxiety and terror, turning over and away in the nick of time. Sometimes I'd doze off for a brief moment then awaken again to feel them coming straight at me and I'd turn away, literally turning in bed and flipping right into my so well-practiced dissociative state. Interspersed with this nighttime chase and turning were flashbacks to all the pregnancies I've had, memories of numbness and dissociation happening with each birth. This is what was rattling through me all night.

I feel like I'm going crazy.

May 20, 2002
I call Chuck in the middle of the night, but can hardly speak. I have so much to say, but I'm all bottled up, twisted with the terror of what I see. I'm tortured into strangled numbness by the *two babies* I see lying on the table, two waxy porcelain figurines.

"There were two babies, twins," I say and then I hang up, silenced by the tiny, ghostly babies that hang suspended before me in the darkness of my bedroom. They have no eyes and no ears, everything closed, sealed up.

"What strange dolls, why are they here?" my child self keeps asking. "I hope they don't give them to me."

Those two tiny babies haunt me all night long and I feel like I'm going crazy one minute and that I'm dead the next, as I toss and turn, unable to sleep. And then I remember that I always had the memory of those two white porcelain babies. They have floated in and out of memory my entire life, palely etched, unidentifiable figures frozen in a forgotten time.

Any real feelings are gone now. I'm stuck in shock and horror.

All day long I'm so numb I can't feel a thing. The ghostly images that haunted me in the night constantly reappear no matter what I do. I just keep seeing those tiny, unfinished babies lying on the table next to me in the doctor's office.

Are they boys; girls? What age? How old would they be if they had lived? Were they, in fact, born alive? The horror is too great. I must push the scene away, though it keeps intruding, forcing me to confront the truth of it, asking me to look closely, to take in the eerie details, to not let this slip back into the past again.

This is reality, it tells me, this is what happened.

Suddenly, I remember the first time I went to a gynecologist. Already in my early twenties, I'd never dared open my legs to a doctor before, fearful of the intimate nature of the exam. Now I was living in Sweden, happily married, and had decided to get a prescription for birth control pills. I geared myself up for the encounter, talked myself through the process ahead of time. I was met only by kindness as soon as I stepped into the doctor's office and my fears immediately calmed. The female doctor took one look at me, barely having touched me, and innocently asked: "When did you have your baby?"

"I didn't have a baby," I replied, shocked by the question.

She made a little sound, like a surprised grunt, but didn't pursue it. She went on with the rest of the exam, gently letting me know what she was doing each step of the way, while I struggled to stay present, the brightness of the day suddenly dropping away as I plunged into darkness.

Afterwards, as I stood on the train platform, the darkness mixed with confusion and terror that dragged me straight into the blackest of depressions, something I constantly fought. I grew angry as I waited for my train. I had been in such a good mood and had in fact spent the better part of the morning preparing myself to go to the appointment, and now here I was heading into a place I'd been struggling to release myself from for years.

Now, as I recapitulate this event, it's clear that something buried deep inside me was attempting to get my attention, but all I wanted to do was send it back into its grave. By the time I got home that day I'd succeeded, for the most part, in pushing it away. Truthfully though, that question—*When did you have your baby?*—haunted me constantly after that. At the time, I turned my anger and discomfort on the doctor, decided she was mean and insensitive, and that I'd never go back to her again, and I never did. Now I know she was only addressing what was so obvious to a professional, and in a kind way, not at all meaning to cause harm or distress.

I had had a baby!—I had had two babies!—I just didn't know it.

Memories of the barn come back to haunt me again too and I know my abuser took me there for torture as I got older, no more games.

"We don't play games anymore; it's just torture, whatever he wants," I say to myself and I know it's true.

Sick, it makes me sick! I'm nauseous again with pain in my stomach, so gripping I can't release it. Bent over trying to work, sucking in the pain and nausea, I hear him whispering in my ear, as if I were complicit, as if I liked it, as if I were really part of it, as if I could ever be part of it.

It was just my body there. I wasn't there. I was never part of it. He changed, or maybe he was different because I had changed. I was no longer a small child and we no longer played childish games. Now I looked different and he treated me differently. Right off the bat, it's straight to business, no more cajoling, no more pretending to be Mr. Nice Guy, straight to the stuff in the toolbox, straight to the torture.

May 22, 2002

We sign the separation agreement, which takes all of ten minutes. I leave the lawyer's office feeling hollow, apprehensive, and depressed, the familiar numbness taking over. I'm lost, swimming in misery, and I'm not sure why. I feel like I should be happy, but I'm so weighed down by the old stuff. The recent recapitulations overshadow every moment of the day.

As the day goes on, I grow increasingly desperate to talk to Chuck, to unburden a little, but I'm stopped in my tracks when a woman friend stops in at the studio with devastating news of her own. Without a moment's hesitation I completely shed my own problems as I rush to put my arms around her and comfort her, a big woman, who cries on my shoulder because her husband is leaving her for another woman. I'm struck that she has real feelings and that she can express them, loudly and succinctly. She's feeling sorry for herself, betrayed, resentful, angry, bitchy, vengeful, and demanding. She's reacting! Her ability to vent is amazing!

She loudly rants and weeps, totally allowing herself to express her disappointment and anger, while I stand and watch, so closed off, unable to access my own feelings. As I take in the immensity of her emotional release, my familiar numbness takes over, creeping into my body, letting me know that I can't go near those kinds of feelings, or any feelings whatsoever. They are buried so deeply that when I say I feel hollow that is precisely the way I feel—empty—no feelings anywhere in sight, nothing, nada. As I take in the enormity of this woman's emotional outburst, I realize just how dead I am inside, how thick a layer of scar tissue I must have between the real me and the trauma that keeps me so disconnected from accessing my feelings and emotions.

It scares me that I can't feel anything, that I can't cry or release anything. I feel so heartless toward myself as I observe this woman fully emoting her disappointment in her partner, but I realize that my lack of feeling is a protective measure, implanted long ago.

If I don't have feelings then no one can hurt me.

I can't feel anything, so I'm safe. There's a barrier surrounding me, a cloak of steel armor, and nothing gets through it. If nothing can get through then nothing will impact me. I permeate my being with numbness to keep out that which is painful, so that the things people say and do won't ever affect me.

May 23, 2002
Although I have no feelings for myself I'm not inhuman. For others I feel immense empathy, sadness, anger, disbelief, and sorrow. I certainly admire emotional expression, but I personally just can't go near it. My sensitive, feeling self is closed up in a ball, safely protected, far from my abuser. As I recapitulate, I discover how I learned to never cry or show weakness, to never let him know that I was physically or emotionally hurt. Why? Because it

wouldn't have mattered, and, if I had let my emotions get the upper hand, I would have been destroyed. And he would have won.

I needed that kind of control and although it was anchored deeply inside, my personal secret in a sense, it was absolutely necessary. If I had not found this most important avenue of self-control, I would not have survived. And even outside of his territory I couldn't let my feelings or emotions out, so full of humiliation and blame, so topped with horror and terror were they, that to express myself even a tiny bit would have created a tidal wave of destruction. I had to keep at bay the moment of annihilation, the moment of disintegration; and dissociation and numbness were the means by which I accomplished this. In my abuser's world, and by default in my own world, death was always just a moment away.

So now, when I rationally know it will be okay to express and feel, I can't just unlock what is stored so deeply inside. My very survival, always at stake, will not release its hold, even though the need no longer really exists. What once was so necessary is now actually a place of deep comfort, and to disrupt that is both frightening and disconcerting. It's as if something that has always been so good for me is threatened with surgical removal, due to be wrenched from me. And really, for what reason?

My survival tactics, long ago honed to perfection, need to be in place. I need to know that they're ready, at all times, just in case. Numbness is the way I've always handled what was so traumatizing, and although it's starting to feel a little odd and unnecessary, I find I can't let it go. It offered the protection I needed as I looked down on that other little girl.

"You're okay, that didn't happen to you. It's that other little girl down there on the ground that the bad stuff happened to. You're okay."

Sometimes I begin to actually *feel* as I recapitulate, and then great anxiety overtakes, disrupting my normal state of control. I fear the power of the memories as I let them go through me. They were much easier to deal with when I was just watching old movies at the far end of that tunnel. As I relive the memories now, I'm stunned by how much my body holds within and equally fascinated by the depth of self-control, but I'm afraid I won't be able to handle the emotional onslaughts. I fear I'll have a total breakdown, that the memories will literally destroy me as I release them—and as I begin *to feel*. And I fear that the shame, humiliation, blame, and hatred of myself will destroy me too.

I continue to guard myself with numbness. I can't seem to control it, its presence firmly embedded in my psychological makeup. Even when I'm with Chuck, feeling safe enough now to talk, its shield is between us. However, as the recapitulation continues I more easily flow with what comes. All I have to do is step into the memories and I immediately feel the pain of them. Somehow I'm able to break through the dissociative numbness of the body memory, acknowledge what happened, fully experience it, understand it, and accept it, but I'm still emotionally shielded from what happened. The emotional memory seems to be a harder nut to crack.

As I recapitulate, I also discover how I used the dissociative state of sinking into the tunnel and the deeper dissociative state of going completely out-of-body to my advantage. They offered the protection of distance. They meant life over the possibility of death at the hands of my abuser. While my abuser did what he wanted with my physical body I was safely ensconced someplace else. However, I realize I never fully returned from either the dissociative state of the numbing tunnel or the out-of-body experiences that gave me a totally different perspective from which to view what was happening to my body. I'm still in such a daze most of the time, partially numb, everything observed from a distance.

It would always be over. I knew that. As I told Chuck the other day I counted on that. And I discovered that I could make it easier on myself by not fighting back physically. I went along with my abuser because it was necessary, aligning with him in order to stay alive, but I never, ever, let him get to me. I closed off as many doors as I could. I locked down my feelings, my emotions, even the pain, in order to survive. No matter what he did, *I would never let him in*. I've carried that decision forward into my adult life.

When I mentioned this attitude, Chuck was reminded of Victor Frankl's book *Man's Search for Meaning* about the experiences of prisoners of concentration camps during the Holocaust. Strikingly similar attitudes were observed among those who survived over those who perished. When he hears that I've never read it, he suggests, in light of my own experiences, that I might find it interesting.

It's true that I've never let anyone in, not my lovers, not even my husbands. It's never been safe enough to let anyone in. Until now; now I'm letting Chuck in, bit by painful bit, breaking one of my oldest personal agreements. It probably wasn't fair that I told him of my fear that he'd forget me when I was leaving the office the other day. I hope he doesn't think I don't trust him. It's not that; it's all about how fragile I feel.

"I feel that as soon as I walk out that door you'll forget everything I've told you, that you won't remember," I said.

"Not very likely," he replied.

May 24, 2002
I'm lying on my bed, feeling pretty relaxed, when I'm hit with such incredible pain that I involuntarily roll into a tight ball. Suddenly I'm chomping my teeth, loudly snapping my jaws, growling like a puppy. I discover that if I growl I can block out what's happening to my body. The pain lessens the faster I chomp my teeth and the louder I growl. I snap and bite the air like a puppy dog, ferocious growls coming from deep inside my belly.

The memory lasts a long time, fifteen to twenty minutes. I have no control over my body, my teeth chomping and biting on their own. I can't stop them, and I can't stop shaking either. I have no control whatsoever. I'm just a weak and frightened puppy dog, with a sharp pain stabbing my clenched stomach.

It takes a few hours to calm down.

In the midst of it I call Chuck. He re-grounds me in this world with simple, practical guidance, but first I have to let down all the barriers so I can even talk to him. I don't even know what those barriers are, so deeply embedded are they, but I feel them standing there, holding everything back, keeping me numb and safe. He's the only one who understands that these things really happened, that the memories are real. Even I don't want to believe them. But then a memory like this hits me so hard, my body riveted in a past experience, that I'm forced to believe not only that these things really did happen, but that they're desperate to tell me so, to get out of my body where they've been trapped for decades. I wonder if all those vague memories, the ones that are still swimming in the murky fog of memory, are going to do this to me too? Am I going to keep getting hit with stuff like this every time I let down my guard and try to relax?

Every time one of these big somatic experiences comes along, the terror and the reality of the abuse hits home and I have to face the truth of it all over again. *Yes, it really happened.* I couldn't make this up. It happened and it wants me to know it, to face it all. It's real. I know it's real. I know it happened.

Today I'm struck, most poignantly, by the sad and miserable truth that I lived a horrible childhood.

May 25, 2002
I feel bruised, fragile and broken, as if someone has been beating on me all night. I don't think the truth of what happened was getting to me before, but it hit me hard last night, very hard; harder than I thought could be possible. Now I have to deal with it again, a second time, but on a different level, the deeper emotional level, as Chuck says. I don't feel very strong and stoical anymore. The feelings hurt too much.

May 27, 2002
I went away for a few days. To travel is very much to be in the moment. Real life seemed so distant while I was away. The intensity of the recapitulation dissipated, though once or twice I felt memories and fear starting to emerge and the smell of something from the past snuck up on me at one point, threatening to send me into collapse mode. But I pushed them all away.

"Not now!" I said as these things teased me. "Not now in this quiet museum, not now in someone else's house. Please not now!"

I'm afraid to run, to do yoga or even breathe deeply, because I'm afraid something will be triggered, that something too difficult to handle will erupt from deep inside. On the other hand, I want to get this pain out of me. I want to get the memories out, to get this recapitulation over with. But at the same time the intensity of that last Doggie game memory was almost too much to handle. I'm afraid I may drop to the floor and go into recapitulating it again at the sound of a dog bark or a yelp of pain. I'm afraid to do something that might shake it awake again.

While I was away, I honestly accepted how damaged I am as a result of what happened to me, how distant and remote I often really am, how disconnected from my own humanly real and emotional self. Often I feel as if I'm nothing more than a plastic replica of a human being. Even when the memories come I've often only been an observer, still dissociated, even as I relive them in excruciating detail. At least that was the case until this last memory, this last one was different. Not only was I acting out every snarling puppy sound, but my body also reenacted every aspect of the memory. *I became the memory itself.* I physically went through every second of that memory in bone chilling and bloodcurdling detail.

All week I've been very far away, so distant. I feel like I'm floating along, not really here, gone somewhere else. I'm looking out at the world, but not fully alive in it, just going through the motions. It's apparently becoming noticeable because people are commenting.

May 29, 2002

I'm going through a really hard time. Feelings are stuck again and it feels like another memory is about to emerge, one of those difficult, powerful ones. The last one still impacts me so incredibly strongly; the trauma of that little girl who was made to play that Doggie game still so palpable and real. My body still holds the memory of it. Even that intense recapitulation seems not to have fully released it. I still feel the energy of it reverberating in my jaw, my throat, my bones, my belly.

Chuck once again reminded me of the *usher*. The usher has come again to usher me into a new, deeper phase of acceptance, as well as into a new experiential process. I admit that although I'm fully into doing this recapitulation journey there is still a part of me that's been fighting the entire process, trying to keep the truth at bay, but the truth won't turn away. It keeps returning, and it will continue to do so until I fully meet it, until I fully face and accept all the truths. But they have to go through me first, and I have to totally release them, only then will I be free and clear of them all.

I've noticed again that running and yoga, and the deeper breathing that both of those physical activities incorporate, seem to trigger the memories, which makes me almost afraid to do them. At the same time, I know how valuable this recapitulation process is and that I won't be able to complete it if I don't allow it to unfold as it will. One method of accessing the memories is probably as valid as another, so I must accept this and just be prepared because the memories will come no matter what I do to control them. They seem to be emerging weekly now and I guess it's not a coincidence that they mostly arrive on the days I do yoga.

Yoga really seems to be a key part of the process. I've noticed that if I go to a yoga class in the morning something inevitably gets stirred and by the end of the day has worked its way through to the point of release. Right now I'm facing another emerging memory. I'm in a fragile and vulnerable state, which is normal as a memory begins poking its head up, looking for a way out.

I'm aware that whatever is coming will hit hard, and also that I must be ready for the onslaught if I am to fully access it. In order to do so, I have to break through the barriers that block my ability to feel to the fullest. This is my greatest challenge, but I understand that in order to fully recapitulate I must feel what happened to my body and psyche in the past. Feeling is also the greatest healing aspect, for only in learning how to feel can I really be humanly present in this life.

My ability to really feel deeply has been almost totally blocked as I have repeatedly dissociated from anything that called upon my emotions. I equate feeling with pain; even feeling a hug is too painful. Dissociating became my method of dealing with the pain and repercussions of the trauma, and now I'm thrown into an incredibly vulnerable place as I'm asked to stop grasping for it, to stop wanting it.

It's an addiction!

Having to remove this protective shield, to stand free and clear of what has kept me safe for so long is a damn scary thing!

May 30, 2002
In a morning yoga class we do lots of breathing work. I feel how I'm tightly holding everything in. I gain a very clear understanding of the way my muscles clamp down. I'm aware that breathing usually stirs things up and I'm a little concerned, but luckily I have a busy day and little time to dwell on my recapitulation process.

I'm thankful for the distraction of work, but in the middle of the day the anguish bubbles up to the surface and the signal that something wants to become known is readily apparent. I'm able to push it back down. I deliberately turn away from what's happening in my body and immediately feel lighter, less heavy, even though I know it's only a temporary solution. Once again I'm thankful that I have my work to focus on.

May 31, 2002
After yesterday's success at pushing the recapitulation process away, today I'm in agony, the agony of holding it all in. My shoulders hunch painfully, my neck is stiff and tight.

"Oh man, this is agony," I thought yesterday in yoga class while doing *bhujangasana*, the cobra pose. It wasn't the pose itself that was agony but the holding in of the old stuff. For the first time really, I felt how my body clenches and holds things back. I could actually feel all the muscles in my body holding onto something, refusing to release it, keeping it close.

Why can't I let it go? I know how good it can feel to release something painful. I know what I'm clenching and holding back and I know what I have to do to release.

So why can't I let it go?

I need to talk about the babies when I meet with Chuck, about feeling sadness for them, those two waxy figurines. I can't stop thinking about the ages they would have been. No matter what my feelings about abortion are, in the end, children of mine *weren't*. There's a little dull ache beginning to grow inside me for those two children. It feels like a new load to carry.

Believing is so hard. Some days I simply refuse to accept the truth of what my body memory is telling me, even though I'm writhing in pain. At other times, I see it all so clearly, all the puzzle pieces falling into place; my life stretching out behind me, a long string of mysteries now revealed, properly put in place. That last crushingly painful memory of the Doggie game made me realize how real it was, how physically tied to it I still am, and how body memory may be stronger and more powerful than mental memory.

"How are you feeling?" Chuck asks me.
I sit there for a long time, numb, unable to give him an answer.
"How am I feeling? How am I feeling? How am I feeling?"
The question rattles around in my head and I just don't know what to say because I can make no sense of it. Sometimes I just

can't figure out how to explain what I'm feeling. If I say I'm sad, well that doesn't really explain my experience because I'm not just feeling emotionally sad, I'm feeling physically sad, energetically depleted and depressed, and that's a different kind of sadness. Sometimes I'm just experiencing a bruised, hurt feeling, not pain per se, but a big lump of sadness, the heavy feeling right before you cry, a welling-up, choking kind of hurt.

I realize the emotional component is still iced over, still inaccessible, cut off a long time ago. Somehow I have to reattach the severed cords, but first I have to find them. I don't even know where they are right now, but every time Chuck asks me how I'm feeling, I know he's asking me to find them, to swim down into the depths of my soul and grab hold of them and sew them back together and get the blood flowing again, so I can *feel* something.

"I feel a great big lump inside my body, but I can't release it."

That's what I tell Chuck after a long silence. Maybe that's what I'm waiting for, for that big lump to release. It feels like I've been waiting forever. That sweet, quiet little girl that I was as a child was in such pain and agony, the fear and terror incredible; the need to protect, to survive, to not be destroyed, incredible too.

I knew what torture was, what never giving in meant, what hanging on by a thread meant. I knew what being able to survive, to live to the next minute, the next hour, the next day, to not let him kill me meant. There came a point where I would say to myself, "He's trying to kill me," and that would make me angry. The fact that he was killing me, and he obviously didn't care, made me angry enough to live.

As I recapitulate this childhood I see the hideous scars. I see the thick layers of ugly scar tissue covering everything.

When I pause—cease thinking about the past for a while and instead turn to the reality of what I've been going through for the past few months—I'm blown away! I'm being taken on an incredible journey as I encounter these powerful memories. Not many people, I assume, would see this as an opportunity, nor would they choose to undertake this kind of very deep inner work, but I feel extremely lucky to be doing this shamanic recapitulation.

In the beginning of this process I knew nothing of such things and now I'm deeply immersed, the world suddenly bigger, expanded beyond expectation and belief. And I'm very lucky to have met Chuck, beyond modest in his capacity as guide, always pointing out the natural unfolding of this process, which in turn allows me to feel how right it is, in alignment with my own nature. It's a journey of a lifetime, one of learning about the self, how the psyche and body work, how the unconscious and the spirit work hand in hand to guide us through life. I'm exactly on the journey I need to be on.

I'm humbled by the attention I've also received from Jeanne, Chuck's deceased wife, as she accompanies me on this journey as well, offering me calming energy at the most desperate of times. I trust that she's with me always, even when I don't feel her, that she's watching over me, helping me from afar, by a means that a year ago I might have dismissed as hokey, but today I know as real. She is definitely a vital energetic presence and I don't doubt that her kindness and compassion are crucially significant to this process of change.

When I began this process, a little over a year ago, when I saw that fox in the road, I sensed that he was showing me something important and meaningful. He was the first *usher*. But who knew where he was really leading me? The usher has come repeatedly since then, taking me deeper into the past, asking me to take a closer look, again and again showing me where to go next. The praying mantis came to help in dreaming, digging into my skull, awakening memories and reminding me that I was once a brave little girl. The tunnel continues to reveal its many secrets, one thing leading to another as I take this unfolding journey into my hidden self. Clarity continues to reign as each veil is swept aside and each memory emerges and becomes real again. As my body relives and recaptures everything, I'm being broken down and pieced back together in a new form, one step at a time.

I'm different now.

All of this is important; it's *my life*. It's important. *I'm important*. Where I go from here is important, where I've been is important. It's my chance to move on to a new phase of being me. I elect to travel onward, to keep taking this recapitulation journey.

Out with the old, in with the new!

Chapter Fifteen

I Feel

June 1, 2002

I'm getting very busy again with work so the heaviness is only periodic, but I sense that I'm storing up for an eventual big release. The dam is holding everything back, but little by little I get brave and lift the floodgates and let a little of the tension out. It tends to manifest in shoulder pain, leg pain, neck pain, and stomachaches. Twinges of old memory stab intermittently as the horror of my past slowly seeps into conscious acceptance. The barbarity of the abuse amazes me, as does the fact that I was able to withstand it, but I also realize that most of the time I left my body, left it with him, while my awareness escaped, fragmented but also protected.

Little memories—smells, touches, sounds—intermix, as if I'm sitting at a great distance from a play, barely able to make out what's happening on stage, but I see that actors are assembling, taking their places. The scene, as it assembles from deep memory, is intermingled with fear and anguish, and I'm struck by a sense that something is going to happen again, that I've been here before and done this already.

Did I even remember the abuse, the torture, from one time to the next? My body and soul remembered, even if my mind and emotions had long ago shut down. I became the ice princess, with a splinter of ice in her heart, so I didn't have to feel. I could be so cold and shut off, my feelings departed, left only with sensations of being tightly held, in stasis, clamped by unseen arms of steel.

June 3, 2002

I dream that a torrential rain, of biblical proportion, is falling, accompanied by a tremendous windstorm. I run out of the house, attempting to save whatever I can, everything being blown and washed away in this powerful storm. As I check out the considerable damage, I notice two life-sized dolls that are about to swirl away and I reach out and grab them at the last minute.

I hear people calling to me from across a flooded field.

"Is any other place badly hit?" they ask.

"I don't know," I call back, wondering if only my property has been struck.

They call out to me again, but I can barely hear them, so I go a little closer. I see them jumping down into the floodwaters. They disappear under the murky water then bob back up again, calling to me. I watch them do this over and over again, bobbing up and down in the water, disappearing one minute and popping back up the next, calling my name.

I'm afraid to get too close because I don't want to get pulled into the water. I sense they might grab me, so I approach very cautiously. Then I realize that they're jumping into open tunnels, huge open drainage ditches, and I see one person swimming toward me along one of these open channels. I carefully step back so he can't grab me and so I won't fall into the churning water. The entire situation is threatening. I'm acutely aware that I must be watchful.

It's still raining and blowing hard. As I stand there and watch the scene before me, I notice that everything that was outside the house, and even things from inside the house, are swirling away in the rushing waters and getting blown by the ferocious wind. Trees are down. Damaged cars and appliances float by, tumbling along in the floodwaters like toy boats. I grab things as they go by, saving what I can. No one else is helping. My kids come out of the house to help, but I send them back inside because it's too dangerous. Once they're safely ensconced back inside I continue my search, scouting about for whatever else I might salvage.

I wake in a nervous, edgy state. I'm a closed container full of anguish, volcanic in intensity, fearful that something is going to get me. I can't settle down at all. It's hard to work or concentrate on anything and my hands shake all day. I'm stretched taut, strained and cranky, like I need to cry, like I'm going to break down into painfully brittle pieces.

I was so busy over the weekend that I was able to keep everything at bay. I even started to relax a little and felt the tension release ever so slightly from my shoulders, finally feeling and hoping that maybe this was going to be the end of the recapitulation. I thought it was a good sign and I'd actually felt lighter and happier over the weekend. I'd even noticed a light in my eyes again, for the first time in months, but now I realize it was only the result of the moments of distraction, a temporary respite. In reality, the past lies waiting, like a monster lurking just beneath the surface of a calm lake, ready to leap up and grab me the minute I'm alone. And it does. It sneaks up and pinches, prods, and pokes.

At this point, I'm exhausted. But I guess I do feel lucky that I'm able to experience this shamanic recapitulation practice, and that I have a wonderful guide through it all. I'm confident that I'll get through it and come out whole and new. But the getting-through is terribly difficult, a twenty-four hour torture, seven days a week, with barely a break. I'm sharp and jagged as I sense the next memory approaching.
Let go of the fear.
Let go of the fear.
Let go of the fear.
Let go of the fear.
Let go of the fear.
Let go of the fear.

At the very end of the day—just completing my last trip of moving furniture back up to the studio after a weekend craft show—I'm hit again. BOOM! The pain, the fear, the anguish explode inside me, the volcano spews while I'm on the stairs, a large box of artwork in my hands. I stumble, almost dropping it, almost collapsing in that moment of stabbing pain.
"Go away! Go away!" I plead.
Panic rising, trying to just breathe, I pass a friend coming around the corner.
"Are you okay!" she asks, deep concern in her voice. "You look, you look... I don't know... you look... freaked out... like you've seen a ghost! Are you okay?"
"Yeah, I'm okay, I've had a freaky day," I'm able to say, and then I know it was only the busyness that has kept the past at bay. Once again I'm thankful for the blessedness of distraction.

June 5, 2002

It's midnight. I can't sleep. Nightmarish memories, too intense to hold back anymore, emerge. I've felt them coming for days, pushing against the brittle surface of my discontent. In the darkness of the night they explode like firecrackers.

I'm being held, tightly clamped against another body, my legs held wide while someone rapes me—two people—both naked. I don't even know if they're both men. Terror and fear rip through me as the memory unfolds, my teeth chattering, but something also feels good. I hear them talking, but I can't clearly hear what they're saying.

I toss and turn, in the throes of disjointed chaos, as more memories explode. Disconnected scenes blur together, unraveling out of me as if pulled by unseen hands. My abuser smokes a pipe. The pipe is being inserted into my vagina. I wonder if he'll light the pipe. Lighting it means something. As I twist and turn in bed more memories emerge and I see him jumping a fence and I admire his physical strength and agility; he's extremely strong and agile. I notice it and almost have feelings of pride that I know someone that strong.

In the morning, I'm ashamed of these feelings, deeply disturbed and wondering how I could have any kind of feeling for him except loathing, fear, and dread.

If I couldn't feel I wouldn't get hurt; if I was cut off and dead he couldn't hurt me, no matter what he did. But I don't want to be that way anymore.

Something changed when I met my new best friend when I was nine, when a little bit of the ice around my heart started to melt and I realized I still had the good me inside. But I also knew I had to keep this good little girl protected; she wasn't safe anywhere, except with this new best friend. So in all other encounters in the world I still kept her hidden.

I remember sitting at a table across from this new best friend, on her back porch, drawing pictures on a warm summer day when she said something that struck at my buried innocence. I don't remember her exact words, but her naïveté touched me deeply and I grabbed onto it for dear life, a life raft sailing towards me, immediately recognizable. Though my own innocence was so isolated as to be almost foreign to me, I was deeply grateful to this little girl for expressing her inner sweetness. Her reflection opened the door to a loving, nonjudgmental self, and in that instant I was utterly human again, sensitive and kind. Love and gratitude poured out of me and gently flowed into the other little girl sitting across the table, as I silently thanked her.

In that instant, I knew I could express my true self under the right circumstances, just as she had done. I saw how she trusted me, without even thinking about it. She said something that the frozen me might have dismissed in a cynical manner, but on that day the tender girl inside me chose to come forth instead. For the moment she felt safe.

I was so happy sitting in the warmth of that summer day, utterly contented and at peace for a while, in touch once again with my true self. It was an unusual, rather magical moment for me and I never forgot it. I was grateful to this new best friend for trusting me and I, in turn, saw that I could trust her. It was only with her that I could sometimes dare to be real, otherwise I existed in a quiet hidden box, tightly guarded, no one allowed in.

June 10, 2002
I got through another busy weekend at the opening of an art exhibit I had curated at the artist's co-operative, everyone congratulating me on a fantastic job, the gallery packed with nearly three hundred people. But now, as a new day dawns, the tensions of the recapitulation return full force and the memories once again swim to the surface. The need to clench has been present all along, but the intensity of last week's work in getting the show up kept me going. At a party after the opening on Saturday night, I felt so tense. I was barely able to stand. Today I'm thoroughly exhausted, though the day has not even begun.

Memories continue to well up from the darkness within. The pipe that appeared in a hint of a memory the other day is now more defined. I see the pipe rack so clearly. I recall anxiously standing next to the display of pipes, afraid of getting into trouble for even being near them. We, my abuser's daughter and I, would dare to pick up the one we liked. He had a pretty, carved white one, made of ivory or bone that I liked best, but then there was the one he used most often, a plain brown one with a thick black stem.

I recapitulate the mounting tension as I watch him pick it up, fill it, and put it in his mouth. Would he light it or not? It meant something. Putting it down meant something and lighting it meant something different.

We look at the round rack of pipes and dare to twirl it on its Lazy Susan base. I see his daughter pointing to the brown one.

"I don't like that one," she says.

"I don't either," I say, nervously. "We better not touch them."

"Oh, it's okay," she says, but then her mother is yelling at us.

"Don't you touch those pipes! Get away from there!"

Startled, we jump away. We are not allowed to touch anything that belongs to him.

Don't touch his chair, and don't ever touch his pipes!

The memory won't leave me, it follows me around all day. Later in the day I sit and do the sweeping breath, allowing the pieces to begin forming a clearer memory, but only as much as I can handle.

He's sitting in his chair looking at me out of the corner of his eye, making sure I'm watching, making sure I see what he's doing, putting down his pipe and walking away. What does it mean?

"It's your turn," my abuser's daughter says, and she turns and walks away.

The pipe is pointing toward me.

June 11, 2002

"I was steeped in incredible anxiety yesterday. I could barely function," I tell Chuck, "and I'm suffering the same today. I feel bruised and hurt."

"Does it go away as the memories come?" asks Chuck.

"No, there's always a new memory with new feelings to replace it, so if there is a respite, it's brief."

We do EMDR around the memory of the pipes.

I stand again next to my abuser's chair, staring at the rack of pipes on the table next to it. Anticipation is high; I'm on high alert, barely able to breathe. My abuser slowly picks up the brown pipe with the black stem. I don't like that pipe. Is he going to light it, or not?

If he lights the pipe the tension will release with the first puff of smoke. It means we're not playing with him today. If he doesn't light the pipe it means something bad will happen. He's looking at me looking at him as he puts the pipe down on the table and slowly spins it in my direction. The black stem points directly at me. He gets out of his chair and, without looking at me, walks toward the back of the house.

"It's your turn," says his daughter, putting her head down, as she turns and slowly walks away.

I know what I'm supposed to do. I turn and see him standing in the darkened hallway, waiting for me by the bathroom door. In a state of resignation, I reluctantly go to him, my feet and body turning to heavy lead. It's my turn today. With his hand on the bathroom door he waits, locking the door behind me as I step into his world. I know what to do. I walk to the end of the long narrow bathroom and stop at the window with the white curtains. I put my hands up on the towel bar beneath the window and wait. He sits behind me on a stool. I see my knuckles, stare at them, white knuckles gripping tighter and tighter.

"He hurts me," is what my child self experiences, but my adult self knows that he is raping me anally. At the moment of penetration I go into my hands; I become my hands, gripping the towel bar. I am no more than four or five years old in this memory and as soon as I enter the bathroom I already know the routine. As soon as I walk over to the towel bar and put my heavy, leaden hands on it, I know that I must pour my energy into it and into my white knuckles if I am to survive. It's how I get through the rapes in the bathroom.

Next we go into the nightmare memory that kept me up all night last week, the two naked people in the barn. Now, as we do EMDR, I clearly see that they are men.

"A man holds me up, pinning my legs and arms, watching while my abuser screws me so violently I think I'm going to die, this time I'll die. I can't breathe," I tell Chuck.

"Take it easy," I hear the naked man say to my abuser. "Hey, take it easy!"

"See you like it," my abuser says when I have an orgasm.

"It's so confusing when he tells me this, because I don't know what to do with those pleasant feelings that come twisted up in this horrific rape," I tell Chuck.

I'm a teenager in this memory, perhaps fourteen years old. I admit to Chuck, and to myself as well, that despite the violence he inflicts on me, I admire my abuser. I see his power and I'm captivated by it.

At the same time that I admit these things, I feel like I'm keeping so much back from myself, and from Chuck, but not on purpose. It's the struggle to fully recapitulate an experience in our limited fifty minute time slot that causes the problem. Sometimes I'm just not ready to fully go back there yet.

June 12, 2002

New sensory memories are emerging now, of being at my abuser's house. I'm around three years old. The smells of that house are of crotch, of smoke, of pipe, of sweat, of man, of earth, of leaves, of sour milk. I feel pain everywhere in my body as these odors go through me. Desperation, despair, and deep loneliness accompany the pain.

As I allow the sensations and feelings to take me deeper, it becomes very clear that there's no one to share my confusion and fear with, no one who understands. The abuse is even unspoken between my abuser's daughter and I. We're silently watchful and on edge when we're together, but rarely speak about it.

"Did he hurt you?" she asked me once when I returned to playing with her after he had raped me in the bathroom.

"Yes," I said.

"Yeah, me too," she said, perhaps satisfying some need to know, and then we went on with our play.

That's what our conversations were limited to, the way we interpreted what he did. *He hurt us.*

I was tongue-tied as a child. Overly anxious and in so much pain, I could barely utter a sound. This was my normal presentation up until adulthood—it's still normal. I still tend to be very quiet, and although it's sometimes profoundly difficult to swim up out of that silence and be vocally present in the world, I think the intense inner loneliness is perhaps the heaviest burden I carry from that time. Handling what was happening to me as best I could was both a silent and a lonely endeavor. I became secretive out of necessity. Under threat of death at my abuser's hands, should I speak of the abuse, I sought inner control, though in truth I was a brave child intent on survival at whatever cost. If that meant silence and loneliness then so be it.

I feel the long-term repercussions of the abuse sitting like a heavy iron knot in the pit of my stomach, as if a man's big hand has been gripping me in silent and lonely imprisonment all these many years.

I wake at eleven in the night, after sleeping for less than an hour, to find myself in the middle of a recapitulation.

I'm left alone, curled up on the floor, possibly the barn floor. I've been raped and I'm just trying to breathe, panting, curled into a ball, just trying to breathe. That's all I can do, just gasp for air. I'm feeling terribly, terribly lonely, shaking, cringing, whimpering, not crying out loud, but silently screaming inside. I'm trying to make sense of all the feelings, of the emotional numbness, the pelvic pain, and the deeply hurt, bruised person I am, as far down in the tunnel as I can go.

I don't know if I can do this recapitulation anymore.

June 13, 2002
I tried to sleep after that recapitulation experience last night. Around two-thirty in the morning another episode started and I just couldn't handle it. I got out of bed and walked around for a while, let the cat in, and then finally went back to bed and tossed and turned the rest of the night.

It's difficult dealing with the loneliness of being cast aside, left abandoned on the floor by my abuser after he'd finished with me. In the memories, and again now as I recapitulate, I'm in shock, numb in body, with occasional physical pain, but mostly it's the emotional hurt that I still hold tightly bottled inside.

I wanted to call Chuck last night, but it was too late, so I just called now and left a message. I'm feeling so ill, physically sick, weak and tired, broken and sad. The men leave me on the floor and go away. They're nearby though. I sense their presence still.

The last time I met with Chuck I mentioned that afterwards, after the rapes in the barn, I just lay on the floor, just lay there. Well, the full truth is, I was a basket case, totally devastated. Last night I relived the fullness of that devastation. In a second experience last night I was in a different place, some place in the woods, but the empty feeling of being left behind to deal with what he had done to me was equally powerful. That was when I got up because I couldn't handle it.

Please call me, Chuck, please call—check your messages, please, please.

I'm not functioning very well. I can't concentrate. Every day, I leave work and go home and just lie down for a while, just curl up, barely breathing.

June 14, 2002

When I meet with Chuck we go back into the memory of lying on the barn floor. I immediately curl up into a ball and relive all the tension and pain that is still balled up in this one memory of being tossed aside after being raped by the two men in the barn.

The men step over me, their big work boots coming down in front of my face. They leave me there, all the deadness rolled up inside my little tortured body, all the emotions, the feelings, the confusions, all the complications I can't figure out, all rolled up there with me, like a tightly rolled newspaper never to be read. Powerful and intense, they inhabit me still, unable to leave until I unroll them and figure them all out. And even though I'm getting to them, actually *feeling* them all over again, as if I'm back there in the past, I'm also still holding back. I can't even make a peep as I recapitulate. I can't cry. I can't say that it hurts. I can barely speak. Until I get out the sounds, I don't think I'll get to the bottom of this. I silently make my way through the memory, giving Chuck very little clue as to what is actually going on.

"I'm still holding tight, still holding in," I finally say.

"Why?"

"I don't know."

"Don't you feel safe yet? Don't you feel safe enough?"

"Maybe not yet. I'm not safe enough yet."

Then I tell Chuck that the thing I'm discovering is that the need to curl up into a ball is necessary, not only because it feels good, but because it's safe there. The longer I stay curled up, the safer I feel, as if I'm protecting myself from my abuser all over again, so he can't get me again as I relive these memories.

In further recapitulating this one incident, I discover that the longer I'm allowed to stay curled up like that, the more it means that he's not coming back, that he's not going to get me again; that this time he's done. And although I may feel safe while lying there on the barn floor or on the ground somewhere in the woods, I'm not really totally safe. It's only a momentary feeling of salvation because I'm already clenched and tight and on my guard against the next time.

I come away from my session with Chuck filled again with the potency of this amazing journey. Although the memories grip me as I go into the details of my past, torturing me all over again, I know I will get through this recapitulation because I'm not alone—I have a guide. The intensity of the work today made me realize that I really can work with Chuck—I *can* trust him, even though my teenage self still hesitates to fully let him in. I know that as she trusts me more, she'll also learn to trust him.

I cling to the regularity of our work together. The presence of another person in the midst of these journeys is so important and necessary. Chuck's presence anchors me as I go off into the muck of the past. He calls me back every few minutes to take a look at what's happening, asking me how I'm doing, patiently mindful of only sending me back into the fray when I'm really ready to handle it. He's like a guarding sentinel, standing off on the side beside my own adult self, who is equally watchful and protective.

My child self discovered today that she can trust his authenticity, integrity, and pure intentions more fully. He will not harm her. He let's her guide us through the process. After all, she's the one who knows the whole story. It's also becoming pretty clear that rather than being fearful, she actually awaits interaction with Chuck now, experiencing the time between sessions as excruciatingly long. She too is learning that the process must unfold in its own way. She's getting used to the short bursts of memory and release and although the process may seem slow at times, the truth is that the body and psyche are really in charge.

Even the adult self gets impatient and experiences the short bursts of memory and release as inadequate sometimes; wanting to really let off steam, to blow a gasket, so to speak; to blow the lid off this thing and finally get the full breadth of it. But I too have begun to respect the process itself, learning that smaller doses are easier to handle. And no matter how bad it makes me feel and no matter how hard it is to comprehend, I must plow through this recapitulation. And, yes, I know I'm not alone.

I did feel like I released something today in the session with Chuck, though it remains mysteriously elusive as to just what it was, perhaps the recognition of why the curling up was so important, why going dead inside and out was so necessary. It wasn't just a bad thing, it meant something good too.

As I write those words the tension immediately creeps back in, my body responding as it always does to the next emerging memory. I wonder what it's going to be!

June 15, 2002

It's happening again, overwhelming fear. I'm going numb and I'm breathing hard, panting. It's different this time—a new memory—terrifying!

I get out of bed in the middle of the night to stop it and walk around the dark house. After a while I return to bed, only to toss and turn. I avoid the emerging memory by turning over all night, rolling back and forth from side to side. I shift away constantly as the night goes on, but am unable to stop an intense experience that starts early in the morning.

I lie in bed laced with anger, sharp black anger in the pit of my stomach, needing to scream bloody murder but not being able to make a sound. Anger, knife-sharp and hard as a spiky metal boot spur is spinning inside me, cutting me apart, shredding my insides. It won't stop; it won't stop! It overwhelms me, spinning out of control.

I'm in agony!

The experience is laced with fear, fear, fear, with chattering teeth, with clenching insides and shaking, shaking, shaking.

"Distractions, distractions may help!" I think, desperately seeking release from the intensity, but I'm so caught in the memory that I can't get out of it.

I roll over in an attempt to instigate the same kind of avoidance that was successful during the night, but now I just succeed in falling deeper into the memory. And this time there's something else waiting for me as I turn. Perched on the edge of the mattress sits a black presence, leering at me, waiting for me to come to it.

I jump out of bed and stay out!

Every time I curl up into a ball I go directly into a memory. I'm met by the fear, the emotions, the confusion, the pain, the anger, and the anxiety of my child self. Everything is in her little curled up body. I have to keep going back to her where she's lying on the floor to sort it all out.

Now, whenever I lie under my covers and curl into a ball, I go to other places too. I'm not always in the barn, but often outside in the woods, in many different places, some that I recognize, some that I don't. I notice that the longer I stay rolled up, the safer I feel. I reconfirm this each time I recapitulate being on the ground, left behind to tend to my wounds alone. The longer I'm safely encased inside that rolled up ball, the more I'm certain that he's not coming back.

The things he did to me had nothing to do with the things my girlfriends and I were trying to figure out about our bodies and our budding sexuality. The words we so daringly and tentatively whispered among ourselves—*sex, fuck, screw*—were tame words, almost pretty compared to what he did. As I recapitulate, I find that I had no words for what he was doing to me, probably also because he was doing them long before I had much of a vocabulary at all.

A new memory is beginning to emerge. Although not yet clear or complete, I get the big picture of it. I sense that it's the last encounter I had with my abuser. I allow myself to go into the memory. I do the sweeping breath, the mountain range on the far wall appearing as I enter the fog of the memory. As I fan my head from side to side, I sweep the fog away and ask the memory to emerge as it will. I ask for the fullness of it to be revealed. The picture clears as I go back in time.

I'm at his daughter's high school graduation party. I'm wearing a pale pink minidress with a row of tiny pearl buttons all the way down the front; the bottom flares out in a little ruffled skirt. He wants to show me the new beehives. I follow him into the orchard.

It's a hot day. The insects sit quietly in the new mown grass between the rows of apple trees. The odors of the day are intense. I feel the summer's heat as we walk far into the orchard adjacent to his property. There's a tree with a short ladder leaning against one of its branches; a large wooden apple crate, perhaps four feet square, lies beneath the tree. He unbuttons all of those pretty little buttons and pushes my dress off my shoulders, pulls my underpants down; no bra; I didn't usually wear one. He lays my clothes over the apple crate.

"Climb up the ladder."

"How far?" I ask, nervous that I'll do it wrong.

"Keep going."

He watches, instructing me to climb to the top of the ladder, pausing occasionally, and then step out onto the thick branch the ladder is leaning against. I steady myself by grabbing another branch above my head, again asking for direction as I begin walking out on the limb, placing one foot carefully in front of the other.

"How far?"

"Keep going," he says, watching me closely.

"Okay," he says, "now stoop down."

Holding onto a branch above my head and sitting on the balls of my feet, I perch on the branch like a scared little bird. He looks at me, touches me, pries my legs further apart and pokes inside me with his rough fingers.

"Okay come down," he says, putting his arms up to catch me.

I hop right down into them, no choice but to do as he says. He carries me to the apple crate and plunks me down on all fours. I hear him unzipping his pants and I'm a little girl again playing Doggie with him. He rubs himself against me until he pushes inside, my head hitting against the crate, butting into the corner of the crate.

Afterwards he tells me to get dressed and get my ass back up to the party. He walks away and I slowly follow. He waits for me by the house, where the chimney juts out.

"Go and get some food," he commands.

I do what he says. I get a plate of food and sit by myself at the end of a long row of chairs and try to eat, try to act normal. I can barely lift the plastic fork to my lips; barely chew. I'm concerned that someone will notice that something is wrong. Over and over again I check that all of my buttons are buttoned, nervously running my fingers over them, soothing myself with their cool pearly soft touch. I leave as soon as I can. I go home, put on my bathing suit and go to the pool. The cold water, the physical activity, the mindless swimming back and forth, and the comforting pressure of the water relieve the physical trauma. Eventually, I forget the rest of it too.

I remember this; I'd often go swimming when I left him, the first shock of cold water severing the attachment to his brutal world. By the time I was done with my swim, I'd have totally blocked out what had happened only minutes or hours before. I'd emerge from the pool dripping and shivering, but once again my familiar, silent, tightly controlled self.

The memories of what he did still hold me in their grip. They're intensely captivating as I recapitulate, but they don't hold the adult me for as long as they've gripped the rolled-up little girl on the floor. I know this because I still feel like that little girl. I'm still lying there on the floor. Part of me never really got up. I've been locked up with her all these years, curled into a tight ball, never imagining it could be any different. It felt safe to stay there. I knew he wasn't coming back to get me again.

It feels good, even now, to roll up like that. It brings back the feelings and memories, but it also feels incredibly calm and quiet. No one else is there, just me. It was also the way I slept at night, rolled into a little ball, tucked far down in the tunnel at the foot of my little bed, safe under my covers. I left my child self back there, rolled up, safe in her knowing that he would not interfere. Now I have to go back and get us both up off the floor and out of that bed, dust us off, and bring us into new life.

I know it's no longer necessary to keep curling up into that ball, though it's what I automatically and instinctually resort to as soon as I feel afraid, resentful, hurt, exhausted, when life becomes too much to handle. Essentially, it's always been a place where I could hide from whatever ailed me, even though I didn't know that what ailed me was something residing inside me, only in memory, but real nonetheless. Now I need to let my child self know that we're no longer going to do that; that the world is safe now; that there are other safe places to go; that we can create our own new, safe places now.

June 16, 2002

He had it all planned. He planned everything; everything was all set up, ready to go. He just needed to get me; he just had to ensnare me. The apple crate had a thin mattress in it, from an old outdoor lounge chair. The ladder was set up in the tree just right, no branches interfering. He'd already cut away what he didn't want so I could easily walk out on the branch. He had the whole thing set up! Earlier, years earlier, in the bathroom of his house, the towel rack never had any towels on it. The maple tree where we played the Tree Branch game had also been prepared, all the branches sawed off, the nubs on the main branch smoothed, prepared by a master.

He planned every detail.

Wherever I am, he is. Wherever I go, he goes. He's in me. I can't get rid of him. He makes me feel like a bad person; he makes me feel disgusting, evil, and loathsome.

June 17, 2002

Monday morning. I'm in agony waiting for my appointment with Chuck tomorrow, keeping it all in, trying to appear normal, doing the routine, but so lost in the past. I don't even dare do the sweeping breath, not wanting to stir anything up today. Instead, I struggle. I constantly push the past away, push its ugly head back down into the darkness inside me. I'm barely able to function. Occasionally, I poke my head up out of the fog, look around and feel slightly more connected, amazed at where I've just been.

"What a trip! What a powerfully intense thing!" I think. "What a mind-blowing experience! Such a privilege being involved in this!"

I guess I wouldn't miss it for anything, but when I'm deeply engrossed, caught in the middle of it, it's horrifying.

June 18, 2002

"I feel like I'm possessed!"

"You are! You're possessed by his energy still inside you. Now the real work begins," says Chuck.

"What do you mean, now the real work begins? What the fuck do you think I've been doing!"

"I didn't mean to imply that you haven't been doing real work, but now the work of releasing his hold on you can really begin in earnest!"

"Well, I can't just let go of it, just like that," I protest. "It doesn't just happen! In fact, I'm fighting to keep it with me, to keep what's familiar. If I keep it in me I'm safe! I know where he is, under my control, and he can't get me."

We do some EMDR around the issue but, try as I might, I just cannot release his evil energy from me. I experience a very physical need to hold onto it. It feels like something my body just cannot bear to be without. I tell Chuck that I never used dolls or stuffed animals to comfort me, but that I kept a firm grip on that bundle of heavy, confusing stuff that I took into bed with me every night. I rolled into a ball with it, hugging it and keeping it firmly under my control. It's as if I've had a baby in my arms my whole life and at one time I'd made a promise to always be there and take care of it. It's as if I'd promised to never let anything bad happen to it, that I'd protect it forever. It became a solemn duty, part of the pact I made with my abuser, and with myself.

As long as I kept that bundle tightly in my clutches then *I* was in control and I could keep the bigger and more intense energy of annihilation away—I could keep *him* far away. And now, letting go, even in a metaphorical sense, is unnerving. It's such a comfortingly real bundle in a way. As I think about the possibility of releasing it, the baby I've held for so long, I feel an unbearable emptiness in my arms, the comforting weight of it gone. And what then? What do I carry then? I still want it, but I understand, as Chuck says, that as long as I carry it then my abuser still has a hold over me, his energy is still in me, and he's still really in charge.

But the baby is dead! It's really just a lifeless bundle that I've been carrying all these years! It offers me nothing! Why am I holding onto a dead baby? And why for so long? Just because it fills a need? Do I really need it so badly? What if I put it down? What will happen then?

I struggle to take in this new reality. Perhaps I don't really need it. On the one hand, at this point in my life, all I'm actually doing is keeping my abuser's energy safely protected, simply because it's so familiar. On the other hand, his hold is so tenaciously tight, his secrets safe in my arms and so deeply satisfying to him, that he refuses to let go. Neither of us wants to give up what we established so long ago, what has so perfectly fitted both our needs.

A battle wages as I grapple with the truthful immensity of this energetic entanglement. I actually feel my abuser's energy as more real and more *foreign* than ever, as I process the reality of this energetic dilemma. But I can't get his tentacles out of me, no matter how hard I try and EMDR just isn't doing the trick.

"Go away! You're a coward!" Chuck yells in an effort to cast my abuser's energy from my body and psyche. "You're evil! Go away! Get out! Leave her alone!"

I can't stand the words. I can't listen. I start to go numb. I cover my ears and sink down into my chair and go blank.

"Can you hear me?" Chuck asks.

"Yes, I can hear you, although I didn't want to listen."

"Why?"

"Because those words feel like such a personal assault. I feel battered."

"Why are they so hard to hear?"

"Because it's about me!"

Each word on top of the next strikes hard and I realize that the reality of the abuse is still sinking in. Part of me still wants to think that maybe it didn't happen, maybe it's not true, maybe it's all a dream. I know it's not, but I still can't fully accept it. It's too much and too exhausting to assimilate and when I hear Chuck yelling like that I shut down because if I have to listen then I also have to *believe*.

The believing is the hard part, believing and going through it all again, all the pain and the reality of knowing that it really did happen just as my body has been telling me—that I suffered indescribable pain and torture as a child. That's why I don't want to let it go, because then I'm admitting to myself, showing myself that it really did happen—*all of it*.

"So, why can't you admit it and accept it?" Chuck asks.

"Why can't I just say, okay, it happened? Because I can only take the truth in small amounts."

I also wonder if it hurts to hear bad things said about my abuser because I haven't fully accepted what he did to me. Or is it because I have feelings for him? Why can't I stand to hear those things said about him? Am I protecting myself from pain, or am I protecting him? What do I really feel about him? Do I really see him as evil? Or do I hold a fondness for him? Is there a whole slough of mixed feelings here? How could I possibly want to protect him from what Chuck is saying? Why don't I want Chuck to say bad things about him? Did I hate him *and* love him?

Chuck mentions that I've worked on this dilemma before in my relationship with my old boyfriend, the one who was twenty years older than me. He reminds me that I got away from that relationship on my own, that I didn't want to play the games anymore and I acted on my own behalf, something inside me pushing me to move on. It was the hardest thing I'd ever done because I'd loved him. I'd totally abandoned myself to him, feeling that I knew him already. There was something that was so utterly familiar, it was almost as if we'd had a past connection. I had loved him deeply, while at the same time I hated him. The relationship we had practically destroyed me.

The deeper emotions I experienced and suffered through when leaving that boyfriend crop up again now. They emerge as I go through this recapitulation and especially this day's work of exorcising foreign, negative energy from my very soul where it planted itself decades ago. The raw, bruised feelings of abandonment and deep loneliness, the *I-can-barely-go-on-with-life pain*, and the *I'm-shredded-to-pieces feelings* that I went through as I broke out of that relationship with my old boyfriend are recognizably present again. They are dear old friends pointing out the pit of depression, as I head straight back into familiar dark territory.

Chuck reminds me that the relationship with that boyfriend was really a re-enactment of the childhood abuse situation, set up for me to remember. I was involved with an older man who was controlling and manipulative, and I played my part perfectly, falling right into the old role, the abused child mesmerized by the circumstances. The turmoils of that relationship sent me back into the deep depression of my childhood too. It was all set up to show me the truth that, yes, I had indeed known this man before, in a previous relationship of similar quality and intensity.

"Your abuser is what the shamans term *predatory energy*," Chuck says, as we return to the challenge at hand. "It's alien energy that inhabited you from a very young age, brainwashed you and fed off your energy. He needed you in order to stay alive."

When Chuck says this I finally get it! *I don't need him—he needs me!* My abuser needed me to fulfill his fantasies and, energetically, he's still attached!

"So, he wants me to love him, he wants me to need him, but he's really sucking off *my* energy?"

"Yes, he's alien energy that took over when you were an easy target, a vulnerable child."

"You're right," I say, "he is a cowardly bastard!"

"Get out! Leave her! You're pathetic!" Chuck yells loudly, but again I react.

"He doesn't like hearing my voice, huh?"

"No, he doesn't."

"Who's reacting here, you or him?"

"It's confusing—I'm not sure. But really, the whole energy thing is simpler to understand now."

I come away with a totally new perspective: *I've lived my entire life inhabited by an evil predator.* He's an alien who took over my being at a very young age—when I was a mere unsuspecting toddler—and he's been inside ever since, wreaking havoc and usurping my abilities to live an uninhibited and joyous life. Getting rid of him is going to take some hard work. As Chuck said: *Now the real work begins!*

June 19, 2002
In a dream, my son and a group of men, most of whom are friends from my past, come to me. Someone has called for an intervention. They've come together with the intention of encouraging me to care about myself and to seriously consider that what happened to me as a child is true. They tell me that I must find a way to begin releasing the pent up energy that is causing me such turmoil. Sitting in a circle, they surround me. I stand in the center while they direct me in techniques of release. They take turns jumping into the circle, trying to scare me, trying to get a reaction out of me. When I don't react they resort to shouting, teaching me how to open my mouth and scream. They yell loudly, showing me how to do it, prompting me, explaining that I need to find an outlet, that somehow I'm just going to have to let loose.

"It's okay," they say, "you can cry, you can scream, you can get angry. No one will care. No one will think you're crazy. Everyone will be so happy if you do."

They suggest that anything I might do to begin the process of expressing my emotions will be good for me. They don't want me to hold in the bad energy anymore. They care about me and they want me to heal.

I wake at 4:30 a.m., extremely tight, under great stress, knowing that in spite of the dream I'm just not able to express my emotions yet. The birds are already awake and chattering noisily, showing what it means to let loose and I can't get back to sleep. Try as I might, it's impossible, so in the midst of the early morning racket I lie in bed and contemplate where I am now and what lies ahead.

School's almost out and plans for the kid's summer schedules have to be determined so I can still work fulltime. A couple of housing possibilities have come along and I'm hoping to make some decisions about buying something and moving out of the shared house before the new school year starts in the fall. It feels like a lot to deal with while in the throes of this incessant recapitulation process.

I've been reading *Running From Safety* by Richard Bach, a book that Chuck recommended. I find similarities in his life philosophy to my own: in order for change to happen you have to let the universe take over to guide and inspire you. If you can trust that, you'll get what you need. If you can just leave the door open, something does eventually come along to carry you forward.

I see it as the optimist's approach, but taking that first step is the biggest challenge. I'm definitely counting on the universe more fully now, daring to trust that I am indeed guided.

One of my brothers recently told me that he always considered me to be "a person of action," as he called it. I haven't always felt like one, but I do know that when I need to be, I certainly am capable of action. Now is one of those times. I've learned, from long periods of habitual inertia, that if you allow yourself to stay locked in an uncomfortable situation, feeling powerless, then nothing will ever change. You have to take action for yourself; no one else can do it for you. It's okay to dream, but it's much better to act. I know that if you don't do A, B, or C, then D, E, and F won't ever happen. If you just take one step you're off on a new journey. Personally, as I dared myself to begin this recapitulation process, I opened a new door to daring to be happy, to finding what I need in this life.

My entire life, in one sense or another, has been spent locked in mortal combat with that alien energy that Chuck and I tussled with the other day. I haven't really understood what it was, but I've been aware of its presence, knowing that something was definitely amiss. The memories are filling that part in, letting me know the reasons for the deep inner conflict. Now I understand that I do need to get rid of it. I must cast out the alien energy, no matter how uncomfortable it feels physically and no matter how great the emotional impact. I must throw down that great bundle of predatory energy that I've been clutching as if it's been the very life of me, and finally move on. I must allow the energy of a new me to take its place.

I must prepare myself to receive my own energy. I must allow everything that is good inside me to finally see the light of day and come to life. I must not be afraid to be who I truly am. The frightened girl inside must not fear her own beauty and her own shadow. To become an evolved person I must get to know myself more fully so I can help that little girl to leave the abuser behind in the shadows of the dark woods where he belongs. I must encourage her to roll out of her little ball of fear and comfort and emerge into the light and follow me, to come with me into a new life of our own making.

It's time to leave the predator behind, to leave the old stuff, the dirty, disgusting, horrid, evil stuff that belongs to him, behind. It's time to leave the pain and hurt and awful memories behind, to shed them along with him. *It's time to let him go.* We've done it his way for long enough. I know it doesn't hold up, it doesn't work. I don't want or need him sucking the life from me anymore. It's time to do life differently. It's time to merge the girl and the woman— taking each other into the warm folds of arms, body, soul, and mind—and become one.

I see how the abuse might have unfolded. First he picked me and then he planned what he would do to me. From the day I first met him he calculatedly plotted and played out his sickness, everything set up, sometimes elaborately; the woods set up exactly as he wanted them. The games were played according to a prescribed format. I see that now in the way he made me go from one area to the other, like trying out rides at a carnival or riding the equipment at a playground, only it was his own terrible playground. It's pretty obvious that he also did the same things to his daughter because we were together with him sometimes, especially early on. But then he started trapping me alone, in calculated, well-planned captures of a little girl.

I see now how he groomed me: first watching and touching, getting me under his spell, getting me to obey, turning me into an obedient, subservient, slave girl. I *was* his slave girl. Then he began penetrating, first anally, with sticks and then his own body, later vaginally, opening me up, using his tools and his body. Planning every step of the way, he was patient and methodical. By the time I was eight or nine it appears that the childish games with sticks had stopped and he began bringing in other men to have full-fledged intercourse, vaginally and anally. I'm appalled by the deviant planning, the crafty evilness of it all!

Chuck is right that there is no way I could have avoided it or stopped it. My abuser had me brainwashed by the age of two, a tiny girl with no chance to fight his insidious evil. I was powerless. What could I do against a man like that?

Did he ever say anything nice to me? Was I totally terrified? I know I was under his spell, it's pretty apparent. I know the zombie-like state of being so well. I hear the phrases that I repeated to myself, my mantras that sent me into oblivion, sending me into the safety of dissociation and out-of-body: *It's happening again. Just bear it. It'll be over soon. It will be over soon. You can stand it, you know you can, and then it will all be over.*

But I did have some power and I still have it because he didn't totally destroy me. There is that great inner strength that has seen me through, from the tiny little girl I once was until now, and it continues to see me through everything. I have, in fact, done remarkably well for someone who went through so much. I have, in fact, survived. It was my own personal holocaust, my own private experiences of terror, and I did survive and I will survive it all over again as I go through this recapitulation. Only this time I'll be freed of it all. I'll be the new me, the real me, fully merged, fully emerged, to live life to the fullest!

In *Running From Safety*, Bach seems to perceive and maintain his inner child as a totally separate being from himself. Why hasn't he merged with him? Does he see him only as someone needing teaching and guidance and once the mentoring is done they move on, separating again? Is this a masculine trait? I don't feel my inner child as separate at all; she's part of me. I've held her at a distance until the time came to meet her on neutral ground, but my intention is to totally work my way toward accepting and absorbing all of her back into me. I don't feel the need to teach her anything; she already knows everything, in fact, she's the one teaching me. I merely need to love and nurture her, the feminine/maternal kind of nurturing, unconditionally accepting her and everything she's been carrying for me because she is me; we are one. And I'm certain that she'll intuitively learn everything else she needs to know about me as we go along.

I can't imagine that I'll ever say goodbye to her or that I'll ever have to leave her alone again. She'll always be a part of me. I'd be incomplete if I walked away from her after all this work in finding and reconnecting with her, and so would she be; all this work for naught. The whole point of recapitulation is to merge and then emerge out of the process a complete whole—psyche, soma, and spirit united—finally at peace.

So, to use Bach's analogy of the pilot, recapitulation is really about learning to be your own pilot, being in control of your aircraft, and owning your own power. Now we're in the midst of a dogfight as I go against everything my abuser installed in me, all the fears, habits and behaviors that I was forced to assimilate in order to uphold his world. I'm taking my power back from my abuser by excising his energy from me, by releasing the fears that have held me in check, making room for my own energy in the process. I'm rescuing the frightened little girl self from his clutches as well, letting her also take the wheel and man the guns, freeing her to experience her personal power in conjunction with my adult awareness of that power, power we've never fully experienced. We're in the midst of a beautiful fight for our sanity, for a future totally freed of the past and all its repercussions.

Not only did my abuser usurp the personal sense of power that would have naturally blossomed had I had a fairly normal childhood, but he also groomed, plotted, and hunted me for years. I never even imagined I could say no to him; it simply wasn't possible. It didn't take long for me to realize that if I tried, if I fought back, protested, kicked, or screamed, I got hit or yelled at, his fierceness and need to be in control were all that mattered. But in reality, he *was* a predator, and he needed me for predatory reasons: to keep him alive and safe so he could act out his fantasies in the comfort of knowing he would not be discovered. In order to be certain of his own safety, he had to start with me when I was very young. Like a master molding his slave to his exact specifications, he trained me to be the perfectly obedient little slave girl that I became, thus being available to fulfill his perverted needs.

I wonder why some people are abusers and some victims, and why he picked me. Was it simply because I was there, because I walked into his territory? I was the innocent who crossed his path. Was it my destiny? Was it my path too? Was I supposed to be abused in this manner as a child, for some reason as yet unknown?

Here I am—almost forty-eight years after it all first started— finally extricating myself from his clutches, realizing where I've been all that time: *in another world*. It's like waking from a dream, a nightmare of a lifetime, and seeing it for the first time—clearly— for what it is.

The nightmare has gone on long enough. I don't want to be in it anymore.

It's nighttime now and the kids are in bed. I'm doing the recapitulation breath, a new memory coming through. I'm a child again, swinging on a swing, actually swaying as I sit on my bed doing the sweeping breath, enjoying it. I love to swing. I'm happy.

"Uh oh! Someone's coming!"

It's him. I see him coming towards me. I stop swinging and stand next to the swing.

"Maybe he's going somewhere else; maybe he doesn't see me in the shade of the trees. If I stay perfectly still maybe he won't see me."

He continues walking towards me. My stomach hurts now. I don't feel happy anymore.

"He's going to make me do something bad."

He pulls up my plaid summer dress, the sleeveless one, and takes off my underpants and makes me put the fat rope dangling from the side of the swing between by legs, the rope that hangs off the bottom of the swing and drags in the dirt, longer on one side than the other. It hurts as he holds the end and pulls it up higher and higher, making me stand on tippy-toes so it doesn't hurt so much.

He makes me sit sideways on the swing, a wooden board, straddling it with the thick rope still between my legs as he pulls me against him, the side of my head thrust into his crotch as he stands next to me. My hands are tightly clasped around one of the long ropes that go far up into the tree in the yard, off on the side of the house where there are no windows. He swings me hard, angrily jerking me off the swing. He picks me up and holds me on his lap as he sits on the wide swing. His penis between my legs feels like wood as he slides me back and forth on top of his erection, roughly swinging, growing excited. He smells of man and smoke, and he's making grunting man sounds. He stops abruptly, pushes me angrily to the ground, calling me bad names.

"Dirty girl! Filthy, nasty, fucked up little girl!" he yells.

I'm a fucked up little four-year-old girl. As I get up off the ground and then bend down to put my underpants back on the heavy swing hits me in the head.

June 20, 2002

In a dream, an acquaintance has died and I'm asked to do a commemorative sculpture in his memory. I begin collecting pieces of old wood, looking for interesting driftwood, walking along roads and into the woods alongside my best friend from childhood. I begin assembling the pieces as we find them. Eventually we need help moving the sculpture because it's too big for us to move alone. Suddenly, we're children again, two little girls playing in the woods. A man comes along riding a strange bike, offering to help us move the huge sculpture, but in order to help he needs to find a trailer. I know he's a pervert and that he wants to have sex with me. I hold him off with a long spike, threatening him, fighting him off.

"Don't touch me, don't come close, don't you dare!" I yell.

My best friend assesses the situation and elects to give herself to him in order to save me. I watch, but only until a certain point. When I see his hands go under the hem of her dress, creeping up her thin, white little girl legs, I can't stand it anymore. I get out my spike again and stab him repeatedly in the back, screaming at him to leave her alone.

I'm doing the sweeping recapitulation breath again, concentrating on getting rid of my abuser, breathing him out. He clings to the edge of my being.

"No! No!" he yells. "You need me! Don't do this! You need me!"

"You're evil!" I yell back. "I don't need you!"

I ignore his cries and continue breathing until I'm not listening anymore and then I begin going numb from my feet up, buzzing and swelling. I feel my whole body marshmallow up as if I'm being inflated, puffing up to the size of a four-hundred-pound person, and then I'm floating like an enormous balloon. The feeling is scary but peaceful at the same time. I know where I'm going. It's okay, it's familiar, but at the same time laced with old panic.

"Oh my God, I'm going again! Does this have to happen again? Why is this happening?" I wonder, as I let myself go deeper into the experience.

Now my head is puffing up, growing bigger. It begins buzzing and vibrating until it suddenly deflates down to a tiny head into which I climb. All of me gets in and sits there inside that tiny vibrating head while my physical body stays huge, a swollen blob, unfeeling and numb far below me. I feel like I'm going to totally leave my body now. I'm sure that I'm going to just vibrate right out of my head, but I stay sitting there a while longer, shrinking into nothing, until I'm barely there. Then I easily seep out. Now my body is empty, with no soul, a blob of nothing down there below me on my bed.

A noisy garbage truck outside the window sends me crashing back into my body. Slowly the vibrations stop and I, and my body, return to normal.

I'm lost in the world of memories as they pour out of me, as I expel my abuser in memory after memory, literally breathing him out using the sweeping recapitulation breath. I suffer through detailed memory sequences complete with visual, sensual, physical, and/or emotional components depending on the clarity of the memory. As I go more deeply into the scenes in the woods and barn I notice that my abuser never looks at me, he doesn't see me at all. He's so preoccupied with what he's doing and, even though I'm the object of his focus, it's as if I don't exist. I personally do not matter.

I relive being with him as he gets excited, as his manner and breathing change, becoming heavy, intense, and threatening. I'm immediately drawn back into his world simply by a brief appearance of him in a memory, of a look or a signal from him, a small hint of the past drawing me right back into his world. I see him from a distance, walking towards me, and everything stops as it once did. I shut down and simply wait for the inevitable to happen. In spite of the certainty that he is going to get me, I notice that I keep a faint hope alive, thinking that perhaps it won't happen this time, perhaps he'll go past me, perhaps he doesn't really mean it, perhaps I'm wrong about him. But no! He heads directly towards me and there is no stopping him whatsoever. He's like a vulture intent on having its prey. Once spotted, I'm doomed, paralyzed by the sight of him. As I wait for him, I go intensely quiet, barely breathing, as fear creeps into my body and deadens it.

I wanted romance and beauty and tenderness as a young girl, but I ended up dealing with the disgustingly loathsome fantasies of a pervert being played out on my person. I missed out on the innocent romance, exploration, and attention of someone my own age, ruined by his intrusions into my body. I didn't have a chance. Everything was distorted from the moment I met him, as I engaged in torturous acts with a grown man who repeatedly told me that I was nasty, filthy and disgusting; a bad, fucked up little girl.

Am I all those things? Was I ever those things?

No! He is! He's disgusting and loathsome and fucked up, not me! But this is what he did to me; this is how he confused me and made me feel responsible for making him do the things he did. He may, in reality be the disgusting one, but I'm the one left with bearing the brunt of it.

Shamanic breathing brings forth memories of my legs being held apart and then I'm curled up on the floor, a length of rope lying across my knees. Then the memory jumps and now my wrists are tied and I'm hanging from a beam in the barn, my feet just reaching the floor. A man comes in. I know he wants me to himself. No one else is around.

"Oh, you're just a baby, just what I like; a baby," he says.

He's big, fat, and ugly, his hands huge. He touches my face. He smells of vomit. He grabs my legs, my buttocks. I'm tied up high enough that he can stand up in front of me and do it.

June 21, 2002

It's eleven at night and I can't sleep. Intense vaginal pain rides in on the memory that started emerging yesterday. I'm tied up in the barn, strange men are coming in, doing what they want. My abuser is selling me to other men.

"Worth every penny! Next time!" I hear them say as they leave.

"Next time! What do they mean?" I wonder when I hear this.

"No, no next time!" I silently plead. "No next time!"

My body is bruised and sore and deep inside I'm painfully hollow as the memory evolves. I'm falling into bottomless, panicking pain.

Ow! Ow! Ow! Ow!

Explosive pelvic pain and clutching stomach pain stab my body. Rocking and curling up, protecting myself from the intensity of it, I recognize it. I know this pain; I've always known this pain. I've been feeling it on and off, fleetingly reminding me of something. It goes away after a while, but lately it's stayed longer and now it envelops me in the deeper memory of it.

He sells me. He ties me up so I can't run away, my feet dangling on the floor, my arms stretched tightly overhead so I can't fight. They come alone or in groups of two or three. There is one fat man with huge fat sausage fingers. He likes babies.

"You're just a baby, just a baby," he repeatedly mutters.

He puts his fat hands on my face, his fat fingers in my mouth, between my legs, on my buttocks, pulling me onto him, raping hard, saying that he likes me, he likes me. Afterwards I can't stand, so I hang, my knees bent, dangling from the rope.

Others come. They hold me down, hold my legs apart while they take turns—hands, bodies, breathing, smells.

"Flip her! Flip her over!" they say in the heat of the games they play with my body.

I feel hands on thighs, hands everywhere, bodies pushing into me. No one cares; no one cares. Later, he comes, my abuser.

"Git! Git, girl! Git outa here! Git outa here, Pussy Girl!"

I see money. He shows me the money, fanning it out, a big wad of bills.

"They'll pay big bucks for girls like you, big bucks. Now git!"

Aching, can't get up and go, lie on floor, stay there a long time, can't move, afraid they'll come back, need to go, need to get away before they come back and get me again.

June 22, 2002
So that's what was happening, he was tying me up and selling me. It wasn't always him doing it to me, there were other men too. I saw the money; he showed me the money. They paid for what they got and did what they wanted. I couldn't protect myself, I couldn't even cover myself. I couldn't get my hands down to cover myself. I couldn't fight.
I'm angry; intensely, bitterly angry!

I can't stand the fear, which is explosive, building in intensity. But I'm so quiet, no cries or screams—they're all stuck inside, all tangled up together. The fear, the anger, the hurt, the pain, the cries, the screams, are all wrapped up together in a thick blanket of disgust. This was my defiance, the need to keep something to myself, safely locking in my feelings, keeping them to myself where no one could get to them. If I didn't do this they would have totally destroyed me and I couldn't let that happen. I couldn't let them totally get me.

I spiral into deep depression as the reality of what was actually happening in the barn sinks in. It's incredible that I even survived, that I was able to walk out of there eventually. That I was able to continue on and have a life is incredible, that I had the strength and capacity to hold it in for so long is incredible. Who am I? Who is this person who could survive all that?

June 23, 2002
The fat guy in the barn becomes even clearer, pieces falling into place: what he wore, what he did, what he said. As I do the recapitulation breath, excruciating details of this memory become clearer. As I fan my head from side to side and take in the energy of the scene that unfolds before me, the pieces fall into place and a fuller memory forms. I see myself standing frozen, my arms tied over my head, tied to the overhead beam, my feet on the ground, until he pulls them up so he can do what he intends. I remain

frozen, while he talks and prods me, probing with his fat fingers, talking the whole time.

"Let's see what we have here... and what's this... and look at that..."

He sticks fat fingers into every orifice. He puts his "little boy thing" into my "little girl thing," holding me up, everything drawn out in excruciating detail.

When he's done, I can't stand up anymore. I can only hang limply from the rafter. My arms so numb, so cold, there is no feeling left in them. They hang like frozen chunks of ice above my head.

I continue the sweeping breath, daring myself to go through the rest of the memory, into what came next. I'm aware that I will not be free of this torment until I complete the picture of what really happened that day in the barn so many years ago.

The next guys untie me and my arms, frozen stumps, fall like dead weights to my sides. There are three or four guys, fast and furious, hands all over me. Touching and holding me down, they take turns. I don't care anymore. I just need to survive. Maybe I pass out. I don't have any more pictures, no more memories, just the frenzy of it, everyone grabbing me, holding me, "flip her, flip her over," and then I'm gone.

Another memory briefly emerges, of another time. Two men take turns, each holding me for the other. I don't know them, I've never seen them before. I stop the recapitulation, stop fanning my head. I can't take anymore. I slowly return to the present and sit in stunned, numb silence.

How many times did he sell me? I don't know.

He made money off me, off Slave Girl.

Getting through the days, depressed, trying to keep busy, always staying busy.

It's thundering and lightning. I'm sitting on my bed in my room late at night in the dark, surrounded by windows on three sides. I begin doing the recapitulation pass, the sweeping breath, seeking to release the energy of the predator and of all the other men too. I breathe them out. Lightning flashes and thunder cracks loudly as I sweep my head back and forth, back and forth, breathing in my own energy, forcing out the predatory energy. The flashing of the lightning and the crashing of the thunder accompany me as I sweep my head back and forth. The rain beats against the windows and the wind whips as the tremendous storm pounds out its flashing, drumming rhythms.

In the dark haziness of my room I'm aware of a scene off to the left and slightly in front of me. The silhouette of a seated figure on top of a mountain ledge appears, clearly discernable through the rain that is pounding down in torrents on this scene, remarkably like the storm raging outside. I'm aware that I am both sitting in my room at this moment and that I am also that figure sitting on the ledge and that I should go to that mountaintop.

Suddenly I'm no longer just sitting on my bed. I'm also in ancient times, sitting on the ledge of a cliff, overlooking a vast valley in the dark of night, on a promontory sticking out into air, into the storm raging all around me. I'm aware of the presence of others behind me in the shelter of a cave, but it's my time to sit in the elements, to brave the forces of nature, to unflinchingly allow myself to sit exposed, unprotected, but fully aware that I have within me the strength and courage to sit here for as long as it takes, until I'm done with this challenge.

The storm rages and someone places a rough-woven, thick woolen blanket over my head and shoulders. This is allowed, the blanket is woven with symbols and icons that will protect and provide me with added strengths. I am a native woman, a tribal woman on a journey. Meanwhile, I'm still in my bedroom, sitting on my bed doing the sweeping breath, breathing in and out, sweeping my head from side to side, the storm continuing to drum as I ride its energy.

Back on the ledge, I become the storm. I breathe it in and out. The thunder, the lightning, the darkness, the earth, the stone ledge I sit upon become one with me. I am earth and sky, water and sound, light and dark. I am journeying and yet sitting solidly at the same time, both on the ledge and on my bed simultaneously. I am strong, committed to taking this journey without fear and without regret. I know this is my duty, my destiny, and my challenge, but also the fulfillment of my shamanic line. I am completing my tests of worthiness and humbleness before all the gods of nature. I am testing my inner strengths, while acknowledging those sitting behind me as my guides. In full awareness, I am marking this moment of my journey, knowing that this is part of my process. I trust all I have experienced in the past, all I am experiencing at this moment, and all that is to come, as necessary, if I am to evolve.

Suddenly, I'm taken into the belly of the storm. I leap into its mouth. I sit upon its tongue. I swallow its saliva. I feel the beat of its pulse. I tremble with the rumble of its heart, and I withstand the blinding light of its intent. I am its apprentice at the same time that I acknowledge its power as my own, simultaneously humbly grateful for it and daringly accepting of it.

When it's done, when the storm subsides, I'm spit out of its mouth. As the winds die down, as the thunder rumbles off into the distance and as the rains slow to a drizzle, I find myself back upon the ledge where I have been sitting for days, still under my blanket, now damp on the outside though warm and dry in the inside. My guides come out of the cave. They lift me by my arms, steadying me upon my feet. Helping me to walk upon my wobbly legs, they take me with them into the warmth and dryness of the cave where they have kept a fire going, where food has been prepared.

"Well done. You have done well," I hear them say.

The mountaintop scene where I have just journeyed disappears from my room as I finish my sweeping breath magical pass. The storm ceases, the thunder rumbles off into the distance and the lightning quiets to intermittent flashes. I'm still sitting on my bed, fully aware of having been in two places at once, having gone on a journey of significance into an ancient experience while expelling alien energy from my current body self. Though I'm not sure what it means, I come away with a greater understanding of myself as wholly in alignment with the greater universe.

I also know that my inner strength and determination are now solidified, firmly aligned with my spirit and with my greater intent to continue trusting this shamanic recapitulation process that I have been allowing myself to take. I also know that I am indeed just beginning my journey, a journey of humbleness and awe, of inner self constantly being asked to make adjustments, to nonjudgmentally acquiesce to the process, to stay in alignment with what comes to guide me. In addition, by constantly pushing myself to keep taking the inner journey, I have found that true self and innocence are completely compatible, trustworthy, reliable, and viable, no matter what world I might find myself in.

I don't know what will happen next, but I've just experienced something otherworldly; not at all like entering my abuser's dark world but a totally different one, full of riches. I understand that I cannot stop this process, that I don't want to stop it either, and that I am indeed on a magical journey.

June 24, 2002

In spite of the journey I took last night, I am once again deeply depressed, deeply sad, back in that barn going over the rapes again and again, but I know I have to keep going back there to fully recapitulate, to release myself from the past, just as I'm releasing the energy of the past from me.

As I open to them, the memories in the barn sweep over me and once again I'm hearing those voices, feeling those frantic hands, the breathing, panting, urging, grunting talk. I'm so lost, so hollow, so scared, so tense, so anxious, holding on until tomorrow when I see Chuck again.

As I recapitulate, I go absolutely still inside, barely breathing, tense, waiting, full of dread, knowing I can't stop what's happening, that it's better to keep quiet. Let it happen and get though it, bundle up the fears and cries, the pain, and don't let them get to me. Don't let them even know they're hurting me. If I keep quiet I'll live. It's my choice. Silence or death?

June 25, 2002

I meet with Chuck and go back into the barn. While going through the memories my arms become numb. Heavy dead weights, they grow to cold icy stumps as my stomach muscles clench and spasm. I clearly hear what each of the men said to me, the fat man talking like a baby, the other guys brutally inattentive, just wanting what they want, all of them just taking what they want from me. The whole thing disgusts me, sickens me, and I'm in agony as I let some of the feelings go through me, bent over and gagging, keeping the wastebasket close in case I throw up. I don't know how old I am, but when Chuck asks, I tell him it feels like I'm about twelve, maybe fourteen at the most.

I come out of the barn and emerge back into Chuck's office deeply depressed and dead inside. We sit there for a few minutes while I return to awareness of the present. Chuck won't let me leave until I assure him that I'm okay to drive. When he next, very gently, tells me that he'll be taking next week off, I feel the floor below my feet drop away and I tumble into a pit of darkness.

"I can't do it, I can't do it alone for two weeks, I barely make it through one," I want to scream, but I just say, "all right, all right."

"I'll be around," he says. "So, if you need to, we can meet."

"I need a break anyway," I say, as I get up to leave. "I don't know if it'll happen, but I've certainly had enough for today."

I can barely stand up and hobble out of the office and even before I get to my car something new starts brewing. I feel it slowly awakening, beginning its slow emergence out of the darkness inside me. I'm already in the grip of it as I start my car and drive away, instructing myself to just focus on the road ahead of me, to just stay focused and in the moment.

June 28, 2002

I'm dreaming that I'm in a dimly lit wide corridor, the ceiling is pretty low and I can't see beyond the immediate space I'm in. The ends of the corridor in either direction are dark. There are large picture windows lined up along the two sides of the room, like at a museum. Behind each large picture window is a display, set in an alcove. I'm running back and forth, naked, under a showerhead that is positioned in the middle of the ceiling. I'm getting thoroughly wet; really letting myself enjoy it. I'm talking freely as I run back and forth. I feel slightly happier and freer than normal and I think I look pretty good too, my slender, naked body reflected in the dimly lit picture windows lining the corridor.

I notice a guy standing off to the side, calmly at ease, leaning against the opposite wall. It's fairly dark in his area and I can't see him clearly. I'm a little miffed and slightly self-conscious when I see that he's watching me, but I sense that he's non-threatening. He's writing on a clipboard, quietly murmuring and nodding, only looking at me occasionally. At first, I think he's a carpenter who's going to fix things in the museum, but then I see he's wearing a Greek fisherman's hat and that it's Chuck. I'm nervous and embarrassed because I'm naked and because I'm talking so much, so out of character, but I keep running back and forth under the shower anyway. I'm aware that whatever I do is perfectly acceptable, that he isn't judging me in any way. He just stands calmly in the dark, writing on the clipboard, documenting everything I say and do.

"It's okay, it's okay," he says reassuringly every now and then. "It's okay."

I go over to one of the large picture windows and rub the dust off it and point out to him that it's my stuff on display there. Things from my past are arranged behind the window, all dusty and dimly lit, but I recognize every one of them.

I don't want to do the memories today—I've been begging them to stop—and I'm not doing the recapitulation sweeping breath either. I need a break. But I'm going crazy because the memories just won't stop. I have no control over them just as I once had no control over the reality that lies behind them. I'm left feeling lonely, lost, and confused; fighting the old demons—as usual.

It helps that the kids are out of school and I'm busy attending to them, but, even so, the memories seep in. Yesterday my arms were going numb, my throat gagging and I kept feeling like I was choking. Last night, while trying to sleep, I felt the dread of a new memory, growing larger since I left Chuck's the other day, preparing to break through the surface.

Somehow I'll just have to get through the next two weeks without contact with Chuck.

June 29, 2002

I try to force a break from the recapitulation process, telling it to stop, saying that I'm going to ignore it, but it doesn't last long. I'm granted a few hours and if I'm lucky a few days of much needed respite, which I'm glad for, but then the past comes rushing back again, triggered by the most insignificant hint of something. A quick flashback, a smell, a voice, a turn of phrase, even a stick lying on the ground can send me back into haunting torture and unbearable agony.

I don't even know what this new memory that's taking it's sweet time to emerge is all about, but I can't deal with the bad feelings about myself, the dirty, nasty, loathsome self—the legacy after fifty years that I still carry inside me. I try to leave it behind by just turning away from it, ignoring it while I try to enjoy myself for a while, but that doesn't last very long. The bad feelings always creep in and take their familiar places. And why would it be any different? After a childhood of brainwashing, of being told I was a fucked up, nasty little girl, I can't expect the self-disgust to wash away overnight. Even though I dreamed a few days ago of running under that shower in the museum, it was only momentary happiness. While dreaming, I did feel slightly lighter, but in reality I feel like I'll never be totally free.

When the bad feelings arise I tend to want to protect myself, the innocent child inside who had to deal with hearing those things said about her. I want to protect her from the bad feelings and from having to be around people. I've always known that if I isolate myself from other people there will be no occasion for any bad feelings to emerge. If I can stay in my own highly controlled world I'm safe, but as soon as people look at me I feel unacceptable, unworthy, like I shouldn't exist. I feel judged, exposed and embarrassed. I want to cover up, to hide, to say: "Don't look at me." And I do get looks—I get lots of looks from men, as I always have—and I get uncomfortable, as if my wounded child self is still controlling how I interpret and react in the world, my feelings enslaved in her past as Slave Girl. She's still tied to the beam in the barn where she learned what men did if you were the kind of girl that she was. That girl knows that looks lead to bad things and those bad things lead to bad feelings. If someone tells you for the first eighteen years of your life that you're a dirty, nasty girl then you're going to believe it. That dirty, nasty little fucked-up girl is going to be cowering in there somewhere, feeling like she doesn't deserve to take up space on the planet.

I recapitulate that when I first learned the Ten Commandments in first grade, at the age of six, I searched for those dirty, nasty girl commandments, anything that hinted at the sins I knew I was partaking in: *Thou shalt not be a dirty, nasty girl who does bad things in the woods. Thou shalt not have sticks poked up your ass. Thou shalt not play naked games with grown men.*

At an early age I had no doubt that I was a sinner. By the time I was in second grade I knew that God was not going to help me and so I rejected him. I decided that I could no longer hold blind allegiance to him just because the nuns and priests at my Catholic school demanded it of me. I'd had my own experiences and God had forsaken me. I sat in the classroom and recognized myself as a doubter the first time the subject came up.

"I'm a doubter, I'm a doubter, I'm a doubter," I'd mutter to myself as I sat through religion class every morning, glad to have found a place to fit in, a doubting Thomas if ever there was one.

After that, I knew God would have nothing to do with me and that I would end up in Hell. I dwelt on the horrors of hell rather than on the beauty and peacefulness of Heaven. Hell was going to be my resting place. It interested me greatly. I was perfectly happy pondering the pictures of flames licking the unhappy sinners, as depicted in the catechism and in art books, deciding where I would stand in order to be out of the fire, on a shelf here or a mountaintop there. Or perhaps I could just sit off on the side away from the biggest fiery pit, away from the pitch forks and the crowds on the road to the giant incinerator at the bottom of deepest Hell. Perhaps I'd just sneak into a crack in a wall and hide out for a few centuries. I wished I'd never been baptized so I could go to Limbo. Spending all eternity in Limbo with the unbaptized babies—which the nuns found so sad—sounded so much better. At least it kept you out of Hell. How bad could that be?

The summer I turned thirteen, when I figure I had that abortion, I was not well. I remember being frail and sickly, cold all the time, as if I were recuperating from a long illness. I remember the sweater I wore all summer, wanting to stay covered up, not wanting to wear summer clothing, not wanting to undress. I took those art classes and my parents hired a babysitter to help take care of my younger siblings, giving my job to a slightly older teenage girl from the neighborhood. I had more kindly attention from my parents and more freedom from chores and responsibilities than ever before. Those art lessons were a complete surprise. Perhaps it was my parents way of expressing something, how they tried to show they loved me or cared about me, though they never hugged me or said anything personally kind regarding the abortion. No words were ever spoken, but perhaps they felt I needed a break, and that was how they decided to do it.

Memories emerge again of going with my abuser up to the spring in the woods where he got his water, a thick black hose running down the mountain into the house. He'd take me up there periodically to threaten me, to remind me that he was boss. He had sex with me there, chewing on my legs and genitals and sticking things into my anus while he held my head down the dark hole of the well. It was meant to keep me quiet. It was very effective.

What follows are the truths that I've been grappling with, the insidiously bare-naked truths that have been emerging with the memories.

Sex, he had *sex* with me. I didn't know what to call it, but that is the correct word to use. *He had sex with me!* Also, he let other people have sex with me.

He started training and grooming me at an extremely early age. I had no choice. It was impossible for me to have had a choice. I wasn't old enough to choose anything. I was so young I didn't know there was a right and a wrong about hardly anything and, at two years old, I certainly didn't know there was anything called sex.

He molded me and trained me to do what he wanted. And I did what he wanted. I did it to protect myself. If I did what he wanted I survived. If I didn't, the consequences were dire.

He used his tools to 'open me up,' and then he had sex with me. He had anal sex with me and then he had vaginal sex with me. Once he had gotten to the point of having vaginal sex it was often followed by anal sex.

He built up my tolerance slowly, one kind of penetration at a time. Even that last memory I have, of going into the orchard with him at his daughter's graduation party, first he had vaginal sex with me in the apple crate, then he pulled me up and, after laying the mattress over the side of the crate, had anal sex. As I recapitulate that memory, I fully experience the physical soreness, the swollen, chafed soreness and the pain, both the exterior pain and the interior pain. I covered myself with my hands afterwards, cupping my hands around my genital area, trying to ease the pain, pressing on it to soothe it, to cool it. I walked around with that pain, that soreness, thinking it must show, that it must be noticeable to everyone.

In my imagination, I've sent him to the spring in the woods behind his house countless times and he's stumbled, fallen in, and drowned. I've killed him over and over again. No, he kills himself, because he's so despicable that he can't stand himself anymore. When he climbs back up out of the spring I push him back down, over and over again. I shove him back down into the black bottomless well where no one will ever find him.

June 30, 2002

I ran today, trying to outrun some of my terrors, but they just jogged alongside me, constantly nattering at me to look at them, to face them.

I keep telling myself I can make it through this week and through next week.

"Just keep busy, keep going, whatever is there will still be there," I tell myself over and over again as the days drag on.

But my abuser's voice interferes now. It's no longer the fifteen-year-old girl who doesn't want things to change, she's already on board, more comfortable now with me in charge, knowing she can trust me and that my judgment is sound and that I'm taking this recapitulation journey on our behalf. No, this time it's him, my abuser, who feels so threatened, and for good reason.

"Don't bother him, leave him alone, he doesn't care, no one cares, don't bother him," he says, telling me to leave Chuck alone, to not call.

"I'm the only one you need. I'm here; I'm always here. You can put me in the old spring, but you can't make me go away. Wherever you are, I am too. I've been with you for decades now; you'll never get rid of me! You'll never fall in love, be able to have sex, or ever trust anyone because of me. I own you. I own you!"

I fight that horrible voice daily, his despicable words rolling through my thoughts, trying to hold onto control. Those words intruding so frequently remind me that I'm not done, that there's still more work to do and more to learn about what happened to me as a child.

I know I shouldn't listen to him, but it does feel like I'll never be able to trust enough to fall in love, to have sex again or allow someone into my life. I feel safer alone. I feel safer keeping things to myself. If I let someone in then I open myself to more abuse, to hurt, to disbelief and judgments from others. Right now I don't see how I could ever open up to anyone, to another relationship. I don't see how I can trust enough to ever let someone touch me. How will I ever be able to have sex again? Won't things just get triggered? How will I deal with that?

I fear it. I'm afraid of intimacy; it's safer to keep my distance.

Something is happening to me. As I'm able to admit that he was actually doing things to me, sexually assaulting me, as I face the truths that are so apparent, I'm actually beginning to *feel* what he was doing. *I feel it.* I don't go numb anymore.

I feel.